BARRY NORMAN'S
BOOK
OF
CRICKET

Barry Norman's Book of Cricket

Quercus

Contents

INTRODUCTION

I suppose I should, first of all, present such credentials as I have for writing this book. As you may be aware, I am not a retired first-class cricketer, still less a former Test match player. The explanation for this is that I was born without any obvious skill at the game, although when I look at some of the people who have represented England in my lifetime I have to wonder what else it was that prejudiced the selectors against me.

What I am, however, is a cricket nut. I know this because two people for whom I had great admiration and affection described me as such. The first was Eric Morecambe, sublime comedian and one-time president of the Lord's

Taverners, a charitable cricketing organization that raises large sums of money for the elderly and infirm and also for the support and encouragement of young cricketers. One day in the mid-1970s, when I was co-presenting the *Today* programme on BBC Radio 4, I had to interview a man whose name, to my eternal shame, I cannot now recall. What I do recall is that when we were chatting before the interview he said: 'I have a message for you from Eric Morecambe and it is this: 'Why isn't Barry Norman, the biggest cricket nut in the country, a member of the Lord's Taverners?' My reply, quite simply, was that nobody had ever asked me. A few days later came the invitation to join and I have been a member of the Taverners, first as a player, now as an occasional umpire, ever since.

A rhapsodic depiction of Lord's by the artist Charles Cundall, painted during the fifth Ashes Test of 1938. Apart from the pavilion and the small buildings around it, the stands have all been replaced. The looming structure on the left is the St John's Wood power station, which was demolished after the Second World War.

The second person who so described me was the immortal Jim Laker, whom I knew fairly well and whom I ran into one evening in the 1970s after a day–night match during the Packer period at the Sydney Cricket Ground and he introduced me thus to John Thicknesse, then the cricket correspondent for the London *Evening Standard*: 'This is my friend Barry – he's a cricket nut.'

Both Eric and Jim were right: cricket is my great passion, right up there with the movies. In my time I have been an opening batsman, a tail-ender, a fast-medium bowler, a leg-spinner and an off-break bowler. I even kept wicket once.

In many of these capacities, as a Taverner I have played with and against some of the great names of this greatest of all games – Colin Cowdrey, Bobby Simpson, Ian Botham, Dennis Lillee, John Snow, Bill and John Edrich, Viv Richards and Keith Miller among them. I never played at Lord's, alas, but I did once turn out at the Oval, where I scored 1 not out, the sort of accomplishment few can boast about – or maybe would even want to.

A PASSION IS BORN

It was my maternal grandfather Harry Crafford, a lifelong supporter of Surrey, who introduced me to the game during the Second World War. He didn't actually take me to watch it; very little cricket was being played anywhere at that time as I recall, what with bombs dropping all over the place. But he told me about it: he told me about Surrey legends of the past called Hitch, Hayward, Hobbs and Sandham, and so infused me with enthusiasm that I borrowed countless books from the public library and soon, without ever having played the game or seen it played, I became a mine of cricket lore.

The first match of any kind that I ever watched was at Lord's in August 1945, an unofficial 'Victory' Test match – England versus the Australian Services. On that glorious, sunny day Cyril Washbrook scored 112, the diminutive Bill Edrich (an immediate idol of mine, later to be joined in my estimation by the incomparable Denis Compton) hit a belligerent 73 and Wally Hammond scorched the earth with his cover drives while he made 83. And all this against an attack that included the soon-to-be-great Keith Miller.

In those days and in succeeding summers, when I became an ardent Middlesex fan, I sat in the free seats or, along with other kids, on the grass in front of the famous Tavern, now sadly long demolished. And there we would remain, our school satchels bulging with Tizer and sandwiches, from pretty well soon after the gates opened until close of play. More than half a century was to pass before I could take my place, as a member of the Marylebone Cricket Club, in the great old Victorian pavilion, the very headquarters of world cricket.

RIGHT *'Oh God, if there be cricket in heaven, let there also be rain,' wrote Sir Alec Douglas-Home in 'Prayer of a Cricketer's Wife'. Here a long-suffering cricket fan waits under his umbrella for the rain to stop and for play to restart, May 1924.*

FINDING MY WAY INTO THE PAVILION

Until the late 1990s when, belatedly, women were permitted not only to enter the pavilion but actually to become members of the MCC (W.G. Grace must have been spinning in his grave), Lord's was an exclusively male enclave, a relic of an earlier, more class- and gender-divided age. Not that it has entirely moved into the 21st century even now; many of the rules that governed behaviour when Lord's moved to its present site in 1814 still pertain in 2009.

This is a place where jeans and trainers are not allowed, where ties and, except in the hottest weather, jackets must always be worn, a place where good manners are almost obligatory and where captains of industry, who outside the ground would treat each other and everyone else with utter ruthlessness, somehow become the very models of courtesy. 'After you, old man.' 'No, no, old boy. After you, please.'

FAREWELL TO THE DON

I have another abiding early memory of Lord's. It was August again, but this time it was 1948, and Don Bradman was playing his last match there, not a Test but simply Australia against the Gentlemen of England. The ground was packed. At 9.30 in the morning the queue stretched from the Grace Gates right round the corner almost to what was then the car park.

It is more than a game, this cricket, it somehow holds a mirror up to English society. ● Neville Cardus

When Bradman made his appearance, number three in the order as usual, trotting down the steps of the Members' stand, everyone stood and applauded and carried on applauding until he had taken his guard. Disappointingly small he seemed to those of us who, in the pre-television era, had never seen him before – until he started to bat.

And then we simply sat and watched, not just admiring but awed, for, I don't know, maybe a couple of hours or however long it took him to score exactly 150, with every shot played all along the ground. Then, the 150 up, he hit a ball – from the England all-rounder Freddie Brown – into the air for the first time, tucked his bat under his arm and was almost halfway back to the pavilion before the New Zealander Martin Donnelly took the catch.

We in the crowd rose again and applauded him all the way back and we were still clapping – and, let's be honest, many of us were weeping – for some time after he had disappeared into the pavilion.

Only cricket, I think, can provide the onlooker with moments like that and, if I hadn't already been hooked on the game, seeing Bradman's farewell to Lord's would have done it for me. But I was hooked and had been since that Victory Test three years earlier. Indeed, I am hooked still and to this day Lord's is one of my favourite places in the world.

But how did it all come about? How did this wonderful pastime grow to become, after football, the most popular game on the planet?

BELOW *An icon of Lord's, the weather vane depicting Father Time was presented in 1926 by Sir Herbert Baker, architect of the old northwestern stand. When this was demolished, he was given a new home on the ground's southeastern side.*

CHAPTER I
A Short History
of Cricket

FROM VILLAGE GAME TO
GLOBAL SPORT

Cricket is the most complex game in the world. It's like chess played on grass, with living pieces and bats and a ball thrown in just to complicate matters even more. Harold Pinter once said: 'I tend to think that cricket is the greatest thing God ever created on earth, certainly greater than sex, although sex is not too bad either.' I'm not going to argue with any of that. Hey, the man won the Nobel Prize for literature – he knew what he was talking about.

But what nobody really knows for sure is when cricket began or even how it got its name. It could have derived from the French word *criquet* (a club), or the Flemish *krick* or *kricke* (a stick) or the Old English *cricc* or *cryce* – with the c's pronounced as k's – which means a kind of staff.

LEFT *Forerunners of the MCC playing a match on Mary-le-Bone Fields in London c.1744, in a painting by Francis Hayman, RA. As was customary for this period, the bowler's delivery is under-arm, the batsman wields a curved-back, cudgel-shaped bat, and the wicket is low, with only two stumps.*

CRICKET'S OPENING OVERS

Whatever, there is a little evidence, though nothing conclusive, that a form of the game was played in England in Saxon times. There's also a theory that it was actually introduced by merchants returning from India or Persia, or even by the Flemish. Say again – the Flemish? *Belgians*? No, no let's be jingoistic and reject that. We thought of it first, right? It's our game, even if some countries (though not Belgium) play it rather better than we do.

In a court case in 1597 there was reference to a game of 'krickett' being played by boys in Surrey, it being regarded then as a pastime for boys rather than grown men. But that soon changed and by the turn of the century or soon after matches were organized on a local basis between neighbouring parishes.

With minor hiccups such as the English Civil War and the coming to power of Oliver Cromwell and his Puritans, who took a sour view of games or any kind of pleasure, come to that, cricket continued to thrive throughout the 17th century, especially after the restoration of the monarchy in 1660, when matches attracted fierce gambling.

By the 18th century, or maybe even earlier, teams were becoming less parochial, adopting the names not just of their villages or towns but of their counties, although the games they played were one-off contests. There's no evidence of anything as organized or official as leagues or cup competitions.

LAWS AND LORD'S

The Laws of Cricket – being the most majestic of games it has no truck with anything as common as 'rules' – were drawn up in a rudimentary way in the 1720s, more significantly in 1744 when the length of the pitch was decreed to be 22 yards and innovations like umpires and a third stump were introduced and, most significantly of all, in 1787 when the Marylebone Cricket Club

(MCC) was formed at Lord's and grandly took it upon itself to be the custodian of the Laws, an honour which it has zealously retained ever since. By then the game had already seen many changes. Until about 1760 bowlers had rolled the ball along the ground, so that batting must have been rather like playing croquet except that the ball approached the striker rather than the other way round. But now bowlers started pitching the ball, flighting it and varying the pace, and to counteract this the old-style bats, which looked much like hockey sticks, were replaced by straighter versions, very similar to those used today.

In the early-to-mid 1700s there had been thriving cricket clubs in London, Kent and Yorkshire but the most famous was the Hambledon club in Hampshire, which was founded in 1760 and became the focal point of the game until the establishment of the MCC. It was Hambledon which, in 1771 after an opposing player with the intriguing name of Shock White had turned up with a bat as wide as the wicket (28"), decreed that in future the maximum width of bats should be no more than 4¼ inches.

ROUND-ARM TO OVER-ARM

More changes were to come in the 19th century. In the 1820s round-arm bowling replaced under-arm, though not without much controversy. There are various theories as to how it came about, the one I like being that, during the Napoleonic Wars, Christiana Willes, sister of the Kent player John Willes, used to bowl to him in the garden and because her hooped skirts were so wide she simply couldn't bowl under-arm but had to deliver the ball from waist height. The well-known pedant and occasional politician John Major says in his book *More Than a Game* (2007) that this probably isn't true because hooped skirts were unfashionable during the Napoleonic Wars, but he was always a spoilsport.

In round-arm bowling, legalized in 1835, the ball was delivered with the hand somewhere between waist and shoulder height; if the hand rose above the shoulder (over-arm) it was a no-ball. Round-arm remained the legitimate form of delivery until the 1860s and indeed it was still used, notably by W.G. Grace, much later than that. But bowlers, seeking as ever to put one over the batters, started raising their hands above the shoulder, sometimes being no-balled sometimes not, until at the Oval in 1862 the All-England bowler James Willsher, playing against Surrey, sent down six over-arm deliveries in a row, was no-balled each time and, in protest, walked off the pitch with all the other professionals in the England team.

This brought matters to a head and the MCC swiftly amended the rules (beg their pardon, Laws) in time for the 1864 season when, for the first time, bowlers were allowed to deliver the ball from any height they wished, whether their hands were above or below the shoulder, so long as they kept their arms straight. And, oh my, what a can of worms the 'straight arm' bit opened up; if you don't believe me ask Muttiah Muralitharan.

BELOW *The statuesque figure of Alfred Mynn, stalwart of his county side for 25 years (1834–59) and one of the greatest all-rounders of his day. For all his imposing physique, however, Mynn almost lost a leg early in his career to the new (and much faster) style of round-arm bowling. His injury prompted the introduction of batting pads.*

Batting pads were introduced in 1836 after the enormous Alfred Mynn of Kent (6 foot-plus and around 23 stone), who was as great a champion in the early part of the century as Grace became in the latter half, was hit so horrendously on the shin while batting that it was feared his leg might have to be amputated. In fact it wasn't and he made a full recovery but his fellow batters said, 'Bloody hell!' (or the Victorian equivalent), 'we'd better do something about that,' and pads were duly invented. Likewise wicketkeepers took to wearing gloves in the 1850s, round-arm bowling probably coming at them at a greater, more stinging, pace than under-arm deliveries.

Things happened rapidly in the 19th century. Gambling on matches became so rife and out of control that in 1817 a leading player, William Lambert, was banned for life for match-fixing. Nothing changes, you see. Old Wm. might have been the first but he was by no means the last to be so ignominiously booted out.

On a more salubrious note Sussex founded the first official County Cricket Club in 1839 and most of the other counties followed suit over the succeeding decades. Overs consisted of four balls until 1889, then five until 1900 when the number of deliveries was raised to six, although in Australia and New Zealand eight-ball overs were bowled between 1922 and 1979. Now the Laws have decreed that the number should be six, wherever the game might be played.

ABOVE *The first England overseas touring side, pictured on board ship in Liverpool just prior to their departure for America, 1 September 1859. Back row (from left to right): Robert Carpenter, William Caffyn, Thomas Lockyer, John Wisden (seated), Heathfield Stephenson, George Parr (captain), James Grundy, Julius Caesar, Thomas Hayward, John Jackson. Front row (l to r): Alfred Diver and John Lillywhite. They won every game.*

THE GAME OF EMPIRE

BELOW An Imaginary
Cricket Match: England v.
Australia, 1887, *by Sir
Robert Ponsonby Staples.
In the right foreground the
Prince of Wales's mistress
Lillie Langtry turns away
as the top-hatted Prince
arrives with Princess
Alexandra (far right).*

Thanks to the British people's long-standing tendency to stuff a few ships with soldiers, nip over an ocean or two and conquer any lands they happened to come across, cricket had been introduced into North America by English colonists during the 17th century and then to the West Indies and India, before arriving in Australia in the late 18th century. New Zealand and South Africa were given the inestimable benefit of the game in the 19th century, so whatever you might think of British imperialism it can't have been all that bad, can it? – not if it spread cricket so far and wide. The first overseas tour took place in 1859 when a team of English pros travelled to the USA and Canada, there to defeat every team they met. The first Test matches, England

Heavenly weather … Cricket weather. Sit around under sunshades. Over after over. ● James Joyce in *Ulysses*

versus Australia, took place in Australia in 1877–8. In between times *Wisden Cricketers' Almanack* – the Bible of the game – was first published in 1864.

The County Cricket Championship began in 1890, those taking part being Gloucestershire, Kent, Lancashire, Middlesex, Nottinghamshire, Surrey (who won it), Sussex and Yorkshire. The years between then and the start of the Great War in 1914 have become known as the 'Golden Age', an era when legendary figures such as Grace, K.S. Ranjitsinhji, C.B. Fry, Sydney Barnes, F.R. Spofforth, Hugh Trumble and Victor Trumper were in (or in Grace's case just past) their pomp. Whether it was known as the Golden Age then is open to doubt: Golden Ages tend to be so named as the result of 20/20 rose-tinted hindsight, but there were certainly some pretty terrific players around in those days.

The growth of Test cricket

In 1909 the Imperial Cricket Conference (ICC) was formed (it would become the International Cricket Conference in 1965, after decolonization had kicked in), its members consisting of England, Australia and South Africa. Three years later what might now be considered the first cricket World Cup, or anyway the first World Championship, was contested when the above-named nations, then the only Test-playing countries, took part in a triangular series in England. The host nation came out on top but nobody really cared; it was such a dismal, rain-ruined competition that it was never tried again.

Besides, between the First and Second World Wars the West Indies, New Zealand and India became Test nations, and Pakistan joined them soon after their country was created in the 1947 Partition of India. Sri Lanka and Zimbabwe acquired Test status in 1981 and 1992 respectively, and Bangladesh became the tenth Test-playing nation in 2000. By then any international competition involving all of them would have been far too lengthy and cumbersome unless the games were made one-day events, which as we know is exactly what happened.

RIGHT *The captains of the three sides contesting the 1912 Triangular Test Tournament line up for a photo-call. From left to right: Frank Mitchell (South Africa), C.B. Fry (England) and Syd Gregory (Australia). Nine matches were played from June to August, with no deciding final. Not for the first or last time, the English summer dampened proceedings, and attendances were poor.*

During the 20th century and especially in its later decades, when attendances at other first-class matches everywhere dwindled pathetically, Test cricket (and also one-day internationals) became increasingly important. Us against Them is all very well when it's a County Championship match, but Us against Them when it's two nations going head-to-head is much more urgent – and it's most urgent of all when the two nations in question are England and Australia with the Ashes at stake.

At various times, with their inbuilt resentment of – and what an Australian once described as their 'cultural cringe' towards – the 'Mother Country', the Aussies will insist that playing the West Indies or India is more important than playing against England, but in their hearts they know it's not. For anyone wearing the baggy green cap, thrashing the Poms and seizing the Ashes is the ultimate achievement.

So let us next look at the history of that often bitterly (though not always, alas, and I speak here as an Englishman, closely) contested series between the Old Enemies.

BELOW *Ricky Ponting, Glenn McGrath and Adam Gilchrist celebrate Australia's unprecedented third successive World Cup victory, which they sealed by beating Sri Lanka in the final at Bridgetown, Barbados, in April 2007.*

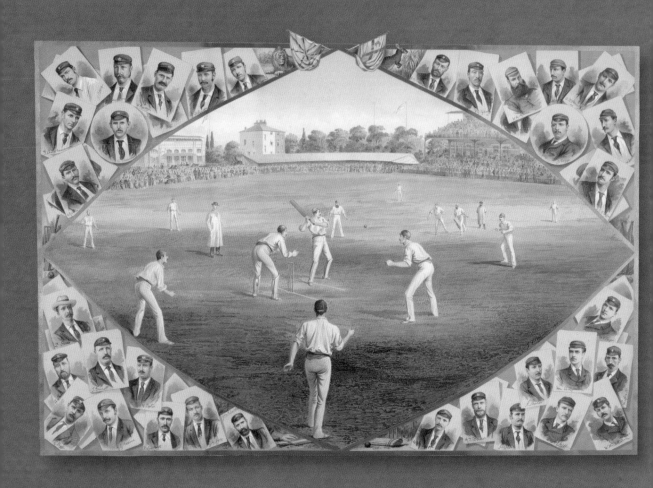

CHAPTER 2
THE LITTLE MATTER
of THE ASHES

TEST CRICKET'S OLDEST AND BITTEREST
RIVALRY: RECORDS AND STATISTICS,
PLUS CELEBRATED FEATS
WITH BAT AND BALL

The first international cricket match took place on 24–25 September 1844, in what now seems the most unlikely setting of New York, when the USA played Canada. Actually, the fact that the game took place at all isn't really surprising. Cricket was widely played in both countries at the time and indeed in the USA it was possibly even more popular than baseball until the Civil War. The Philadelphia club was particularly strong in the 1880s and when they toured England in 1889 their star player, J. Barton ('Bart') King, was reckoned to be one of the best fast bowlers in the world.

However, that first match can't have been much fun to watch. Canada scored only 82 and 63, the USA an even more pathetic 64 and 58, and Canada won by 23 runs. By all accounts the most exciting aspect of the contest was the betting that took place around it, an estimated $120,000 (which equates to an astronomical sum these days) being wagered on the outcome.

BEGIN AS YOU MEAN TO GO ON

But all that is no more than a historical oddity because the really serious stuff didn't begin until nearly 33 years later when, on 15 March 1877 at Melbourne, England and Australia faced each other for the first time. The visitors, captained by James Lillywhite of Sussex, had not got off to a good start. Several of England's leading players, W.G. Grace among them, had turned down the invitation to tour and the party, which only numbered 12 to begin with, was rapidly reduced to 11 when the wicketkeeper, Ted Pooley of Surrey, got into a fight over a bet in New Zealand and ended up in jail, so Lillywhite and the others arrived for the first Test in Australia without him.

Nor was that the end of their troubles because the deputy 'keeper, Henry Jupp, who was widely regarded as clinically insane, was having one of his bad spells and couldn't be entrusted with the gloves. But, *faute de mieux*, there being only 11 players left, he had to be picked as a batsman and, in fact, ended up as England's top scorer in the game with 63, so obviously there was some kind of method in his madness.

The first ball in real Test cricket was bowled by Alfred Shaw of Nottinghamshire to Charles Bannerman, who scored the first run and went on to make the first century – 165 retired hurt, out of a total of 245. To his records can be added that of Billy Midwinter who, when England batted and were dismissed for 196, took 5 for 78, thus recording the first five-for (or as we movie buffs like to call it, Michelle) in

LEFT Vignettes of English and Australian cricketers surround a scene from the Lord's Test of 19–21 July 1886. England, dominant for much of the 1880s, won by an innings and 106 runs.

BELOW England's Alfred Shaw, bowler of the very first ball in Test cricket, pictured late in his career (1895) at the age of 53.

Test history. Australia then managed only 104 in their second knock, leaving England to score a mere 153 to win.

But, alas, as was to happen all too often in the future, they were simply not up to it. Skittled for 108, England lost the inaugural Test by 45 runs. Mind you, the same 11 players (Pooley still languishing in clink) did much better in the second match, also at Melbourne, which they won by four wickets, thus squaring the series.

England, this time captained by the autocratic Lord Harris, later to govern Bombay, returned to Australia in 1878–9 and lost the only Test by 10 wickets, the Aussie fast bowler Fred ('the Demon') Spofforth taking the first hat-trick in a Test match. In 1880, when Australia came to England for the first time, England – and Lord Harris – got their revenge with a one-nil win. Back in Australia in 1881–2, however, the Aussies, captained by W.L. Murdoch, beat Alfred Shaw's England two-nil in a four-match series.

But all these games were merely opening skirmishes in the never-ending war that was to come…

HOWZAT! William Midwinter, born in Gloucestershire in 1851, is the only man to have played both for and against Australia. An all-rounder who emigrated to Oz, he turned out for Australia in the inaugural Test between the two countries at Melbourne, then returned to his homeland, played for Gloucestershire and toured Australia in 1881–2 as a member of Alfred Shaw's team, opening the bowling for England in two Tests. After that, commuting between the two countries and ever the cheerful mercenary, he represented Australia again in 1882–3 and 1886–7 and toured England with the Aussies in 1884. Altogether he played eight Tests for Australia and four for England. Sadly, however, this unique cricketer ended his life tragically. After the deaths of his wife and children he became insane and died in a lunatic asylum in 1890.

THE MOTHER OF CRICKETING RIVALRIES

England versus Australia at cricket is significant for all manner of historical and cultural reasons. When the series of matches began England, or rather Britain, was the predominant nation in the world, Australia simply one of its colonies, its population consisting (in the lofty English view) largely of descendants of deported criminals. To an extent this was probably true, but the Aussies rather resented what they regarded with some justification as English patronage and condescension. And they still do.

Consider this: 'England versus Australia is *the* cricketing rivalry, the one that matters above all others: the Empire versus the Colony, Victorian manners versus Victorian Bushrangers, men representing the Queen against men representing the Queen's Land.' I don't know how eloquent 'the Demon'

Spofforth was but he might well have said this towards the end of the 19th century, although in fact the words were written by Geoff Lawson, the former Australian fast bowler, in his foreword to Simon Briggs's book *Stiff Upper Lips and Baggy Green Caps*, published in 2006.

Never mind that England, or even Britain, doesn't have an empire any more or that the last vestige of Victorian manners (some might say any kind of good manners) disappeared from the British Isles decades ago; the Australian perception of toffee-nosed Englishmen continuing to look down on their humble colonial cousins clearly still persists. And it doesn't matter that this is a misconception. English cricket-lovers respect and admire (albeit a touch grudgingly) Australian cricket and its champions, the Bradmans, Warnes, McGraths, Waughs and Pontings. Deep down we wish they had belonged to us, not them. But the Aussies won't have it. The colonial resentment, inferiority complex if you like, instilled in them by us in Victorian times lingers on. And it is this – along with the Ashes – that gives a unique edge to every series of cricket matches between England and Australia.

THE INVENTION OF THE ASHES

The early games between the two countries were played hard enough but the introduction of the Ashes gave all future contests a particularly sharp focus. The Ashes were created, or rather invented, after the only Test of the 1882

BELOW An engraving of the famous Oval match in late August 1882 that brought the first Australian victory on English soil and gave rise to the Ashes. Frederick 'the Demon' Spofforth, seen here bowling to W.G. Grace, was the hero of the hour, taking 7 for 28 in the second innings to skittle the home side out for 77, 8 short of their target.

series at the Oval. The captains for this historic match were A.N. ('Monkey') Hornby for England and W.L. Murdoch for Australia. (The Australians, at this point anyway, obviously took the game too seriously to have silly nicknames.) In dull, damp conditions Australia batted first and were all out for 63. In reply England made 101. For the home side, so far so good – and things looked even better when, second time around, the Aussies could manage only 122, thanks partly to a bit of gamesmanship by W.G. Grace when he unsportingly ran out Sammy Jones who, having comfortably completed a run, had wandered down the wicket to replace a divot. Actually, this wasn't nearly as smart a move as W.G. might have supposed: his conduct really got up the nose of the 'Demon' Spofforth who, when England went in to bat again needing only 85 to win, destroyed them with a mixture of medium-paced off-breaks, break-backs and cutters. Spofforth ended the match with an analysis of 14 for 90 and England lost by seven runs. The tension towards the end of the game was such that one spectator is said to have died of a heart attack, while another apparently bit through the handle of his brother-in-law's umbrella, though which of them was actually holding the umbrella at the time is not known.

What is most important about the game, however, is the aftermath. On the Saturday after the match Reginald Shirley Brooks published the following mock obituary in the *Sporting Times*:

We have come to beard the kangaroo in his den – and try to recover those Ashes. ● Hon. Ivo Bligh, 1882

Enter now the Hon. Ivo Bligh, who that winter took an England team to Australia and kept harping on about 'the ashes'. At first this didn't strike much of a chord in Aussies, few of whom were known to read the *Sporting Times*, but eventually the message got through that, somehow, something called the Ashes were at stake in the four Tests the teams were to play. The series ended two-all but, for various reasons, only the first three games were regarded as official Tests and since England won those two-one Bligh was reckoned to have regained the Ashes, which – literally – is what he did.

There are several theories about the actual creation of the Ashes but the most widely accepted is that at a country-house party hosted by Sir William Clarke at his estate in Victoria, either before the series started or after the third Test, the England team – or, anyway, the amateurs among them; nobody invited pros to country-house parties – were presented by a bunch of Melbourne ladies with an urn, possibly a former perfume jar, about six inches high and made of terracotta, containing… what? Some say it was either the ashes of a cricket bail, or a stump, or the outer casing of a ball or – gruesome thought – even the dusty remains of King Cole, who had toured England with an Australian Aboriginal team in 1868. Most people, including the MCC, now believe that the urn contains the remnants of a bail.

HOWZAT! Albert Trott, who was born in 1872 and represented Victoria, made three appearances for Australia against A.E. Stoddart's team in 1894–5, scoring 205 runs at an average of 102.5 and taking nine wickets at 21.33. Good enough, you might have thought, to get him into the Aussie touring team of 1896, especially as it was captained by his brother, George Henry (Harry) Trott. But apparently not. Spurned by the selectors, Albert made his own way to the Mother Country, joined Middlesex, threw in his lot with England and played two Tests against South Africa in 1898–9. In the summer of 1899 he rubbed a little salt into Aussie wounds when, playing for Middlesex, he hit a ball from Monty Noble, captain of the Australian tourists, over the top of the pavilion at Lord's, a feat nobody has ever been able to equal.

ASHES RECORDS: ENGLAND

Most Ashes appearances

	Span	T
M.C. Cowdrey	1954–75	43
G.A. Gooch	1975–95	42
D.I. Gower	1978–91	42
J.B. Hobbs	1908–30	41
W. Rhodes	1899–1926	41

Highest innings totals

Score	Ground	Match date
903–7d	The Oval	20 Aug. 1938
658–8d	Trent Bridge	10 June 1938
636	Sydney	14 Dec. 1928
627–9d	Old Trafford	6 July 1934
611	Old Trafford	23 July 1964

Note: England's lowest-ever total was 45 at Sydney in 1887.

Top ten batting averages (qualification: 10 matches)

		T	I	NO	R	HS	Av.
H. Sutcliffe	1924–34	27	46	5	2741	194	66.85
K.F. Barrington	1961–8	23	39	6	2111	256	63.96
M. Leyland	1929–38	20	34	4	1705	187	58.83
L. Hutton	1938–55	27	49	6	2428	364	56.47
J.B. Hobbs	1908–30	41	71	4	3636	187	54.26
K.P. Pietersen	2005–7	10	20	2	963	158	53.50
W.R. Hammond	1928–47	33	58	3	2852	251	51.85
J.H. Edrich	1964–75	32	57	3	2644	175	48.96
F.S. Jackson	1893–1905	20	33	4	1415	144*	48.79
M.P. Vaughan	2002–5	10	20	0	959	184	47.95

Highest run-scorers

		T	I	NO	R	HS	Av.
J.B. Hobbs	1908–30	41	71	4	3636	187	54.26
D.I. Gower	1978–91	42	77	4	3269	215	44.78
G. Boycott	1964–81	38	71	9	2945	191	47.50
W.R. Hammond	1928–47	33	58	3	2852	251	51.85
H. Sutcliffe	1924–34	27	46	5	2741	194	66.85

Most centuries

	T	100s
J.B. Hobbs	41	12
D.I. Gower	42	9
W.R. Hammond	33	9
H. Sutcliffe	27	8
G. Boycott	38	7
J.H. Edrich	32	7
M. Leyland	20	7

The most celebrated of all England opening partnerships, Jack Hobbs and Herbert Sutcliffe come out to bat during the 1928–9 series in Australia. Hobbs and Sutcliffe amassed a total of 11 century partnerships against the Aussies.

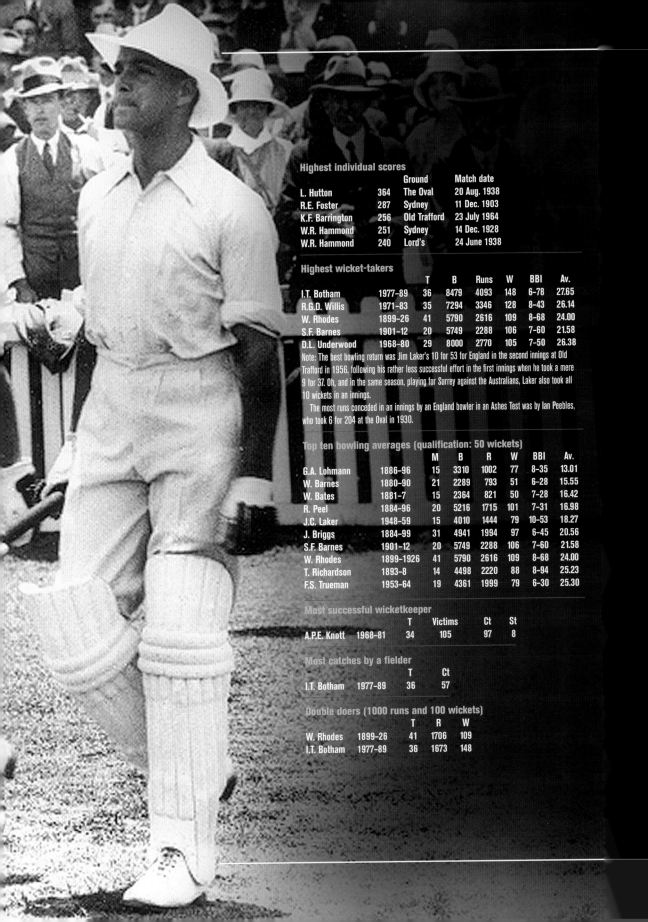

Highest individual scores

		Ground	Match date
L. Hutton	364	The Oval	20 Aug. 1938
R.E. Foster	287	Sydney	11 Dec. 1903
K.F. Barrington	256	Old Trafford	23 July 1964
W.R. Hammond	251	Sydney	14 Dec. 1928
W.R. Hammond	240	Lord's	24 June 1938

Highest wicket-takers

		T	B	Runs	W	BBI	Av.
I.T. Botham	1977–89	36	8479	4093	148	6–78	27.65
R.G.D. Willis	1971–83	35	7294	3346	128	8–43	26.14
W. Rhodes	1899–26	41	5790	2616	109	8–68	24.00
S.F. Barnes	1901–12	20	5749	2288	106	7–60	21.58
D.L. Underwood	1968–80	29	8000	2770	105	7–50	26.38

Note: The best bowling return was Jim Laker's 10 for 53 for England in the second innings at Old Trafford in 1956, following his rather less successful effort in the first innings when he took a mere 9 for 37. Oh, and in the same season, playing for Surrey against the Australians, Laker also took all 10 wickets in an innings.

The most runs conceded in an innings by an England bowler in an Ashes Test was by Ian Peebles, who took 6 for 204 at the Oval in 1930.

Top ten bowling averages (qualification: 50 wickets)

		M	B	R	W	BBI	Av.
G.A. Lohmann	1886–96	15	3310	1002	77	8–35	13.01
W. Barnes	1880–90	21	2289	793	51	6–28	15.55
W. Bates	1881–7	15	2364	821	50	7–28	16.42
R. Peel	1884–96	20	5216	1715	101	7–31	16.98
J.C. Laker	1948–59	15	4010	1444	79	10–53	18.27
J. Briggs	1884–99	31	4941	1994	97	6–45	20.56
S.F. Barnes	1901–12	20	5749	2288	106	7–60	21.58
W. Rhodes	1899–1926	41	5790	2616	109	8–68	24.00
T. Richardson	1893–8	14	4498	2220	88	8–94	25.23
F.S. Trueman	1953–64	19	4361	1999	79	6–30	25.30

Most successful wicketkeeper

		T	Victims	Ct	St
A.P.E. Knott	1968–81	34	105	97	8

Most catches by a fielder

		T	Ct
I.T. Botham	1977–89	36	57

Double doers (1000 runs and 100 wickets)

		T	R	W
W. Rhodes	1899–26	41	1706	109
I.T. Botham	1977–89	36	1673	148

Sir Ivo, later to become Lord Darnley, kept the trophy until his death in 1927 when his widow, the former Florence Morphy, one of the Melbourne ladies who made the original presentation, handed it to the MCC for safe keeping and, apart from a couple of courtesy visits to Australia, it has remained at Lord's ever since.

These days the winners of the Ashes (usually Australia, it grieves me to say) are presented with a slightly larger-than-life replica of the urn made of Waterford crystal, but the Ashes themselves have a permanent home in the Lord's museum. Nevertheless, their very existence has added a particular zest to every Anglo-Australian encounter since 1882.

INTO THE 20TH CENTURY

For a while England held the upper hand. In 12 series (counting Bligh's) until 1897–8, England won 11 times, after which the pendulum swung briefly the other way. Australia won the next four series but then the Empire struck back again and won four of the six contests between 1903–4 and 1912.

That was the end of the Golden Age. Grace was gone from the English team, along with Ranji, Archie MacLaren, C.B. Fry and the rest. Gone, too, from the Australian line-up were Trumper, Spofforth, Clem Hill and other

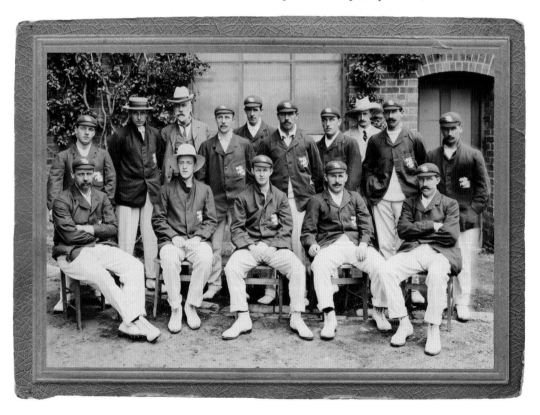

early greats like Hugh Trumble. But some who had made their mark in the latter part of this period – Jack Hobbs, Wilfred Rhodes and Warwick Armstrong among them – would continue to play significant parts when hostilities were resumed after the First World War.

England–Australia contests had been temporarily shelved after 1912 on account of infinitely nastier hostilities breaking out in 1914. But when that dispute was resolved, not to anybody's satisfaction really, the Ashes series resumed with a vengeance, Australia regaining titular possession of the urn with a five-nil walloping of England – the first whitewash, though not, sadly, the last – in 1920–1. The winning captain then was the massive Warwick Armstrong, a fine all-rounder, who stood 6' 3" and didn't so much hit the scales at around 22 stone as cause them grievous bodily harm. His opposite number, J.W.H.T. Douglas, whose dour batting caused his initials to be interpreted as meaning 'Johnny Won't Hit Today', was a former Olympic middleweight boxing champion, but in this series he and his team were seriously overmatched (see Warwick's Wonders, pages 233–240).

So, too, was the England side of 1921 when Armstrong and his gang thrashed them three-nil on home soil, thanks largely to the fact that Australia had created something of a precedent by opening their attack with two truly fast bowlers, J.M. Gregory and E.A. McDonald, who between them took 46 wickets in the series at a joint average of comfortably under 30. Until then Test attacks had often been opened by a fast bowler at one end and some sort of spinner at the other, a practice still adhered to in English county cricket for many years. In 1947 I can remember seeing Middlesex kicking off with the fast-medium Laurie Gray and the left-arm spinner Jack Young.

NOBLESSE OBLIGE AND PROFESSIONAL QUALITY

England's captain for most of the 1921 series was the Hon. Lionel Tennyson, grandson of the former poet laureate Alfred of that ilk. He was not a bad batsman, but you can't help feeling that he got the job because, even after the War, cricket in England was still regarded as a pastime for gentlemen with nothing much better to do. The words of Lord Hawke, of Yorkshire, a snob's snob – 'Pray God, no professional shall captain England' – retained a strong resonance with the selectors. And indeed no professional was to captain England regularly until well after the Second World War, although the Nottinghamshire professional Arthur Shrewsbury had led the side for seven matches in the mid-1880s. In 1924–5 England lost again, four-one, but, glory be, they finally won a post-war series (one-nil) in 1926, thanks to Jack Hobbs and Herbert Sutcliffe opening the second innings with a stand of 172 on a sticky wicket in the final match at the Oval.

Now, though, the old order began to change and new heroes emerged. The first of these, for England, was Walter Hammond of Gloucestershire,

FAR LEFT After Australia had won the thrilling 1902 Ashes series in England 2–1, Pelham Warner's MCC side toured Australia in 1903–4, pulling off an equally close 3–2 win to regain the Ashes. Back row (from left to right): Herbert Strudwick, Len Braund, J. A. Murdock (manager) Albert Knight, Edward Arnold, Arthur Fielder, Wilfred Rhodes, Reginald Foster, Albert Relf, John Tyldesley. Front row (l to r), Tom Hayward, Bernard Bosanquet, Pelham Warner, George Hirst and Arthur Lilley. Three decades later, 'Plum' Warner was England's manager on the infamous Bodyline tour.

BELOW *Groundsman
'Bosser' Martin poses
proudly with his heavy
roller in front of a
scoreboard displaying
England's final score in the
fifth Test at the Oval,
1938. Bosser's behemoth,
which he used to prepare
the wicket with a mixture
of cow dung and clay,
played no small part in the
match, creating a flat strip
on which batsmen could
post huge scores.*

who in 1928–9 scored a staggering 905 runs at an average of 113.12 in a series resoundingly won four-one by A.P.F. Chapman's touring England team. Surely – no question – here was the best batsman in the world, destined to bestride the cricket scene for years to come.

Well, alas, no. For also playing in that series was a 20-year-old from Bowral, New South Wales, one Donald Bradman. He did very well – 468 runs at 66.85 – but that hardly put him in Hammond's class. The Aussies had what they regarded as an even better prospect in the 19-year-old Archie Jackson, who scored 164 on his debut to become the youngest player, till then, to make a hundred in a Test match. Sadly, Jackson was to die of tuberculosis only four years later, his promise unfulfilled.

What, though, of Bradman? Not a bad player, England thought – until 1930 when he proceeded to smash Hammond's record by notching up 974 runs at 139.14 in a series won two-one by W.M. Woodfull's Australians. From then until his retirement in 1948 Bradman was, give or take the odd glitch, to dominate international cricket, not only the greatest batsman of his time but surely the greatest ever to play the game.

England, led by the saturnine Douglas Jardine, ably abetted by the hostile fast bowling of Harold Larwood and Bill Voce, did manage to clip his wings in 1932–3 – the infamous 'Bodyline' series, which we'll discuss elsewhere (see pages 265–269). With only 396 runs at 56.75, Bradman seemed almost mortal that year but back in England in 1934, when the Australians regained the Ashes two-one, it was business as usual with the Don scoring 758 runs at 94.75. By 1936–7 (Aussies winning again, three-two) he was the team captain and remained so until the end of his career. Oh, and he also managed a little matter of 810 runs at an average of 90. It seemed almost unfair. Why should God, who as every Englishman knows was a founder-member of the MCC, gift Australia, of all nations, such a prodigy? What had the English done that He should play such a dirty trick on us?

The 1938 series, with England now captained by Wally Hammond, who had turned amateur to gain this privilege, was a one-all draw, notable for the final game at the Oval when England made the record total of 903 for 7 declared and won by an innings and 579 (another record), helped, for good measure, by yet a third record in the shape of Len Hutton's score of 364, then the highest individual innings in Test history.

And that was it for the next several years, thanks to a certain Adolf Hitler, whose Austrian upbringing sadly didn't include cricket – surely he would have been a much better man if it had – plunging the world into the most God-awful chaos.

Resuming hostilities after the war

England did not visit Australia again until 1946–7, when Bradman's team beat Hammond's three-nil, thanks not only to Bradman who, boringly, topped the batting averages again, but also to the emergence of the formidable Aussie fast-bowling combination of Keith Miller and Ray Lindwall. And, from the English point of view, things were no better in 1948 when Bradman's 'Invincibles' (see pages 240–247) beat England, now captained by Norman Yardley, four-nil, or in 1950–1 when Australia, led by A.L. Hassett, beat Freddie Brown's England four-one.

By now, 'the Colonials' had held the Ashes for 15 years, but at last things began to look up for 'the Empire' (what Empire? It was disintegrating in front of their eyes). England under Hutton – their first professional captain, and not before time – regained the urn one-nil in 1953 and retained it three-one in 1954–5, thanks to the demon bowling of Frank Tyson, well supported by Brian Statham. Peter May then took over from Hutton and Ian Johnson from Hassett for the 1956 series in which, on the way to a two-one victory, Jim Laker slaughtered the Aussies at Old Trafford by taking 19 wickets in the match (see Laker's Match, pages 214–216). We English take particular relish in such feats because nothing much like them happens too often.

BELOW *Denis Compton and Bill Edrich make their way to the Oval pavilion through a sea of delighted spectators, as England win the final test of the tense 1953 series by 8 wickets to take the series 1–0 and regain the Ashes. England thereby ended a period of Australian supremacy that dated back to 1934.*

The brief period of English supremacy, however, was not to last. Richie Benaud's team beat May's four-one in 1958–9 and two-one in 1961, then drew one-each with Ted Dexter's tourists in 1962–3. After that R.B. (Bobby) Simpson took over for Australia to beat Dexter's lot one-nil in 1964 before sharing a one-all draw with M.J.K. Smith's XI in 1965–6. In 1968 Colin Cowdrey was captain when England drew the series one-apiece with W.M. (Bill) Lawry's Aussies. Another six series had gone by without Australia losing but things started to look up for the Old Country again when the gritty Yorkshireman Ray Illingworth led England to a two-nil win in 1970–1.

RETURN OF THE FAST MEN

In that series Geoff Boycott scored 657 runs at 93.86 but it was John Snow, with 31 wickets at 22.84, whose seriously quick bowling really won the Ashes. At Sydney Snow nearly caused a riot when he hit the Aussie leg-spinner and tail-ender Terry Jenner a frightful crack on the head with a bouncer (see right). As a result beer cans and bottles were thrown at England's deep fielders and Illingworth took his team off the field in protest. Snow, a clergyman's son and a published poet, was uncontrite, writing later of opposing batsmen in general: 'I never let them forget the game is played with a very hard ball.'

ABOVE Echoes of Bodyline? Australian tail-ender Terry Jenner is felled by a bouncer from England paceman John Snow on the second day of the seventh Test in Sydney, 13 February 1971. The crowd at the SCG, never renowned for their restraint, responded by hurling bottles and cans onto the pitch.

During this series the Australian selectors, probably more ruthless than their English counterparts, ditched their captain, the dour Bill Lawry, without bothering to tell him in person and replaced him with Ian Chappell, a much feistier character, whose team in 1972 held Illingworth's England to a two-two draw, the most notable feat being Bob Massie's 16 for 137 at Lord's.

The Aussies had always played their cricket hard – Bradman was not exactly a softie – but under Ian Chappell they became harder still, especially in 1974–5 when the England captain Mike Denness saw not only English wickets but English bones broken under a furious new-ball onslaught from Dennis Lillee and Jeff Thomson, the latter probably bowling as fast as anyone ever has and remarking, with more candour than charm, that he enjoyed hitting batsmen even more than bowling them out. Thomson took 33 wickets at 17.93 and Lillee 25 at 23.84 and England lost that series four-one, only gaining the single win because Thommo missed the last Test with an injury. Australia's star batsman in the 1974–5 series was another Chappell, Ian's equally bloody-minded younger brother Greg, who scored 608 runs at 55.27. In 1975, under Tony Greig, England lost again (one-nothing).

HOWZAT! Syd Gregory (Australia) was dismissed for a duck 11 times in Ashes Tests, and Ian Botham and Shane Warne 10 times each. Clem Hill for Australia was dismissed in the 90s five times. Nine players have carried their bats throughout an innings; of these, Bill Brown of Australia made the highest score, 206* at Lord's in 1938 and Jack Hobbs (England) the lowest, 23* at Adelaide in 1908. Bill Woodfull (Australia) is the only player to have carried his bat twice: 30* at Brisbane in 1928 and 73* at Adelaide in 1933.

LEFT *Ian Botham takes a catch to dismiss Graham Yallop off John Emburey's bowling during the fourth Test match at Edgbaston, 1981. Botham then put on a devastating display of aggressive swing bowling, taking 5 wickets for just 1 run in 28 balls to pull off an unlikely victory and give England a 2–1 series lead. A series that had begun ignominiously, with a loss and a draw and Botham's resignation as captain, ended in a 3–1 England triumph.*

Taking fresh guard after the century

In 1976–7 Greig took England to Melbourne for one match celebrating the centenary of the continuing strife between the two countries. With what the Aussies probably regarded as a pleasing symmetry Australia won that game, as they had won the very first, by 45 runs, notwithstanding a heroic century by Derek Randall for England. In this single contest the Ashes weren't up for grabs, not that it would have mattered because Australia held them anyway.

Soon after this, however, the Australian tycoon Kerry Packer upset everybody's apple-cart by waving fat cheques at most of the world's best players, thus wooing them away from their national teams to establish his rival, and unofficial, World Series Cricket (see The Packer Revolution, pages 269–272). It would be quite wrong to say that this decimated the Australian squad (even Packer wasn't ruthless enough to kill one in ten of them) but Australia certainly suffered more than most.

Greg Chappell captained them in 1977 but his Packer-distracted team were beaten three-nil by J.M. Brearley's England, a series notable for Bob Willis's 27 wickets at 19.77 and Boycott's return from a self-imposed exile from Test cricket to make a six-hour 100 at Trent Bridge (after running out the local hero, Derek Randall) on the way to amassing 442 runs at 147.33. In 1978–9, with Chappell having succumbed to the mogul's money, a weakened Australia under Graham Yallop were thrashed five-one by Brearley and

FAR LEFT *Jeff Thomson's unique slinging-style action, which generated incredible pace, is perfectly illustrated in this action shot by celebrated cricket photographer Patrick Eagar. Thomson – who took 100 Ashes wickets at 24.18 in 21 matches – once memorably gave a no-nonsense account of his bowling method: 'I just roll up and go whang!'*

company, although the home fast bowler Rodney Hogg returned the remarkable figures of 41 wickets at 12.85. A year later England toured again under Brearley and lost three-nothing to a full-strength Australia, a sort of whitewash in that only three Tests were played. But it had been decreed, much to Australian indignation after the event, that the Ashes would not be at stake this time so England weren't too bothered.

Besides, next came 1981, Ian Botham's year (see Botham's Match, pages 220–222), during which England, captained again by Brearley, defeated Australia, led by Kim Hughes (he who would later, famously, resign in tears after a defeat by the West Indies), by the emphatic margin of three-one. The visiting hero was the right arm fast-medium Terry Alderman, who took nine wickets in the match on his debut at Lord's, on the way to snaffling 42 at 21.26 in the series.

However, with Greg Chappell back in charge Australia beat Bob Willis's England two-one in 1982–3, England being somewhat weakened by the fact that Graham Gooch had taken a rebel side on tour to South Africa. After this Allan Border became the Australian skipper and remained so for five series, the first of which his team lost to England, led by David Gower, in 1985 by three-one when Gower scored 732 runs at 81.33, and the second of which saw England, now skippered by Mike Gatting, win two-one in 1986–7 despite being rubbished in advance as useless in English as well as Australian newspapers.

ENGLISHMEN OF A SENSITIVE DISPOSITION SHOULD LOOK AWAY NOW

At this point, here endeth the good news – for English readers anyway. Between 1989 and 2002–3, Australia, led three times by Border, three times by Mark Taylor and twice by Steve Waugh, won eight series in a row. In that time England were captained variously by Gower, Graham Gooch, Mike Atherton, Alec Stewart and Nasser Hussain – none of whom could do much more than look on helplessly as Australia rattled up 18 victories to England's paltry seven.

In these encounters there was little enough for England to cheer. In 1989, a six-Test series, Australia won four-nothing, with Mark Taylor notching up 838 at 83.80 and Terry Alderman taking 41 wickets at 17.36. In 1990–1 the victory margin was three-nothing, this time largely thanks to the left-arm fast-medium Bruce Reid taking 27 wickets at the miserly rate of 16.00.

Shall I go on? Yes, I suppose I'd better, painful though it is. 1993 saw the advent of Shane Warne and 'the ball of the century', his first in Ashes cricket, the one he bowled to a bemused Mike Gatting at Old Trafford, the prodigious leg-break that appeared to pitch on the square-leg umpire's boot before turning enough to hit off-stump. (Gatting was famous for his healthy appetite, prompting Graham Gooch to say of the ball of the century: 'If that had been a cheese roll it would never have got past him.') Gooch scored 673 runs in the series at 56.08 but Warne took 34 wickets at 25.79 and Australia won four-one.

When the pressure point comes, English cricketers crumble. ● Shane Warne sledges the Poms, 1997

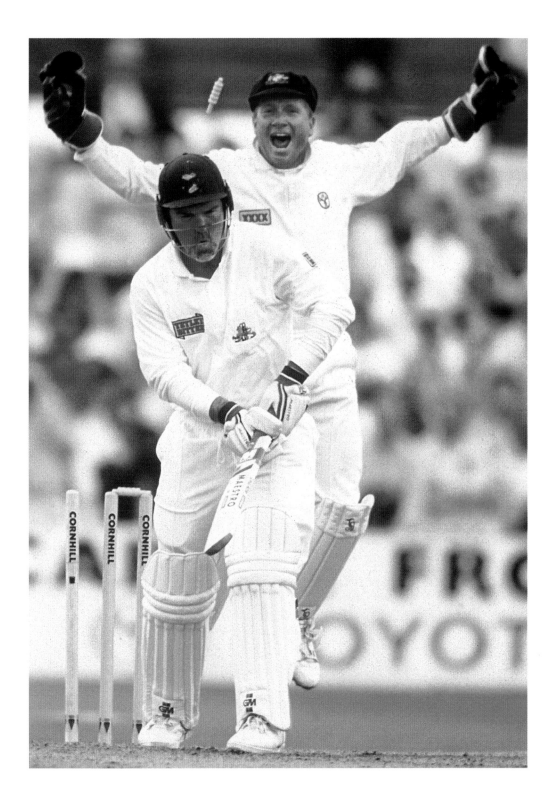

ASHES RECORDS: AUSTRALIA

Most Ashes appearances

	Span	T
S.E. Gregory	1890–1912	52
A.R. Border	1978–93	47
S.R. Waugh	1986–2003	46
W.W. Armstrong	1902–21	42
R.W. Marsh	1970–83	42

Note: Sydney Edward Gregory (1870–1929), a right-handed batsman who toured England with Australia eight times, is the only man to appear in more than 50 Ashes Tests to date.

Highest innings totals

Score	Ground	Match date
729–6d	Lord's	27 June 1930
701	The Oval	18 Aug. 1934
695	The Oval	16 Aug. 1930
659–8d	Sydney	13 Dec. 1946
656–8d	Manchester	23 July 1964

Note: Australia's lowest-ever total was 36 at Edgbaston in 1902.

Top ten batting averages (qualification: 10 matches)

		T	I	NO	R	HS	Av.
D.G. Bradman	1928–48	37	63	7	5028	334	89.78
S.R. Waugh	1986–2003	46	73	18	3200	177*	58.18
A.R. Border	1978–93	47	82	19	3548	200*	56.31
G.R.J. Matthews	1985–91	10	16	5	589	128	53.55
D.M. Jones	1986–91	17	28	2	1320	184*	50.77
A.R. Morris	1946–55	24	43	2	2080	206	50.73
K.R. Stackpole	1966–72	13	24	1	1164	207	50.61
J. Langer	1998–2007	21	38	5	1658	250	50.25
R.B. Simpson	1958–66	19	31	3	1405	311	50.18
M.E. Waugh	1991–2001	29	51	7	2204	140	50.09

Highest run–scorers

		T	I	NO	R	HS	Av.
D.G. Bradman	1928–48	37	63	7	5028	334	89.78
A.R. Border	1978–93	47	82	19	3548	200*	56.31
S.R. Waugh	1986–2003	46	73	18	3200	177*	58.18
C. Hill	1896–1912	41	76	1	2660	188	35.46
G.S. Chappell	1970–83	35	65	8	2619	144	45.94

Most centuries

	T	100s
D.G. Bradman	37	19
S.R. Waugh	46	10
G.S. Chappell	35	9
A.R. Border	47	8
A.R. Morris	24	8

Highest individual scores

		Ground	Match date
D.G. Bradman	334	Headingley	11 July 1930
R.B. Simpson	311	Old Trafford	23 July 1964
R.M. Cowper	307	Melbourne	11 Feb. 1966
D.G. Bradman	304	Headingley	20 July 1934
D.G. Bradman	270	Melbourne	1 Jan. 1937

Highest wicket-takers

		T	B	R	W	BBI	Av.
S.K. Warne	1993–2007	36	10,757	4535	195	8–71	23.25
D.K. Lillee	1971–82	29	8516	3507	167	7–89	21.00
G.D. McGrath	1994–2007	30	7280	3286	157	8–38	20.92
H. Trumble	1890–1904	31	7895	2945	141	8–65	20.88
M.A. Noble	1898–1909	39	6845	2860	115	7–17	24.86

Don Bradman, on his first tour of England, hits out on his way to 131 in his second innings of the first Test at Trent Bridge, 17 June 1930. The England wicketkeeper is George Duckworth, with Hammond in the gully and Woolley at slip.

Top ten bowling averages (qualification: 50 wickets)

		T	B	R	W	BBI	Av.
C.T.B.Turner	1887–95	17	5195	1670	101	7–43	16.53
R.M. Hogg	1978–83	11	2629	952	56	6–74	17.00
F.R. Spofforth	1877–87	18	4185	1731	94	7–44	18.41
H. Trumble	1890–1904	31	7895	2945	141	8–65	20.88
G.D. McGrath	1994–2007	30	7280	3286	157	8–38	20.92
D.K. Lillee	1971–82	29	8516	3507	167	7–89	21.00
T.M. Alderman	1981–91	17	4717	2117	100	6–47	21.17
G.E. Palmer	1880–6	17	4517	1678	78	7–65	21.51
K.R. Miller	1946–56	29	5717	1949	87	7–60	22.40
R.R. Lindwall	1946–59	29	6728	2559	114	7–63	22.44

Note: The best bowling in an Ashes Test match (or any Test match) by an Australian was by R.A.L. Massie, who took 16 for 137 at Lord's (on his Test debut) in 1972. The most expensive bowling in an Ashes contest (or any Test) was by Leslie ('Chuck') Fleetwood-Smith who, against England at the Oval in 1938, returned a match analysis of 1 for 298.

Most successful wicketkeeper

		T	Victims	Ct	St
R.W. Marsh	1970–83	42	148	141	7

Most catches by a fielder

		T	Ct
G.S. Chappell	1970–83	35	61

Double doers (1000 runs and 100 wickets)

		T	R	W
G. Giffen	1881–96	31	1238	103
M.A. Noble	1898–1909	39	1905	115

Note: K.R. Miller scored 1511 Ashes runs on top of his 87 wickets, while S.K. Warne scored 946 runs as well as taking 195 wickets.

1994–5 saw England, now under Mike Atherton ('Captain Grumpy'), beaten three-one. They did rather better in another six-match series in 1997, losing only three-two, with England's second win, at the Oval, coming courtesy of 11 wickets by the beer-swilling, fag-puffing left-arm spinner Phil Tufnell, of whom Ian Chappell said: 'The other advantage for England when Tufnell's bowling is that he isn't fielding.'

Warne missed the first four Tests in 1998–9, not that England found much comfort in that because his replacement, Stuart MacGill, took 27 wickets at 17.70 as Australia won three-one. But Warne was back to take 31 wickets at 18.70 when Steve Waugh took over the Australian captaincy in 2001 to give England a four-one spanking. Glenn McGrath did even better with 32 at 16.93. It was four-one again in 2002–3, though at least there was some solace for England in that Michael Vaughan played better than he ever did before or since to score 633 runs at 63.30, including three centuries.

But, oh, the shame of it – and, once again, the unfairness. Once more God had done the dirty on England by gifting Australia not only with a mighty array of batsmen – Border, Steve Waugh and his brother Mark, Ricky Ponting, Matthew Hayden and Justin Langer among them – but, just to make the odds even more uneven, He'd also given them the world's greatest spinner in Warne and one of its very finest fast-medium bowlers in McGrath.

England's year in the sun

Yet, at last, in 2005 the sun broke through and shone benignly on England, who regained the Ashes by a score of two to one, thanks in part to a superlative all-round performance by Andrew ('Freddie') Flintoff (24 wickets at 27.29 and 402 runs at 40.20), one particularly heroic innings by Kevin Pietersen, a crucial dropped catch by Warne and an injury to McGrath. Now England – or so we thought – had a great team, with splendid fast bowlers in Steve Harmison, Flintoff, Simon Jones and Matthew Hoggard, a champion batsman in Pietersen and an astute captain in Michael Vaughan. We'd beaten the best, so now we were the best. 'Bring it on, Aussies!', we said.

And unfortunately they did. In 2006–7 an England team, captained by Flintoff in the absence of the injured Vaughan, might just as well have posted the Ashes to Australia and not even bothered to tour (see Ponting's Party-Poopers, pages 258–262). They were thrashed, walloped, massacred five-nil, which is where matters now rest with the record between the two countries reading:

ABOVE *Steve Waugh, holding the Waterford Crystal Ashes replica, and Adam Gilchrist celebrate Australia's 4–1 victory in the 2002–3 Ashes series, after the final Test at the SCG on 6 January 2003.*

OPPOSITE *Still unsteady on their feet after a marathon victory bender, England's 2005 Ashes stars Andrew Flintoff and Kevin Pietersen arrive at 10 Downing Street for an official reception with prime minister Tony Blair. The Aussies took the view that England had celebrated their triumph just a little too well, and duly prepared a horrible revenge.*

Matches played:	316
Won by England:	97
Won by Australia:	131
Drawn:	88

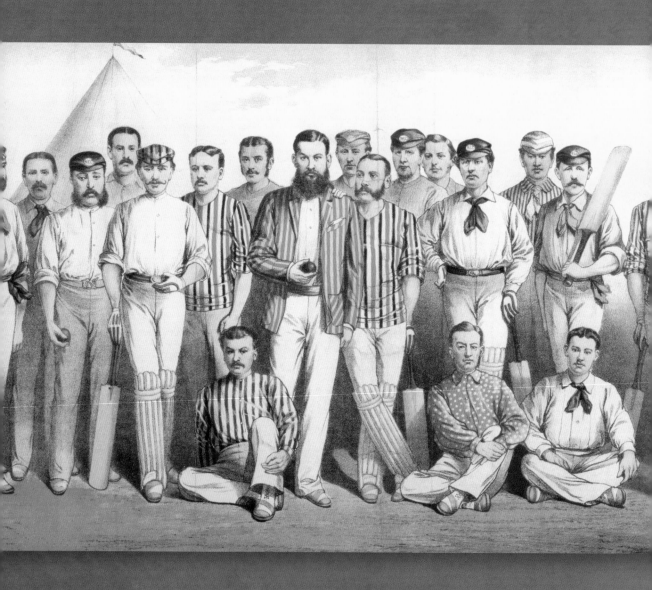

CHAPTER 3
THE ENGLISH GAME

THE 18 FIRST-CLASS COUNTIES:
HISTORY, HONOURS, RECORDS, NOTABLE
PLAYERS AND FASCINATING FACTS

I n England the hub of the first-class game is the County Championship, which first took an officially recognized shape in 1890. Before then there had been a very unofficial championship, often decided by newspapers, which printed the results of such county games as were played and arbitrarily anointed a champion side. But this led to much confusion and in 1889 the counties got together, laid down the rules and the official Championship was born and recognized by *Wisden* which, being the Bible of the game, is the final arbiter on all matters worthy of record.

Somerset joined the original eight first-class counties in 1891 and Derbyshire, Essex, Hampshire, Leicestershire and Warwickshire brought the numbers up to fourteen in 1895. Worcestershire joined them in 1899, Northants in 1905, Glamorgan in 1921 and finally Durham made it an even eighteen in 1992.

UP AND DOWN

Until 1999 the counties all played together in one league, but in 2000 the Championship was divided into two divisions of nine teams each, with promotion and relegation decided on a three-up, three-down basis, though this was later changed to two-up and two-down.

The argument – or anyway one argument – in favour of changing the system was that over the years the Championship had become a cosy, even listless, affair, especially towards the end of the season when it was usually quite obvious that only two or three sides had a chance of winning the title and the rest had nothing much to play for except their wages. Relegation and promotion battles, it was suggested, would give the players added incentive, concentrate their minds and keep them on their toes from start to finish.

This certainly proved to be the case in 2008 when, until the last two or three games of the season, any eight of the nine teams could have ended up either as First Division champions or relegated. But in cricket, unlike in football, I doubt if it makes much difference to the supporters which division their team is playing in; they still tend to turn up in as large – or, rather, as small – numbers as they did before. Nor, really, is there any marked difference between the strength of the teams in the two divisions – on paper anyway. You can, for instance, find England players like Alastair Cook and Ravi Bopara of Essex, Andrew Strauss and Owais Shah of Middlesex and Monty Panesar of Northamptonshire turning out in Division Two, while Sussex, when they won the Championship in 2006, had no current England players at all.

On the other hand you have to be pretty quick off the mark to find any of England's Test squad appearing for their counties because their international contracts with the England and Wales Cricket Board (ECB) preclude their

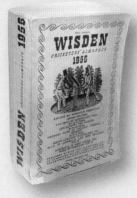

ABOVE Wisden Cricketers' Almanack *first appeared in 1864 and has been published annually without interruption ever since. The distinctive woodcut of two Victorian cricketers that was the* Almanack's *principal cover illustration from 1938 until 2003 was the work of the artist Eric Ravilious.*

LEFT *'Famous English Cricketers', a coloured lithograph of 1880 from* The Boy's Own Paper.

THE FIRST-CLASS GAME

First-class matches are played over three, four or five days. One-dayers and Twenty20 don't count. They have their place, of course, and their champions but, please, don't mention them in the same breath as first-class matches. Indeed, there are purists even now who don't regard them as proper cricket, arguing that if God had wanted all cricket matches to produce a winner and a loser he'd have made them timeless. As a matter of fact, until the Second World War a lot of games – particularly Tests – were timeless, but even that didn't always work. At Durban in 1938–9 England played South Africa over 10 days and it still ended in a draw on account of England having a boat to catch. This made the purists – and, for all I know, God – very happy.

playing more than at most a handful of county matches each year. In 2006, for instance, when Middlesex were relegated from Division One their captain Andrew Strauss didn't turn out for them once, being too busy opening the innings for England.

Imagine how such a situation would go down in football. What interesting shade of enraged purple might Sir Alex Ferguson turn if someone told him that Wayne Rooney was no longer available for Manchester United because of his England commitments?

Even so, winning Division One, which is to say the County Championship, is still something to be prized. Well, ask anyone from Sussex who, though founder-members of the thing, had to wait 113 years before they gained their first title in 2003. They've made up for lost time since, having won it again in 2006 and 2007.

But over the years – though not lately – Yorkshire have been by far the most successful county, having won the Championship 31 times; Surrey, with 28 wins, are their closest rivals. The least successful are Gloucestershire, Somerset and Northamptonshire, who have never won. Admittedly, Northamptonshire did win the Second Division title in its inaugural year, but it's not the same, is it?

At the other end of the scale the battle for most wooden spoons is more evenly fought, with Derbyshire having propped up all the rest 14 times and Somerset (13) and our old friends Northamptonshire (11) running them close.

THE ARRIVAL OF THE ONE-DAY GAME

Cricket changed forever in 1963 with the introduction in England of the first one-day competition, the Gillette Cup. Attendances at three-day county matches were waning year by year so a brisk, one-day, 60-overs knockout tournament was dreamt up as a way to revive interest. Little could the instigators have realized what they had done. Their new, quicker version of the noble game proved so popular that six years later the 40-overs, Sunday-afternoon John Player League was introduced, followed in 1972 by the Benson & Hedges Cup, both of which drew the crowds. Now the floodgates were open and within little more than a generation the one-day game, by attracting huge audiences, was to dominate cricket all over the world, especially in India. Even Test matches, where the game is played at its highest, subtlest, most devious level, no longer attract, day by day, the sort of crowds that will flock to a Twenty20 contest. The Twenty20 Cup – a mere 20 overs an innings of bash and clout, admittedly sometimes clever and often exciting bashing and clouting – was inaugurated in England in 2003, though since

1890

Team	P	W	L	D	Pts
1 Surrey	14	9	3	2	6
2 Lancashire	14	7	3	4	4
3 Kent	14	6	3	5	3
4 Yorkshire	14	6	3	5	3
5 Nottinghamshire	14	5	5	4	0
6 Gloucestershire	14	5	6	3	-1
7 Middlesex	12	3	8	1	-5
8 Sussex	12	1	11	0	-10

Points system: 1 for a win, 0 for a draw, -1 for a loss

LEFT *George Lohmann played for Surrey from 1884 to 1896, taking a career-best 220 wickets in the 1890 County Championship.*

2008

Division One

		P	W	L	Tie	D	Abandoned	Batting bonus points	Bowling bonus points	Deduct	Pts	
1	Durham	16	6	3	0	6	1	37	41	0	190	
2	Nottinghamshire	16	5	3	0	7	1	37	43	0	182	
3	Hampshire	16	5	4	0	7	0	33	47	0	178	
4	Somerset	16	3	2	0	11	0	44	44	0	174	
5	Lancashire	16	5	2	0	8	1	24	40	0	170	
6	Sussex	16	2	2	0	12	0	45	38	0	159	
7	Yorkshire	16	2	5	0	9	0	50	45	0	159	
8	Kent	16	4	6	0	6	0	30	44	0	154	Relegated to Division 2
9	Surrey	16	0	5	0	10	1	45	36	1	124	

Division Two

		P	W	L	Tie	D	Abandoned	Batting bonus points	Bowling bonus points	Deduct	Pts	
1	Warwickshire	16	5	0	0	11	0	53	46	0	213	Promoted to Division 1
2	Worcestershire	16	6	2	0	7	1	40	45	5	196	
3	Middlesex	16	4	5	0	7	0	46	45	0	175	
4	Northamptonshire	16	3	3	0	10	0	52	35	0	169	
5	Essex	16	5	6	0	5	0	36	45	3	168	
6	Derbyshire	16	4	3	0	9	0	33	46	4	167	
7	Leicestershire	16	3	4	0	9	0	29	43	0	150	
8	Glamorgan	16	3	5	0	7	1	26	36	0	136	
9	Gloucestershire	16	0	5	0	11	0	42	38	2	122	

Points system: Win: 14 points. Tie: 7 points. Draw: 4 points. Loss: No points awarded. Teams also collect bonus points for their batting and bowling performances in the first 130 overs of each innings. These points are retained regardless of the outcome of the match.

then (see Twenty20, pages 298–303) it's been hijacked by India where the Indian Premier League threatens, at the time of writing, to dominate all of cricket, thanks to its financial clout. It's an interesting enough game in its own limited way, but one that has precious little to do with real cricket.

So far in England the County Championship is still more important and prestigious than any national knockout cup or the One-Day League. But to spectators brought up on the ever-shifting images of television and thus equipped with the attention span of fruit-flies or, to put it more kindly, with less free time than their predecessors, it's the one-day game that rules.

Today the knockout cups in England are played over 50 overs and every now and then – like the Championship itself – change their names as new sponsors, prosperous firms either eager to show their devotion to the game or to hitch a ride on cricket's popularity, take over from each other. The counties' achievements in all the competitions are detailed in the pages that follow.

THE MINOR COUNTIES: A SHORT HISTORY

What are the Minor Counties? Well, they are the counties which were not accorded first-class status when the County Championship began in 1890 and formed their own championship in 1895. As we have seen, four of them – Worcestershire in 1899, Northants in 1905, Glamorgan in 1921 and Durham in 1992 – were later given first-class status.

In the early days the first-class counties' second XIs also competed in the Minor Counties Championship and, both before and after the Second World War, won it quite often. In 1959, however, the Second XI Championship was established and thereafter fewer second XIs played with the Minors. Yorkshire Seconds were the last to win the title in 1971 and Somerset Seconds were the last to appear in the Minor Counties Championship in 1987.

From the start professionals like the great Sydney Barnes turned out for the Minor Counties' sides, but mostly the teams consisted of amateurs. The Championship games were organized in batches so that players could arrange their summer holidays around them. For many years the teams played between eight and a dozen or so two-day matches, usually against neighbouring counties to keep the travelling down. But in 1983 the competition was changed into a two-division affair, ten teams in each division and each team playing six three-day matches with the

divisional winners having a play-off to decide the Championship.

Also in 1983 the Minor Counties Cricket Association Knockout Cup was started to mirror the first-class counties' knockout competitions. Like most one-day cup contests it has changed its name a number of times and between 1998 and 2002 involved 38 teams, among them the first-class counties' cricket boards. In 2002 it was won by the Warwickshire Cricket Board XI, but since then the competition has been streamlined and is now contested only by Minor Counties sides.

The Minor Counties Championship has been won most often by Staffordshire (ten times), but it's probably fair to say that Durham (nine wins, including two shared titles) would have surpassed them had they not joined the top flight. Devon have won it six times, including one shared title, and three counties – Cheshire, Hertfordshire and Oxfordshire – have been champions four times. Wales (which represents all the Welsh counties except Glamorgan) has never won it, but has only taken part since 1983.

Norfolk and Devon (four times) have been the most frequent winners of the Knockout Cup. Cheshire are close behind with three wins, while six counties – including poor old Wales – have yet to record a final victory.

THE FIRST-CLASS COUNTIES

DERBYSHIRE

Founded: 1870
HQ: County Ground, Derby
County Champions: 1936
One-Day League Champions: 1990
**Gillette Cup/NatWest Trophy/C&G
Trophy/Friends Provident Trophy:** 1981
Benson & Hedges Cup: 1993

Derbyshire supporters will forgive me (or maybe not) for saying that theirs is not exactly a fashionable county. On the whole the clamour of players wishing to join has, certainly in recent years, been easily drowned out by the clamour of those keen to get out. One thinks of such former stalwarts – and Test players – as Kim Barnett and Dominic Cork, who decided in the last 10 years or so that better futures awaited them at, respectively, Gloucestershire and Lancashire, while in 2008 Rikki Clarke came from Surrey to be Derbyshire's captain, soon gave up the job and, before the season was over, had joined Warwickshire. In the same year Nayan Doshi also joined from Surrey and also left before the end of the summer.

In the late 19th century the county had almost come to financial grief when its then assistant secretary dipped his fingers liberally into the till before scarpering to Madrid, there to become tailor to the king of Spain. His crime, curiously enough, was brought to light by none other than

F.R. Spofforth, the 'Demon' bowler, who had married a local girl, played briefly for Derbyshire and, for reasons best known to himself, took a close interest in the county's financial affairs. But every county has its ups as well as its downs and Derbyshire, too, has its warm memories, though fewer perhaps than many of their rivals: 1936 when, under the captaincy of A.W. Richardson, they were county champions, was their biggest year. And 1981, when they became the first winners of the NatWest Trophy, was not bad either.

Notable players: T.S. (Stan) Worthington who, at the Oval in 1936 made 128 against India, became the only Derbyshire player to score a century for England. R.W. (Bob) Taylor, the best in a line of Derbyshire 'keepers who played for England, claimed 174 victims in 57 Tests (1971–84), and more first-class victims (1649) than any other wicketkeeper. The all-rounder Geoff Miller, who

BELOW Derbyshire's Devon Malcolm limbers up before the start of the sixth Test match between England and the West Indies at the Oval in 1995.

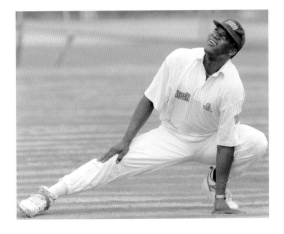

HOWZAT! In 1887 the Derbyshire wicketkeeper William Storer became the first professional to score a century in each innings of a first-class match.

— DERBYSHIRE RECORDS —

Highest Total For: 801-8d vs Somerset, Taunton, 2007
Highest Total Against: 662 by Yorkshire, Chesterfield, 1898
Lowest Total For: 16 vs Nottinghamshire, Nottingham, 1879
Lowest Total Against: 23 by Hampshire, Burton upon Trent, 1958
Highest Innings For: 274 by G.A. Davidson vs Lancashire, Manchester, 1896
Highest Innings Against: 343* by P.A. Perrin for Essex, Chesterfield, 1904
Best Bowling For: 10-40 by W. Bestwick vs Glamorgan, Cardiff 1921
Best Bowling Against: 10-45 by R.L. Johnson for Middlesex, Derby, 1994
Most Runs in a Season: 2165 by D.B. Carr, 1959
Most Runs in a Career: 23,854 by K.J. Barnett, 1979-98
Most 100s in a Season: 8 by P.N. Kirsten, 1982
Most 100s in a Career: 53 by K.J. Barnett, 1970-98
Most Wickets in a Season: 168 by T.B. Mitchell, 1935
Most Wickets in a Career: 1670 by H.L. Jackson 1947-63
Most Career Dismissals by a Wicketkeeper: 1304 (1157 ct, 147 st) by R.W. Taylor, 1961-84
Most Career Catches by a Fielder: 563 by D.C. Morgan, 1950-69

later went to Essex, won 34 caps for England and in 2008 became chairman of the national selectors. Donald Carr scored more runs in a season than any other Derbyshire player but is perhaps most notable for the fact that in 1945, having just left Repton School, he played for England in a Victory 'Test' against Australia. Later he played in two real Tests. For the most part, however, the stalwarts of Derbyshire cricket, with the exception of imports like the South African Eddie Barlow, who captained the side in the 1970s, have been fine county pros, who occasionally (and in some cases more than occasionally) played for England – men like the fast bowlers Bill Copson in the 1930s, Cliff Gladwin (1940s and 50s), Les Jackson in the 1950s, Mike Hendrick and Alan Ward in the 1970s, the all-rounder George Pope (1930s and 40s) and the leg-spinner Tommy Mitchell (1930s) along with Dominic Cork and the batsman Denis Smith who in the 1930s and 1940s was the county's most prolific scorer until Barnett came

along. Then, too, there was the Jamaican-born fast bowler Devon Malcolm who took 128 wickets for England, and who, in a Test against South Africa in 1994, was struck on the helmet by a ball from Fanie de Villiers and was so incensed that he announced to his opponents: 'You guys are history!' and proved it by taking 9 for 57 in the South African second innings.

DURHAM

Founded: 1882
HQ: The Riverside, Chester-le-Street
County Champions: 2008
Friends Provident Trophy: 2007
NatWest Pro 40 League: 2007 (Division Two)

As new boys to the Championship (they only joined in 1992) Durham understandably took time to settle but in 2008 they nailed the big one – the County Championship – to go along with a couple of one-day trophies and the nine Minor County Championships (two of them shared) that they won between 1901 and 1984. Their other distinction before they joined the big boys was to be the first minor county to beat a first-class side when they defeated Yorkshire in the Gillette Cup in 1973. In the first few years after promotion Durham depended heavily on imports from other counties and countries, such as Wayne Larkins, Ian Botham and David Graveney, later chairman of the England selectors, and David Boon and Dean Jones from Australia. Success was slow to come but in 2005, captained by the Australian Mike Hussey, they were promoted to the first divisions of both

of the West Indies, have given sterling service. But Durham is surely proudest of its home-grown talent – Collingwood, one of the mainstays of England's Test batting and for a while the country's captain in ODIs; Steve Harmison, extremely fast, eternally erratic but a potential match-winner who was briefly rated the best bowler in the world; Plunkett, whose talent has yet to be fulfilled; and Mustard, who can count himself unlucky not to have won at least one Test cap.

the County Championship and the National Cricket League. And in beating Hampshire for the Friends Provident Trophy in 2007 they broke the record for most runs scored in the final of a 50-overs tournament in making 312 for 5. Latterly, the county has produced its own stars and now boasts Paul Collingwood, Steve Harmison and Liam Plunkett, all of whom have played Test cricket – with distinction in the first two cases – and Phil Mustard, who has kept wicket and opened the batting for England in one-day internationals. Nor should we forget Gary Pratt, whose outstanding fielding as a substitute helped England regain the Ashes in 2005 and caused Ricky Ponting to throw a notorious hissy fit.

Notable players: In the early first-class years Botham, Boon, Dean and Larkins lent glamour if not a lot of success to the club. For some time Larkins was Durham's leading run-scorer and still holds the record for most runs scored in a single season. More recently Hussey and Shivnarine Chanderpaul and Ottis Gibson, both

---

— DURHAM RECORDS —

Highest Total For: 645–6d vs Middlesex, Lord's, 2002
Highest Total Against: 810–4d by Warwickshire, Birmingham, 1994
Lowest Total For: 67 vs Middlesex, Lords, 1996
Lowest Total Against: 56 by Somerset, Chester-le-Street, 2003
Highest Innings For: 273 by M.L. Love vs Hampshire, Chester-le-Street, 2003
Highest Innings Against: 501* by B.C. Lara for Warwickshire, Birmingham, 1994
Best Bowling For: 10–47 by O.D. Gibson vs Hampshire, Chester-le-Street, 2007
Best Bowling Against: 9–36 by M.S. Kasprowicz for Glamorgan, Cardiff, 2003
Most Runs in a Season: 1536 by W. Larkins, 1992
Most Runs in a Career: 7856 by J.J.B. Lewis, 1997–2006
Most 100s in a Season: 6 by P.D. Collingwood, 2005
Most 100s in a Career: 14 by J.E. Morris, 1994–9, and P.D. Collingwood, 1996–2008
Most Wickets in a Season: 80 by O.D. Gibson, 2007
Most Wickets in a Career: 518 by S.J.E. Brown, 1992–2002
Most Career Dismissals by a Wicketkeeper: 194 (189 ct, 5 st) by M.P. Speight, 1997–2001
Most Career Catches by a Fielder: 116 by P.D. Collingwood, 1996–2008

 HOWZAT! The wicketkeeper Phil Mustard is known as the Colonel, after the murder suspect Colonel Mustard in the board game 'Cluedo'.

ESSEX

Founded: 1876
HQ: County Ground, Chelmsford
County Champions: 1979, 1983, 1984, 1986,
1991, 1992. Division Two: 2002
One-Day League: 1981, 1984, 1985, 2005, 2006
**Gillette Cup/NatWest Trophy/
C&G Trophy/Friends Provident Trophy:**
1985, 1997, 2008
Benson & Hedges Cup: 1979, 1998

For much too long after being admitted to the Championship in 1895 Essex did little more than make up the numbers. They had some pretty decent players, from C.J. Kortright, who was reckoned to be the fastest bowler in the world around the turn of the 20th century, to Percy Perrin, who scored nearly 30,000 runs, including 66 centuries, between 1896 and 1928 but never played for England. Initially Essex's problem was that it was close to London but less fashionable than Middlesex

*LEFT Charles Jesse Kortright
(Essex and England). His
obituary in the 1953
Wisden eulogized him as
'probably the fastest bowler
in the history of the game'.*

or Surrey and therefore not very attractive to the top amateurs. Also it wasn't very well off and therefore not very attractive to the top pros either. Indeed, the county was often in financial difficulties and in 1924 was obliged to raise £1000 through an emergency appeal simply to stay in business. Later it had to sell its home base at Leyton and led a peripatetic existence until it acquired the Chelmsford ground in 1967 and more or less settled down. Even so, Essex produced some distinguished players, among them J.W.H.T. Douglas who captained both England and Essex on either side of the First World War. Particularly prominent in the late 1930s was the England fast bowler Ken Farnes, who was killed in the Second World War. In the post-war years, the Essex stars were the Test players Trevor Bailey, Doug Insole and T.P.B. (Peter) Smith who, like his cousin Ray, gave splendid service as an all-rounder. They were followed by Keith Fletcher, who went on to captain England. But it wasn't until the late 1970s that Essex began to show its muscle, collecting four Championships and five other trophies between 1979 and 1986. And the county has been doing pretty well ever since, usually there or thereabouts if you overlook a sojourn in Division Two of the Championship.

Notable players: To those already mentioned must be added the names of Graham Gooch (see also pages 85–86) and Nasser Hussain, both of whom captained England. Gooch, who bagged a pair in his first Test against Australia in 1975, is nevertheless the best player Essex has ever produced. Hussain's record is less distinguished but he was a notable player both for his county and his country (he won his first cap in 1990 and made 5764 Test runs at 37.18). Of the present

HOWZAT! In 1948 Essex were the only team to bowl out Bradman's Invincibles in a single day. Mind you, they did concede 721 runs in the process.

squad, Alastair Cook has become the youngest player to score 2000 runs for England and Ravi Bopara has appeared in both Tests and ODIs.

ESSEX RECORDS

Highest Total For: 761–6d vs Leicestershire, Chelmsford, 1990
Highest Total Against: 803–4d by Kent, Brentwood, 1934
Lowest Total For: 30 vs Yorkshire, Leyton, 1901
Lowest Total Against: 14 by Surrey, Chelmsford, 1983
Highest Innings For: 343* by P.A. Perrin vs Derbyshire, Chesterfield, 1904
Highest Innings Against: 332 by W.H. Ashdown for Kent, Brentwood, 1934
Best Bowling For: 10–32 by H. Pickett vs Leicestershire, Leyton, 1895
Best Bowling Against: 10–40 by E.G. Dennett for Gloucestershire, Bristol, 1906
Most Runs in a Season: 2559 by G.A. Gooch, 1984
Most Runs in a Career: 30,701 by G.A. Gooch, 1973–97
Most Wickets in a Season: 172 by T.P.B. Smith, 1947
Most Wickets in a Career: 1610 by T.P.B. Smith, 1929–51
Most Career Dismissals by a Wicketkeeper: 1231 (1040 ct, 191 st) by B. Taylor, 1949–73
Most Career Catches by a Fielder: 519 by K.W.R. Fletcher, 1962–88.

GLAMORGAN

Founded: 1888
HQ: Sophia Gardens, Cardiff
County Champions: 1948, 1969, 1997
One-Day League: 1993, 2002, 2004

Glamorgan joined the Championship in 1921, won their first match against Sussex (by 23 runs), managed only one more victory that summer and

HOWZAT! On 31 August 1968 at Swansea, the great West Indian all-rounder Gary Sobers became the first man ever to hit six sixes in an over in first-class cricket. The unhappy, possibly even distraught, recipient of this brutal treatment was Malcolm Nash, Glamorgan's medium-slow left-arm bowler. And, no, Nash wasn't bowling for a declaration – he was really trying.

finished bottom of the county table, a position with which they became fairly familiar over the next decade or so. Their finances were dodgy, so they could afford few decent professionals and relied heavily on amateurs – notably, in the 1930s, Maurice Turnbull, captain throughout the decade, and J.C. Clay, spin bowler and club secretary. Turnbull, a triple international who was killed during the Second World War, played rugby union and hockey for Wales and was the first Welshman to win an England cap at cricket, versus New Zealand in 1929–30. Things looked up for the county after 1945 and, under the new captain Wilf Wooller and with a team composed of indigenous talent and a few imports, Glamorgan won the Championship in 1948.

With the emergence of a number of very good Welsh cricketers, including the batsman Alan Jones and the bowler Don Shepherd, this triumph was repeated in 1969 under the captaincy of Tony Lewis, who also captained England. During the 1990s and the first half of the 2000s the county did pretty well, too, but it's interesting that only 17 players have been capped for England in Tests and ODIs while playing for Glamorgan. Of them the off-spinner Robert Croft, with 21 caps between 1996 and 2001, has had the longest Test career. Were the others not good enough – or is Glamorgan simply not a fashionable county and therefore hardly impinges on the selectors' consciousness? The unluckiest of all Glamorgan players was Alan Jones, who represented England against the Rest of the World in 1970 but, unhappily for him, the matches in that series were not regarded as official Tests.

Notable players: The early stalwarts for the county were Turnbull, who played nine times for England, and Clay, who was capped only once (1935) but played on until his 50th year, taking 1317 wickets and helping Glamorgan's post-war revival. Wilf Wooller, though never quite good enough to become a Test player, took nearly 1000 wickets and scored 13,593 runs in first-class cricket and was the county's driving force, both as player and captain and later as an administrator, for many years. Other Welsh-born Glamorgan heroes include Tony Lewis, scorer of more than 20,000 first-class runs (and captain of England on the 1972–3 tour of India and Pakistan), Matt Maynard, who made 54

centuries for the county (1985–2005), the off-spinner Robert Croft and I.J. (Jeff) Jones and his son Simon, both of whom were extremely fast bowlers whose promising England careers were, alas, curtailed by injury. Steve James, who played twice for England, scored 309 not out versus Sussex in 2000 and also made five double-centuries during his county career. Don Shepherd, a right-arm fast-medium and off-break bowler, took 2218 wickets at 21.38 in all first-class cricket between 1950 and 1972. He was unlucky not to win an England cap. Distinguished overseas players for the county include Viv Richards (West Indies) and the Pakistanis Majid Khan and Javed Miandad, who made four double-hundreds for Glamorgan.

GLAMORGAN RECORDS

Highest Total For: 718-3d vs Sussex, Colwyn Bay, 2000
Highest Total Against: 712 by Northamptonshire, Northampton, 1998
Lowest Total For: 22 vs Lancashire, Liverpool, 1924
Lowest Total Against: 33 by Leicestershire, Ebbw Vale, 1965
Highest Innings For: 309* by S.P. James vs Sussex, Colwyn Bay, 2000
Highest Innings Against: 322 by M.B. Loye for Northamptonshire, Northampton, 1998
Best Bowling For: 10-51 by J. Mercer vs Worcestershire, Worcester, 1936
Best Bowling Against: 10-18 by G. Geary for Leicestershire, Pontypridd, 1929
Most Runs in a Season: 2276 by H. Morris, 1990
Most Runs in a Career: 34,056 by A. Jones, 1957-83
Most Wickets in a Season: 176 by J.C. Clay, 1937
Most Wickets in a Career: 2174 by D.J. Shepherd, 1950-72
Most Career Dismissals by a Wicketkeeper: 933 (840 ct, 93 st) by E.W. Jones, 1961-83
Most Career Catches by a Fielder: 656 by P.M. Walker, 1956-72.

GLOUCESTERSHIRE

Founded: 1870
HQ: County Ground, Bristol
One-Day League: 2000. Division Two: 2006
Gillette Cup/NatWest Trophy/
C&G Trophy/ Friends Provident Trophy:
1973, 1999, 2000, 2003, 2004
Benson & Hedges Cup: 1977, 1999, 2000

Gloucestershire's record really isn't that great; in fact, give or take a positive rash of one-day trophies between 1999 and 2006 it's pretty poor – not a single County Championship to boast of. Even so Gloucs holds a special place in the history of the game – it was the home of W.G. Grace, grand-daddy of cricket, and later of Walter

ABOVE *Gloucestershire in 1894. Back row (left to right): H. Wrathall, J.R. Painter, Smith (scorer), W.H. Murch, F.G. Roberts. Middle row (l to r): E.M. Grace (captain), A.T.H. Newnham, W.G. Grace, J.J. Ferris, S.A.P. Kitcat. Front row (l to r): W. Troup, J.H. Board, H.W. Brown.*

Hammond, one of the truly great batsmen. In its early years it was dominated by the Grace brothers, E.M., G.F. and W.G., and with them aboard was very successful in the years before the official County Championship was formed. Later Gilbert ('the Croucher') Jessop, who was reckoned to be one of the hardest-hitting batsmen the game has ever seen, the all-rounder Charlie Townsend and George Dennett performed well but received little support. Much the same was true between

the wars. Hammond was peerless then among English batsmen but the attack relied too heavily on the spinners, Tom Goddard and Charlie Parker. Indeed, Gloucestershire has produced a

HOWZAT! Jack Russell was and is an eccentric eater and tea-drinker, imbibing as many as 20 cuppas a day. Derek Randall insists that during the Oval Test of 1989 Russell used the same teabag on all five days – 100 cups in all.

number of fine spinners, including David Allen and John Mortimore in the post-war period, when the county's stars were the likes of Tom Graveney (later to move to Worcestershire), Arthur Milton (who played cricket and football for England), the Test wicketkeeper Jack Russell and the overseas players Mike Procter (South Africa), Zaheer Abbas (Pakistan) and Courtney Walsh (West Indies). The recent one-day successes owed a great deal to the coach, John Bracewell of New Zealand, and the captaincy of Mark Alleyne.

GLOUCS RECORDS

Highest Total For: 653-6d vs Glamorgan, Bristol, 1928
Highest Total Against: 774-7 declared by the Australians, Bristol, 1948
Lowest Total For: 17 vs the Australians, Cheltenham, 1896
Lowest Total Against: 12 by Northamptonshire, Gloucester, 1907
Highest Innings For: 341 by Craig Spearman vs Middlesex, Gloucester, 2004
Highest Innings Against: 319 by C.J.L. Rogers for Northamptonshire, Northampton, 2006
Best Bowling For: 10-40 by E.G. Dennett vs Essex, Bristol, 1906
Best Bowling Against: 10-66 by A.A. Mailey for the Australians, Cheltenham, 1921, and by K. Smales for Nottinghamshire, Stroud, 1956
Most Runs in Season: 2860 by W.R. Hammond, 1933
Most Runs in a Career: 33,664 by W. R. Hammond, 1920-51
Most Wickets in a Season: 222 by T.W.J. Goddard in 1937 and 1947
Most Wickets in a Career: 3170 by C.W.L. Parker, 1903-35
Most Career Dismissals by a Wicketkeeper: 1054 (950 ct, 104 st) by R.C. Russell, 1981-2004
Most Career Catches by a Fielder: 719 by C. A. Milton, 1948-74

HAMPSHIRE

Founded: 1863
HQ: The Rose Bowl, Southampton
County Champions: 1961, 1973
One-Day League: 1975, 1978, 1986
Gillette Cup/NatWest Trophy/C&G Trophy/Friends Provident Trophy: 1991, 2005
Benson & Hedges Cup: 1988, 1992

Hampshire, thanks to the Hambledon club, is widely regarded as one of the birthplaces of cricket, but for more than 65 years after being admitted to the County Championship did little of note. In the decade or so after the First World War they were particularly disappointing because, on the face of it, they had a strong team captained by the Hon. Lionel Tennyson and including the prolific batsman Phil Mead and George Brown, the wicketkeeper-batsman. In the 1930s these were replaced by men like Johnny Arnold, who played for England at both cricket and football, and another good wicketkeeper in Neil McCorkell, and in the 1950s came the outstanding fast-medium bowler Derek Shackleton. But it was not until 1961 under the dashing Colin Ingleby-Mackenzie, and with the West Indian Roy Marshall leading the batting, that the county won its first Championship. That feat was repeated in 1973, in which decade Hampshire had an attractive team that included the West Indians Gordon Greenidge and Andy Roberts, as well as Barry Richards from South Africa. Indeed, the county has never been short of attractive players, many of them imported, such as Malcolm Marshall, Robin Smith and Shane Warne. In

ABOVE C.P. (Phil) Mead of Hampshire and England. Only Jack Hobbs, Frank Woolley and 'Patsy' Hendren made more first-class runs, and nobody made more for one team than the 48,892 Mead scored for Hampshire.

recent years under Warne the team looked capable of winning the Championship but had to be content with success in shorter forms of the game.

Notable players: Hampshire has never had a player to rival Phil Mead, who scored 55,061 runs in all first-class cricket, including 153 centuries (four of them for England), took 277 wickets and held 675 catches. George Brown's record is pretty nifty too: 25,649 first-class runs, 568 catches and 78 stumpings, and 626 wickets as a medium-fast

bowler. How's that for an all-rounder? Ingleby-Mackenzie was a huge influence on the club as was Shackleton, who took 2857 first-class wickets at 18.65, was unlucky to play only seven times for England and whose accuracy was so phenomenal that it caused astonishment in 1964, his 40th year, when he was seen to bowl a long hop. Roy Marshall opened the batting for Hampshire for nearly 20 years, scoring 35,725 runs in all first-class cricket. Robin Smith, who like his brother Chris qualified for England when South Africa were excluded from international sport, scored 4236 runs at 43.67 in 62 Tests and for some years was one of the mainstays of Hampshire's batting. Three other notable imports were David Gower (from Leicestershire), John Crawley (from Lancashire) and, more recently, Kevin Pietersen (from Nottinghamshire).

—HAMPSHIRE RECORDS—

Highest Total For: 714-5d vs Nottinghamshire, Southampton, 2005
Highest Total Against: 742 by Surrey, the Oval, 1909
Lowest Total For: 15 vs Warwickshire, Birmingham, 1922
Lowest Total Against: 23 by Yorkshire, Middlesbrough, 1965
Highest Innings For: 316 by R.H. Moore vs Warwickshire, Bournemouth, 1937
Highest Innings Against: 303* by G.A. Hick for Worcestershire, Southampton, 1997
Best Bowling For: 9-25 by R.M.H. Cottam vs Lancashire, Manchester, 1965
Best Bowling Against: 10-46 by W. Hickton for Lancashire, Manchester, 1870
Most Runs in a Season: 2854 by C.P. Mead, 1928
Most Runs in a Career: 48,892 by C.P. Mead, 1905-36
Most Wickets in a Season: 190 by A.S. Kennedy, 1922
Most Wickets in a Career: 2669 by D. Shackleton, 1948-69
Most Career Dismissals by a Wicketkeeper: 700 (630 ct, 70 st) by R.J. Parks, 1980-92.
Most Career Catches by a Fielder: 629 by C.P. Mead, 1905-36.

HOWZAT! As Hampshire's captain, Colin Ingleby-Mackenzie laid down one stern rule: all players should be in bed before breakfast on match days.

KENT

Founded: 1859
HQ: St Lawrence Ground, Canterbury
County Champions: 1906, 1909, 1910, 1913, 1970, 1977, 1978
One-Day League: 1972, 1973, 1976, 1995, 2001
Gillette Cup/NatWest Trophy/C&G Trophy/Friends Provident Trophy: 1967, 1974
Benson & Hedges Cup: 1973, 1976, 1978
Twenty20 Cup: 2007

Kent's success in the early years of the 20th century had much to do with the fact that in 1897 the county had, with great foresight, established a nursery at Tonbridge. From there emerged such local heroes as Colin Blythe, Frank Woolley and A.P. ('Tich') Freeman. Alas, for whatever reason – maybe the 1914–18 war had something to do with it – the supply seemed to dry up and it wasn't until the 1970s that Kent were again something of a force in the land. Blythe, by all accounts the very model of a left-arm spinner, was killed in the First World War but Freeman and Woolley continued playing until 1936 and 1938 respectively. They, along with the likes of A.P.F. Chapman, who captained both Kent and England, L.E.G. Ames, a superb wicketkeeper-batsman (see page 99), Doug Wright, the leg-spinner, and batsmen such as B.H. Valentine and Arthur Fagg, provided the backbone of a series of underachieving teams between the wars.

Later, the emergence of players like Godfrey Evans, Colin Cowdrey, Alan Knott, Bob Woolmer and Derek Underwood, plus a recruiting policy that brought in John Shepherd from Barbados and Asif Iqbal from Pakistan, led to a revival that began with winning the Gillette Cup in 1967 and the Championship under Mike Denness in 1972. More recently the appearance of two more Cowdreys, Colin's sons Chris (who like his father captained England) and Graham, and Test players Robert Key and Geraint Jones have provided Kent with teams that are usually there, or anyway thereabouts, and, as they proved in winning the Twenty20 Cup in 2007, tend to play entertaining cricket.

Notable players: Colin Blythe was one of the great slow left-arm bowlers, a master of accuracy and flight. An emotional man subject to epileptic fits, between 1899 and 1914 he took 2506 wickets in first-class cricket, including 100 in 19 Tests for England. The leg-spinner 'Tich' Freeman was both a phenomenon and an enigma, almost unplayable in county cricket but a huge disappointment in Tests, especially against the Australians, who pretty well slaughtered him in 1924–5. Yet only Wilfred Rhodes has taken more than his 3776 first-class wickets. He took 200 wickets in a season eight times, his best return being 304 in 1928. He was only 5' 2" but should have been a giant of the game. That he wasn't must have been to do with a failure of temperament on the big occasions. Woolley, like Colin Cowdrey and Underwood, certainly was

HOWZAT! Douglas Carr, a purveyor of the then little-known googly, first played for Kent in 1909 at the age of 37. Within weeks he was turning out for England versus Australia at the Oval, where he took 7 for 282. That was his one and only Test appearance. His first-class career ended in 1914.

ABOVE *Fragile in health, but deadly with ball in hand: Kent's left-arm spinner Colin Blythe, c.1905. Blythe, who took 2506 first-class wickets at 16.81 apiece between 1897 and 1914, was 38 when he was killed by shell-fire near Passchendaele on 8 November 1917.*

one of the greats of the game and is dealt with elsewhere (see page 98). Chapman, whose later years were marred by alcoholism, captained England in two Ashes series (1928–9 and 1930). He was, apparently, a dashing batsman and outstanding fielder but his overall record (16,309 runs at 31.97) hints strongly at underachievement. Ames was the most remarkable of wicketkeepers – the only one to have scored 100 centuries and to have done the 'keepers' double (1000 runs and 100 dismissals in a season) three times – while his successors, Evans and Knott, though unable to match him as batsmen, may well have been his superiors behind the stumps. Denness, apart from Douglas Jardine the only Scotsman to have captained England, won the Championship and cups for Kent before moving on to Essex, and Key kept up the tradition of fine Kent batsmen who have gone on to play for their country (2002).

LANCASHIRE

Founded: 1864
HQ: Old Trafford, Manchester
County Champions: 1897, 1904, 1926, 1927, 1928, 1930, 1934, 1950. Division Two: 2005
One-Day League: 1969, 1970, 1989, 1998, 1999. Division 2: 2003
Gillette Cup/NatWest Trophy/C&G Trophy/Friends Provident Trophy:
1970, 1971, 1972, 1975, 1990, 1996, 1998
Benson & Hedges Cup: 1984, 1990, 1995, 1996

Lancashire's early stars included Archie MacLaren, scorer of the first quadruple century in first-class cricket in 1895, and R.H. Spooner. But the golden period was between the wars. The brothers John and Ernest Tyldesley, both Test batsmen, were prolific scorers, as later were Eddie Paynter and the young Cyril Washbrook. The bowling in the 1920s was led by Ted McDonald, the Australian quickie, and the slow right-arm of Dick Tyldesley, no relation to John and Ernest but himself one of four brothers who all played for Lancashire. After the Second World War, however, there was little to enthuse about, except in cup matches, although the county produced a number of excellent players, Brian Statham paramount among them. Despite a line-up that included such Test players as Ken Cranston, Ken Grieves, Winston Place and Geoff Pullar among the batsmen and Roy Tattersall and the slow left-armer Malcolm Hilton among the bowlers, Lancashire managed little in the Championship. On the other hand a run of cup successes began with the appointment of Jack Bond as captain in 1968. Under him the county won five one-day trophies, thanks largely to the recruitment of overseas players such as the Indian wicketkeeper Farokh Engineer and Clive Lloyd, the West Indies captain. The 1990s, too, produced a plethora of cup victories. Even so, a county of such tradition – come on, it used to be a power in the land – can hardly be happy with only one Championship in 74 years.

Notable players: MacLaren epitomized both the classic batsman and authoritarian captain of the Victorian age. His 424 against Somerset at Taunton is still the highest first-class score by an Englishman. Reginald Spooner, who played cricket and rugby union for England, was another elegant batsman, who continued playing until 1923, although his best years were before the First World War. The same was true of John Tyldesley, who also retired after 1923 having made 37,897

BELOW *Michael Atherton of Lancashire leaps to avoid a drive by Yorkshire's Darren Gough during a Roses Match at Old Trafford, July 1998.*

HOWZAT! One of Lancashire's early stars, bowler Walter Brearley, played four Tests in the early years of the 20th century, taking 17 wickets for an average of 21.11. He was alleged to be so conceited that he would ask of strangers: 'Don't you know me really? I am the famous Walter Brearley.'

first-class runs. Younger brother Ernest scored 38,874 runs and is the only Lancashire batsman to make 100 centuries. Eddie Paynter, famous for rising from his sick-bed to score a heroic 83 against Australia and help win the Brisbane Test during the Bodyline tour of 1932–3, was shamefully neglected by England; he played only 20 Test matches despite averaging 59.23. George Duckworth, a superb wicketkeeper, played 24 Tests and was denied more by Leslie Ames's superior batting ability. In a career that spanned 31 years (1933–64) Washbrook (34,101 first-class runs at 42.67) was an immensely reliable opening bat, both for Lancashire and, in partnership with Len Hutton, for England. Brian Statham (see pages 90–1) was simply one of England's finest-ever fast bowlers. The off-spinner Roy Tattersall would certainly have won more than 16 Test caps in the 1950s but for the misfortune of coming along at the same time as Jim Laker. Jack Bond was never more than a journeyman county batsman but a brilliant captain in one-day cricket (see also Cricket in the Dark, pages 294–295). Michael Atherton, one of the most obdurate of opening batsmen for both Lancashire and England, played 115 Tests, scoring 16 centuries. Although his average (37.69) is the lowest of anyone who has made more than 6000 Test runs, he was much better than that suggests. Atherton's misfortune was to be the mainstay of a generally weak England side at a time (1989–2001) when many other countries had formidable opening attacks. Lancashire's latest star is Andrew ('Freddie') Flintoff, who did so much to win the Ashes in 2005 but whose career has been sorely afflicted by injury (see also pages 100–1).

LANCS RECORDS

Highest Total For: 863 vs Surrey, the Oval, 1990
Highest Total Against: 707-9d by Surrey, the Oval, 1990
Lowest Total For: 25 vs Derby, Manchester, 1871
Lowest Total Against: 22 by Glamorgan, Liverpool, 1924
Highest Innings For: 424 by A.C. MacLaren vs Somerset, Taunton, 1895
Highest Innings Against: 315* by T.W. Hayward for Surrey, the Oval, 1898
Best Bowling For: 10-46 by W. Hickton vs Hampshire, Manchester, 1870
Best Bowling Against: 10-40 by G.O.B. Allen for Middlesex, Lord's, 1929
Most Runs in a Season: 2633 by J.T. Tyldesley, 1901
Most Runs in a Career: 34,222 by E. Tyldesley, 1909-36.
Most Wickets in a Season: 198 by E.A. McDonald, 1925
Most Wickets in a Career: 1816 by J.B. Statham, 1950-68
Most Career Dismissals by a Wicketkeeper: 925 (635 ct, 290 st) by G. Duckworth, 1923-38
Most Career Catches by a Fielder: 555 by K.J. Grieves, 1949-64

LEICESTERSHIRE

Founded: 1879
HQ: Grace Road, Leicester
County Championship: 1975, 1996, 1998
One-Day League: 1974, 1977
Benson & Hedges Cup: 1972, 1975, 1985
Twenty20 Cup: 2004, 2006

Leicestershire's early years were pretty undistinguished, lower-table mediocrity being their general lot, although in 1935 they were the

ABOVE *David Gower of Leicestershire and England unfurls a characteristic drive. Frances Edmonds, wife of Gower's England team-mate Philippe Edmonds, once wrote of the elegant left-hander: 'He looked so frail and wispish, like a pedigree two-year-old filly.'*

first county to appoint a professional captain in W.E. Astill. For the most part their mainstays before the Second World War were Astill and George Geary, both all-rounders who played for England, the batsman Les Berry and the New Zealander C.S. Dempster. Things got better in the late 1950s with the signing of Willie Watson from Yorkshire and the development of the opening batsman Maurice Hallam. Then Tony Lock joined from Surrey to inject a bit of aggro into the side and finally success arrived under the captaincy of another import, Ray Illingworth, who led the team to the County Championship in 1975. Their biggest star then and since was David Gower (see page 86), who first played for Leicestershire in 1975 but was not around for their two further Championship wins in 1996 and 1998, having decamped to Hampshire. A fair few Leicester players have been picked for England – Darren Maddy, Alan Mullally and Chris Lewis among them, all since 1990 – but none really stuck around for very long. Right now the county is in the second division of both the Championship and the One-Day League. But with the likes of the wicketkeeper Paul Nixon, who has played ODIs for England, and Jeremy Snape it has shown a healthy appetite for the Twenty20 game.

Notable players: With the exception of Gower, who was one of the country's finest ever left-hand bats, Leicestershire seem to have depended largely on players from other counties nearing the end of their careers (Illingworth and Watson for example), overseas imports and a succession of nearly-men, good enough to be picked for England but not to stay long in the team. Their most prolific player, Les Berry, never played for England at all. Chris Lewis won 32 caps as a classy but frustratingly underachieving all-rounder while Alan Mullally, who performed consistently well for the county, was in and out of the England team from 1996 to 2001. Among their few true stars were Jack Walsh, a teasing left-arm spinner (1946 until 1956), who would surely have played for his native Australia had it not been for the Second World War, and Phil Simmons, who played 26 times for the West Indies and was a huge influence on the successful county side of the middle-to-late 1990s. Recently Aftab Habib, Jimmy Ormond and Maddy (before leaving for Warwickshire in 2008) have won a few Test caps, but Leicestershire have lately shown a disturbing tendency to lose promising young talent, such as Stuart Broad, son of the former England batsman Chris, and Luke Wright to other counties, respectively Nottinghamshire and Sussex, while relying over-heavily on 'Kolpak' players from overseas (see pages 317–319).

HOWZAT! In 1911 against Yorkshire the Leicestershire opening batsman C.J.B. Wood performed the then-unparalleled feat of carrying his bat in both innings, for 107* and 117*.

LEICS RECORDS

Highest Total For: 701-4d vs Worcestershire, Worcester, 1906
Highest Total Against: 761-6d by Essex, Chelmsford, 1990
Lowest Total For: 25 vs Kent, Leicester, 1912
Lowest Total Against: 24 by Glamorgan, Leicester, 1971, and by Oxford University, Oxford, 1985
Highest Innings For: 309* by H.D. Ackerman vs Glamorgan, Cardiff, 2006
Highest Innings Against: 341 by G.H. Hirst for Yorkshire, Leicester, 1905
Best Bowling For: 10-18 by G. Geary vs Glamorgan, Pontypridd, 1929
Best Bowling Against: 10-32 by H. Pickett for Essex, Leyton, 1895
Most Runs in a Season: 2446 by L.G. Berry, 1937
Most Runs in a Career: 30,143 by L.G. Berry, 1924-51
Most Wickets in a Season: 170 by J.E. Walsh, 1948
Most Wickets in a Career: 2131 by W.E. Astill, 1906-39
Most Career Dismissals by a Wicketkeeper:
903 (794 ct, 109 st) by R.W. Tolchard, 1965-83
Most Career Catches by a Fielder: 427 by M.R. Hallam, 1950-70

MIDDLESEX

Founded: 1864
HQ: Lord's
County Champions: 1903, 1920, 1921, 1947, 1949, 1976, 1977, 1980, 1982, 1985, 1990, 1993
One-Day League: 1992
**Gillette Cup/NatWest Trophy/
C&G Trophy/Friends Provident Trophy:**
1977, 1980, 1984, 1988
Benson & Hedges Cup: 1983, 1986
Twenty20 Cup: 2008

Two of Middlesex's Championships were shared – in 1949 with Yorkshire and in 1977 with Kent – but theirs is a pretty impressive record however you

look at it. What's more, the invention of the googly – a significant contribution to the development of cricket – was made by a Middlesex player, B.J.T. Bosanquet, at the beginning of the 20th century. Indeed, the history of the county is studded with names that have gone down in cricket lore – from A.E. Stoddart, an early captain of England at both cricket and rugby union, to Frank Tarrant and Albert Trott, each of whom played for both Australia and England, the cousins J.T. and J.W. Hearne, G.O.B. ('Gubby') Allen, who refused to bowl 'Bodyline' on the 1932–3 Australian tour, Francis T. Mann and his son Francis G., both captains of England, and E.H. ('Patsy') Hendren, who performed heroically for county and country. Middlesex did well immediately after the Second World War under the captaincy of R.W.V. Robins and F. G. Mann, much helped by the mature talents of W.J. (Bill) Edrich, Denis Compton and Jack Robertson, but the best period came with numerous wins in several competitions between 1977 and 1993. Led for much of that time by J.M. Brearley, one of the most astute captains cricket has ever seen, and Mike Gatting, Middlesex then had a particularly strong side that included such England regulars as the 'spin twins' John Emburey and Phil Edmonds and the fast-medium bowler Angus Fraser – whose Test record (177 wickets at 27.32

BELOW *Mike Brearley (right), pictured in 1979 with his England team-mates Bob Willis (centre) and Ian Botham (left).*

HOWZAT! In his benefit match against Somerset in 1907 Albert Trott took four wickets in four balls and then did another hat-trick in the same innings. Not surprisingly, the game finished early, with very little gate money taken, leaving Trott to muse bitterly that he had bowled himself 'into the workhouse'.

runs apiece in 46 matches) would have been far better but for injury – along with Clive Radley, the West Indian quick Wayne Daniel and the England wicketkeeper Paul Downton. Success and trophies – apart from winning the Twenty20 Cup in 2008 – dried up in the 2000s, despite the presence of Test players like Andrew Strauss, Owais Shah, Ed Smith and Shaun Udal (recruited from Kent and Hampshire respectively), Aussie Justin Langer, and promising youngsters such as Billy Godleman. A rapid turnover in captains – going from Strauss to Ben Hutton to Smith and then, at the end of the 2008 season, Udal – can't have helped much.

— MIDDLESEX RECORDS —

Highest Total For: 642-3d vs Hampshire, Southampton, 1923
Highest Total Against: 850-7d by Somerset, Taunton, 2007
Lowest Total For: 20 vs MCC, Lord's, 1864
Lowest Total Against: 31 by Gloucestershire, Bristol, 1924, and by Glamorgan, Cardiff, 1997
Highest Innings For: 331* by J.D.B. Robertson vs Worcestershire, Worcester, 1949
Highest Innings Against: 341 by C.M. Spearman for Gloucestershire, Gloucester, 2004
Best Bowling For: 10-40 by G.O.B. Allen vs Lancashire, Lord's, 1929
Best Bowling Against: 9-38 by R.C. Robertson-Glasgow for Somerset, Lord's, 1924
Most Runs in a Season: 2669 by E.H. Hendren, 1923
Most Runs in a Career: 40,302 by E.H. Hendren, 1907-37
Most Wickets in a Season: 158 by F.J. Titmus, 1955
Most Wickets in a Career: 2361 by F.J. Titmus, 1949-82
Most Career Dismissals by a Wicketkeeper: 1224 (1024 ct, 200 st) by J.T. Murray, 1952-75
Most Career Catches by a Fielder: 561 by E.H. Hendren, 1907-37

Notable players: Bosanquet, obviously, though perhaps less for what he did than for what his invention enabled people like Shane Warne to do later. The Hearnes, Tarrant and Trott all gave splendid service to the county over the years. With his 57,611 first-class runs and 170 centuries Hendren was one of the near-greats of the game and Bill Edrich was not far behind him. In 1938 Edrich made 1000 runs before the end of May and in 1947 scored 3539, an aggregate bettered only by Compton's 3816 in the same year. (For Compton himself, see pages 82–83.)

LEFT '*Middlesex Twins' Bill Edrich and Denis Compton walk out to bat at the Oval during their* annus mirabilis *of 1947.*

Jack Robertson should have played more than 11 times for England but was kept out of the side by Lancashire's Cyril Washbrook. Denis Compton's brother Leslie was an excellent wicketkeeper-batsman for nearly 20 years and John Murray, who made 1527 first-class dismissals, was an even better one. Brearley was a fine county player but, except as captain, an underachiever for England. Gatting's England record (4409 runs at 35.55) is also disappointing but he was a phenomenal county batsman (28,411 runs). Emburey and Edmonds were as good a pair of spinners as any county has had in recent years. Apart from the import Daniel, Middlesex have been light on fast bowlers, though both Alan Moss (1950s) and John Price (1960s and 70s) played Test cricket.

NORTHAMPTONSHIRE

Founded: 1878
HQ: County Ground, Northampton
Gillette Cup/ NatWest Trophy/C&G
Trophy/Friends Provident Trophy: 1976, 1992
Benson & Hedges Cup: 1980

As trophy cupboards go, that of Northants is hardly better stocked than Mother Hubbard's. They were second in the Championship in 1912 and fourth in 1913, but in 24 seasons between 1919 and 1948 were never in the top 10. Furthermore, they were lucky to join the elite at all in 1905 when, as *Wisden* rather spikily put it, but for their fast-medium bowler George Thompson 'it is safe to say that Northamptonshire would not have been given a place among the first-class teams'. Thompson

ABOVE *Colin Milburn of Northants hitting out against the West Indies in 1966. Three years later, his career was sadly cut short when he lost his left eye in a car crash.*

became the first Northants player to be capped for England (versus Australia in 1909) but not too many others from the county followed suit in those particularly barren years, although there were a few good players such as the all-rounder Vallance Jupp, the batsman Fred Bakewell and the fast bowler E.W. ('Nobby') Clark. Even so, between 1935 and 1939 the county had the dismal record of 99 Championship matches without a single win. After 1945 Northants produced the opening batsman Dennis Brookes, the tearaway fast bowler Frank Tyson and the wicketkeeper Keith Andrew, as well as poaching the likes of Freddie Brown and Raman Subba Row from Surrey and Jock Livingston and George Tribe from Australia, but still didn't win

have been had he not lost an eye in a car crash? Over the years, however, Brookes was the county's most reliable and consistent batsman. The bespectacled, grey-haired Steele, once described as looking like 'a bank clerk who went to war', was called up at the age of 33 for Test cricket in 1975 and acquitted himself as well there as he did in the county game. At his peak Tyson (see page 92), who devastated the Australian batting in 1954–5, was the fastest bowler in the world, but his career was curtailed by injury. And for years Andrew was one of the best wicketkeepers in the country.

any Championships. Their successors have been able to do no better even though since the 1960s they have included Colin Milburn, Allan Lamb, Peter Willey, David Steele, Graeme Swann and Monty Panesar, as well as – at various times – such overseas stars as Curtly Ambrose, Matthew Hayden, Kapil Dev and Mike Hussey. The pity of it is that all the above-named didn't come along at the same time; you could have chosen a pretty decent XI from that lot.

Notable players: The overseas contingent apart, Lamb (who was himself born in South Africa) was Northants' most noted batsman with 79 caps for England, although who knows how good Milburn – nicknamed Ollie because of his physical resemblance to Oliver Hardy – might

—NORTHANTS RECORDS—

Highest Total For: 781-7d vs Nottinghamshire, Northampton, 1995
Highest Total Against: 673-8d by Yorkshire, Leeds, 2003
Lowest Total For: 12 vs Gloucestershire, Gloucester, 1907
Lowest Total Against: 33 by Lancashire, Northampton, 1977
Highest Innings For: 331* by M.E.K. Hussey vs Somerset, Taunton, 2003
Highest Innings Against: 333 by K.S. Duleepsinhji for Sussex, Hove, 1930
Best Bowling For: 10-127 by V.W.C. Jupp vs Kent, Tunbridge Wells, 1932
Best Bowling Against: 10-30 by C. Blythe for Kent, Northampton, 1907
Most Runs in a Season: 2198 by D. Brookes, 1952
Most Runs in a Career: 28,980 by D. Brookes, 1934-59
Most Wickets in a Season: 175 by G.E. Tribe, 1955
Most Wickets in a Career: 1102 by E.W. Clark 1922-47
Most Career Dismissals by a Wicketkeeper: 810 (653 ct, 157 st) by K.V. Andrew, 1953-66
Most Career Catches by a Fielder: 469 by D.S. Steele 1963-84

HOWZAT! In a Test in 1979 Northants all-rounder Peter Willey caught Dennis Lillee off the bowling of Graham Dilley – in other words 'Lillee caught Willey bowled Dilley'.

NOTTINGHAMSHIRE

Founded: 1841
HQ: Trent Bridge, Nottingham
County Champions: 1907, 1929, 1981, 1987,
2005. Division Two: 2004
One-Day League: 1991
**Gillette Cup/NatWest Trophy/C&G
Trophy/Friends Provident Trophy:** 1987
Benson & Hedges Cup: 1989

The history of Nottinghamshire cricket is dotted with great names of the past, such as the 19th-century bowler Alfred Shaw (see page 21) and batsman Arthur Shrewsbury ('Give me Arthur,' said W.G. Grace, when asked to pick an England team) and George Gunn, who played for the county from 1902 to 1932 and scored 119 in his first Test innings in 1907. The Gunns were an important Nottinghamshire family. George's older brother John (first-class career: 1896–1925) and their uncle William (first-class career: 1880–1904) also played for England and George's son G.V. turned out for the county in the 1920s and 30s. The Joe Hardstaffs, father and son, also played for England, dad five times during a career lasting from 1902 to 1926. And, of course, there was the great Harold Larwood, scourge of Bradman in the 'Bodyline' series, along with his almost equally deadly county and England colleague, Bill Voce. Before the Second World War it was said that if you whistled down a pit shaft in Nottinghamshire up

would come a fast bowler and indeed there were times when the county fielded six former miners. Honours have not come along too often for Notts but fine players have: the batsmen R.T. Simpson, Derek Randall and Chris Broad and the Test wicketkeepers Bruce French and Chris Read among them. Overseas players have also been important to the county, the Australian leg-spinning all-rounder Bruce Dooland being a vital influence in the 1950s. Later came Garfield Sobers, followed by Richard Hadlee of New Zealand and the South African Clive Rice, both of whom starred in the 1987 team that won both the Championship and the NatWest Trophy. Another New Zealander, Stephen Fleming, led the county to the Championship in 2005. That triumph was followed by relegation in 2006 and, more agreeably, by promotion again the following year.

Notable players: Arthur Shrewsbury, who used to say as he went out to bat, 'Bring me a cup of tea at four o'clock', was the first of a line of great Nottingham characters. George Gunn, whose 15 Tests were spread between 1907 and 1930, was another. On his 50th birthday he scored 164 not out against Worcestershire. (For Larwood, see page 89.) Bill Voce played 27 Tests and, in a career lasting from 1927 to 1952, took 1558 first-class wickets, 98 of them for England. Joe Hardstaff junior, a better player than his dad, was an England stalwart in the 1930s. Reg Simpson made 30,546 first-class runs, captained the

LEFT *Derek Randall jokes after being made Man of the Match in the Centenary Test at Melbourne in 1977 for his magnificent second-innings score of 174.*

A view of the Pavilion End at Trent Bridge, home of Nottinghamshire CCC, during the fourth Ashes Test, August 2005. This famous ground has hosted county cricket since 1841, and Test cricket since 1899.

HOWZAT! In 1931 George Gunn, aged 52, scored 183 against Warwickshire, and his son G.V. Gunn made 100 not out in the same innings – a family double unique in first-class cricket.

county from 1951 until 1960 and in 1950–1 at Melbourne scored 156 not out in England's first win over Australia for 13 years. Derek Randall, who made 174 in the Centenary Test against Australia in 1977 and was one of the greatest of all fielders, was known as 'the clown prince of cricket'. After ducking a vicious bouncer from Dennis Lillee he said: 'No good hitting me there, mate. Nothing to damage.' He scored 2470 runs and seven centuries for England. Dooland, who played three Tests for Australia, and took 770 wickets for Notts in five seasons, was another major performer for the county, as were Sobers, Hadlee, Rice and Fleming. Chris Read, probably the best 'keeper in the country in the 2000s, was unlucky to have a limited Test career because he was considered not quite good enough to bat at number seven for England.

NOTTS RECORDS

Highest Total For: 791 vs Essex, Chelmsford, 2007
Highest Total Against: 781-7d by Northamptonshire, Northampton, 1995
Lowest Total For: 13 vs Yorkshire, Nottingham, 1901
Lowest Total Against: 16 by Derbyshire, Nottingham, 1879, and by Surrey, the Oval, 1880
Highest Innings For: 312* by W.W. Keeton vs Middlesex, the Oval, 1939
Highest Innings Against: 345 by C.G. Macartney for the Australians, Nottingham, 1921
Best Bowling For: 10-66 by K. Smales vs Gloucestershire, Stroud, 1956
Best Bowling Against: 10-10 by H. Verity for Yorkshire, Leeds, 1932
Most Runs in a Season: 2620 by W.W. Whysall, 1929
Most Runs in a Career: 31,592 by G. Gunn, 1902-32
Most Wickets in a Season: 181 by B. Dooland, 1954
Most Wickets in a Career: 1653 by T.G. Wass, 1896-1920
Most Career Dismissals by a Wicketkeeper: 957 (733 ct, 224 st) by T.W. Oates, 1897-1925
Most Career Catches by a Fielder: 466 by A.O. Jones, 1892-1914

SOMERSET

Founded: 1875
HQ: County Ground, Taunton
One-Day League: 1979
Gillette Cup/NatWest Trophy/ C&G Trophy/Friends Provident Trophy: 1979, 1983, 2001
Benson & Hedges Cup: 1981, 1982
Twenty20 Cup: 2005

In the 1890s and 1900s the Somerset team was distinguished, if it was distinguished at all, by the presence of such Test players as Lionel Palairet and Sammy Woods (who played for both Australia and England). In the 1920s and 30s they were succeeded by the left-arm spinner Jack ('Farmer') White and the opening batsman Harold Gimblett. For too long, though, the county side was made up mostly of journeyman pros and such good amateurs as could spare the time – and it showed. For four consecutive seasons from 1952 they finished bottom of the table. Nor did matters improve that much with the recruitment of Colin McCool and Bill Alley from Australia (1950s) and Brian Close from Yorkshire (1971). But then, later in the 1970s, Ian Botham and the great West Indians Viv Richards and Joel Garner came along and, at last, under the captaincy of Brian Rose, Somerset began to win things. However, when Peter Roebuck took over as skipper the New Zealander Martin Crowe was signed as the overseas pro, Richards and Garner were sacked and, in protest, Botham shoved off to Worcestershire (1986). Since then trophies have been few, despite the presence of outstanding players like Marcus Trescothick, Andy Caddick, the Aussies Justin Langer and Jamie Cox and the South African captain Graeme Smith, under whom Somerset won the Twenty20 Cup in 2005.

Notable players: Harold Gimblett's debut is legendary in Somerset: summoned as a 20-year-old last-minute replacement against Essex in 1935, he went in with Somerset 107 for 6, hit a century in 63 minutes and finished 17 minutes later with 123. He played a few times for England, fewer perhaps than he should, and scored more runs for his county than anyone else. But he suffered from depression, retired abruptly from the game and in 1978 committed suicide. Arthur Wellard, a much sunnier character, was a fast-medium bowler and prodigious hitter of the ball. He, too, played a couple of games for England. Jack White was England's left-arm spinner between Rhodes and Verity and Somerset's most prolific wicket-taker. Bill Alley, a belligerent all-rounder overlooked by Australia, joined Somerset in 1957 when he was 38 and played 350 games before retiring at 49 to become an umpire. (Botham, Richards and Garner are dealt with on pages 100, 148 and 151–152.) Trescothick is the best batsman Somerset has produced, with 5825 Test runs at 43.79 and a top score of 219. A superb opening bat and first-rate slip fielder, he would certainly have played far more often for England if depression had not brought his withdrawal from Test cricket in 2006. With 234 Test wickets at 29.91 Andy Caddick, who was born in New Zealand but threw in his lot with Somerset and England, rates as the county's best-ever fast bowler.

ABOVE *In September 1986 the illustrious trio of Ian Botham, Viv Richards, and Joel ('Big Bird') Garner played together for the last time as Somerset team-mates. The county decided against renewing the two West Indians' contracts, and Botham departed in sympathy.*

— SOMERSET RECORDS —

Highest Total For: 850-7d vs Middlesex, Taunton, 2007
Highest Total Against: 811 by Surrey, the Oval, 1899
Lowest Total For: 25 vs Gloucestershire, Bristol, 1947
Lowest Total Against: 22 by Gloucestershire, Bristol, 1920
Highest Innings For: 342 by J.L. Langer vs Surrey, Guildford, 2006
Highest Innings Against: 424 A.C. MacLaren for Lancashire, Taunton, 1895
Best Bowling For: 10-49 by E.J. Tyler vs Surrey, Taunton, 1895
Best Bowling Against: 10-35 by A. Drake for Yorkshire, Weston-super-Mare, 1914
Most Runs in a Season: 2761 by W.E. Alley, 1961
Most Runs in a Career: 21,142 by H. Gimblett, 1935–54
Most Wickets in a Season: 169 by A.W. Wellard, 1938
Most Wickets in a Career: 2165 by J.C. White, 1909–37
Most Career Dismissals by a Wicketkeeper: 1007 (698 ct, 309 st) by H.W. Stephenson, 1948–64
Most Career Catches by a Fielder: 381 by J.C. White, 1909–37

HOWZAT! In 1924 the Somerset batsman Jack MacBryan enjoyed the most nondescript of all Test careers: his one match (against South Africa at Manchester) was so ruined by rain that he never made it to the crease.

SURREY

Founded: 1845
HQ: The Oval, Kennington
County Champions: 1890, 1891, 1892, 1894,
1895, 1899, 1914, 1950, 1952, 1953, 1954, 1955,
1956, 1957, 1958, 1971, 1999, 2000, 2002.
Division Two: 2006
One-Day League: 1996, 2003. Division Two: 2000
**Gillette Cup/NatWest Trophy/C&G
Trophy/Friends Provident Trophy:** 1982
Benson & Hedges Cup: 1974, 1997, 2001
Twenty20 Cup: 2003

Surrey have enjoyed two outstanding decades – the
1890s and the 1950s. The leading players in the
earlier period were the batsmen Tom Hayward and
Bobby Abel and three top-class bowlers in George
Lohmann, Bill Lockwood and Tom Richardson.
Already a prolific batsman before the First World
War, the great Jack Hobbs was even more prolific
thereafter. Other Surrey favourites of the post-war
period included Andy Sandham, Percy Fender, Alf
Gover and Douglas Jardine. Championship success
did not return until 1950, however, when the title
was shared with Lancashire. After that, under Stuart
Surridge and then Peter May, Surrey won it seven
times in eight years. That was possibly the best
county team ever, with batsmen such as May and
Ken Barrington, the Bedser twins, Alec and Eric,
and the phenomenal spin partnership of Jim Laker
and Tony Lock. Success later on was more
intermittent despite the emergence of other Test
stalwarts such as John Edrich, Graham Thorpe and
Alec Stewart, whose father Mickey also played for
Surrey and England. At various times the side has
been strengthened by overseas imports such as
Intikhab Alam, Waqar Younis and Saqlain Mushtaq,
to say nothing of the theft of the prolific Mark
Ramprakash from Middlesex. The tragic Ben
Hollioake, killed in a car crash in 2002, shone briefly,
as did his brother Adam, a good all-rounder and
excellent captain, especially in the one-day game.

Notable players: The diminutive Bobby Abel
(5' 4") carried his bat against Australia at Sydney in
1891–2 for 132 not out, and played until 1904 when
he was 47. Tom Hayward played in 35 Tests and

BELOW *Long famed for the gasometers (built in 1853) that still loom over the ground, Surrey's home at the Kennington Oval presented a far more rural picture in the early 19th century, as shown in this contemporary print.*

ABOVE *Mark Ramprakash began his career with Middlesex, but moved to Surrey in 2001.*

centuries, along with 5138 runs at 43.54 for England. Thorpe, a clever, gritty left-handed bat, made a century in his debut Test and went on to play 100 times for England, scoring 6744 runs at 44.66. Alec Stewart did even better – he played 133 Tests, scored 8463 runs and claimed 241 victims (227 caught, 14 stumped) behind the wicket. For years Martin Bicknell was one of the best fast bowlers in the country. Of late Mark Butcher and Mark Ramprakash, a truly great county batsman but so disappointing at Test level, have done most to hold the Surrey innings together. In 2006 and 2007 Ramprakash averaged more than 100 and in 2008 became only the 25th player to score 100 centuries in first-class cricket. But his Test record – 2350 runs in 52 matches, average 27.32 – was a poor reflection of his outstanding talent.

scored 1000 runs or more in 20 consecutive seasons. The medium-fast Lohmann and the fast bowler Richardson were also outstanding players in the earlier years. Andy Sandham, Hobbs's opening partner, was the first man to score a triple-hundred in a Test: 325 against the West Indies in 1929–30. Hobbs (see page 80) was one of the finest batsmen of all time. Fender, another gifted all-rounder, was noted for his powerful hitting; in 1920 he scored a century in 35 minutes at Northampton. Surridge was a sound county player and a superb captain. (For Alec Bedser, Laker, May and Barrington, see pages 89–90, 83 and 84.) In another era Eric Bedser, a good batsman and off-spinner, would probably also have played for England; Lock, of course, did – taking 174 wickets in 49 Tests. After leaving Surrey he captained both Leicestershire and Western Australia. In 1977 John Edrich, cousin of Bill, became only the third left-hander (after Philip Mead and Frank Woolley) to score 100 first-class

SURREY RECORDS

Highest Total For: 811 vs Somerset, the Oval, 1899
Highest Total Against: 863 by Lancashire, the Oval, 1990
Lowest Total For: 14 vs Essex, Chelmsford, 1983
Lowest Total Against: 16 by MCC, Lord's, 1872
Highest Innings For: 357* by R. Abel vs Somerset, the Oval, 1899
Highest Innings Against: 366 by N.H. Fairbrother for Lancashire, the Oval, 1990
Best Bowling For: 10-43 by T. Rushby vs Somerset, Taunton, 1921
Best Bowling Against: 10-28 by W.P. Howell for the Australians, the Oval, 1899
Most Runs in a Season: 3246 by T.W. Hayward, 1906
Most Runs in a Career: 43,554 by J.B. Hobbs, 1905–34
Most Wickets in a Season: 252 by T. Richardson, 1895
Most Wickets in a Career: 1775 by T. Richardson, 1892–1905
Most Career Dismissals by a Wicketkeeper: 1221 by H. Strudwick (1035 ct, 186 st) 1902–27
Most Career Catches by a Fielder: 605 by M.J. Stewart, 1954–72

HOWZAT! In 2007 in a Friends Provident Trophy match against Gloucestershire, Surrey set a world record for the highest score in a 50-overs game – 496 for 4. Ali Brown, who hit 176 in 97 balls, and James Benning (152) put on 294 for the first wicket. No fewer than 320 of Surrey's runs came in boundaries (22 sixes and 47 fours).

SUSSEX

Founded: 1839
HQ: County Ground, Hove
County Championship: 2003, 2006, 2007.
Division Two: 2001
One-Day League: 1982, 2008.
Division Two: 1999, 2005
Gillette Cup/NatWest Trophy/
C&G Trophy/Friends Provident Trophy:
1963, 1964, 1978, 1986, 2006

Sussex is the oldest county club but despite boasting outstanding players such as K.S. Ranjitsinhji and C.B. Fry (right) at the turn of the 20th century, followed by Ranji's nephew K.S. Duleepsinhji, the Langridge brothers James and John, Maurice Tate, David Sheppard, Jim Parks and his lad Jim junior, Ted Dexter and John Snow they couldn't win a damn thing until 1963. Mind you, they made up for this embarrassing lack of success with five trophies – including three Championships – between 2003 and 2007 under the captaincy of Chris Adams. Sussex has the tradition of being a family club, as witness the presence in the team at various times of such sets of brothers as the Langridges, Charlie and John Oakes, Harry and Jim Parks senior and Tony and Ian Greig, not to mention the father-and-son tradition of Fred and Maurice Tate, the George Coxes senior and junior, and the two Jim Parks. But it can't have been nepotism that weakened the side and caused the long wait for honours because they were all good players, several of whom represented England, and in most cases the sons were better than the fathers. Perhaps what earlier sides had lacked was the all-for-one team spirit that Adams injected into his

highly efficient but hardly star-studded XI. Well, that and – in the Championship years – the deadly leg-spin bowling of Pakistan's Mushtaq Ahmed.

Notable players: Ranji and Fry were stars of the Golden Age, Ranji the inventor of the leg glance and Fry simply a phenomenon, whose exceptional talents reached far beyond the boundary. James Langridge was a fine batsman and left-arm spinner while John is often described as the best batsman never to have played for England. Maurice Tate was a stalwart for many years for both country and county (see page 98), while Jim Parks the elder is the only man to have scored 3000 runs and taken 100 wickets in a season (1937). Dexter was one of the game's near-greats, a thrilling batsman, useful medium-pacer and a superb amateur golfer. Tony Greig had a fine record for England (3599 runs and 141 wickets)

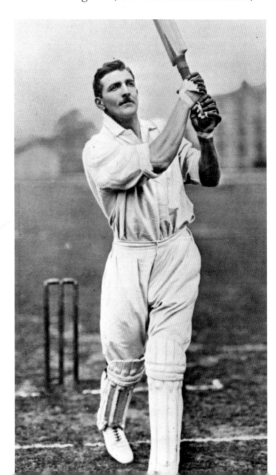

and captained the county well before succumbing to the lure of Kerry Packer (see page 270). John Snow was one of England's greatest post-war fast bowlers (202 Test wickets at 26.66). Chris Adams didn't cut it in Tests but is an inspirational county batsman and captain, while Mushtaq Ahmed, latest in a list of overseas players that has included Imran Khan and Javed Miandad, did more than most to win the county its recent honours. Nor should we forget Sir C. Aubrey Smith, a fairly average player who turned out for England (as captain) in one Test in South Africa (1888–9) and went on to become a Hollywood movie star.

SUSSEX RECORDS

Highest Total For: 705-8d vs Surrey, Hastings, 1902
Highest Total Against: 726 by Nottinghamshire, Nottingham, 1895
Lowest Total For: 19 vs Surrey, Godalming, 1830, and vs Nottinghamshire, Hove, 1873
Lowest Total Against: 18 by Kent, Gravesend, 1867
Highest Innings For: 335* by M.W. Goodwin vs Leicestershire, Hove, 2003
Highest Innings Against: 322 by E. Paynter for Lancashire, Hove, 1937
Best Bowling For: 10-48 by C.H.G. Bland vs Kent, Tonbridge, 1899
Best Bowling Against: 9-11 by A.P. Freeman for Kent, Hove, 1922
Most Runs in a Season: 2850 by J.G. Langridge, 1949
Most Runs in a Career: 34,152 by J.G. Langridge, 1928–55
Most Wickets in a Season: 198 by M.W. Tate, 1925
Most Wickets in a Career: 2211 by M.W. Tate, 1912–37
Most Career Dismissals by a Wicketkeeper:
1176 (911 ct, 265 st) by H.R. Butt, 1890–1912
Most Career Catches by a Fielder:
779 by J.G. Langridge, 1928–55

 HOWZAT! C.B. Fry, who was known at Oxford as 'Almighty' for his sporting prowess (he was a Triple Blue), went on to represent his country not only at cricket, but also at football and athletics. Legend has it that he was once offered the throne of Albania.

WARWICKSHIRE

Founded 1882
HQ: Edgbaston, Birmingham
County Championship: 1911, 1951, 1972, 1994, 1995, 2004
One-Day League: 1980, 1994, 1997
Gillette Cup/NatWest Trophy/ C&G Trophy/Friends Provident Trophy: 1966, 1968, 1989, 1993, 1995
Benson & Hedges Cup: 1994, 2002

Warwickshire have probably owed more than most counties to their overseas players. The fast bowling of New Zealand's Tom Pritchard (along with the leg-spin of Eric Hollies) had much to do with their Championship win in 1951. The West Indian off-spinner Lance Gibbs played a key role in their 1972 win, while Brian Lara made the world-record first-class score of 501 not out for Warwicks against Durham (see page 149) as the county became champions again in 1994. There have also been home-grown heroes, including the wicketkeeper-batsman E.J. ('Tiger') Smith, Tom Dollery, Dennis Amiss (the first Warwickshire-born man to score a century for England), Tom Cartwright, one of the most accurate of medium-fast bowlers, M.J.K. Smith, an international for England at rugby union and cricket who always played in spectacles but still scored 39,832 runs. In 1981 and 1982, however, Warwicks gave away more than 45 runs for each wicket they took, a record of which no other side is eager to deprive them. Things looked up in the 1990s, mostly under Dermot Reeve, especially in 1994 when they achieved a remarkable treble, and there has been a modicum of success in this decade.

HOWZAT! In 1922 against Derbyshire William Quaife and his son Bernard batted for 10 minutes or so against the bowling of another father-and-son partnership, Billy and Robert Bestwick. This is a unique event in first-class cricket.

Notable players: W.G. Quaife, batsman and leg-spinner, was one of the county's earliest stars in a career that lasted from 1894 to 1928, along with Frank Foster, another all-rounder, who scored 305 not out against Worcestershire in 1914. Inter-war stalwarts included R.E.S. Wyatt, who captained England and also played for Worcestershire, Dollery and Hollies, later renowned as the man who bowled Bradman for a duck in his last Test innings. Bob Barber was an attacking left-handed opener and useful leg-spinner who, in 1965–6, made a thrilling 185 in a Test against Australia. Bob Willis (see pages 96–97) was a notable recruit from Surrey, as was Nick Knight from Essex. Others who have lent lustre to Warwickshire sides include Gladstone Small, a very quick bowler despite apparently lacking a neck to separate his head from his shoulders, Ashley Giles (a better Test player than his 143 wickets at 40.60 would suggest), Dermot Reeve, an inspiring captain and useful all-rounder, Gibbs (see page 150), Lara (right) and South African fast bowler Allan Donald (see page 138) and, most recently, Ian Bell.

WORCESTERSHIRE

Founded: 1865
HQ: New Road, Worcester
County Championship: 1964, 1965, 1974, 1988, 1989. Division Two: 2003
One-Day League: 1971, 1987, 1988, 2007
Gillette Cup/NatWest Trophy/C&G Trophy/Friends Provident Trophy: 1994
Benson & Hedges Cup: 1991

In the early years of the 20th century Worcestershire were known as 'Fostershire' because seven brothers of that name, sons of a Malvern clergyman, would turn out for the county, sometimes four in the same match. The best of them was R.E. (known as 'Tip') who, on his debut

HOWZAT! In the early days Worcestershire struggled. In 1914 there was a move to wind up the club altogether and in 1919 the county decided that, for all manner of reasons, they were too weak to take part in the Championship. When they returned in 1920 they lost three consecutive games by an innings and more than 200 runs.

for England, scored 287 against Australia at Sydney in 1903–4. The county struggled, both financially and on the field, between the wars when among their few stars were the Test batsman Cyril Walters, Fred Root (an early exponent of leg theory, later to be used with devastating effect in Australia by Jardine and his henchmen), the fast bowler Reg Perks and the all-rounder Dick Howarth. Success, however, didn't arrive until the 1960s when Don Kenyon captained a side that included such recruits as Tom Graveney from Gloucestershire and Basil D'Oliveira. Championships and other trophies in future decades, too, owed much to the shrewd recruitment, or poaching, of players like New Zealander Glenn Turner (see page 164), the Zimbabwe-born Graeme Hick, Steve Rhodes from

Yorkshire and Ian Botham from Somerset. In the last few years the county has suffered much financial damage due to the flooding of its lovely ground.

Notable players: Foster's 287 is still the highest score by any Englishman in a Test in Australia. In 1949 Perks, Howarth and the leg-spinner Roly Jenkins made up as good an attack as any in the country. Peter Richardson was a fine left-handed opener who played for England in the late 1950s, as (just once) did his brother Dick. Kenyon, though not quite up to it in Test cricket, was a superb county player. Graveney was one of the near-greats of English cricket, scorer of 47,793 runs, 4882 of them, including 11 hundreds, for England (average 44.38). D'Oliveira, who was

Worcestershire's photogenic New Road ground, nestling in the shadow of Worcester cathedral. In the days when visiting Test sides played several warm-up matches against county sides, this was traditionally their first port of call.

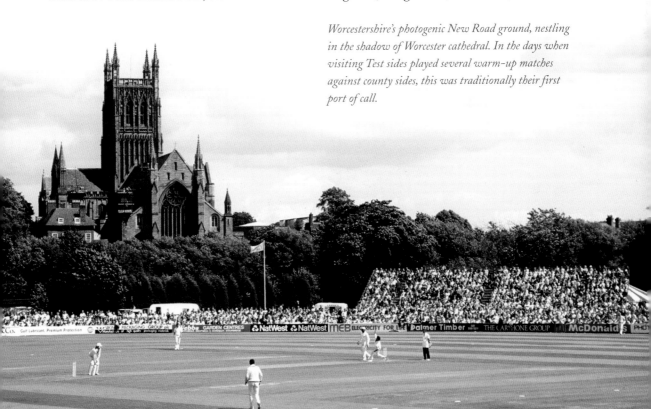

debarred from playing for South Africa because he was a 'Cape Coloured', qualified for Worcestershire and England in his thirties and was a supremely talented right-hand batsman and medium-pace bowler. For England he scored 2484 runs in 44 Tests, average 40.06, and took 47 wickets at 39.55. Norman Gifford, the left-arm spinner and county captain from 1971 to 1980, took 2068 first-class wickets, 33 of them for England. The Australian batsman Tom Moody had a big influence on the side which he captained from 1995 to 1999. As for Graeme Hick, who announced his retirement in 2008, what can one say except that, along with Mark Ramprakash, he was one of the almost tragic 'nearly men' of English cricket. His England record (3383 runs in 65 Tests at 31.32) is modest. But his overall achievement – 41,112 first-class runs, including 136 centuries, at 52.23 is outstanding. He should have been, as everyone hoped he would be, England's star batsman of the 1990s. But, as with Ramprakash, he lacked the temperament to transfer his prodigious talent into Test cricket. Oh, what a pity.

─ WORCS RECORDS ─

Highest Total For: 701-6d vs Surrey, Worcester, 2007
Highest Total Against: 701-4d by Leicestershire, Worcester, 1906
Lowest Total For: 24 vs Yorkshire, Huddersfield, 1903
Lowest Total Against: 30 by Hampshire, Worcester, 1903
Highest Innings For: 405* by G.A. Hick vs Somerset, Taunton, 1988
Highest Innings Against: 331* by J.D.B. Robertson for Middlesex, Worcester, 1949
Best Bowling For: 9-23 by C.F. Root vs Lancashire, Worcester, 1931
Best Bowling Against: 10-51 by J. Mercer for Glamorgan, Worcester, 1936
Most Runs in a Season: 2654 by H.H.I. Gibbons, 1934
Most Runs in a Career: 34,490 by D. Kenyon, 1946–67
Most Wickets in a Season: 207 by C.F. Root, 1925
Most Wickets in a Career: 2143 by R.T.D. Perks, 1930–55
Most Career Dismissals by a Wicketkeeper: 1095 (991 ct, 104 st) by S.J. Rhodes, 1985–2004
Most Catches by a Fielder: 487 by G.A. Hick, 1984–2008

YORKSHIRE

Founded: 1863
HQ: Headingley Carnegie Stadium, Leeds
County Championship: 1893, 1896, 1898, 1900, 1901, 1902, 1905, 1908, 1912, 1919, 1922, 1923, 1924, 1925, 1931, 1932, 1933, 1935, 1937, 1938, 1939, 1946, 1949, 1959, 1960, 1962, 1963, 1966, 1967, 1968, 2001
One-Day League: 1983
Gillette Cup/NatWest Trophy/ C&G Trophy/Friends Provident Trophy: 1965, 1969, 2002
Benson & Hedges Cup: 1987

Despite, or maybe because of, its tradition – unbroken until the signing of Sachin Tendulkar in 1992 – of choosing only players born in the county, Yorkshire's record in the Championship is incomparable. They have won the title outright 30 times and shared it with Middlesex in 1949. After the First World War other counties strove to break Yorkshire's stranglehold by importing players from all over but they were sneeringly dismissed in the Ridings as 'League o' Nations teams'. Lord Hawke, first as captain for 28 years then as chairman, had much to do with Yorkshire's early success, but it's hard to explain how one county could produce so many outstanding players and teams for so long.

What is equally difficult to explain is why – if you look at the records – the supply seems pretty well to have dried up since the late 1960s. Brian Close was controversially sacked as captain in 1970; so was Boycott in 1978. In 1982 Ray Illingworth, brought back from Leicestershire to manage the county, replaced Chris Old as captain at the age of 50; amidst much uproar Boycott was not offered a

ABOVE *(left to right) England's Yorkshiremen Matthew Hoggard, Craig White, Michael Vaughan and Darren Gough at Headingley, August 2000.*

new contract in 1983, though the committee later changed its mind; Illingworth was dismissed as team manager in 1984 and the rumblings seem to have continued on and off ever since. Perhaps, too, dropping the 'natives only' policy was a mistake, for with the exception of the Australian Darren Lehmann few of the overseas imports have been very successful. In the county's glory days it was said that if Yorkshire did well, so did England. For England's sake then we should all hope that Yorkshire manage to put together another decent homegrown side as soon as possible. They might have managed it already if players like Michael Vaughan and Matthew Hoggard had been made available more often by England.

Notable players: The roll of honour of great Yorkshire players goes on and on, from George Hirst and Wilfred Rhodes, through Percy Holmes, Herbert Sutcliffe and Hedley Verity, to Len Hutton, Freddie Trueman and Geoff Boycott, to, most recently, Darren Gough and Michael Vaughan.

 HOWZAT! During a rain-interrupted Test in the 1990s the England team were trying to recall the Seven Wonders of the World. They got six but stalled on the seventh until Darren Gough piped up: 'Ayoop, lads, Ah've got it – t'Hanging Baskets o' Babylon.'

Hirst, with his 36,323 runs and 2739 wickets (plus his unique feat of 2385 runs and 208 wickets in 1906), only just misses the England's Greats list. Holmes, who with Sutcliffe shared a then world-record opening partnership of 555 against Essex in 1932, would surely have played more than seven times for England if Hobbs hadn't been around. Maurice Leyland, Bill Bowes, Johnny Wardle, Bob Appleyard and Chris Old would have been outstanding in any era. Like Gough, who left for Essex, became a ballroom-dance champion on TV and then returned to Yorkshire as captain, they were all excellent Test cricketers. But then in those years of dominance Yorkshire seemed to turn out Test players on a conveyor belt. Vaughan, who quit as England captain in 2008, was a splendid Test skipper who led his side to more victories than any other Englishman (26 with 11 draws in 51 matches), and a very good batsman, who had one patch of greatness in 2002–3, when he scored 900 runs in seven Tests against Sri Lanka and India and 633 at 63.30 in the Ashes series in Australia.

— YORKSHIRE RECORDS —

Highest Total For: 887 vs Warwickshire, Birmingham, 1896
Highest Total Against: 681-7d by Leicestershire, Bradford, 1996
Lowest Total For: 23 vs Hampshire, Middlesbrough, 1965
Lowest Total Against: 13 by Nottinghamshire, Nottingham, 1901
Highest Innings For: 341 by G.H. Hirst vs Leicestershire, Leicester, 1905
Highest Innings Against: 318* by W.G. Grace for Gloucestershire, Cheltenham, 1876
Best Bowling For: 10-10 by H. Verity vs Nottinghamshire, Leeds, 1932
Best Bowling Against: 10-37 by C.V. Grimmett for the Australians, Sheffield, 1930
Most Runs in a Season: 2883 by H. Sutcliffe, 1932
Most Runs in a Career: 38,561 by H. Sutcliffe, 1919–45
Most Wickets in a Season: 240 by W. Rhodes, 1900
Most Wickets in a Career: 3608 by W. Rhodes, 1898–1930
Most Career Dismissals by a Wicketkeeper: 1186 (863 ct, 323 st) by D. Hunter, 1888–1909
Most Career Catches by a Fielder: 665 by J. Tunnicliffe, 1891–1907

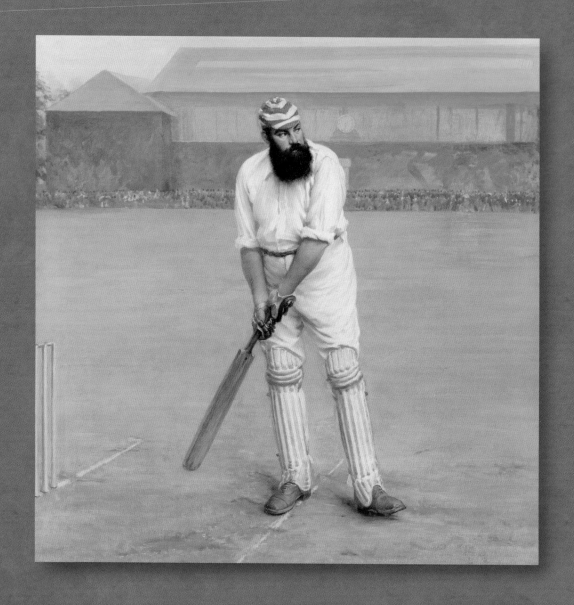

CHAPTER 4
ENGLAND'S GREATS

PROFILES OF ENGLAND'S FINEST,
PLUS THEIR TEST AND
FIRST-CLASS RECORDS

W

hat follows is a perfectly arbitrary list of, in my opinion – and in chronological order – the greatest of English cricketers. You will, of course, disagree. Good – draw up your own list. Meanwhile here we go with…

THE BATSMEN

W.G. GRACE (1848–1915)
Gloucestershire and London County

You have to start with the Doctor, although by rights he belongs among the all-rounders. Not only was he universally regarded as the champion cricketer of his era but he alone did more to popularize cricket than any other individual. Whenever he appeared admission prices rose, partly to accommodate the large fees this so-called amateur demanded but also because, in the public mind, he *was* cricket. As the writer C.L.R. James put it, he was, 'the best-known Englishman of his time'. By the standards of that time he was huge – 6' 2" and, except in his youth, heavily bearded and built like the proverbial brick s**thouse – and his achievements were equally massive. He played first-class cricket from 1865 to 1908, was the first man to make 100 centuries, scored 152 on his Test debut against Australia in 1880, played his last Test (again against Australia) when he was 50, did the double (1000 runs and 100 wickets) eight times – bowling slow, flighted round-arm or even under-arm – scored

1000 runs in May when he was 46 and made 1000 runs in a season 28 times, all the while playing on what today would be regarded as virtually unprepared wickets (hence his, by modern standards, comparatively low batting average). In the 1871 season only 17 first-class hundreds were scored and Grace made 10 of them. He was a colossus, immensely powerful, probably not pretty to watch, probably not a very nice man – he was financially greedy – but a giant to whom cricket owes an enormous debt.

Even today, nearly 100 years after his death, murmur 'W.G.' and people who can't tell a stump from a bail will know who you mean.

LEFT *W.G. Grace at the crease, resplendent in MCC cap, 1890. Archibald Wortley's painting was commissioned by the MCC through subscriptions of £1 from its members.*

ABOVE *Invitation card to a banquet in Bristol in 1895 to celebrate W.G. Grace's 100th first-class century.*

Test batting and fielding

T	I	NO	R	HS	Av.	100	50	Ct
22	36	2	1098	170	32.29	2	5	39

Test bowling

T	B	Runs	W	BBI	Av.
22	666	236	9	2-12	26.22

First-class batting and fielding

M	I	NO	R	HS	Av.	100	50	Ct	St
880	1493	105	54,896	344	39.55	126	254	876	5

First-class bowling

M	R	W	BB	BBM	Av.
880	51,545	2876	10-49	17-89	17.92

J.B. ('JACK') HOBBS
(1882–1963) *Surrey*

Probably the greatest opening batsman of all time. He scored more first-class runs and made more centuries than anyone else, more than half those hundreds coming after his 40th birthday, and when he was 46 he became the oldest man ever to score a century in a Test. If Grace, against whom he played in his first match, was 'the Champion' then Hobbs was 'the Master'. His career, which began in 1905, covered 29 years, 22 of them as a Test player. God knows what his statistics would have been like had he not missed four years because of the First World War and had he been as greedy for runs as, say, Bradman. Unlike the Don he was inclined to get himself out – or as someone said, 'abdicate' – after passing 100 (though maybe not

in Tests) to let someone else have a go. He was born in Cambridge, was self-taught, never had a coach but was a classically stylish player with an immaculate straight bat, and though playing in a time of uncovered wickets he seemed to have an answer to every kind of bowling. In 1953 he became the first professional cricketer to be knighted and, an even greater accolade, in 2000 *Wisden* named him as one of the Five Cricketers of the Century.

Test batting and fielding

T	I	NO	R	HS	Av.	100	50	Ct
61	102	7	5410	211	56.94	15	28	17

(Bowling: Hobbs took 1-165 in Tests, best 1-19)

First-class batting and fielding

M	I	NO	R	HS	Av.	100	50	Ct
826	1315	106	61,237	316*	50.65	197	273	342

First-class bowling

M	B	R	W	BBI	Av.
826	5217	2704	108	7-56	25.03

HERBERT SUTCLIFFE
(1894–1978) *Yorkshire*

Maybe the second-greatest opening batsman of all time, with the highest Test average (60.73) of any Englishman. He reached 1000 Test runs in only 12 innings (Bradman needed 13). Because of the 1914–18 war he was 24 before he made his first-class debut in 1919 and nearing 30 when he played his first Test, against South Africa in 1924, scoring 122 in his second innings. From then on his Test average never dropped below 60 and he and Hobbs became England's finest opening pair. Like Hobbs he could play any kind of bowling on any kind of wicket, a master of the dead-bat shot but also, when circumstances required, a ferocious hooker of the short, fast ball. In 1927 he could have become Yorkshire's first professional captain but declined the

LEFT *Well might Jack Hobbs have smiled in 1925, the season in which he scored a record 3024 first-class runs, including 16 centuries. This record stood for more than 20 years until beaten by Denis Compton in 1947 (see page 62).*

invitation, probably aware that in such a class-conscious age his appointment might have been divisive.

Test batting and fielding								
T	I	NO	R	HS	Av.	100	50	Ct
54	84	9	4555	194	60.73	16	23	23

First-class batting and fielding								
M	I	NO	R	HS	Av.	100	50	Ct
747	1088	123	50,138	313	51.95	149	230	474

WALTER HAMMOND
(1903–65) *Gloucestershire*

Bradman chose Hammond, his nearest rival for the title of the world's greatest batsman throughout the 1930s, in his all-time world XI. 'Nuff said. Hammond scored 36 double-centuries (one fewer than Bradman's world record), stands third in the list of most century-makers, has the highest average of those who made more than 50,000 first-class runs and in Australia in 1928–9 scored 905 Test runs – only Bradman has exceeded that. Again you wonder what his record might have been had he not lost six years to the Second World War, two years having to qualify for Gloucester (because he was born in Kent) and the 1926 season through illness – possibly syphilis because he was a noted swordsman as well as batsman. He made his county debut in 1923, scored 1000 runs in May in 1927, was powerful, athletic, the master of the cover drive and among the best of all slip-fielders. He alone has held 10 catches in a match – versus Surrey in 1928, in which year he took a record 78 catches altogether. He was also a useful fast-medium bowler. In 1938 he became an 'amateur' (in name anyway) in order to captain England and made his last first-class appearance in 1951 before emigrating to South Africa where he died. He was not, by all accounts, a particularly likeable man but many experts consider him, alongside Grace, Hobbs and Bradman, as one of the four greatest batsmen of all time.

ABOVE *Wally Hammond in 1936. The Gloucestershire batsman held the record for the most runs scored in Test cricket for 33 years, from 1937 to 1970.*

Test batting and fielding								
T	I	NO	R	HS	Av.	100	50	Ct
85	140	16	7249	336*	58.45	22	24	110

Test bowling						
T	B	R	W	BBI	BBM	Av.
85	7969	3138	83	5–36	7–87	37.80

First-class batting and fielding								
M	I	NO	R	HS	Av.	100	50	Ct	St
634	1005	104	50,551	336*	56.10	167	185	820	3

First-class bowling					
M	B	R	W	BB	Av.
634	51,579	22,389	732	9–23	30.58

 HOWZAT! Hammond's reputation as a womanizer was neatly summed up by Eddie Paynter, who said: 'Wally? Well, yes, he liked a shag.'

ABOVE *Len Hutton lofts a ball from Athol Rowan in the final Test against South Africa at the Oval, 1947.*

LEN HUTTON
(1916–90) *Yorkshire*

Hutton made his first-class debut at 17 in 1934, first played Test cricket (against New Zealand) in 1937 and in 1938, at the Oval, made the record Test score – a record that stood for 20 years – of 364 against Australia, when he batted for 13 hours and 17 minutes. A wartime injury resulted in his left arm being two inches shorter than his right, but he recovered to become the foundation-stone of England's immediate post-war batting and to score 3249 runs in 1949. With Cyril Washbrook he achieved England's record first-wicket partnership of 359 at Jo'burg in 1948–9. In 1952 he

became England's first professional captain since Arthur Shrewsbury 65 years earlier and in 1953 regained the Ashes for the first time in 20 years. He was a classic stroke-maker, who eschewed risks and regarded himself, over-modestly, as 'a Roundhead to Denis Compton's Cavalier'. In its obituary *Wisden* named him 'one of the greatest batsmen the game has produced'. He retired in 1956 and was knighted the same year.

Test batting and fielding								
T	I	NO	R	HS	Av.	100	50	Ct
79	138	15	6971	364	56.67	19	33	57

(A part-time leg-spinner, he took three Test wickets for 232 runs, average 77.33; best bowling 1–2)

First-class batting and fielding								
M	I	NO	R	HS	Av.	100	50	Ct
513	814	91	40,140	364	55.51	129	177	400

First-class bowling					
M	B	R	W	BBI	Av.
513	9774	5106	173	6–76	29.51

D.C.S. COMPTON
(1918–97) *Middlesex*

With Denis it wasn't so much what he did as the way he did it, although what he did was remarkable enough – 3816 runs, including 18 centuries, in 1947 for starters. At Trent Bridge in 1938 in his first match against Australia, aged 19, he had to be woken up to be told it was his turn to bat and then scored a century. Against North-Eastern Transvaal in 1948–9 he scored 300 in three hours and one minute. More than almost anyone else he approached cricket as if it were a joy, not a job. He could play every shot in the book and some known only to himself. He once swept Tom Goddard for four while tripping over his own feet and falling flat on his face. He was also a fine footballer who won 12 wartime caps for England and, with Arsenal, a League Championship medal in 1948 and an FA Cup-winners medal in 1950. A knee injury, incurred while playing football, seriously handicapped the latter part of his career, which, as with Hutton, would have been even more glorious but for the War. He was a useful bowler of left-arm chinamen, which he never took seriously, and an appalling runner

HOWZAT! Denis and his elder brother Leslie, a wicketkeeper-batsman and England international centre-half, won County Championship medals with Middlesex in 1947 and Football League Championship medals with Arsenal in 1948. They are the only brothers to have done that double.

between the wickets. His career with Middlesex lasted from 1936 to 1957, though he played the occasional first-class game until 1964.

Test batting and fielding

T	I	NO	R	HS	Av.	100	50	Ct
78	131	15	5807	278	50.06	17	28	49

Test bowling

T	B	R	W	BBI	Av.
78	2710	1410	25	5–70	56.40

First-class batting and fielding

M	I	NO	R	HS	Av.	100	50	Ct
515	839	88	38,942	300	51.85	123	183	416

First-class bowling

M	B	R	W	BBI	Av.
515	36,640	20,074	622	7–36	32.27

P.B.H. MAY
(1929–94) Cambridge University and Surrey

Peter May (right) is thought by many to be the best and most graceful of all post-war English batsmen. He was regarded as a prodigy at both Charterhouse School and Cambridge University, made his debut for Surrey in 1950 and for England against South Africa in 1951, when he scored 138. He was part of and, for two seasons, captain of the Surrey team that won the County Championship eight times between 1950 and 1958 and captained England when the Ashes were retained in 1956.

Though he lost the Ashes in 1958–9 and again in 1961, he won 20 of his 41 games as England skipper. (Only Michael Vaughan has since won more matches.) In 1957 he scored 285 not out in a fourth-wicket partnership of 411 with Colin Cowdrey (154) against West Indies – England's highest stand for any wicket. Richie Benaud once said that May was the *only* great English batsmen to emerge since the War.

Test batting and fielding

T	I	NO	R	HS	Av.	100	50	Ct
66	106	9	4537	285*	46.77	13	22	42

First-class batting and fielding

M	I	NO	R	HS	Av.	100	50	Ct
388	618	77	27,592	285*	51.00	85	127	282

(May never bowled in Tests and delivered only 17 overs (for 49 runs and no wickets) in first-class cricket)

M.C. COWDREY
(1932–2000) Oxford University and Kent

Colin Cowdrey's dad was obviously in no doubt that his son would be a great cricketer and gave him the initials MCC (M for Michael) to concentrate his mind. It worked – he was a schoolboy prodigy who at 13 became the youngest player ever to appear at Lord's (in a school match for Tonbridge versus Clifton), made his debut for Kent at 17 and went on to captain the county, Oxford University and (on 27 occasions) England. He was a plump rather than athletic figure but a fine slip-fielder and a seemingly effortless stroke-maker, who shares with Hammond and Geoffrey Boycott the record number of centuries for England (22). At Lord's in 1963 he enabled England to draw the match with West Indies by going in with a broken arm, ready to bat one-handed if necessary against Wes Hall. Fortunately, he didn't have to face a ball. He toured Australia six

ABOVE *Colin Cowdrey playing against Australia in 1968. Despite his less than svelte figure, Cowdrey was a natural sportsman who excelled at golf, rackets and squash as well as cricket.*

times, the last time in 1974–5 when, aged 41, he was sent out as emergency replacement in the shell-shocked, Thomson-and-Lillee-battered England side. After retirement in 1976 he became president of the MCC, chairman of the ICC, a knight in 1992 and a life peer (Baron Cowdrey of Tonbridge) in 1997.

Test batting and fielding

T	I	NO	R	HS	Av.	100	50	Ct
114	188	15	7624	182	44.06	22	38	120

(Cowdrey took 0–104 in Tests in 17.2 overs. He played in one ODI, scoring 1 run.)

First-class batting and fielding

M	I	NO	R	HS	Av.	100	50	Ct
692	1130	134	42,719	307	42.89	107	231	638

First-class bowling

M	B	R	W	BBI	Av.
692	4876	3329	65	4–22	51.21

KEN BARRINGTON
(1930–81) *Surrey*

After Herbert Sutcliffe and Eddie Paynter, Ken Barrington has the third highest Test average of any England batsman. He made his debut for Surrey in 1953 and for England in 1955 against South Africa, scoring a duck in his first innings. After two games he was dropped for four years, in which time he converted himself from a free-scoring, attacking batsman into a bloody-minded stonewaller. Thereafter he was frequently the backbone of the England team but, such is selectorial gratitude, after taking seven hours to score 137 against New Zealand in 1965 he was dropped for hanging about too long. But, boy, did England need him against Australia – in 23 Ashes Tests he averaged 63.96. And his highest score was against Australia in 1964. He may not have been pretty to watch but his figures speak for themselves. Oh, and he bowled decent leg-spin, too. He retired after a mild heart attack in 1968 and died after another heart attack in the West Indies while acting as assistant manager and coach to Ian Botham's touring team in 1981.

Test batting and fielding

T	I	NO	R	HS	Av.	100	50	Ct
82	131	15	6806	256	58.67	20	35	58

Test bowling

T	B	R	W	BBI	Av.
82	2715	1300	29	3–4	44.82

First-class batting and fielding

M	I	NO	R	HS	Av.	100	50	Ct
533	831	136	31,714	256	45.63	76	170	514

First-class bowling

M	B	R	W	BBI	Av.
533	17,301	8905	273	7–40	32.61

HOWZAT! Sometime during the 1980s I was playing for the Lord's Taverners against Barclays Bank, captained by Colin Cowdrey, in Manchester. In our team was the great Bobby Charlton – Man U, England, World Cup '66, you name it. Our skipper threw him the ball: 'Have a bowl, Bobby.' Charlton looked up, saw he was going to bowl to Cowdrey, turned to me with a huge, delighted grin and said: 'This is my dream!'

HOWZAT! Dennis Lillee on Boycott: 'The only fellow I've met who fell in love with himself at a young age and has remained faithful ever since.'

GEOFFREY BOYCOTT
(b.1940) *Yorkshire*

Geoff Boycott would probably tell you himself that he was one of the finest of all opening batsmen and he would be right. He could also probably describe for you, ball by ball, every innings he ever played. A highly complex man, who started in first-class cricket wearing spectacles before converting to contact lenses, he made himself into a great batsman by intensive practice and minute attention to detail. His first-class career lasted from 1962 to 1986 and he made his Test debut, against Australia, in 1964. At Yorkshire, whom he captained from 1971 until 1978, he was a contentious and divisive figure and in 1974 he opted out of Test cricket for three years, saying he had lost his appetite for it. (Some said he resented being passed over for the England captaincy in favour of Mike Denness.) Boycott returned to Test matches in 1977 and on his comeback, versus Australia at Trent Bridge, scored a century and another – his 100th hundred – at Headingley. In 1971 he became the first English

BELOW *In front of his home crowd at Headingley, and playing in his 100th Test match, Geoffrey Boycott on-drives Australian bowler Greg Chappell to reach his 100th hundred, 11 August 1977.*

batsman to average more than 100 in a season and in 1979 became the second. Like Barrington he could play attacking shots but preferred defensive ones and was sometimes accused by colleagues of playing for himself rather than the team. He once said to me: 'There's only one thing I hate and that's getting out.' His whole approach to the game seemed to prove that.

Test batting and fielding								
T	I	NO	R	HS	Av.	100	50	Ct
108	193	23	8114	246*	47.72	22	42	33
(In Tests he took 7 wickets for 382 runs, average 54.57, best 3-47)								

First-class batting and fielding								
M	I	NO	R	HS	Av.	100	50	Ct
609	1014	162	48,426	261*	56.83	151	238	264

First-class bowling					
M	B	R	W	BBI	Av.
609	3685	1459	45	4-14	32.42

ODI batting and fielding								
M	I	NO	R	HS	Av.	100	50	Ct
36	34	4	1082	105	36.06	1	9	5
(Boycott took 5 wickets for 105 in ODIs, average 21.00)								

GRAHAM GOOCH
(b.1953) *Essex*

Goochie was, so far, the last great England opener. A big, dark, powerful man with a droopy moustache and head hair that is (thanks to transplants) younger than its owner. He played first-class cricket from 1973 to 2000, marked his Test debut (versus Australia in 1975) with a pair, was dropped for three years, was dropped again after taking a 'rebel' tour to South Africa in 1982 but is nevertheless England's highest run-scorer. Against India at Lord's in 1990 he became the only man to score a triple century and a hundred (333 and 123) in the same match. That aggregate is the highest by anyone in a single Test. His match-winning 154 not out against West Indies the following year was then rated the highest-ranking innings of all time by the ICC. He began, like Barrington, as a free-scorer, then switched, successfully, to making himself

ABOVE *Graham Gooch in 1993. Gooch enjoyed an Indian summer as a Test batsman, making 11 of his 20 centuries for England in the last four years of his career (1991–5).*

hard to dismiss. As England captain his insistence on physical fitness did not always make him popular with his team-mates but he was perhaps the ultimate professional. If you include the runs he made in top-class one-day cricket (22,211) he actually scored more than Jack Hobbs. He also bowled right-arm medium.

Test batting and fielding

T	I	NO	R	HS	Av.	100	50	Ct
118	215	6	8900	333	42.58	20	46	103

Test bowling

T	B	R	W	BBI	Av.
118	2655	1069	23	3-39	46.47

First-class batting and fielding

M	I	NO	R	HS	Av.	100	50	Ct
581	990	75	44,846	333	49.01	128	217	555

First-class bowling

M	B	R	W	BBI	Av.
581	18,785	8457	246	7-14	34.37

ODI batting and fielding

M	I	NO	R	HS	Av.	100	50	Ct
125	122	6	4290	142	36.98	8	23	45

ODI bowling

M	B	R	W	BB	Av.
125	2066	1516	36	3-19	42.11

DAVID IVON GOWER
(b.1957) *Leicestershire and Hampshire*

Boycott grafted, so did Gooch. Gower merely caressed the ball, sending it delicately on its way to the boundary. His strokeplay, even in the most tense situations, had the elegance that is found so often in left-handers. And that was his problem. He made batting look so easy that, when dismissed, he was frequently accused of playing a 'lazy' shot. Yeah, right. He was so lazy that he played 117 Tests and retired as England's then-highest run-scorer, that retirement being hastened by a falling-out with his England captain, Gooch. The craftsman Gooch believed that people should be seen to be working hard; Gower, the artist, surely worked as hard as anyone at his game (as his record indicates), but chose not to let the effort show. Poles apart they were. What Gower did show, however, was his own relish of cricket, which he took seriously but never solemnly. His record as a captain was indifferent – an Ashes win in 1985 set against two whitewashes by the West Indies and an Ashes defeat in 1989. But in time such details will be forgotten and what will be remembered is the pleasure he derived from the game and shared with his audience.

Test batting and fielding

T	I	NO	R	HS	Av.	100	50	Ct
117	204	18	8231	215	44.25	18	39	74

First-class batting and fielding

M	I	NO	R	HS	Av.	100	50	Ct	St
448	727	70	26,339	228	40.08	53	136	280	1

ODI batting and fielding

M	I	NO	R	HS	Av.	100	50	Ct
114	111	8	3170	158	30.77	7	12	44

(Gower kept wicket very occasionally and bowled right-arm off-breaks hardly more often. In Tests he took 1-20 (best 1-1); in first-class matches 4-227 (best 3-47); and in ODIs 0-14.)

KEVIN PETER PIETERSEN (b.1980)
KwaZulu-Natal, Nottinghamshire and Hampshire

Super-confident and wonderful to watch when batting, Pietersen made a hash of his short spell as England captain. Appointed in the summer of 2008 he resigned in January 2009, after three Tests (one

ABOVE *Kevin Pietersen hits a six against Sri Lanka at Edgbaston in 2006 with a characteristically flamboyant reverse sweep.*

won, one lost), nine ODIs (four won, five lost) and a falling-out with the England coach Peter Moores (see Postscript, page 325). Pietersen is a cricketing mercenary in that he rejected the land of his father (South Africa) in favour of the land of his mother and England can only be grateful for that because he's an inspired and inspiring batsman, exciting and innovative – witness his one-legged 'stork' shot that whips the ball through mid-wicket and his six-hitting reverse sweep that converts him temporarily into a left-hander. His 158 on the last day of the Oval Test in 2005 was instrumental in helping England regain the Ashes. Pietersen is a man for the big occasion, as he showed with his century at Lord's in 2008 against South Africa, who still hate him for 'deserting' them. His self-confidence is sometimes indistinguishable from narcissism and he is not universally popular. He fell out with Nottinghamshire before decamping for Hampshire. But he is utterly professional; having begun in South Africa as an off-spinner who batted a bit, he has probably worked harder than any of his contemporaries to convert himself into one of the outstanding batsmen of his age. As he approaches his prime there seems no limit to what he might achieve – always providing he doesn't fall out with too many more people.

Test batting and fielding

T	I	NO	R	HS	Av.	100	50	Ct
50	91	4	4445	226	51.09	16	14	31

(Bowling: 4–518, average 129.50, best 1–11)

First-class batting and fielding

M	I	NO	R	HS	Av.	100	50	Ct
135	225	16	10,817	254*	51.75	38	43	111

First-class bowling

M	B	R	W	BBI	Av.
135	5539	3229	61	4–31	52.93

ODI batting and fielding

M	I	NO	R	HS	Av.	100	50	Ct
87	78	15	3047	116	48.36	7	20	31

(Bowling: he has taken 5–201, average 40.20, best 2–22)

So that's twelve great batsmen (counting Grace, the all-rounder). But what, you say, no Tom Hayward, Ranji or Fry? No Jessop, 'Patsy' Hendren or Eddie Paynter? No Ted Dexter or Tom Graveney, no Graham Thorpe or Marcus Trescothick? Well, such lists are never comprehensive – that's the beauty of them and why they cause such argument. But now let's move on to…

S.F. BARNES (1873–1967)
Staffordshire, Warwickshire, Lancashire

Impossible to substantiate now because there's probably nobody alive who ever saw him play, but Sydney Barnes (below) has the reputation of being the greatest bowler that ever lived. A stroppy, cantankerous man who resented authority, he largely shunned county cricket, except for a few seasons, because he could make more money playing in the leagues and for Staffordshire. But he was so good that he was selected for England while playing only league cricket. By all accounts he bowled right-arm medium-fast seam and swing, leg-cutters and off-cutters and could spin the ball fiercely either way. When it was put to him that he never bowled the googly, he said he never needed it. Even bearing in mind that he played mostly on wickets more conducive to bowling than batting, his achievements are still remarkable. In Australia in 1911–12 he took 34 wickets at 22.88; in 1912 in the Triangular Tournament with Australia and South Africa he had 39 at 10.35, and in four Tests in South Africa in 1913–14 claimed 49 at 10.93. Playing for Wales in 1928, when he was 55, he took 7 for 51 and 5 for 67 against West Indies. The following year, for the Minor Counties against South Africa he took 8 for 41 in 32 overs. Of his 106 Ashes wickets, 77 were taken on the flatter, truer pitches of Australia. The man was a brooding, saturnine phenomenon, a master of his craft who was still playing Minor Counties and league cricket well into his sixties.

Test bowling

T	B	R	W	BBI	BBM	Av.
27	7873	3106	189	9–103	17–159	16.43

Test batting and fielding

T	I	NO	R	HS	Av.	100	50	Ct
27	39	9	242	38*	8.06	0	0	12

First-class bowling

M	B	R	W	BBI	Av.
133	31,527	12,289	719	9–103	17.09

First-class batting and fielding

M	I	NO	R	HS	Av.	100	50	Ct
133	173	50	1573	93	12.78	0	2	72

HAROLD LARWOOD
(1904–95) *Nottinghamshire*

Of unusual build for a fast bowler (medium-height, lean and wiry), 'Lol' Larwood was reckoned by his contemporaries to be the quickest of them all and certainly the most fearsome of his age. His speed was estimated at well in excess of 90 mph and it was said that his action was so explosive that after delivery the knuckles of his right, bowling, hand would brush the ground. At 14 he began work as a miner but at 18 was offered a contract by Nottinghamshire. In 1926, his first full season, he made his Test debut against Australia but

HOWZAT! Superb in Tests and first-class cricket, Sydney Barnes was all but unplayable everywhere else. For Staffordshire he took 1441 wickets at 8.15 and in league cricket 4069 at 6.03.

HOWZAT! Larwood's county captain Arthur Carr knew how to get the best out of him – feed him plenty of beer. 'Lol' would knock back up to four pints at lunchtime before knocking over even more wickets in the afternoon.

was at his best in 1932–3 (see Bodyline, pages 264–269), reducing Bradman to mortal level and taking 33 wickets at 19.51. That was both the peak and the nadir of his career because he refused to apologize for the Bodyline tactics and was never picked for England again. That was England's loss. In 1953 he emigrated to Australia, where he died, two years after being awarded the MBE.

Test bowling

T	B	R	W	BBI	BBM	Av.
21	4969	2212	78	6-32	10-124	28.35

Test batting and fielding

T	I	NO	R	HS	Av.	100	50	Ct
21	28	3	485	98	19.40	0	2	15

First-class bowling

M	B	R	W	BBI	Av.
361	58,027	24,994	1427	9-41	17.51

First-class batting and fielding

M	I	NO	R	HS	Av.	100	50	Ct
361	438	72	7290	102*	19.91	3	23	234

HEDLEY VERITY
(1905–43) *Yorkshire*

Verity, who followed Wilfred Rhodes (see page 97) as Yorkshire's – and England's – left-arm spinner became, like his predecessor, one of the best in the history of the game: a master of every aspect of his art – pace, flight, spin. On drying wickets he was lethal. His list of

spectacular returns includes 19.4-16-10-10 (including a hat-trick) against Nottinghamshire in 1932, the best bowling figures of all time, and against Essex in 1933 he took 17 wickets for 91 in a single day. He made his debut for Yorkshire in 1930 and for England (against New Zealand) the following year. In 1934 he performed the amazing feat of taking 14 wickets in a day against Australia in a Test match. Between 1932–3 and 1938 he played 16 Tests against Australia and dismissed Bradman eight times, leading the Don to say he could never 'completely fathom Hedley's strategy' – a rare compliment. Verity was also a useful batsman, who once emulated Rhodes in opening for England against Australia. In the Second World War he became a captain in the Green Howards and died of wounds in a prison camp in Sicily.

Test bowling

T	B	R	W	BBI	BBM	Av.
40	11,173	3510	144	8-43	15-104	24.37

Test batting and fielding

T	I	NO	R	HS	Av.	100	50	Ct
40	44	12	669	66*	20.90	0	3	30

First-class bowling

M	B	R	W	BBI	Av.
378	84,219	29,146	1956	10-10	14.90

First-class batting and fielding

M	I	NO	R	HS	Av.	100	50	Ct
378	416	106	5603	101	18.07	1	13	269

ALEC BEDSER
(b.1918) *Surrey*

Alec Bedser began his Test career with 11 wickets in each of his first two matches against India in 1946. From then on he was the mainstay of England's bowling into the 1950s and of Surrey's attack in the eight championship-winning years of that decade. A big, powerful man, he was one of the greatest right-arm fast-medium bowlers, in the mould of the also illustrious Maurice Tate (see page 98), and the first

ABOVE *Alec Bedser in 1954, aged 36.*

England bowler to take 200 wickets in Tests. His enormous hands enabled him to bowl seam, swing, cutters and, when he felt like it, quick leg-breaks. With his twin brother Eric, a gifted all-rounder, he made his Surrey debut in 1938, and in 1946, the first post-war season, took 100 wickets and breezed into the England side. Bradman admitted to finding him one of the most difficult bowlers to face. His best year was 1953 when, already 35, he took 39 wickets in the Ashes-winning series at 17.48. A stolid tail-end batsman, his greatest feat was scoring 79 as nightwatchman against Australia in 1948. After retiring in 1960 he served as an England selector for 23 years and was knighted for services to cricket in 1996, thus becoming the first England bowler to be knighted since Francis Drake, boom, boom.

Test bowling

T	B	R	W	BBI	BBM	Av.
51	15,918	5876	236	7–44	14–99	24.89

Test batting and fielding

T	I	NO	R	HS	Av.	100	50	Ct
51	71	15	714	79	12.75	0	1	26

First-class bowling

M	B	R	W	BBI	Av.
485	106,118	39,279	1924	8–18	20.41

First-class batting and fielding

M	I	NO	R	HS	Av.	100	50	Ct
485	576	181	5735	126	14.51	1	13	289

JAMES CHARLES LAKER
(1922–86) *Surrey and Essex*

If Jim Laker wasn't the greatest of orthodox off-spinners (and I think he was) then he certainly had the greatest analysis – 19 for 90 versus Australia at Old Trafford in 1956 (see Laker's Match, pages 214–216). His overall figures in the Test series that year were 46 wickets at 9.60, a record against the Aussies. The Second World War had delayed his entry into first-class cricket until 1946, but with his high, classic action, sharp spin, accuracy and flight he swiftly broke into the England team and toured the West Indies in 1947–8. Bradman's Invincibles, however, punished him severely in 1948 and it was 1956 (his *annus mirabilis,* when he took all 10 Aussie wickets in an innings for Surrey as well as England) before he gained a regular spot in the Test team. Previously his most notable achievements had been to take 8 for 2 in a Test Trial in 1950 and to spearhead Surrey's all-conquering Championship attack alongside Bedser, Tony Lock and Peter Loader. He left Surrey in 1959 before returning to cricket after three years to play a couple of seasons for Essex. Later he became a noted, knowledgeable and laconic cricket commentator for BBC television.

Test bowling

T	B	R	W	BBI	BBM	Av.
46	12,027	4101	193	10–53	19–90	21.24

Test batting and fielding

T	I	NO	R	HS	Av.	100	50	Ct
46	63	15	676	63	14.08	0	2	12

First-class bowling

M	B	R	W	BBI	Av.
450	101,974	35,791	1944	10–53	18.41

First-class batting and fielding

M	I	NO	R	HS	Av.	100	50	Ct
450	548	108	7304	113	16.60	2	18	270

JOHN BRIAN STATHAM
(1930–2000) *Lancashire*

In the 1950s Brian Statham, popularly known as 'George', was part of two deadly England fast-bowling combinations – first with Frank 'Typhoon' Tyson, then with Fred Trueman. Though perhaps not as quick as the other two, he was by no means the junior partner, being renowned (as was Bedser) for relentless accuracy, line and length. Unlike most fast bowlers he didn't use the bouncer very often, but his yorker could crush a batsman's foot. He made his debut for Lancashire in 1950 and served the county exceedingly well, for three years as captain, until 1968. In the winter of 1950–1 he was flown to Australia as a replacement in the England team and there made his Test debut, going on to play in more Tests than any fast bowler before him. His best for England was 7 for 39 against South Africa in 1955 and in 1958–9, as May's England lost the Ashes four-nil, he still took 7 for 59 against Australia at Melbourne. He retained his form till the end and indeed in his final county match he took 6 for 31 against the old enemy Yorkshire. His first-class average is the lowest of any bowler who has

taken 2000 first-class wickets since 1900, and second only to that of his fellow-Lancastrian Johnny Briggs, who operated in the far more bowler-friendly conditions of the 19th century.

Test bowling

T	B	R	W	BBI	BBM	Av.
70	16,056	6261	252	7–39	11–97	24.84

Test batting and fielding

T	I	NO	R	HS	Av.	100	50	Ct
70	87	28	675	38	11.44	0	0	28

First-class bowling

M	B	R	W	BBI	Av.
559	100,955	36,999	2260	8–34	16.37

First-class batting and fielding

M	I	NO	R	HS	Av.	100	50	Ct
559	647	145	5424	62	10.80	0	5	230

ABOVE *Lancashire and England fast bowler Brian Statham (right) is congratulated by Ted Dexter (left) and Fred Trueman (behind) after taking his 237th Test wicket at Adelaide, 26 January 1963. Statham thereby surpassed Alec Bedser as England's highest Test wicket-taker. Just over a month later Trueman beat Statham's record in New Zealand.*

FRANK HOLMES TYSON
(b.1930) *Northamptonshire*

For a short – alas, too short – period 'Typhoon' Tyson was surely one of the quickest bowlers of all time and certainly the fastest of his own era. Richie Benaud thought he was the quickest he had ever seen. After trials for his native Lancashire, he first appeared for Northants in 1952 but – probably because of the violence of his delivery, his run-up (once reckoned to be about 50 yards) and a not particularly fluent action – he was subject to frequent injury and was forced to retire in 1960. Still, his feats in Australia in 1954–5, when he blew the Aussies away, taking 7 for 27 at Melbourne and helping England to retain the Ashes, earn him an entry among the legends of the game. His Test career was brief but explosive, as his figures show, and one cannot but wonder wistfully what he might have achieved if he had been fitter for longer. Unusually for a Test-class fast bowler he was a university graduate (Durham) and a scholarly bloke, who – like Harold Larwood – emigrated to Australia, where he became a school headmaster.

FREDERICK SEWARDS TRUEMAN
(1931–2006) *Yorkshire*

'Fiery' Fred is way up there in the pantheon of great fast bowlers, the first man ever to take 300 wickets in Tests. ('All I can say is that t' next booger to do it will be bloody tired,' he said on achieving the feat.) Only 5' 10" but powerfully built, he first played for Yorkshire in 1949 and for England in 1952 when he took 24 wickets in three Tests (including 8 for 31 at Leeds) and terrified the Indian batsmen. As the rip-roaring speed of his youth diminished, he developed into a crafty but still very quick exponent of right-arm swing and seam, whose skill was too often denied to England through his own contrariness. Of the 118 Tests England played during his career he missed 51, usually as a result of annoying the selectors. He was extremely strong and aggressive, able and willing to bowl all day and an exponent of deadly out-swing. Gary Sobers thought him one of the most difficult of all bowlers to bat against.

He retired from Yorkshire in 1969 but later played a few one-day matches for Derbyshire. He also became a commentator on BBC Radio's *Test Match Special* with an ill-concealed contempt for the modern game, his favourite phrase being an exasperated 'Ah just don't know what's goin' off out there!' His Test and first-class figures are impressive by any standards.

Test bowling

T	B	R	W	BBI	BBM	Av.
17	3452	1411	76	7-27	10-130	18.56

Test batting and fielding

T	I	NO	R	HS	Av.	100	50	Ct
17	24	3	230	37*	10.95	0	0	4

First-class bowling

M	B	R	W	BBI	Av.
244	38,173	16,030	767	8-60	20.89

First-class batting and fielding

M	I	NO	R	HS	Av.	100	50	Ct
244	316	76	4103	82	17.09	0	13	85

Test bowling

T	B	R	W	BBI	BBM	Av.
67	15,178	6625	307	8-31	12-119	21.57

Test batting and fielding

T	I	NO	R	HS	Av.	100	50	Ct
67	85	14	981	39*	13.81	0	0	64

First-class bowling

M	B	R	W	BBI	Av.
603	99,701	42,154	2304	8-28	18.29

First-class batting and fielding

M	I	NO	R	HS	Av.	100	50	Ct
603	713	120	9231	104	15.56	3	26	439

 HOWZAT! A fellow Yorkshireman once said: 'Tha's got a big arse, Fred.' To which Trueman replied: 'Well, tha' needs a big hammer to drive a big nail.'

Fast bowlers are a breed apart, and Fred Trueman was apart from the breed. ● Denis Compton

Fred Trueman takes his 300th Test wicket by dismissing Australia's Neil Hawke (caught in the slips by Cowdrey) at the Oval, 15 August 1964.

Derek Underwood traps John Inverarity, the last Australian batsman, leg before wicket on the last day of the fifth and final Test at the Oval, 27 August 1968. Underwood's 7 for 50 in Australia's second innings brought England victory by 226 runs and squared the series 1–1. The England players, a roll-call of greats of the 1960s and 1970s, are (from left to right) Illingworth, Graveney, Edrich, Dexter, Cowdrey, Underwood, Knott, Snow, Brown, Milburn and D'Oliveira.

DEREK LESLIE UNDERWOOD
(b.1945) *Kent*

It was obvious 'Deadly' Derek would be a good 'un when, aged 18, he became the youngest player to take 100 wickets in his maiden first-class season. He was a left-arm spinner with a unique style – medium rather than slow, decidedly brisk when he wanted to be and a match-winner, as he proved against Australia at the Oval in 1968 when he took four wickets in 27 balls to square the series. He had an ungainly, flat-footed run-up but a mastery of flight and length. By the time he was 25 he had taken his 1000th wicket, a feat only Wilfred Rhodes and George Lohmann managed at a younger age. Against that he was 39 before he scored his only first-class hundred. In Tests he took nearly 300 wickets and would have nabbed many more had he not joined World Series Cricket in the late 1970s and then totally blotted his copybook by joining a 'rebel' tour of South Africa in 1982. But he was obviously forgiven for these misdemeanours for, in October 2008, he became president of the MCC.

Test bowling

T	B	R	W	BBI	BBM	Av.
86	21,862	7674	297	8–51	13–71	25.83

Test batting and fielding

T	I	NO	R	HS	Av.	100	50	Ct
86	116	35	937	45*	11.56	0	0	44

First-class bowling

M	B	R	W	BBI	Av.
676	139,783	49,993	2465	9–28	20.28

First-class batting and fielding

M	I	NO	R	HS	Av.	100	50	Ct
676	710	200	5165	111	10.12	1	2	261

ODI bowling

M	B	R	W	BB	Av.
26	1278	734	32	4–44	22.93

ODI batting and fielding

M	I	NO	R	HS	Av.	100	50	Ct
26	13	4	53	17	5.88	0	0	6

ROBERT GEORGE DYLAN WILLIS
(b.1949)
Surrey, Warwickshire, Northern Transvaal

Bob Willis's method was simple – from a 30-yard run-up, arms flapping, and a height of 6' 5", he bowled straight and fast at around 90 mph with a nasty bouncer and a good yorker. When he was at his best that was enough for most batsmen. He first played for Surrey in 1969 and was flown to Australia in 1970–1 as a replacement for the injured Alan Ward. But because of his own injuries it was some time before he

BELOW *A tousle-headed Bob Willis sprints from the field after bowling England to victory at Headingley, 21 July 1981 (with Gatting, Gooch and Willey in happy pursuit). Ian Botham's rumbustious 149 not out allowed England to set Australia a modest fourth-innings target of 130, but Willis's inspired fast bowling left them 19 runs short.*

established himself in the Test team. In 1972, when Surrey still wouldn't give him his county cap, he moved to Warwickshire. He had two knee operations in his twenties and rarely bowled without pain, though that never seemed to affect his speed. His greatest achievement was in 'Botham's Match' against Australia at Leeds in 1981 (see pages 220–222) when he took 8 for 43 to clinch victory. Two years later he became only the fourth bowler to take 300 Test wickets and in 1984 played his last Test, against the West Indies. Since retirement he has become a well-known cricket commentator for Sky TV.

Test bowling

T	B	R	W	BBI	BBM	Av.
90	17,357	8190	325	8-43	9-92	25.20

Test batting and fielding

T	I	NO	R	HS	Av.	100	50	Ct
90	128	55	840	28*	11.50	0	0	39

First-class bowling

M	B	R	W	BBI	Av.
308	47,986	22,468	899	8-32	24.99

First-class batting and fielding

M	I	NO	R	HS	Av.	100	50	Ct
308	333	145	2690	72	14.30	0	2	134

ODI bowling

M	B	R	W	BB	Av.
64	3595	1968	80	4-11	24.60

ODI batting and fielding

M	I	NO	R	HS	Av.	100	50	Ct
64	22	14	83	24	10.37	0	0	22

So who have I left out this time? Names to conjure with include Bobby Peel and Colin Blythe, great left-arm spinners both; the fast-medium George Lohmann with a Test record of 112 wickets at only 10.75; Bill Voce, the best left-arm fast bowler of his time; Darren Gough, who could bowl a yorker even faster than he can twirl a dance partner; Tony Lock, another deadly left-arm spinner and outstanding fielder; John Snow, one of the finest of England's post-war quicks. Well, again you can make your own list, meanwhile let's have a look at…

THE ALL-ROUNDERS

We've dealt with Grace, so we'll begin with…

WILFRED RHODES
(1877–1973) *Yorkshire*

Rhodes's career spanned 32 years, from 1898 to 1930. In that period, bearing in mind he lost four years to the First World War, he took 100 wickets in a season a record 23 times, scored 1000 runs 21 times, did the double on 16 occasions and as a truly great left-arm spinner became the only man ever to take more than 4000 first-class wickets. As a right-handed batsman he started at number 11 with Yorkshire and rose to open the England innings alongside Hobbs, with whom he made England's then-record opening stand of 323 against Australia in 1911–12, Rhodes hitting 179. Eight years earlier he had taken 15 for 124 against Australia at Melbourne, and at Edgbaston in 1902 when Australia were dismissed for 36, their lowest-ever total, Rhodes took 7 for 17. His all-round accomplishments indeed are not only phenomenal – they're unbeatable. In 1926, when he was 48, he was recalled to the England team at the Oval and took 6 for 79, notably 4 for 44 in the second innings, to help regain the Ashes. He played his last Test, in Jamaica, in 1929–30, at the age of 52. His attributes as a bowler included devious variations of flight, sharp spin and unerring accuracy, and as a batsman solid defence allied to a sound judgement of when to attack.

Test batting and fielding

T	I	NO	R	HS	Av.	100	50	Ct
58	98	21	2325	179	30.19	2	11	60

Test bowling

T	B	R	W	BBI	BBM	Av.
58	8225	3425	127	8-68	15-124	26.96

First-class batting and fielding

M	I	NO	R	HS	Av.	100	50	Ct
1106	1528	237	39,802	267*	30.83	58	198	765

First-class bowling

M	R	W	BBI	Av.
1106	69,993	4187	9-24	16.71

FRANK EDWARD WOOLLEY
(1887–1978) *Kent*

Not only was Frank Woolley, by general acclaim of his
peers, a great all-rounder; many would say he was the
most composed and majestic of all left-handed
batsmen. That being so, his Test figures hardly seem
to do him justice. Had he carried his county form into
international cricket he might well be regarded as the
English all-rounder par excellence. He played for Kent
from 1906 to 1938, scoring 1000 runs in a season 28
times, equalling Grace's record, and took 100 wickets
in a season eight times. In those eight years he did the
double, on the way becoming the only man to score
2000 runs and take 100 wickets four times. He bowled
left-arm spin with much turn and accuracy but batting
(only Jack Hobbs has scored more runs) was his forte:
by all accounts he scored nearly as fast as Gilbert
Jessop. In 1928 he made 3352 runs
at an average of 60.94. He first
played for England, against
Australia, in 1909 and in 1912,
again versus Australia, returned
match-winning figures of 62
runs and 10 for 49 in the
game. In the previous winter
versus Tasmania he had
scored 305 not out, at that
time the fastest (3 hours 25
minutes) triple-century ever
recorded. At Lord's against
Australia in 1921 he had
the unhappy experience of
being out for 95 and 93.

Test batting and fielding
T	I	NO	R	HS	Av.	100	50	Ct
64	98	7	3283	154	36.07	5	23	64

Test bowling
T	B	R	W	BBI	BBM	Av.
64	6495	2815	83	7–76	10–49	33.91

First-class batting and fielding
M	I	NO	R	HS	Av.	100	50	Ct
979	1536	84	58,969	305*	40.75	145	295	1018

First-class bowling
M	R	W	BBI	Av.
979	41,066	2068	8–22	19.85

*ABOVE Sussex and England all-rounder Maurice Tate
(seen here in 1928) is credited with having invented
modern seam bowling. A large and amiable man, with
a broad grin and large feet, 'Chubby' Tate was a gift to
contemporary cartoonists.*

MAURICE WILLIAM TATE
(1895–1956) *Sussex*

Son of the unfortunate Fred (see pages 211–213),
Maurice 'Chubby' Tate began as a hard-hitting
batsman and right-arm medium-paced off-spinner. He
was 27 before he converted to bowling fast-medium
and became one of the greatest exponents of that
particular skill. Off a short run-up, around eight yards,
and with a high action he appeared to make the ball hit
the pitch fast and come off even faster. He first
appeared for Sussex in 1912 and for England in 1924
when, on his debut, he took a wicket with his first ball
and ended up with 4 for 12 as he and Arthur Gilligan
(6 for 7) dismissed South Africa for 30. He took 100
wickets in a season 14 times, scored 1000 runs 12 times
and did the double eight times, or nine if you include
his feats on the 1926–7 tour of India and Ceylon. In
three successive seasons from 1923, he scored more
than 2000 runs and took over 100 wickets. As a big
man with powerful shoulders he was a solid rather
than elegant free-hitting batsman. His chief claim
to greatness lies in his bowling, but he was certainly
a genuine all-rounder.

Test batting and fielding								
T	I	NO	R	HS	Av.	100	50	Ct
39	52	5	1198	100*	25.48	1	5	11

Test bowling						
T	B	R	W	BBI	BBM	Av.
39	12,523	4055	155	6–42	11–228	26.16

First-class batting and fielding								
M	I	NO	R	HS	Av.	100	50	Ct
679	970	103	21,717	203	25.04	23	93	283

First-class bowling					
M	B	R	W	BBI	Av.
679	150,461	50,571	2784	9–71	18.16

LESLIE ETHELBERT GEORGE AMES
(1905–90) *Kent*

Anyone cursed with a name like Ethelbert would have
to be good at something to make up for it, and Les
Ames was very good indeed at both wicketkeeping and
batting, so good that he was worthy of a place in the
Test team for either of his skills. The list of his records
is deeply impressive – the only wicketkeeper to score
100 centuries, the first 'keeper to do the double of 1000
runs and 100 victims, a feat he accomplished three
times (only John Murray of Middlesex has done it
since), the most dismissals in an English season (127
in 1929), the most stumpings in an English season (64
in 1932) and a share, with 'Gubby' Allen, in England's
highest eighth-wicket partnership – 246 against New
Zealand in 1931. He even bowled a bit, taking 24 first-
class wickets at 33.37. He was England's first-choice
'keeper from 1931 to 1938. For Kent his record was
greatly helped by keeping to the prolific 'Tich' Freeman,
'st Ames b Freeman' being a frequent entry in the score-
books. He played for Kent from 1926 to 1951 and was
a Squadron Leader in the RAF during the Second
World War.

Test batting and fielding									
T	I	NO	R	HS	Av.	100	50	Ct	St
47	72	12	2434	149	40.56	8	6	74	23

First-class batting and fielding									
M	I	NO	R	HS	Av.	100	50	Ct	St
593	951	95	37,248	295	43.51	102	176	703	418

ALAN PHILIP ERIC KNOTT
(b.1946) *Kent, Tasmania*

Knottie was England's finest post-war wicketkeeper;
during a Test career from 1967 to 1981, which at one
point included 65 consecutive games, he was probably
the best in the world. Nimble and acrobatic, collar
always turned up, sleeves always rolled down,
constantly doing callisthenics to keep his muscles
loose, introspective and a seeker after perfection, he
was equally brilliant close to the stumps or standing
back. The combination of Knott and Underwood –
with Knottie, Mr Punch profile and all, breathing
menacingly into the batsman's ear – provided
numerous wickets for Kent and England. He could
bat, too, with a quick-footed, idiosyncratic style that
favoured the cut and the sweep. Seeking a like-for-like
replacement at number seven in the batting order has

Test batting and fielding									
T	I	NO	R	HS	Av.	100	50	Ct	St
95	149	15	4389	135	32.75	5	30	250	19

First-class batting and fielding									
M	I	NO	R	HS	Av.	100	50	Ct	St
511	745	134	18,105	156	29.63	17	97	1211	133

(First-class bowling (off-breaks): 2-87; BBI 1-5)

ODI batting and fielding									
M	I	NO	R	HS	Av.	100	50	Ct	St
20	14	4	200	50	20.00	0	1	15	1

given the England selectors a pretty-well permanent headache ever since his retirement. Usually he was a quick scorer, either against pace or spin, but in 1967–8 at Georgetown he batted for four hours for 73 not out to save the match and win the series for Cowdrey's team. In 1977 he joined Packer's WSC mob but swiftly regained his England place and finished his Test career in some style by scoring 70 not out at the Oval in the 1981 Ashes series.

IAN TERENCE BOTHAM
(b.1955) *Somerset, Worcestershire and Durham*

'Iron Bottom', as Indian fans called him, was England's greatest all-rounder – one of the greatest anywhere, ever. A rumbustious, assertive, charismatic man, not always popular with the Test authorities (they dropped him in 1986 for smoking pot) his deeds read like something out of *The Boy's Own Paper*. 'Both' (or 'Beefy'; he answers to either) was a match-winner, not only in 1981 (see Botham's Match, pages 220–222) but frequently. Between 1977 and 1992, he took more Test wickets than any other England bowler and reached the doubles of 1000 runs and 100 wickets, 2000 runs and 200 wickets and 3000 runs and 300 wickets faster

than anyone else in history. He was the first player to score a century and take 10 wickets in a Test (versus India in 1980) and five times scored 100 and took five wickets in an innings in the same match. He was a brilliant attacking batsman, a hostile fast-medium swing bowler and a superb slip-fielder. Towards the end injury and anno domini marred his overall figures but he was still a tremendous player, though as England captain not so good. He skippered England 12 times in 1980 and 1981, losing four and drawing eight – though nine of these matches were against the all-conquering West Indies. He played for Somerset from 1974 to 1985, appeared for Worcestershire between 1986 and 1991, joined Durham in 1992 and retired midway through the 1993 season. He was an indefatigable worker, and walker, for charity, raising more than £10 million for Leukaemia Research. In 2007 he was deservedly knighted for services to both cricket and charity. 'Arise, Sir Beefy!'

ANDREW FLINTOFF
(b.1977) *Lancashire*

With his 402 Test runs and 24 wickets in the 2005 Ashes series, Freddie was certainly a world-class all-rounder, England's best since Botham. If his overall figures – batting average less than it should be, bowling average a shade too high for a top-class strike bowler – don't quite reflect his exceptional ability, a series of debilitating injuries, especially to his left ankle, could be held to blame. Standing 6' 4" and powerfully built, he is, at his best, a ferociously hard-hitting batsman, a superb slip-fielder and a consistently accurate 90 mph bowler capable of blasting any team aside. His early years, though, were to say the least erratic – Test debut at 20 and then in and out of the Lancashire side for a year or so, probably through lack of motivation and application as he bloated himself into, on his own admission,

RIGHT *'Freddie' Flintoff exults at taking the wicket of Damien Martyn during a marathon spell of fast bowling that brought him five Australian wickets on the penultimate day of the final Test match at the Oval, 11 September 2005. Flintoff's Herculean performance helped England to secure a draw – and thereby to win the series and regain the Ashes.*

Test batting and fielding

T	I	NO	R	HS	Av.	100	50	Ct
102	161	6	5200	208	33.54	14	22	120

Test bowling

T	B	R	W	BBI	BBM	Av.
102	21,815	10,878	383	8–34	13–106	28.40

First-class batting and fielding

M	I	NO	R	HS	Av.	100	50	Ct
402	617	46	19,399	228	33.97	38	97	354

First-class bowling

M	B	R	W	BBI	Av.
402	63,547	31,902	1172	8–34	27.22

ODI batting and fielding

M	I	NO	R	HS	Av.	100	50	Ct
116	106	15	2113	79	23.21	0	9	36

ODI bowling

M	B	R	W	BB	Av.
116	6271	4139	145	4–31	28.54

'a fat lad'. But after a stint at Rod Marsh's ECB Academy in 2001 he got his act together and since then has been, by and large and when fit, pretty well the first name on any England team-sheet. In 2003 his belligerent 95 at the Oval helped win the series against South Africa and in 2005 he was the undoubted hero of England's Ashes win – as he was of the monumental boozing bender that followed it. As a captain he was, like Botham, promoted too soon and would probably be happy to forget the 2006–7 whitewash in Australia along with the night in the West Indies at the 2007 World Cup when he was stripped of the England vice-captaincy after being found drunk in charge of a pedalo. His injuries then kept him out of Tests for 18 months but he came back strongly in 2008 to be named Man of the Series in the four-nil ODI thrashing of South Africa.

Test batting and fielding

T	I	NO	R	HS	Av.	100	50	Ct
74	121	8	3595	167	31.81	5	25	51

Test bowling

T	B	R	W	BBI	BBM	Av.
74	13,974	6886	211	5–58	8–156	32.63

First-class batting and fielding

M	I	NO	R	HS	Av.	100	50	Ct
176	278	22	8739	167	34.13	15	51	180

First-class bowling

M	B	R	W	BBI	Av.
176	21,639	10,473	331	5–24	31.64

ODI batting and fielding

M	I	NO	R	HS	Av.	100	50	Ct
138	120	16	3391	123	32.60	3	18	43

ODI bowling

M	B	R	W	BB	Av.
138	5510	4025	163	5–56	24.69

Okay, okay. Where are Alec Stewart (who nearly made the squad), George Hirst, Ted Dexter (again), Tony Greig or – if you like – Trevor Bailey? Maybe you can think of a few others I've overlooked but while you're doing that and disagreeing with my choices just think of the cracking teams you could pick from the players I *did* name.

ENGLAND'S
TEST RECORDS

Tests – played 884; won 305, lost 257, drawn 322. Not great but not bad. Only against Australia and West Indies have England lost more games than they have won.

In ODIs – played 503; won 240, lost 240, tied 5, no result 18.

In Tests England's highest total remains 903–7d against Australia at the Oval in 1938. The lowest is 45, also against Australia at Sydney in 1887, closely followed by 46 versus West Indies, Port-of-Spain, 1994.

Most Test appearances

	T
A.J. Stewart	133
G.A. Gooch	118
D.I. Gower	117
M.A. Atherton	115
M.C. Cowdrey	114

Highest individual Test scores

	R	Opp.	Ground	Match date
L. Hutton	364	Australia	The Oval	20 Aug. 1938
W.R. Hammond	336*	New Zealand	Auckland	31 Mar. 1933
G.A. Gooch	333	India	Lord's	26 July 1990
A. Sandham	325	West Indies	Kingston	3 Apr. 1930
J.H. Edrich	310*	New Zealand	Headingley	8 July 1965

Highest Test batting averages (qualification: 15 Tests or more)

	T	Av.
H. Sutcliffe	54	60.73
E. Paynter	20	59.23
K.F. Barrington	82	58.67
W.R. Hammond	85	58.45
J.B. Hobbs	61	56.94

Highest Test run-scorers

	Span	T	I	NO	R	HS	Av.
G.A. Gooch	1975–95	118	215	6	8900	333	42.58
A.J. Stewart	1990–2003	133	235	21	8463	190	39.54
D.I. Gower	1978–92	117	204	18	8231	215	44.25
G. Boycott	1964–82	108	193	23	8114	246*	47.72
M.A. Atherton	1989–2001	115	212	7	7728	185*	37.69

Most Test centuries

	T	100
G. Boycott	108	22
M.C. Cowdrey	114	22
W.R. Hammond	85	22
K.F. Barrington	82	20
G.A. Gooch	118	20

Note: Gooch holds the England record for most fifties (46).

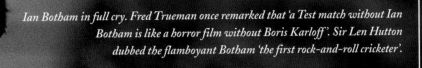

Ian Botham in full cry. Fred Trueman once remarked that 'a Test match without Ian Botham is like a horror film without Boris Karloff'. Sir Len Hutton dubbed the flamboyant Botham 'the first rock-and-roll cricketer'.

Most Test ducks

	T	I	NO	0s
M.A. Atherton	115	212	7	20
A.R. Caddick	62	95	12	19
M.J. Hoggard	67	92	27	19
D.L. Underwood	86	116	35	19
S.J. Harmison	57	75	20	18

Highest Test partnerships

	R	W	Opp.	Ground	Match date
P.B.H. May, M.C. Cowdrey	411	4	West Indies	Edgbaston	30 May 1957
L. Hutton, M. Leyland	382	2	Australia	The Oval	20 Aug. 1938
W.J. Edrich, D.C.S. Compton	370	3	South Africa	Lord's	21 June 1947
J.H. Edrich, K.F. Barrington	369	2	New Zealand	Headingley	8 July 1965
L. Hutton, C. Washbrook	359	1	South Africa	Johannesburg	27 Dec. 1948

Highest Test wicket-takers

		T	B	R	W	BBI	Av.
I.T. Botham	1977–92	102	21,815	10,878	383	8–34	28.40
R.G.D. Willis	1971–84	90	17,357	8190	325	8–43	25.20
F.S. Trueman	1952–65	67	15,178	6625	307	8–31	21.57
D.L. Underwood	1966–82	86	21,862	7674	297	8–51	25.83
J.B. Statham	1951–65	70	16,056	6261	252	7–39	24.84

Note: The best overall bowling average was returned by G.A. Lohmann who, between 1886 and 1896, took 112 wickets at the astonishingly low average of 10.75. Four men have taken nine or more wickets in an innings – Laker (twice in a match, Old Trafford, 1956) Lohmann, Devon Malcolm and S.F. Barnes. Against South Africa in 1913–14 Barnes took 49 wickets in four matches. Laker's 46 in five games in 1956 is the next best.

Most dismissals by a wicketkeeper in a Test career

		T	Victims	Ct	St
A.P.E. Knott	1967–81	95	269	250	19

Note: Bob Taylor took seven catches in an innings vs India, Bombay, 1980; in 1995 Jack Russell took 11 in a match vs South Africa, Johannesburg. During that series he made 27 dismissals (25 ct, 2 st).

Most catches by a fielder in a Test career

	T	Ct
I.T. Botham	102	120
M.C. Cowdrey	114	120

Leading all-rounders (1000 runs [average of 20 or more] and 100 wickets)

	T	R	Bat. av.	W	Bowl. av.	Tests for 1000/100
T.E. Bailey	61	2290	29.74	132	29.21	47
I.T. Botham	102	5200	33.54	383	28.40	21
J.E. Emburey	64	1713	22.53	147	38.40	46
A. Flintoff	74	3595	31.81	211	32.63	43
A.F. Giles	54	1421	20.89	143	40.60	43
A.W. Greig	58	3599	40.43	141	32.20	37
R. Illingworth	61	1836	23.24	122	31.20	47
W. Rhodes	58	2325	30.19	127	26.96	44
M.W. Tate	39	1198	25.48	155	26.16	33
F.J. Titmus	53	1449	22.29	153	32.22	40

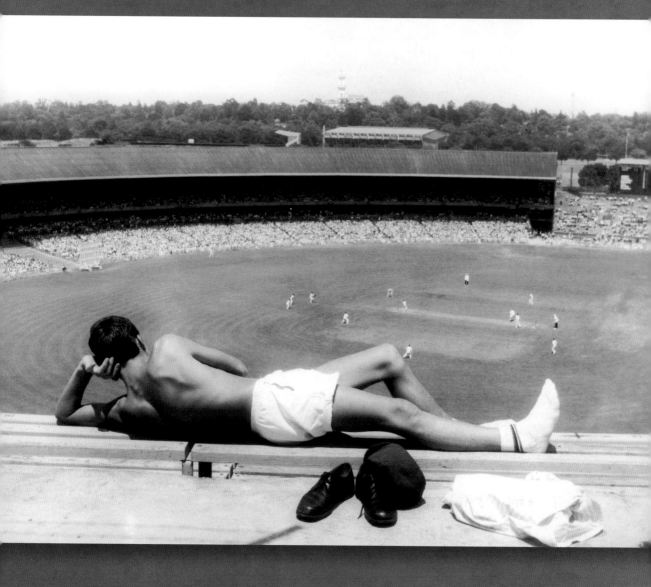

CHAPTER 5
CRICKET IN AUSTRALIA

THE DOMESTIC GAME DOWN UNDER,
PLUS PROFILES AND TEST AND FIRST-CLASS
RECORDS OF AUSTRALIA'S ALL-TIME GREATS

Australia is the dominant power in world cricket and has been for the best part of 20 years. Australians enjoy this enormously; the rest of the world does not. The rest of the world finds it very boring. Not that Australia win all the time, of course; sometimes they lose individual matches and even series, but in the last 10 years under Steve Waugh and then Ricky Ponting they have twice won 16 Tests in a row, pretty much against all-comers. And what makes matters even more irritating for everyone else is that as fast as their champions drop out a new bunch pops up to take over.

Australia have played more than 700 Test matches and won nearly 47 per cent of them, while losing only about 25 per cent. They have been top of the ICC Test Championship table since its inception in 2001, except for a brief period when they were usurped by South Africa; they are also dominant in one-day internationals and have won the World Cup four times, the last three in succession while remaining undefeated in their last 29 games.

Come on, guys – give the rest of us a break. Or at least share your secret with us. Is it that you take sport more seriously than anyone else or do you just want to win more than anyone else? The answer, I suspect, is yes in both cases. It was, after all, the Australians who invented sledging (see pages 278–281) to give them a psychological advantage on the field, though even that might be no more dispiriting to the opposition than the sound of the triumphal song emana-ting from the Aussie changing-room after each win.

It's called 'Under the Southern Cross', authorship attributed to Rodney Marsh, and it goes like this: 'Under the Southern Cross I stand/A sprig of wattle in my hand/A Native of my native land/Australia you f***ing beauty.' The responsibility of leading the team in this doggerel is passed from player to player and currently rests with the unfortunate Michael Hussey.

Australia's opponents have heard it far too often – the English, most painfully, five times in succession in 2006–7. We already know the Aussies' overall record against England but since they are, by some distance, the world's outstanding cricketing nation it's worth taking a look at how they have fared against everyone else. Non-Aussies of a sensitive disposition, averse to hearing bad news, might care to skip the statistics box that follows on page 106.

LEFT *A sun-baked fan enjoys a bird's-eye view of a Test match at the Melbourne Cricket Ground, 1960.*

BELOW *Master batsman and master drinker David Boon leads the singing of 'Under the Southern Cross I Stand', 1989.*

Australia vs South Africa
Tests – played 82: won 47, lost 17, drawn 18
ODIs – played 72: won 37, lost 32, tied 3

Australia vs Pakistan
Tests – played 52: won 24, lost 11, drawn 17
ODIs – played 74: won 43, lost 27, tied 1, no result 3

Australia vs West Indies
Tests – played 105: won 50, lost 32, tied 1, drawn 22
ODIs – played 119: won 58, lost 57, tied 2, no result 2

Australia vs Sri Lanka
Tests – played 20: won 13, lost 1, drawn 6
ODIs – played 68: won 46, lost 20, no result 2

Australia vs New Zealand
Tests – played 48: won 24, lost 7, drawn 17
ODIs – played 117: won 80, lost 32, no result 5

Australia vs Zimbabwe
Tests – played 3, won 3
ODIs – played 27, won 25, lost 1, no result 1

Australia vs India
Tests – played 76: won 34, lost 18, tied 1, drawn 23
ODIs – played 96: won 57, lost 32, no result 7

Australia vs Bangladesh
Tests – played 4, won 4
ODIs – played 16, won 15, lost 1

AUSTRALIA'S DOMESTIC COMPETITIONS

So there the Aussies stand, atop the world and, credit where it's due, deservedly so. But how did it all begin? Well, the game has been played Down Under for more than 200 years, although the first serious domestic competition, the Sheffield Shield, was not organized until 1892, by which time Australia and England had already been locked in grim combat for the Ashes for 10 years. The shield itself was donated by Lord Sheffield, who had financed W.G. Grace's English tourists of 1891–2, and was contested much like the County Championship in England until 1982–3, since when instead of the top team in the league being declared champions it has to take on the runners-up in what amounts to a cup final.

Another change came in 1999 when the competition found a sponsor in the National Food Company and changed its name to the Pura Cup. But in 2008 Pura dropped out and the Sheffield Shield was restored. So, after all these years, the states were back where they started – vying with each other for a trophy graciously gifted to them by a Pom. Bit of a choker for them, I should think.

In its inaugural season, and for many years thereafter, the only contestants for the Shield were Victoria, New South Wales and South Australia, then mere colonies of the Mother Country. In 1926–7 they were joined by Queensland. Western Australia first took part in 1947–8 and Tasmania in 1977–8. Not surprising, therefore, that the most frequent winners of the trophy, whatever its name, are New South Wales (45) and Victoria (27), followed by Western Australia (15), South Australia (13), Queensland (six) and Tasmania with a solitary victory in 2006–7.

The most important one-day competition is the Ford Ranger Cup, which began under a different name and different sponsorship in 1969–70 and featured the six Australian states plus New Zealand, the inaugural winners. But New Zealand withdrew after 1974–5, no doubt highly satisfied with winning the thing three times in six years, since when it has been an all-Aussie affair that is now organized on a round-robin basis, each team playing the others home and away before the best two come together in the final. This is a form of cricket that suits Western Australia best: so far they have appeared in 21 finals, winning 11. New South Wales are next best with nine wins, followed by Queensland with eight. For the rest, Victoria have four victories, Tasmania three and South Australia two.

The aptly named KFC Twenty20 Big Bash − cheap and cheerful cricket, not for gourmets, sponsored by a cheap and cheerful fast food chain, also not for gourmets − was introduced in 2005−6 and has been dominated by Victoria, which won the first three competitions.

HEROES OF THE SHEFFIELD SHIELD

The highest average in Australia's domestic first-class cricket belongs to Bradman − who else? − at 110.19 in 96 innings between 1929 and 1949 while playing for New South Wales and South Australia. And the highest score, 452 not out for NSW against Queensland in 1929−30 was also made by Bradman. But the most runs in a season − 1506 at 94.12 − were scored by Simon Katich (NSW) in 2007−8 and the most in a career, 13,635, by Darren Lehmann (SA/Vic) between 1987 and 2008. Lehmann, incidentally, also scored most centuries (45) in Shield/Cup matches.

The highest team total was Victoria's 1107 (talk about overkill) against New South Wales at Melbourne in 1926−7 and the lowest, 27, was recorded by South Australia against New South Wales at Sydney in 1955−6.

Of the bowlers the leg-spinner Clarrie Grimmett (Vic/SA) took most career wickets − 513 at 25.29 in 79 games between the early 1920s and 1941. But the most wickets in a season − 67 in 11 games − were claimed by Colin Miller (Tasmania) in 1997−8. (Mind you, this feat, commendable though it is, rather pales when compared with the achievement of the left-arm spinner 'Chuck' Fleetwood-Smith of Victoria, who dismissed 60 batsmen in only six games in 1934−5.) The best career average was that of Bill O'Reilly, possibly the greatest of leg-spinners until Shane Warne came along, who took 203 wickets at 17.10.

The most successful of all wicketkeepers in Australian domestic cricket is Darren Berry (SA/Vic), who claimed 546 victims (499 caught, 47 stumped) in 139 games. Berry toured England with Australia in 1997 but never played in a Test, being a contemporary of Ian Healy and Adam Gilchrist. Many in Australia thought he was a

BELOW *Gum trees surrounding Yarra Park provide ideal vantage-points for spectators at the Melbourne Cricket Ground in 1864.*

superior 'keeper but the other two were better batters and in Tests it's runs that count.

It was tough on Berry, but what his record and lack of international recognition tend to exemplify is Australia's continuing and enviable strength in depth. Time after time one of the Test team's stars drops out for one reason or another and, just as the opposition is breathing a sigh of relief, somebody equally good steps in. In the 2005–6 series against the West Indies, for instance, Justin Langer had to miss the game at Brisbane. His replacement was Mike Hussey of Western Australia who, at 30, seemed a bit old to be making his Test debut and with scores of 1 and 29 was hardly impressive. But look what he did then – in his next 25 Tests he scored 2325 runs with eight hundreds at an average of 68.38. Other nations can only keep their fingers crossed that the Aussies don't have any more old blokes like him ready to step into the breach. The sobering fact, however, is that they probably do.

RETIREMENTS, DEFEATS AND RECOVERY

On the other hand... In late 2008 things changed rather drastically. Australia lost series away to India and at home to South Africa. Well, India is different – anyone can lose there – but defeat by South Africa was a catastrophe and by year's end the Aussies were barely clinging on as the number one Test nation.

What's more, Hayden had retired, Hussey's average – around 80 at the beginning of the year – had plummeted, the likes of Brett Lee, Stuart Clark, Shane Watson and Andrew Symonds were injured and no new old blokes and, worse still, no new young blokes had come through. Good, said the rest of the world, high time somebody else took over.

But then Australia went to South Africa for the return series and – come on, you've really got to hand it to them – the whole team rose like the Phoenix from its own ashes. An old bloke, well, oldish at nearly 30, called Marcus North made a century on debut; a very young bloke, Phil Hughes, 20 and a bit, became the youngest ever to score two hundreds in a Test (and that in only his second game); and a trio of fast bowlers, the right-armers Peter Siddle and Andrew McDonald, led by the left-armer Mitchell Johnson, the veteran among them with all of 18 caps before the visit to South Africa, contributed mightily to thrashing the Proteas.

While it might have been premature to claim that the West Indies were a power again after their dodgy home series win over England in March 2009, only a fool would now regard Australia as second to anybody. Okay, with the retirement of Stuart McGill they didn't have a single spinner much better than a pie-chucker but who's to say they wouldn't unearth one when they needed him?

They really are that bloody good and that bloody resilient. Curse them.

THE BATSMEN

The following list is in chronological order except that, well, it would be absurd not to begin with the Don because he was, quite simply, the greatest of them all.

DONALD GEORGE BRADMAN
(1908–2001) *New South Wales and South Australia*

Bradman was a small man (only 5' 7") but he towers over the game like a giant of restricted growth. His deeds, especially his Test batting average, seem like figments of the imagination. Surely nobody could have been that good, could have accumulated runs quite so remorselessly? But he was and he did and for 20 years he was, as Bill Woodfull put it, 'worth three batsmen to Australia'. He began at 19 for NSW with a century on his debut, hit 79 and 112 in his second Test, made the then-highest first-class score of 452

not out against Queensland in 1928–9 and in 1930 amassed 974 runs against England, 309 of them made in one day at Leeds on the way to a world record Test score of 334. The Bodyline series of 1932–3 trimmed his wings a little but only a little – he still averaged 56.57 – and thereafter the runs and records kept coming. On average he scored 50 or more in every second innings he played and is the only Australian to make 100 centuries. As *Wisden* said, he 'reinvented the game' and in so doing achieved a standard nobody else is ever likely to reach. And to think that for two years in his late teens he gave up cricket for tennis – what a loss that would have been. Only at the end did the gods decide that enough was enough, that a Test batting average of 100 would be ridiculous and so arranged his second-ball duck at the Oval in 1948 to prove that even the Don wasn't quite perfect (see page 246).

Test batting and fielding

T	I	NO	R	HS	Av.	100	50	Ct
52	80	10	6996	334	99.94	29	13	32

Test bowling

T	I	B	R	W	BBI	BBM	Av.
52	9	160	72	2	1-8	1-15	36.00

First-class batting and fielding

M	I	NO	R	HS	Av.	100	50	Ct
234	338	43	28,067	452*	95.14	117	69	131

First-class bowling

M	B	R	W	BBI	Av.
234	2114	1367	36	3-35	37.97

VICTOR THOMAS TRUMPER
(1877–1915) *New South Wales*

Trumper was, they say, a genius – a right-handed batsman of fluent, elegant grace whose hundred before lunch against England on a rain-affected wicket at Manchester in 1902 is still thought to be one of the

HOWZAT! The postal address of the Australian Broadcasting Corporation, is PO Box 9994 – Bradman's Test average, give or take a decimal point. Coincidence? The po-faced ABC says it is. Why don't they just lighten up and glory in this association with Australia's greatest native son?

HOWZAT! The young Arthur Mailey first met Trumper when he bowled against him in a Grade cricket match and dismissed him. Afterwards Mailey said: 'I felt terrible. I felt as if I had shot a dove.'

ABOVE *The legendary Australian batsman Victor Trumper batting at the Oval, in G.W. Beldam's iconic photograph.*

Test batting and fielding

T	I	NO	R	HS	Av.	100	50	Ct
48	89	8	3163	214*	39.04	8	13	31

Test bowling

T	I	B	R	W	BBI	BBM	Av.
48	15	546	317	8	3–60	3–87	39.62

First-class batting and fielding

M	I	NO	R	HS	Av.	100	50	Ct
255	401	21	16,939	300*	44.57	42	87	173

First-class bowling

M	B	R	W	BBI	Av.
255	3822	2008	64	5–19	31.37

CLEM HILL
(1877–1945) *South Australia*

One of the great left-handers, in 1902 Hill became the first player to score 1000 Test runs in a calendar year (nobody was to do it again for 45 years) and when he retired (in 1912) had scored more Test runs than anyone else at the time. He was sound and patient in defence, highly effective with the drive, hook and cut,

finest innings ever played. In his time, like Grace before him and Bradman later, he was regarded as the world's greatest batsman with the ability to thrive in, to others, unplayable conditions. Against England in 1903–4 on a dreadful wicket at Melbourne he made 74 of Australia's total of 122. In that series he scored 574 at 63.77 and against South Africa in 1910–11 he made 661 runs at an average of 94.42. He was, apparently, able to adapt to any kind of bowling and, according to conditions, to switch from orthodox to unorthodox while still making batting look the easiest thing in the world. If his overall figures seem unremarkable it's because much of his cricket was played on pitches that would be deemed unacceptable today.

and particularly good on hard, Australian wickets. His Sheffield Shield aggregate of 6274 runs at 52.28 was a record until Bradman beat it. Normally he batted at number three and, with Trumper, formed the backbone of the Australian team. But at Melbourne in 1897–8, when he was 21, he came in against England at 58 for 6 and scored 188 to win the game. Ten years later he and Roger Hartigan put on 243, still the record Australian stand for the eighth wicket. In addition to his seven Test hundreds he was also out four times in the nineties, three of them in consecutive Tests against England in 1901–2.

Test batting and fielding								
T	I	NO	R	HS	Av.	100	50	Ct
49	89	2	3412	191	39.21	7	19	33

First-class batting and fielding								
M	I	NO	R	HS	Av.	100	50	Ct
252	416	21	17,213	365*	43.57	45	83	168

(Hill never bowled in a Test and in first-class cricket took 10 wickets at 32.30. Like Bradman he brought off one stumping as a stand-in wicketkeeper.)

CHARLES GEORGE MACARTNEY
(1886–1958) *New South Wales and Otago*

Charlie Macartney, known to his fellow-countrymen as 'the Governor General', was a brilliant, attacking right-handed batsman, who could dominate an attack better than anyone until Bradman. He usually batted at number three and, it is said, had a shot – orthodox or unorthodox, he didn't care – for every ball. But on his first tour of England in 1909 he was played mostly as a slow left-arm bowler and won the Headingley Test by taking 11 for 85. The following year he scored a century against South Africa and after the 1914–18 war established himself among Australia's greatest players. In the 1920–1 Ashes series, he scored 170 at Sydney and topped the batting averages with 86.66. Against Nottinghamshire in 1921 he scored 345 in

LEFT *Clem Hill (seated third from left) pictured c.1900 with his fellow South Australians, and team-mates in the Australian Test side, (left to right) Joe Darling, George Giffen and Ernie Jones.*

less than four hours and against England at Leeds made a hundred before lunch. He did that again, also at Leeds, in 1926, while putting on 235 for the second wicket with Bill Woodfull. He played for Australia from 1907 until 1926 when, once again, he topped the Test averages with 473 runs at 94.60.

Test batting and fielding								
T	I	NO	R	HS	Av.	100	50	Ct
35	55	4	2131	170	41.78	7	9	17

Test bowling							
T	I	B	R	W	BBI	BBM	Av.
35	45	3561	1240	45	7-58	11-85	27.55

First-class batting and fielding								
M	I	NO	R	HS	Av.	100	50	Ct
249	360	32	15,019	345	45.78	49	53	102

First-class bowling					
M	B	R	W	BBI	Av.
249	24,228	8782	419	7-58	20.95

STANLEY JOSEPH McCABE
(1910–68) *New South Wales*

Len Hutton said of Stan McCabe: 'He had qualities that even Bradman hadn't got.' After McCabe had scored 232 in less than four hours against England at Trent Bridge in 1938, Bradman himself said: 'If I could play an innings like that I'd be a proud man.' But perhaps McCabe's finest hour was at Sydney in 1932–3 when he scored 187 and tore England's 'Bodyline' attack apart, hooking the ferocious bouncers with rare courage and panache. He was a short, stocky right-handed batsman with great attacking flair, who played for Australia from 1930 until the Second World War, which brought his Test career to an end, although he was not yet 30. He was also a useful fast-

medium bowler who, when Australia lacked good fast men in the 1930s, often opened the bowling for them.

[Stan McCabe, career statistics]								
Test batting and fielding								
T	I	NO	R	HS	Av.	100	50	Ct
39	62	5	2748	232	48.21	6	13	41
Test bowling								
T	I	B	R	W	BBI	BBM	Av.	
39	62	3746	1543	36	4–13	4–38	42.86	
First-class batting and fielding								
M	I	NO	R	HS	Av.	100	50	Ct
182	262	20	11,951	240	49.38	29	68	138
First-class bowling								
M	B	R	W	BBI	Av.			
182	13,440	5362	159	5–36	33.72			

ARTHUR ROBERT MORRIS
(b.1922) *New South Wales*

Arthur Morris made his first-class debut against Queensland when he was 18 and scored a hundred in each innings. He went on from there to become one of Australia's finest left-handers. For Bradman's 'Invincibles' in 1948 he topped the averages with 696 runs at 87.00. Altogether in 24 Tests against England he hit seven centuries, including two in one match in 1946–7, and scored 2080 runs at 50.73. His form declined after 1950, at which time he had a Test average of 67.77, but he was still good enough to score 153 against England in the 1954–5 series before Frank Tyson began to dominate the Australian batsmen. An elegant, compact opening bat, particularly effective in partnership with Sidney Barnes and recently voted Australia's best opener since the war, he retired from Tests in 1955 but continued in the first-class game for another eight years.

Test batting and fielding								
T	I	NO	R	HS	Av.	100	50	Ct
46	79	3	3533	206	46.48	12	12	10
First-class batting and fielding								
M	I	NO	R	HS	Av.	100	50	Ct
162	250	15	12,614	290	53.67	46	46	73
(An occasional left-arm spinner, Morris took 2 Test wickets at 25.00 and altogether 12 first-class wickets at 49.33)								

ROBERT NEIL HARVEY
(b.1928) *Victoria and New South Wales*

Neil Harvey had three brothers – Merv, Mick and Ray – who also played for Victoria; Merv even played one game for Australia. But Neil was incomparably the best of them, indeed one of the greatest of all left-handers. In his second Test (against India) aged 19 and three months, he became the youngest batsman to score a century for Australia. In 1948 he made another hundred on his debut against England. In his first 13 Test innings he scored six centuries and averaged more than 100. He was a flamboyant, attacking batsman – 'technically perfect' in shot selection, according to Bradman – who was also regarded as the finest fielder of his time. Against the South African tourists in 1952–3 he made 834 runs in the Tests, beating even Bradman's record against them. In fact when Harvey retired only the great Don had scored more Test runs and centuries for Australia. Later he became a Test selector and was included in the Australian Cricket Board's official 'Test Team of the 20th Century'.

BELOW *The mercurial left-hander Neil Harvey played in 79 tests for Australia between 1947 and 1963.*

Test batting and fielding

T	I	NO	R	HS	Av.	100	50	Ct
79	137	10	6149	205	48.41	21	24	64

(As an occasional off-spinner Harvey took 3 wickets at 40.00 in Tests)

First-class batting and fielding

M	I	NO	R	HS	Av.	100	50	Ct
306	461	35	21,699	231*	50.93	67	64	228

First-class bowling

M	B	R	W	BBI	Av.
306	2574	1106	30	4–8	36.86

GREGORY STEPHEN CHAPPELL
(b.1948) *South Australia, Queensland and Somerset*

A member of Australia's most famous cricketing dynasty and the best of them. His grandfather, Vic Richardson, played Test cricket, so did his brothers Ian and Trevor. Indeed, only Trevor didn't get to be captain of the side. A tall, composed and elegant right-handed batsman, Greg scored a century in his first Test, another in his last and in between made two in his first match as skipper. He captained Australia 48 times, winning 21 matches and losing 13. As skipper he lost the Ashes in 1977 and regained them in 1982–3. A fine player of fast bowling and a superb fielder, he also developed into an effective bowler of medium-paced seam-up, a skill he learned during a couple of years with Somerset. At home, he began with South Australia, then moved to Queensland as captain before joining Kerry Packer's World Series Cricket, thus missing 24 Tests. He was the finest Australian batsman of his generation and a ruthless captain who, in 1981, notoriously made his brother Trevor bowl the last ball of an ODI against New Zealand under-arm and along the ground to stop the batsman from hitting a match-winning six. In 2005 he became coach to the Indian team but fell out with Sourav Ganguly (which hardly makes him unique) and resigned after the 2007 World Cup.

Test batting and fielding

T	I	NO	R	HS	Av.	100	50	Ct
87	151	19	7110	247*	53.86	24	31	122

Test bowling

T	I	B	R	W	BBI	BBM	Av.
87	88	5327	1913	47	5–61	5–61	40.70

First-class batting and fielding

M	I	NO	R	HS	Av.	100	50	Ct
321	542	72	24,535	247*	52.20	74	111	376

First-class bowling

M	B	R	W	BBI	Av.
321	20,926	8717	291	7–40	29.95

ODI batting and fielding

M	I	NO	R	HS	Av.	100	50	Ct
74	72	14	2331	138*	40.18	3	14	23

ODI bowling

M	I	B	R	W	BB	Av.
74	67	3108	2097	72	5–15	29.12

HOWZAT! In a Test against New Zealand at Wellington in 1973–4 Greg Chappell scored a century in each innings and so did his brother Ian. This is the only time two brothers have achieved such a feat. At the time Greg's aggregate of 380 runs – 247 not out and 133 – was a record in a Test match.

ALLAN BORDER

(b.1955) *New South Wales, Queensland, Essex, Gloucestershire*

A.B. is a man of many Test records – the fastest Aussie to 1000 runs, the first to play 100 matches, 93 consecutive games as captain and the first man to score two 150s (versus Pakistan, 1979–80) in the same match. At one time he also held the record for most Test runs and has still appeared in more consecutive matches (153) than anyone else. An obdurate middle-order left-handed bat and useful left-arm spinner, he first came into an Australian side weakened by the absence of WSC players in 1978–9, but kept his place to become an initially reluctant and underrated skipper, who nevertheless led his team to World Cup triumph in 1987, regained the Ashes two years later and eventually handed on to Mark Taylor the makings of a world-beating side. He celebrated his 100th Test by taking 7 for 46 against the West Indies. He was not the prettiest of batsmen but always a difficult man to get out – often at his best when the going was tough for lesser players – and particularly sure and nimble against spin. His dedication to Australian cricket, first during the WSC period and then in 1985 when seven of the national squad defected in favour of a rebel tour of South Africa, was recognized by the fact that nowadays Australia's Cricketer of the Year is awarded the Allan Border Medal.

Test batting and fielding								
T	I	NO	R	HS	Av.	100	50	Ct
156	265	44	11,174	205	50.56	27	63	156

Test bowling							
T	I	B	R	W	BBI	BBM	Av.
156	98	4009	1525	39	7-46	11-96	39.10

First-class batting and fielding								
M	I	NO	R	HS	Av.	100	50	Ct
385	625	97	27,131	205	51.38	70	142	379

First-class bowling					
M	B	R	W	BBI	Av.
385	9750	4161	106	7-46	39.25

ODI batting and fielding								
M	I	NO	R	HS	Av.	100	50	Ct
273	252	39	6524	127*	30.62	3	39	127

ODI bowling					
M	B	R	W	BB	Av.
273	2661	2071	73	3-20	28.37

STEPHEN RODGER WAUGH

(b.1965) *New South Wales*

Known to his team-mates, predictably, as 'Tugga', Steve Waugh is the most-capped player in Test history. At first a free-scoring right-handed batsman and right-arm medium-pace bowler, he remodelled his game after being dropped from the national team, cut out the frills and returned to become an avaricious run-gatherer and Australia's captain during the record run (later to be equalled by Ricky Ponting's team) of 16 consecutive Test wins. He was less attractive to watch than his gifted twin brother Mark, but a remorseless opponent, both as batsman and skipper, and an unashamed exponent of sledging to gain a psychological edge. He was in the Armstrong–Bradman–Chappell tradition of Aussie hard men. His record – twice Ashes-winning and twice World Cup-winning captain, a double-century to help win a series against West Indies in 1994–5 and two

LEFT *A tinny and a trophy: if there's anything Australians enjoy even more than an ice-cold beer, it's thrashing England. Allan Border celebrates winning back the Ashes in 1989 by a thumping 4–0 margin.*

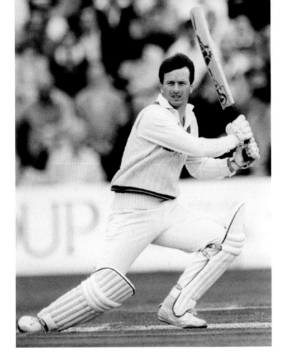

ABOVE *'Iceman' Steve Waugh was instrumental in turning the Australian team of the late 1990s and early 2000s into an unstoppable cricketing juggernaut.*

hundreds to win the game (and, as it turned out, the Ashes) at Old Trafford in 1997 – puts him up there among cricket's greatest achievers. Neither as batter nor captain did he show mercy and it was he who turned an already highly successful Australian team into the dominant unit that Ponting inherited.

Test batting and fielding

T	I	NO	R	HS	Av.	100	50	Ct
168	260	46	10,927	200	51.06	32	50	112

Test bowling

T	I	B	R	W	BBI	BBM	Av.
168	150	7805	3445	92	5-28	8-169	37.44

First-class batting and fielding

M	I	NO	R	HS	Av.	100	50	Ct
356	551	88	24,052	216*	51.94	79	97	273

First-class bowling

M	B	R	W	BBI	Av.
356	17,428	8155	249	6-51	32.75

ODI batting and fielding

M	I	NO	R	HS	Av.	100	50	Ct
325	288	58	7569	120*	32.90	3	45	111

ODI bowling

M	I	B	R	W	BB	Av.
325	207	8883	6761	195	4-33	34.87

MATTHEW HAYDEN (b.1971)
Queensland, Northamptonshire and Hampshire

Matt Hayden was a great big, thumping thug of a batsman, a left-handed opener who hammered the ball to all parts, though mostly through the off side. Although he made a century on his first-class debut for Queensland, the Aussie selectors didn't fancy him much at first and from 1994 he was in and out of the side for six years until establishing himself by scoring 539 runs (average 109.80) in a three-Test series against India in 2000–1. After that he made more than 1000 Test runs in each of five successive years as well as notching up Australia's highest individual score – 380 (admittedly against the hapless Zimbabwe) in 2003. His critics called him a 'flat-track bully' and sneered that he was rubbish against England's pace attack in 2005. But then so was Ricky Ponting. Anyway, Hayden did very well after that and his overall record is formidable by any standards. He has the highest Test average of any Australian opening batsman. Only two Australians (Ricky Ponting and Steve Waugh) have made more Test 100s. He was a sound slip-fielder, an occasional right-arm medium bowler and he captained Northants in 1999 and 2000.

Test batting and fielding

T	I	NO	R	HS	Av.	100	50	Ct
103	184	14	8625	380	50.73	30	29	128

First-class batting and fielding

M	I	NO	R	HS	Av.	100	50	Ct
295	515	47	24,603	380	52.57	79	100	296

ODI batting and fielding

M	I	NO	R	HS	Av.	100	50	Ct
161	155	15	6133	181*	43.80	10	36	68

(Hayden's bowling record is 0-40 in Tests; 17-671, average 39.47 in first-class games; BBI 3-10. In ODIs he took 0-18.)

HOWZAT! It's reported that when he first saw the massive Hayden come out to bat, equipped with helmet and full body-armour, England's Paul Collingwood exclaimed: 'By God, it's Buzz Lightyear.'

RICKY THOMAS PONTING
(b.1974) *Tasmania and Somerset*

'Punter' Ponting ('Punter' because of his love of greyhound racing) is the archetypal modern Australian cricketer – a feisty, pugnacious right-handed batsman, fluent against fast bowling, though sometimes iffy against top-class spin, and a superb fielder. He broke into the Test team in 1995, scoring 96 against Sri Lanka. There followed a few years in which he was in and out of the side, due to attitude, fluctuating form and an admitted drink problem, which he has now conquered. But since establishing himself at number three he has built up a formidable record – only Tendulkar has scored more Test centuries. He succeeded Steve Waugh as captain of the ODI side in 2002 and of the Test team in 2004, promptly losing the Ashes the following year. But he regained them with a vengeance in 2006–7. He also led the team to a record-equalling 16 straight Test wins. Under Ponting Australia retained the World Cup in 2007, when he scored 140 in the final. What's more, he was the first player to score a century in each innings of his 100th Test (against South Africa in 2006) and the first Australian to score 10,000 runs in ODIs. Many think he's the best Australian batsman since Bradman.

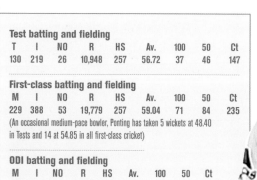

Test batting and fielding

T	I	NO	R	HS	Av.	100	50	Ct
130	219	26	10,948	257	56.72	37	46	147

First-class batting and fielding

M	I	NO	R	HS	Av.	100	50	Ct
229	388	53	19,779	257	59.04	71	84	235

(An occasional medium-pace bowler, Ponting has taken 5 wickets at 48.40 in Tests and 14 at 54.85 in all first-class cricket)

ODI batting and fielding

M	I	NO	R	HS	Av.	100	50	Ct
310	301	35	11,365	164	42.72	26	66	137

(Ponting has taken 3 ODI wickets at 34.66)

RIGHT *After a mainly successful spell as Australian Test captain from 2004 onwards, Ricky Ponting contemplates harder times ahead, as his side loses the final Test against India in Nagpur in November 2008, and with it the series (2–0).*

So there you are – 12 of the best and already I can hear cries of outrage. What, no Woodfull or Ponsford, no Sidney Barnes or Justin Langer or Mike Hussey? I could – you could – go back even further to find men worthy of inclusion. But you'll have to do that by yourselves because that's my choice and now I move on to…

THE BOWLERS

FREDERICK ROBERT SPOFFORTH

(1853–1926) *New South Wales, Victoria and Derbyshire.*

Tall, lanky, black hair parted sharply in the middle and with a moustache that looked as though some furry creature had attached itself to his upper lip, 'the Demon' was right-arm fast-medium rather than really quick. But he could swing the ball into right-handers and was equally effective with both the faster and the slower ball. In short, he was Australia's first truly great bowler and the nemesis of W.G. Grace, who never mastered him. In a career that spanned 1874 to 1897, he made his debut for Australia in the second-ever Test in 1876–7, having refused to play in the first because the NSW wicketkeeper Billy Murdoch hadn't been chosen. In 1878 the Aussie tourists dismissed the MCC twice in a day at Lord's for scores of 33 and 19, Spofforth taking 10 for 20 in all and bowling Grace for a duck. But his greatest moment came in 1882 when he took 14 for 90 at the Oval to clinch the series in the first Ashes match (see page 24). He was the first bowler to take a Test hat-trick and claimed 10 wickets in a Test four times. He dropped out of Test cricket in 1886, moved to England and played for Derbyshire from 1889 until 1891.

HUGH TRUMBLE

(1867–1938) *Victoria*

In his day Trumble was regarded as an all-rounder but only his bowling record is really impressive, though he was a useful bat and did the double in England in 1899. He was a tall, medium-paced off-break bowler with a command of length, flight and enough spin to trouble batsmen on any wicket. On poor wickets he was said to make the ball bite, turn and lift quite venomously. He was the first great off-spinner and W.G. Grace thought him 'the best bowler Australia has sent us'. Trumble made his Test debut in 1890 but only gained a regular place in 1896. A slow developer, he reached his peak in 1901–2 when, captaining the side at the age of 34, he took 28 wickets at 20.03 – including a hat-trick at Melbourne. In 1902 he took 26 wickets at 14.26. The following year he retired briefly from Test cricket but was persuaded to return against England for the last four matches of the 1903–4 tour, snaffling 24 victims and finally bowling out on a dramatic high note by taking 7 for 28, including another hat-trick, to win the game for Australia. After that he retired, having taken more wickets than anyone else in Tests.

Test bowling

T	I	B	R	W	BBI	BBM	Av.
18	30	4185	1731	94	7–44	14–90	18.41

Test batting and fielding:

T	I	NO	R	HS	Av.	100	50	Ct
18	29	6	217	50	9.43	0	1	11

First-class bowling

M	B	R	W	BBI	Av.
155	30,593	12,759	853	9–18	14.95

First-class batting and fielding

M	I	NO	R	HS	Av.	100	50	Ct
155	236	41	1928	56	9.88	0	3	83

Test bowling

T	I	B	R	W	BBI	BBM	Av.
32	57	8099	3072	141	8–65	12–89	21.78

Test batting and fielding

T	I	NO	R	HS	Av.	100	50	Ct
32	57	14	851	70	19.79	0	4	45

First-class bowling

M	B	R	W	BBI	Av.
213	44,060	17,134	929	9–39	18.44

First-class batting and fielding

M	I	NO	R	HS	Av.	100	50	Ct
213	344	67	5395	107	19.47	3	20	329

CLARENCE VICTOR GRIMMETT
(1891–1980) *Victoria, South Australia and Wellington*

Clarrie Grimmett's record is quite amazing. A small, wizened man, known as 'the Gnome' (see page 308), he was born in New Zealand, bowled leg-spin, made his Test debut against England in 1924–5 at the age of 34 and took 11 wickets for 82, going on to become the first player ever to make his debut after 30 and take 100 Test wickets. By the time he finished in 1936, he had become the first bowler to take 200 Test wickets – at the rate of nearly six a game. That achievement is all the more striking given that throughout his career he was either vying for a place with, or bowling alongside, two other great leg-spinners in Arthur Mailey and Bill O'Reilly. Grimmett was a more parsimonious bowler than Mailey and not as quick as O'Reilly. With an almost round-arm action he was exceptionally accurate in length and flight, relying mostly on leg-breaks and top-spinners, though he could also bowl the googly and is credited with inventing the flipper. Against South Africa in 1935–6 he set an Australian record by taking 44 wickets in the series. O'Reilly thought him 'the best spin bowler the world has seen'.

Test bowling							
T	I	B	R	W	BBI	BBM	Av.
37	67	14,513	5231	216	7–40	14–199	24.21

Test batting and fielding:								
T	I	NO	R	HS	Av.	100	50	Ct
37	50	10	557	50	13.92	0	1	17

First-class bowling					
M	B	R	W	BBI	Av.
248	73,987	31,737	1424	10–37	22.28

First-class batting and fielding								
M	I	NO	R	HS	Av.	100	50	Ct
248	321	54	4720	71*	17.67	0	12	140

WILLIAM JOSEPH O'REILLY
(1905–92) *New South Wales*

Bill O'Reilly, aptly known as 'Tiger', purveyed ferocious leg-breaks, googlies and top-spinners from a low trajectory at a brisk medium-pace. His attitude towards batsmen was much like that of a really nasty fast bowler

BELOW *'Tiger' O'Reilly in action in England in 1934.*

who seriously wanted to hurt them. *Wisden* described him as 'hostile'; batsmen thought so, too. Bradman described him as the best bowler he had ever seen and, chipping in again in 1939, *Wisden* said he was 'emphatically one of the greatest bowlers of all time'. A tall man (6' 2") who batted left-handed, he first appeared for Australia against South Africa in 1931–2 and for the next two or three years he and Grimmett were the most lethal leg-spin bowling combination cricket has known. In the 'Bodyline' series O'Reilly was Australia's most successful bowler, taking 27 wickets at 26.81, including a ten-for in the Melbourne match to secure the home side's only win. In 1934 against England O'Reilly took 28 wickets, Grimmett 25 and the other Aussie bowlers 18 between them. Against South Africa in 1935–6 O'Reilly had 27 victims and Grimmett his record-breaking 44. When Grimmett was then dropped for the awful sin of being 45 years old, O'Reilly became the hub of the Australian attack and remained so until the Second World War. In 1945–6 he appeared in the first post-war Test, against New Zealand, took 5 for 14 and 3 for 19, and then called it a day, later becoming an outspoken commentator on the game. His figures are damned good anyway but even better when you remember that he bowled mostly on shirt-front wickets.

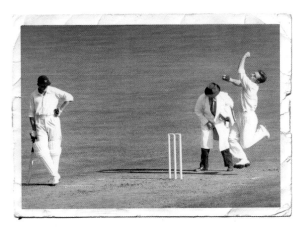

ABOVE *Ray Lindwall's classic side-on action is well illustrated in this photograph of him bowling at the Oval in 1953. The batsman is England's Tom Graveney.*

a bit, he had a classically smooth run-up and an action that generated ferocious pace and swing in both directions. His Test debut was against New Zealand in 1946 but it was in the 1946–7 Ashes series that he made his presence felt, scoring a century in the third match – he was a more-than-useful batsman – and taking 7 for 63 in the last. In the 1948 series, revealing the kind of pace no Englishman had shown since Larwood (Lindwall's role model, incidentally) he took 27 wickets, including 6 for 20 at the Oval when England were skittled for 52. Then and for the best part of a decade he and Keith Miller formed one of the deadliest pairs of opening bowlers in the game's history. Lindwall used the bouncer rarely and in fact more than 40 per cent of his Test victims were clean-bowled.

Test bowling

T	I	B	R	W	BBI	BBM	Av.
27	48	10,024	3254	144	7–54	11–129	22.59

Test batting and fielding

T	I	NO	R	HS	Av.	100	50	Ct
27	39	7	410	56*	12.81	0	1	7

First-class bowling

M	B	R	W	BBI	Av.
135	37,064	12,850	774	9–38	16.60

First-class batting and fielding

M	I	NO	R	HS	Av.	100	50	Ct
135	167	41	1655	56*	13.13	0	1	65

RAYMOND RUSSELL LINDWALL
(1921–96) *New South Wales and Queensland*

Ray Lindwall was Australia's first great fast bowler since the days of Jack Gregory and Ted McDonald in the 1920s. Broad of chest and shoulder, standing 5' 10" and

Test bowling

T	I	B	R	W	BBI	BBM	Av.
61	113	13,650	5251	228	7–38	9–70	23.03

Test batting and fielding:

T	I	NO	R	HS	Av.	100	50	Ct
61	84	13	1502	118	21.15	2	5	26

First-class bowling

M	B	R	W	BBI	Av.
228	43,215	16,956	794	7–20	21.35

First-class batting and fielding

M	I	NO	R	HS	Av.	100	50	Ct
228	270	39	5042	134*	21.82	5	19	123

DENNIS KEITH LILLEE
(b.1949) *Western Australia*

Dennis Lillee is notorious for attempting to use an aluminium bat in a Test against England in 1979, for betting on England to win at the long odds of 500–1 at Headingley in 1981 (see Botham's Match, pages 220–222), and for aiming a kick at Javed Miandad in a Test against Pakistan, also in 1981. (Well, lots of people have wanted to kick Javed.) What Lillee is rightly famous for is being one of the finest, paciest (once timed at 97 mph) fast bowlers of them all. Alone, or in partnership with Jeff Thomson in 1974–5, he was an inveterate destroyer of English batsmen. Well, of almost any batsmen, really. A tough, belligerent, rather rebellious character, he made a remarkable comeback from serious back injury early in his career, joined Packer's World Series Cricket with predictable success and then returned to the Test arena and took 35 wickets in six matches against West Indies and England in 1979–80. With a splendid action, speed, control, a vicious bouncer and sheer aggression (most fast bowlers have attitude; Lillee had it in spades) he ended his career with the then world-record number of Test wickets, 95 of them caught behind the stumps by Rod Marsh.

ABOVE *The most feared fast bowlers in Australian Test history? Dennis Lillee (left) and Jeff Thomson. 'Ashes to ashes, dust to dust/If Thomson don't get ya, Lillee must'* ran a cartoon caption in the Sydney Telegraph.

Test bowling

T	I	B	R	W	BBI	BBM	Av.
70	132	18,467	8493	355	7–83	11–123	23.92

Test batting and fielding

T	I	NO	R	HS	Av.	100	50	Ct
70	90	24	905	73*	13.71	0	1	23

First-class bowling

M	B	R	W	BBI	Av.
198	44,806	20,695	882	8–29	23.46

First-class batting and fielding

M	I	NO	R	HS	Av.	100	50	Ct
198	241	70	2377	73*	13.90	0	2	67

ODI bowling

M	I	B	R	W	BB	Av.
63	63	3593	2145	103	5–34	20.82

ODI batting and fielding

M	I	NO	R	HS	Av.	100	50	Ct
63	34	8	240	42*	9.23	0	0	10

HOWZAT! In the Melbourne Centenary Test of 12–17 March 1977, Dennis Lillee's outstanding bowling figures of 6–26 and 5–139 played a major part in steering Australia to a 45-run victory – exactly the same winning margin Australia recorded in the very first Test match 100 years earlier.

SHANE KEITH WARNE
(b.1969) *Victoria and Hampshire*

Named as one of the Five Cricketers of the Century in the 2000 edition of *Wisden*, Warne is quite simply the greatest spin-bowler ever. Between 1992 and his international retirement in 2007, he was the first player to take 600 and then 700 Test wickets and in all international matches claimed more than 1000 victims with a baffling variety of viciously spun leg-breaks, googlies, flippers, zooters, sliders and anything else he cared to dream up, plus pinpoint accuracy and devilish mind-games. Best remembered, of course, is 'the ball of the century' with which, in his first Ashes Test in 1993, he bowled Mike Gatting (see page 37). Off the field he sometimes resembled a soap opera character, being involved in numerous scrapes with women to whom he wasn't married and even being banned for failing a drug test (he had taken a diuretic, actually). But on the field he was a genius. In the 2005 Ashes contest he virtually *was* the Australian attack, taking 40 wickets in the series. Towards the end of his career he was an inventive captain of Hampshire for three years. But for his larrikin image he would surely have captained Australia, too.

Test bowling
T	I	B	R	W	BBI	BBM	Av.
145	273	40,705	17,995	708	8–71	12–128	25.41

Test batting and fielding
T	I	NO	R	HS	Av.	100	50	Ct
145	199	17	3154	99	17.32	0	12	125

First-class bowling
M	B	R	W	BBI	Av.
301	74,830	34,449	1319	8–71	26.11

First-class batting and fielding
M	I	NO	R	HS	Av.	100	50	Ct
301	404	48	6919	107*	19.43	2	26	264

ODI bowling
M	I	B	R	W	BB	Av.
194	191	10,642	7541	293	5–33	25.73

ODI batting and fielding
M	I	NO	R	HS	Av.	100	50	Ct
194	107	29	1018	55	13.05	0	1	80

GLENN DONALD McGRATH
(b.1970) *New South Wales*

No other fast bowler has taken more Test wickets than the lean, lanky McGrath. There have been many faster bowlers than he, but it was not speed but relentless accuracy that was McGrath's most formidable weapon. A tall (6' 6") right-arm bowler with a high action, he believed in keeping bowling simple, relying on line, length, seam movement and sharp bounce, tactics which led, for instance, to him dismissing Mike Atherton a record 19 times. But then the opposition's leading batsmen were always McGrath's main targets. He was supremely confident, an inveterate sledger – indeed he could be a bad-tempered bugger at times – and perhaps second only to Lillee as Australia's greatest fast bowler. He played one season for Worcestershire and later a few games for Middlesex and ended his career by being named Man of the Series during Australia's successful 2007 World Cup campaign.

Test bowling
T	I	B	R	W	BBI	BBM	Av.
124	243	29,248	12,186	563	8–24	10–27	21.64

Test batting and fielding
T	I	NO	R	HS	Av.	100	50	Ct
124	138	51	641	61	7.36	0	1	38

First-class bowling
M	B	R	W	BBI	BBM	Av.
189	41,759	17,414	835	8–24	10–27	20.85

First-class batting and fielding
M	I	NO	R	HS	Av.	100	50	Ct
189	193	67	977	61	7.75	0	2	54

ODI bowling
M	I	B	R	W	BB	Av.
250	248	12,970	8391	381	7–15	22.02

ODI batting and fielding
M	I	NO	R	HS	Av.	100	50	Ct
250	68	38	115	11	3.83	0	0	37

Only eight names there, you notice. But that's because some of Australia's finest bowlers have also been talented multi-taskers, as we shall see from the following list of…

THE ALL-ROUNDERS

MONTAGUE ALFRED NOBLE
(1873–1940) *New South Wales*

At the time of his death Monty Noble was reckoned by many to have been Australia's finest ever all-rounder. His bowling, off-spin and swerve at paces varying from slow to medium, was his stronger point but he was also a stylish right-hand batsman, capable of fierce attack or staunch defence, and an astute captain. Noble was one of the stars of the 'Golden Age' and perhaps his crowning achievement was in the 1901–2 Ashes series when he took 32 wickets at 19 each. As a batsman who scored seven double-centuries in first-class cricket, he never quite showed his best at Test level, although at Manchester in 1899 he saved Australia by scoring 60 not out in three hours and then 89 in five hours.

Test batting and fielding

T	I	NO	R	HS	Av.	100	50	Ct
42	73	7	1997	133	30.25	1	16	26

Test bowling

T	I	B	R	W	BBI	BBM	Av.
42	71	7159	3025	121	7-17	13-77	25.00

First-class batting and fielding

M	I	NO	R	HS	Av.	100	50	Ct
248	377	34	13,975	284	40.74	37	66	187

First-class bowling

M	B	R	W	BBI	Av.
248	33,112	14,443	626	8-48	23.14

WARWICK WINDRIDGE ARMSTRONG
(1879–1947) *Victoria*

'The Big Ship', as he was known, transformed himself from the tall, slim Test debutant of 1901–2 into the 22-stone Falstaffian figure who retired 20 years later. In the meantime, despite the First World War intervening, he became one of Australia's finest all-rounders, a cussed, confident right-hand batsman, a purveyor of fast-medium stuff and leg spin and in 1920–1 captain of the first side to whitewash England

(see Warwick's Wonders, pages 232–240). He was, if you like, the W.G. Grace of the early 20th century, a massive, dominant, rather haughty presence both on and off the field. As skipper he beat England eight times in a row with the kind of ruthless attitude emulated by almost every Australian captain since.

Test batting and fielding

T	I	NO	R	HS	Av.	100	50	Ct
50	84	10	2863	159*	38.68	6	8	44

Test bowling

T	I	B	R	W	BBI	BBM	Av.
50	80	8022	2923	87	6-35	7-166	33.59

First-class batting and fielding

M	I	NO	R	HS	Av.	100	50	Ct
269	406	61	16,158	303*	46.83	45	57	273

First-class bowling

M	B	R	W	BBI	Av.
269	43,297	16,405	832	8-47	19.71

JOHN MORRISON GREGORY
(1895–1973) *New South Wales*

Jack Gregory's Test career was brief but glorious. A left-handed batsman, he scorned batting gloves but still scored a century in 70 minutes against South Africa in 1921. As a right-arm bowler of awesome pace he was a mighty contributor to the whitewash of England in 1920–1 and, alongside Ted McDonald, to Australia's subsequent three-nil series win in England. Along with all that he was a

RIGHT *As well as being a demon fast bowler, Jack Gregory was a class act with the bat and in the field.*

superb fielder who held a record 15 catches in the 1920–1 series. He was a bowler who charged to the wicket, ending his run-up with a huge leap and a delivery of blistering pace, and a batsman who regarded the ball as being there to wallop out of sight. But for injury his would have been a particularly outstanding career. He broke down during the 1926 tour of England and again in the first Test at Brisbane in 1928–9 when he had to leave the field, never to play for his country again.

Test batting and fielding								
T	I	NO	R	HS	Av.	100	50	Ct
24	34	3	1146	119	36.96	2	7	37

Test bowling							
T	I	B	R	W	BBI	BBM	Av.
24	42	5582	2648	85	7-69	8-101	31.15

First-class batting and fielding								
M	I	NO	R	HS	Av.	100	50	Ct
129	173	18	5659	152	36.50	13	27	195

First-class bowling					
M	B	R	W	BBI	Av.
129	22,014	10,580	504	9-32	20.99

ABOVE *Keith Miller hits out on the way to 145 not out in the third Test at Sydney, January 1951. Miller's innings paved the way for victory over England by an innings and 13 runs.*

KEITH ROSS MILLER
(1919–2004) *Victoria and New South Wales*

Keith ('Nugget') Miller was about as naturally gifted as a cricketer could be – an attacking batsman, who made 181 on his first-class debut for Victoria, a superb fielder and a bowler who, off a short run, could send down deliveries of lightning speed, life-threatening bouncers or, according to his whim, leg-breaks. Either with bat or ball he could change the course of a game. High, wide and handsome was 'Nugget' and so sometimes was his bowling. He'd been a fighter pilot in the Second World War and realized better than most that cricket was not a matter of life and death but something to be enjoyed. The game was never dull when Miller was involved. He would probably have captained Australia, and done it well, had he not fallen foul of Bradman on the 1948 Ashes tour. Well into the Aussies' record score of 721 in a day against Essex, Miller deliberately allowed himself to be bowled first ball, having no taste for taking part

in one-sided slaughter. Bradman never forgave him. Miller was that rare commodity – a player worthy of a Test place either as batsman or bowler – and is the only man to have his name on the honours board at Lord's in both capacities, having scored a century and also taken a five-for there.

Test batting and fielding								
T	I	NO	R	HS	Av.	100	50	Ct
55	87	7	2958	147	36.97	7	13	38

Test bowling							
T	I	B	R	W	BBI	BBM	Av.
55	95	10,461	3906	170	7-60	10-152	22.97

First-class batting and fielding								
M	I	NO	R	HS	Av.	100	50	Ct
226	326	36	14,183	281*	48.90	41	63	136

First-class bowling					
M	B	R	W	BBI	Av.
226	28,070	11,087	497	7-12	22.30

ALAN KEITH DAVIDSON
(b.1929) *New South Wales*

An accurate, miserly left-arm fast-medium bowler and hard-hitting lower order left-handed batsman, Davidson was one of the mainstays of the Australian team during the 1950s and early 60s. Bowling was his strong point; he swung the ball late, conceded fewer than two runs an over and many rank him alongside Wasim Akram as the best left-arm quick in the game's history. But his batting, too, was far from negligible. In the tied Test against West Indies at Brisbane in 1960–1 (see pages 217–219) he became the first player ever to score 100 runs (44 and 80) and take 10 wickets (5 for 135 and 6 for 87) in a Test match. Six-foot tall and powerfully built, he started off bowling chinamen and only switched to pace when his local team was short of a fast bowler. It was the best move he ever made because it helped him to become an all-rounder of the very highest class.

Test batting and fielding

T	I	NO	R	HS	Av.	100	50	Ct
44	61	7	1328	80	24.59	0	5	42

Test bowling

T	I	B	R	W	BBI	BBM	Av.
44	82	11,587	3819	186	7–93	12–124	20.53

First-class batting and fielding

M	I	NO	R	HS	Av.	100	50	Ct
193	246	39	6804	129	32.86	9	36	168

First-class bowling

M	B	R	W	BBI	Av.
193	37,704	14,048	672	7–31	20.90

RICHIE BENAUD
(b.1930) *New South Wales*

Now best known as the peerless doyen of cricket commentators, Richie Benaud was also a world-class all-rounder – a leg-spinner in the great Aussie tradition, an attractive attacking batsman, a brilliant close-to-the-wicket fielder and one of the shrewdest and most astute of captains. In his first series as skipper in 1958–9 he took 31 wickets to win the Ashes back for Australia and in 1961 took 6 for 70 at

ABOVE *Richie Benaud*, eminence grise *of TV cricket commentary, during the fifth and final Ashes Test match at the Oval, September 2005. This was the last Test match that Benaud commentated on in England.*

Old Trafford to stop England regaining them. He was first chosen for Australia as a batsman who could bowl but in the event the batting did not quite live up to expectations while the bowling far surpassed them. In 1963 he became the first player to score 2000 runs and take 200 wickets in Test matches. When he retired in 1964 he was Australia's leading Test wicket-taker.

Test batting and fielding

T	I	NO	R	HS	Av.	100	50	Ct
63	97	7	2201	122	24.45	3	9	65

Test bowling

T	I	B	R	W	BBI	BBM	Av.
63	116	19,108	6704	248	7–72	11–105	27.03

First-class batting and fielding

M	I	NO	R	HS	Av.	100	50	Ct
259	365	44	11,719	187	36.50	23	61	254

First-class bowling

M	B	R	W	BBI	Av.
259	60,481	23,370	945	7–18	24.73

RIGHT *Adam Gilchrist hits a six on his way to the second fastest century in Test history, in the third Ashes Test match at Perth, 16 December 2006. In a uniquely hard-hitting career, Gilchrist smashed more sixes in Test matches (100) than any other batsman.*

ADAM CRAIG GILCHRIST
(b.1971) *New South Wales, Western Australia*

Adam Gilchrist was one of the most thrilling players in the game. Whether opening the batting in ODIs or coming in at number seven in Tests, he could tear an attack apart in a matter of minutes with hitting that sometimes seemed positively brutal. The England attack at Perth in the 2006–7 Ashes series can vouch for that because he scored a hundred off them in 57 balls. In all Tests his strike rate was 82 runs per 100 deliveries. As a wicketkeeper he was not the greatest but he was good enough to hold the world record of 436 Test dismissals until South Africa's Mark Boucher overtook him. Although his batting declined a bit towards the end, especially in the 2005 Ashes series, he must rank as the finest wicketkeeping all-rounder the game has seen.

Test batting and fielding

T	I	NO	R	HS	Av.	100	50	Ct	St
96	137	20	5570	204*	47.60	17	26	379	37

First-class batting and fielding

M	I	NO	R	HS	Av.	100	50	Ct	St
190	280	46	10,334	204*	44.16	30	43	756	55

ODI batting and fielding

M	I	NO	R	HS	Av.	100	50	Ct	St
287	279	11	9619	172	35.89	16	55	417	55

HOWZAT! Richie Benaud has a simple rule-of-thumb for good cricket commentary: 'My mantra is: put your brain into gear and if you can add to what's on the screen then do it, otherwise shut up.'

AUSTRALIA'S TEST RECORDS

Australia's highest-ever total in Tests is 758–8d against West Indies at Kingston in 1955; the lowest 36 against England at Birmingham in 1902.

Most Test appearances

	T
S.R. Waugh	168
A.R. Border	156
S.K. Warne	145
R.T. Ponting	130
M.E. Waugh	128

Highest individual Test scores

	R	Opp.	Ground	Match date
M.L. Hayden	380	Zimbabwe	Perth	9 Oct. 2003
M.A. Taylor	334*	Pakistan	Peshawar	15 Oct. 1998
D.G. Bradman	334	England	Headingley	11 July 1930
R.B. Simpson	311	England	Old Trafford	23 July 1964
R.M. Cowper	307	England	Melbourne	11 Feb. 1966

Highest Test batting averages
(qualification: 15 Tests or more)

	T	Av.
D.G. Bradman	52	99.94
R.T. Ponting	130	56.72
M.E.K. Hussey	36	56.26
G.S. Chappell	87	53.86
J. Ryder	20	51.62

Highest Test run-scorers

	Span	T	I	NO	R	HS	Av.
A.R. Border	1978–94	156	265	44	11,174	205	50.56
R.T. Ponting	1995–2009	130	219	26	10,948	257	56.72
S.R. Waugh	1985–2004	168	260	46	10,927	200	51.06
M.L. Hayden	1994–2009	103	184	14	8625	380	50.73
M.E. Waugh	1991–2002	128	209	17	8029	153*	41.81

Most Test centuries

	T	100
R.T. Ponting	130	37
S.R. Waugh	168	32
M.L. Hayden	103	30
D.G. Bradman	52	29
A.R. Border	156	27

	T	I	NO	0s
G.D.McGrath	124	138	51	35
S.K. Warne	145	199	17	34
S.R. Waugh	168	260	46	22
M.F...gh	128	209	17	19
I.A. ...	119	182	23	18

Highest Test partnerships

	R	W	Opp.	Ground	Match date
W.H. Ponsford, D.G. Bradman	451	2	England	The Oval	18 Aug. 1934
S.G. Barnes, D.G. Bradman	405	5	England	Sydney	13 Dec. 1946
W.H. Ponsford, D.G. Bradman	388	4	England	Headingley	20 July 1934
S.R. Waugh, G.S. Blewett	385	5	South Africa	Jo'burg	28 Feb. 1997
W.M. Lawry, R.B. Simpson	382	1	West Indies	Bridgetown	5 May 1965

Highest Test wicket-takers

		T	B	R	W	BBI	Av.
S.K. Warne	1992–2007	145	40,705	17,995	708	8–71	25.41
G.D. McGrath	1993–2007	124	29,248	12,186	563	8–24	21.64
D.K. Lillee	1971–84	70	18,467	8493	355	7–83	23.92
B. Lee	1999–2008	76	16,531	9554	310	5–30	30.81
C.J. McDermott	1984–96	71	16,586	8332	291	8–97	28.63

Note: The best bowling average belongs to J.J. Ferris (48 wickets at 14.25) but he only played in eight games. Of those who have enjoyed a long career Alan Davidson is best with 186 wickets at 20.53 in 44 Tests. Clarrie Grimmett took the most wickets in a series with 44 (at 14.59) against South Africa in 1935–6; Arthur Mailey's 9–121 against England at Melbourne in 1921 was the best return in a single innings but the best bowling figures in a match were returned by Bob Massie with 16–137, also against England, at Lord's in 1972.

Most dismissals by a wicketkeeper in a Test career

		T	W	Ct	St
A.C. Gilchrist	1999–2008	96	416	379	37

Note: Rodney Marsh holds the record for most dismissals in a series: 28, all caught, in five games against England in 1982–3. Against New Zealand at Hamilton in 2000 Gilchrist took 10 catches in the match.

Most catches by a fielder in a Test career

	T	Ct
M.E. Waugh	128	181

Note: J.M. Gregory took 15 catches in the series against England in 1920–1.

Leading all-rounders (1000 runs [at an average of 20 or more] and 100 wickets)

	T	R	Bat. Av.	W	Bowl. Av.	Tests for 1000/100
R. Benaud	63	2201	24.45	248	27.03	32
A.K. Davidson	44	1328	24.59	186	20.53	34
G. Giffen	31	1238	23.35	103	27.09	30
B. Lee	76	1451	20.15	310	30.81	53
R.R. Lindwall	61	1502	21.15	228	23.03	38
K.R. Miller	55	2958	36.97	170	22.97	33
M.A. Noble	42	1997	30.25	121	25.00	27

Shane Warne, Australia's leading Test wicket–taker, rejoices in one of his 708 Test dismissals. Aside from his many cricketing accolades, Warne also has the curious distinction of being the only leg–spin bowler to be immortalized in a musical.

CHAPTER 6
CRICKET IN SOUTH AFRICA

THE DOMESTIC GAME IN THE RAINBOW NATION, PLUS PROFILES AND TEST AND FIRST-CLASS RECORDS OF SOUTH AFRICA'S ALL-TIME GREATS

Cricket was introduced to South Africa by the English (natch), who also played the first Test match in that country, on a matting wicket, in 1888–9. England won by eight wickets on the second day.

In that first match England were captained by Sir C. Aubrey Smith, of Sussex, who took 5 for 19 in the first innings. It was his only Test. He missed the second match because of illness and England were led by Monty Bowden, of Surrey, a wicketkeeper-batsman who, at 23 years and 144 days was England's youngest captain. It was Bowden's second – and last – Test appearance. Afterwards he stayed on in South Africa and played for Transvaal, dying at the age of 26 after a fall from an ox-wagon.

CONTESTING THE CURRIE CUP

The following year (1889–90) a domestic competition, the Currie Cup – named for Sir Donald Currie who donated it – was introduced. Not much of a competition, really, because at first only two sides, Kimberley and Transvaal, took part.

However, it quickly caught on and expanded, probably reaching its peak of popularity in the 1970s and 80s when, thanks to the government's apartheid policy, South Africa was shunned and isolated from international sport. At that time domestic cricket was the only show in town, apart from a few rebel tours of which most people, including liberal-minded white South Africans, disapproved.

FAR LEFT *Jacques Kallis straight-drives during a match against Bangladesh A in 2008. A prodigious all-rounder, Kallis has not only played in more Tests, scored more Test runs and more Test centuries, and taken more Test catches than any other South African, he is also his country's fourth most successful Test bowler in terms of wickets taken.*

LEFT *The South African team that toured England in 1907. Back row (left to right): G.A. Faulkner, A.D. Nourse, J.H. Sinclair, G. Alsop (manager), S.D. Snooke, A.E. Vogler, G.C. White; middle row (l to r): M. Hathorn, R.O. Schwarz, P.W. Sherwell (captain), J.J. Kotze, W.A. Shalders, L.J. Tancred; front row (l to r): S.J. Snooke and H. Smith. England took the three-Test series one-nil.*

But after 1990, when apartheid had bitten the dust and South Africa was welcomed back into the international community, interest in the domestic game began to wane. In 1990–1 the national trophy ceased to be the Currie Cup and became the Castle Cup instead. It remained so until 1996–7, when it changed its name again to the SuperSport Series.

Even that, though, failed to do the trick and in 2004–5 there was a considerable overhaul of the competition. Six new franchises incorporating the 11 existing provincial teams were introduced in the hope of producing more and better sides at the top level: Cape Cobras (Western Province and Boland), Dolphins (KwaZulu-Natal), Eagles (Free State and Griqualand

West), Lions (Gauteng/Transvaal and North West), Titans (Easterns and Northerns) and Warriors (Eastern Province and Border).

Over the years Transvaal have been the most successful side, winning the competition outright 25 times. Natal are next with 21 wins, followed by Western Province (18), Free State, Orange or otherwise (3), Eastern Province (2) and Easterns and Kimberley (one each). The title has been shared five times.

Various one-day trophies with a bewildering tendency to change their names are also played for. The Benson & Hedges Series, introduced in 1981–2, became the Standard Bank Cup in 1996–7. The Gillette Cup, first contested in 1969–70, turned into the Datsun Shield in 1977–8 and the Nissan Shield in 1983–4. Sometimes the games were played over 60 overs, sometimes 50 and sometimes 45. In all of them the most powerful teams have tended to be Western Province and Transvaal.

THE D'OLIVEIRA AFFAIR AND EXCLUSION

Thanks to the bigotry of the Pretoria regime, South African cricket was completely screwed up by apartheid. Under this charming system only white people were allowed to represent the nation at any sport and then they could only play against other white teams. West Indies, India, Pakistan? Forget it.

In the late 1960s, though, South Africa's chickens came home to roost. England were due to tour in 1968–9. Fine, no problem – until Tom Cartwright dropped out of the touring party and was replaced by Basil D'Oliveira, who should have been in it to start with. But D'Oliveira had been born in South Africa and – oh, horror! – he was coloured. Well, South Africa couldn't have that – a black man mixing on equal terms with white people in their country? Hey, man, no way. The republic's prime minister B.J. Vorster declared that Dolly's selection was both political and unacceptable. The MCC, which had chickened out of picking Dolly in the first place, now showed some cojones, refused to be intimidated by Vorster and the tour was cancelled.

A mistake, cried some – including, no doubt, the people who had offered Dolly money to make himself unavailable for the tour. We should build bridges, they said, keep our sporting links with South Africa open to show them the error of their ways – and a fat lot of good *that* had done in the past.

In 1970 the International Cricket Council (ICC) made disapproval of South Africa's politics pretty well unanimous by suspending the country from international cricket indefinitely, or anyway until apartheid was gone. That was tough on the players because South Africa had a cracking team at the time (see The Super Springboks, pages 247–251). They had just murdered Bill Lawry's Aussies four-nothing, and outstanding players like Barry Richards, the Pollock brothers (Graeme and Peter), Mike Procter and Eddie Barlow were in their prime. Now their Test careers were over.

FAR LEFT *South Africa's discriminatory and racist policy of apartheid towards its black majority led to the country being increasingly ostracized from international sporting competition. The Springboks' tour of England in 1965 attracted vehement protest; here, a policeman looks on as demonstrators carry placards outside the team's base at the Waldorf Hotel in central London. Earlier that year, under the Group Areas Act, the authorities in Pretoria had prohibited any mixed-race sport within South Africa.*

In the years to come, however, the international ban worked nicely for England and Australia, with such South Africans as Tony Greig, Robin Smith and Allan Lamb choosing to qualify for the former and Kepler Wessels doing the same for the latter before returning to play for his native land when South Africa was reinstated as a Test nation in 1991.

AFTER APARTHEID

Since that date the national team has had mixed success. They have produced splendid players in Jacques Kallis, Shaun Pollock (son of Peter), Allan Donald, Makhaya Ntini and Dale Steyn and in 2007 were, briefly, top of the ICC One-Day International rankings. But against that they acquired a reputation as 'chokers' by reaching the semi-finals of the World Cup three times without progressing any further.

There was also the little matter of their captain Hansie Cronje owning up to match-fixing and being drummed out of the game (see pages 276–277). And the introduction of a racial quota policy, which decreed that a certain number of non-white players must be in the international squad, if not indeed the team, and led in 2006 to Ashwell Prince becoming the first non-white to captain South Africa, has not been without its problems.

It was because of the alleged lack of opportunity due to the quota policy that Kevin Pietersen opted to qualify for England. In 2007 the fast bowler Andre Nel, who is white, reacted furiously to being leapfrogged for a place in the South African touring party to India by the Cape Coloured bowler Charl Langeveldt. Just to add complication Langeveldt also withdrew, rather honourably, because he felt Nel was the better player. But gradually the quota problems seemed to sort themselves out, and with a Rainbow Nation of players like Graeme Smith, Steyn (who took 74 wickets in 13 Tests in 2008, at an exceptionally good strike rate), Kallis, Ntini, Prince, Hashim Amla, A.B. de Villiers, the promising young fast bowler Morne Morkel and J.P. Duminy, who scored 166 against Australia in his second Test, they put together their best team since the days of Richards and the Pollock brothers.

By the end of 2008, during which they won 11 Tests, South Africa had not lost a series in more than two years and in the previous 12 months had drawn with India, beaten England in England and, best of all, had won a series in Australia for the first time ever. However, the Aussies gained swift revenge in the return series in South Africa in February–March 2009, their series victory preventing the hosts from usurping the Aussies' cherished No. 1 spot in the ICC Test Championship.

HOWZAT! In the 1999 World Cup semi-final in England Herschelle Gibbs dropped the Australian captain Steve Waugh at a critical point of the game. 'Mate,' said Waugh, 'you've just dropped the World Cup.' And so, as it turned out, he had.

THE BATSMEN

BRUCE MITCHELL
(1909–95) *Transvaal*

Bruce Mitchell was 17 when he made his debut for Transvaal and took 11 wickets with leg-breaks and googlies. But after that his batting took over and he developed into one of the finest batsmen his country has produced, a tidy, obdurate opener who played in all South Africa's 42 Tests from 1929 to 1949. His 164 not out at Lord's in 1935 had much to do with securing South Africa's first win in England. In 1947 at the Oval he batted for more than 13 hours while scoring two centuries (120 and 189 not out) in the match. For much of his international career South Africa's batting was inconsistent and Mitchell was obliged to play the anchor role. But he was not entirely defensive. He possessed the full range of strokes and, when the conditions were right, could score freely and quickly enough. He was an excellent fielder. Although he eventually became only an occasional bowler, he did manage a five-for – against Australia in 1935–6.

Test batting and fielding

T	I	NO	R	HS	Av.	100	50	Ct
42	80	9	3471	189*	48.88	8	21	56

Test bowling

T	I	B	R	W	BBI	BBM	Av.
42	39	2519	1380	27	5–87	5–87	51.11

First-class batting and fielding

M	I	NO	R	HS	Av.	100	50	Ct
173	281	30	11,395	195	45.39	30	55	228

First-class bowling

M	B	R	W	BBI	Av.
173	12,360	6382	249	6–33	25.63

ARTHUR DUDLEY NOURSE
(1910–81) *Natal*

Of South Africans who have completed full Test careers only Graeme Pollock has a higher batting average than Dudley Nourse. The son of Arthur ('Old Dave') Nourse, himself a South African Test player, Dudley was an aggressive, hard-hitting right-handed batsman, particularly strong off the back foot, and an outstanding fielder. His most memorable innings was at Trent Bridge in 1951 when, as captain and playing with a broken thumb, he scored 208 in nine hours to lead South Africa to their first Test victory in 16 years. In his first Test against England in 1935 he scored 4; in his last, also against England, in 1951, he made 4 and 4. But in between times he had consistently been his country's leading player, among his notable scores being 231 against Australia in 1935–6.

Test batting and fielding

T	I	NO	R	HS	Av.	100	50	Ct
34	62	7	2960	231	53.81	9	14	12

First-class batting and fielding

M	I	NO	R	HS	Av.	100	50	Ct
175	269	27	12,472	260*	51.53	41	54	135

(Nourse's bowling record was 0–9 in Tests and 0–124 in first-class matches)

ROBERT GRAEME POLLOCK
(b.1944) *Eastern Province and Transvaal*

Bradman reckoned Graeme Pollock and Gary Sobers were the finest left-hand batsmen he ever saw. Well, both of them were geniuses at the game and certainly it's hard to think of anyone better than Pollock, whose

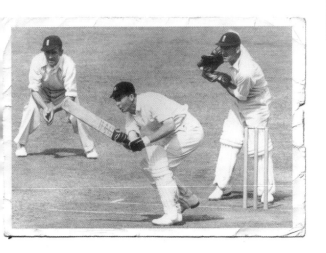

LEFT *Bruce Mitchell takes a single off England's Doug Wright to reach the first of his twin centuries in an epic batting display in the fifth Test match at the Oval, August 1947.*

ABOVE *Graeme Pollock (left) and his fast-bowling older brother Peter, at the Oval in 1965. The Pollock siblings excelled in that summer's three-match Test series against England, Graeme scoring 291 runs at 48.50 and Peter bagging 20 wickets at 18.30 apiece.*

Test career was abruptly halted when South Africa were ostracized. Before then he was probably the most thrilling batsman in the world, a player of awe-inspiring ability, combining power, grace and immaculate timing with a voracious appetite for runs. The younger brother of the fast bowler Peter Pollock and uncle of the all-rounder Shaun, Graeme scored his first first-class hundred when he was 16 and his first Test century, against Australia, in 1963–4 when he was 19. After that he simply got better and better. The high points of an all-too-brief career include 125 made in appalling Trent Bridge gloom against England in 1965, 209 while batting with a pulled thigh muscle against Australia in 1966–7 and what

was then the highest score by a South African, 274 – also against Australia – in 1969–70. And that was the end of it. At 26, because of politics, he was gone – about four years before he would have reached his peak.

Test batting and fielding								
T	I	NO	R	HS	Av.	100	50	Ct
23	41	4	2256	274	60.97	7	11	17
(In Tests Pollock, an occasional leg-spinner, took 4 wickets at an average of 51.00)								

First-class batting and fielding								
M	I	NO	R	HS	Av.	100	50	Ct
262	437	54	20,940	274	54.67	64	99	248

First-class bowling					
M	B	R	W	BBI	Av.
262	3743	2062	43	3-46	47.95

BARRY ANDERSON RICHARDS

(b.1945) *Natal, Transvaal, Hampshire, South Australia*

God alone knows how good Richards might have been but for South Africa's exclusion from Test cricket. Four Tests against Australia, when he was only 24, and that was his lot. But those Tests, his performances in Kerry Packer's World Series Cricket and his general first-class form suggest he would have become one of the greatest of the greats. He was naturally gifted, an attacking opening batsman, graceful and thrilling, who once made 325 in a day for South Australia. Technically and temperamentally he was faultless, except for a tendency to lose interest when the bowling wasn't challenging enough. He was also a superb slip-fielder and an effective occasional off-spinner.

Test batting and fielding								
T	I	NO	R	HS	Av.	100	50	Ct
4	7	0	508	140	72.57	2	2	3
(Richards took 1-26 in 12 overs in Tests)								

First-class batting and fielding								
M	I	NO	R	HS	Av.	100	50	Ct
339	576	58	28,358	356	54.74	80	152	367

First-class bowling					
M	B	R	W	BBI	Av.
339	6126	2886	77	7-63	37.48

GRAEME CRAIG SMITH
(b.1981) *Western Province and Somerset*

Until the end of 2008 it might have seemed a little early to mention Smith and greatness in the same breath. But in that year he scored more than 1600 Test runs, including match-winning centuries against both England and Australia, and skippered his side to its first series victory in England since 1965 and its first ever series win in Australia. A tall, left-handed opening bat, at 22 he became South Africa's youngest captain in March 2003. Kevin Pietersen may once have dismissed him as 'an absolute muppet', but his record indicates otherwise. In 2003 he scored two double-centuries against England, including 277 – the highest Test score by a South African. In 2008 he and Neil McKenzie put on a world record 415 for the first wicket, though admittedly that was only against Bangladesh. He's not as gifted as Pollock or Richards but then few people are. In his early days he could be arrogant, in your face or surly, but he appears to have mellowed since and his achievements, both as captain and batsman, certainly rank him among South Africa's finest.

Test batting and fielding								
T	I	NO	R	HS	Av.	100	50	Ct
76	133	9	6330	277	51.04	18	25	101

(Smith has taken 8 Test wickets at 100.12)

First-class batting and fielding								
M	I	NO	R	HS	Av.	100	50	Ct
114	197	14	9293	311	50.78	26	35	159

(In first-class matches he has taken 11 wickets at 95.27)

ODI batting and fielding								
M	I	NO	R	HS	Av.	100	50	Ct
136	134	9	5111	134*	40.88	7	37	72

(In ODIs Smith has 18 wickets at 52.83)

HUGH JOSEPH TAYFIELD
(1929–94) *Rhodesia, Natal, Transvaal*

'Toey' Tayfield – so-called because of his habit of stubbing his toe into the ground before each delivery – was an immaculate off-spinner, a master of line, length and crafty variations of spin and flight. In 1955 he took his 100th wicket in only his 22nd Test and in 1956–7, also against England, he took 37 wickets in the series, including 9 for 113 in the second innings at Johannesburg. He did not turn the ball as much as Jim Laker but he was, nevertheless, one of the best off-spinners the game has seen. He bowled mostly over the wicket and close to the stumps. At Melbourne in 1952–3 he took 13 wickets to secure South Africa's first win over Australia in 42 years. He was not only a brilliant bowler but a fine fielder, a useful bat and a great optimist as anyone who, like him, married five times would have to be.

Test bowling							
T	I	B	R	W	BBI	BBM	Av.
37	61	13,568	4405	170	9–113	13–165	25.91

Test batting and fielding								
T	I	NO	R	HS	Av.	100	50	Ct
37	60	9	862	75	16.90	0	2	26

First-class bowling						
M	B	R	W	BBI	BBM	Av.
187	54,848	18,890	864	9–113	13–165	21.86

First-class batting and fielding								
M	I	NO	R	HS	Av.	100	50	Ct
187	259	47	3668	77	17.30	0	10	149

HOWZAT! When Hugh Tayfield took his 9–113 against England at Johannesburg in 1956–7, the final catch was held by his brother Arthur, fielding as a substitute.

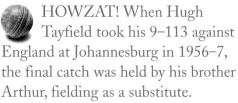

SOUTH AFRICA'S TEST RECORDS

Tests – played 343; won 119, lost 121, drawn 103.
ODIs – played 418; won 260, lost 141, tied 5, no result 12.

South Africa's highest Test total is 682–6d against England
at Lord's in 2003; the lowest 30, which they achieved
twice against England – at Port Elizabeth in 1896
and at Birmingham in 1924.

Highest individual run-scorers in Tests

	Span	T	I	NO	R	HS	Av.
J.H. Kallis	1995–2009	129	218	32	10,092	189*	54.25
G. Kirsten	1993–2004	101	176	15	7289	275	45.27
G.C. Smith	2002–9	76	133	9	6330	277	51.04
H.H. Gibbs	1996–2008	90	154	7	6167	228	41.95
D.J. Cullinan	1993–2001	70	115	12	4554	275*	44.21

Most Test appearances

	T
J.H. Kallis	129
M.V. Boucher	124
S.M. Pollock	108
G. Kirsten	101
H.H. Gibbs	90

Most Test centuries

	T	100s
J.H. Kallis	129	30
G. Kirsten	101	21
G.C. Smith	76	18
D.J. Cullinan	70	14
H.H. Gibbs	90	14

Highest individual Test scores

	R	Opp.	Ground	Match date
G.C. Smith	277	England	Edgbaston	24 July 2003
D.J. Cullinan	275*	New Zealand	Auckland	27 Feb. 1999
G. Kirsten	275	England	Durban	26 Dec. 1999
R.G. Pollock	274	Australia	Durban	5 Feb. 1970
G.C. Smith	259	England	Lord's	31 July 2003

Most Test ducks

	T	I	NO	0s
M. Ntini	98	112	41	21
A.A. Donald	72	94	33	17
M.V. Boucher	124	175	21	17
G. Kirsten	101	176	15	13
W.J. Cronje	68	111	9	11

Highest Test batting averages
(qualification: 15 Tests or more)

	T	Av.
R.G. Pollock	23	60.97
J.H. Kallis	129	54.25
A.D. Nourse	34	53.81
G.C. Smith	76	51.04
K.C. Bland	21	49.08

Highest Test partnerships

	R	W	Opp.	Ground	Match date
J.A. Rudolph, H.H. Dippenaar	429*	3	Bangladesh	Chittagong (MAA)	24 Apr. 2003
N.D. McKenzie, G.C. Smith	415	1	Bangladesh	Chittagong (CDS)	29 Feb. 2008
G.C. Smith, H.H. Gibbs	368	1	Pakistan	Cape Town	2 Jan. 2003
E.J. Barlow, R.G. Pollock	341	3	Australia	Adelaide	24 Jan. 1964
G.C. Smith, H.H. Gibbs	338	1	England	Edgbaston	24 July 2003

Highest Test wicket-takers

		T	B	R	W	BBI	Av.
S.M. Pollock	1995–2008	108	24,353	9733	421	7–87	23.11
M. Ntini	1998–2009	98	20,198	10,905	386	7–37	28.25
A.A. Donald	1992–2002	72	15,519	7344	330	8–71	22.25
J.H. Kallis	1995–2009	129	16,860	7931	257	6–54	30.85
H.J. Tayfield	1949–60	37	13,568	4405	170	9–113	25.91

Note: The best bowling figures in an innings were recorded by Hugh Tayfield who took 9-113 against England in 1957. Ntini and Tayfield (twice) have taken 13 wickets in a match: Ntini's figures being 13-132 vs West Indies, 2005 and Tayfield's 13-165 vs Australia, 1952 and 13-192 vs England, 1957.

Most dismissals by a wicketkeeper in a Test career

		T	W	Ct	St
M.V. Boucher	1997–2009	124	471	449	22

Most catches by a fielder in a Test career

	T	Ct
J.H. Kallis	129	141

Leading all-rounders (1000 runs [at an average of 20 or more] and 100 wickets)

	T	R	Bat. Av.	W	Bowl. Av.	Tests for 1000/100
N. Boje	43	1312	25.23	100	42.65	43
T.L. Goddard	41	2516	34.46	123	26.22	36
J.H. Kallis	129	10,092	54.25	257	30.85	53
S.M. Pollock	108	3781	32.31	421	23.11	26

Against the spectacular backdrop of Table Mountain, South Africa battle it out against Australia in the first Test of the 2006 series at Newlands in Cape Town.

Test bowling							
T	I	B	R	W	BBI	BBM	Av.
72	129	15,519	7344	330	8-71	12-139	22.25

Test batting and fielding								
T	I	NO	R	HS	Av.	100	50	Ct
72	94	33	652	37	10.68	0	0	18

First-class bowling					
M	B	R	W	BBI	Av.
316	58,801	27,680	1216	8-37	22.76

First-class batting and fielding								
M	I	NO	R	HS	Av.	100	50	Ct
316	370	139	2785	55*	12.05	0	1	115

ODI bowling					
M	B	R	W	BB	Av.
164	8561	5926	272	6-23	21.78

ODI batting and fielding								
M	I	NO	R	HS	Av.	100	50	Ct
164	40	18	95	13	4.31	0	0	28

ABOVE *Allan Donald and England's Mike Atherton exchange frosty glances during their classic duel in the fourth Test at Nottingham, 26 July 1998. Atherton's dogged 98 not out helped England to an eight-wicket victory.*

ALLAN ANTHONY DONALD
(b.1966) *Free State and Warwickshire*

Allan Donald has to be up there in the pantheon of great fast bowlers. Certainly he was South Africa's greatest – decidedly quick and always menacing. He made his debut in 1992 in South Africa's first Test after exclusion, but for which his record would surely be even better. They called him 'White Lightning' because of his speed and scowling aggression, the latter most notable during a furious onslaught on Mike Atherton at Trent Bridge in 1998 when Atherton had declined to 'walk' after gloving the ball to the keeper and being given not out. In England, Donald had a long, successful career with Warwickshire whom he went on to coach. He was the first South African bowler to reach 300 Test wickets and for years, until joined by Shaun Pollock, was the only world-class bowler in the national team. As such, the injuries caused by his excessive workload contributed to his retirement from Test cricket in 2002.

MAKHAYA NTINI
(b.1977) *Border, Warwickshire*

In March 1998 against Sri Lanka, Ntini became the first black South African to represent his country at cricket. A year later his career nearly came to an end when he was convicted of rape. But he was acquitted on appeal and since then has gone on to be only the third South African to take 300 Test wickets. As a right-arm fast bowler, just short of great pace but with an action modelled on that of Malcolm Marshall, he tends to bowl from wide of the crease, moving the ball off the seam and in the air. For some years he has been described as 'the engine-room' of the South African attack, his best performance being 13 for 132 against West Indies in 2005. In 2003 he became the first South African to take 10 wickets in a Test at Lord's. As a batsman he is one of nature's number 11s.

RIGHT *Makhaya Ntini with Ashwell Prince (right) and A.B. De Villiers. Ntini was the first black African cricketer to represent South Africa, while Prince became its first black captain when he briefly replaced the injured Graeme Smith in July 2006.*

Test bowling

T	I	B	R	W	BBI	BBM	Av.
98	185	20,198	10,905	386	7–37	13–132	28.25

Test batting and fielding

T	I	NO	R	HS	Av.	100	50	Ct
98	112	41	684	32*	9.63	0	0	25

First-class bowling

M	B	R	W	BBI	Av.
170	31,697	17,267	607	7–37	28.44

First-class batting and fielding

M	I	NO	R	HS	Av.	100	50	Ct
170	197	69	1211	34*	9.46	0	0	39

ODI bowling

M	B	R	W	BB	Av.
171	8597	6444	265	6-22	24.31

ODI batting and fielding

M	I	NO	R	HS	Av.	100	50	Ct
171	45	22	188	42*	8.17	0	0	30

THE ALL-ROUNDERS

Like Australia, South Africa has been rich in all-rounders, of whom the following are outstanding examples.

GEORGE AUBREY FAULKNER
(1881–1930) *Transvaal*

Aubrey Faulkner was one of the earliest and, in his time, greatest exponents of slow-medium googly bowling and an excellent bat. At Headingley in 1907 he took six English wickets for 17 in 11 overs, while against Australia at Melbourne in 1910–11 he scored 204. As a bowler he could turn the ball sharply either way and also deliver a quickish yorker; as a right-hand batsman he was not particularly attractive but assured and hard to dismiss. He began in domestic cricket as a bowler, then developed as a batsman and was for many years a dominant figure in South African cricket. One of Faulkner's greatest all-round achievements was to score 153 and take 6 for 64 in the match to help A.C. MacLaren's XI beat Warwick Armstrong's otherwise all-conquering Australians in 1921. He won the DSO as an army major in the 1914–18 war, opened London's first cricket academy after his retirement from the game and, sadly, died there by his own hand.

Test batting and fielding

T	I	NO	R	HS	Av.	100	50	Ct
25	47	4	1754	204	40.79	4	8	20

Test bowling

T	I	B	R	W	BBI	BBM	Av.
25	43	4227	2180	82	7–84	9–75	26.58

First-class batting and fielding

M	I	NO	R	HS	Av.	100	50	Ct
118	197	23	6366	204	36.58	13	32	94

First-class bowling

M	B	R	W	BBI	Av.
118	16,624	7826	449	7–26	17.42

MICHAEL JOHN PROCTER

(b.1946) *Rhodesia, Natal, Orange Free State, Western Province, Gloucestershire*

Mike Procter was another highly talented South African robbed of a Test career by politics. He is therefore now best remembered for his vital contributions to Gloucestershire over 13 seasons – and also for scoring six centuries in consecutive innings for Rhodesia in 1970. He was a right-arm fast bowler, whose chest-on delivery meant he appeared to bowl off the wrong foot but was nevertheless very quick, and a powerful, fast-scoring, right-hand middle-order batsman. Later in his career, after knee injuries, he purveyed cunning off-spin. All his Tests were played in two series against Australia, both of which South Africa won. Twice in county cricket he scored a century before lunch and in 1970 won the Gillette Cup for Gloucestershire (sometimes known as 'Proctershire' in recognition of his massive contribution) by scoring 94 and taking two wickets. Procter was a giant of the first-class game and there's little reason to doubt that he would have fared just as well over a lengthy Test career.

Test batting and fielding

T	I	NO	R	HS	Av.	100	50	Ct
108	156	39	3781	111	32.31	2	16	72

Test bowling

T	I	B	R	W	BBI	BBM	Av.
108	202	24,353	9733	421	7–87	10–147	23.11

First-class batting and fielding

M	I	NO	R	HS	Av.	100	50	Ct
186	267	55	7023	150*	33.12	6	35	132

First-class bowling

M	B	R	W	BBI	Av.
186	39,067	15,508	667	7–33	23.25

ODI batting and fielding

M	I	NO	R	HS	Av.	100	50	Ct
303	205	72	3519	130	26.45	1	14	108

ODI bowling

M	B	R	W	BB	Av.
303	15,712	9631	393	6–35	24.50

Test batting and fielding

T	I	NO	R	HS	Av.	100	50	Ct
7	10	1	226	48	25.11	0	0	4

Test bowling

T	I	B	R	W	BBI	BBM	Av.
7	14	1514	616	41	6–73	9–103	15.02

First-class batting and fielding

M	I	NO	R	HS	Av.	100	50	Ct
401	667	58	21,936	254	36.01	48	109	325

First-class bowling

M	B	R	W	BBI	Av.
401	65,404	27,679	1417	9–71	19.53

SHAUN MACLEAN POLLOCK

(b.1973) *Natal, Warwickshire*

What a glittering dynasty are the Pollocks – peerless left-hander Graeme, fast bowler Peter and all-rounder Shaun, son of Peter. Shaun, South Africa's record Test-wicket taker, batted and bowled right-handed. His batting average is respectable, his bowling average a lot better than that. He was fast-medium rather than quick, and comparable in his immaculate line and length to Richard Hadlee and Glenn McGrath. A lot of South Africa's success in the later 1990s was due to his new-ball partnership with Allan Donald. In later years he lost some of his pace but not his accuracy and ability to move the ball both ways. As Test captain in 2000 after the disgrace of Hansie Cronje, he was none too successful and soon lost the job to Graeme Smith. His critics say he should have done more with the bat but he was still a pretty damn useful player to send in at number seven or eight.

MARK VERDON BOUCHER
(b.1976) *Border*

In the modern tradition of wicketkeepers who must be able to bat, Mark Boucher has long been an integral part of the South African team, at one point playing 75 consecutive Tests. He was the first wicketkeeper to claim 400 Test victims, holds the record for the most dismissals by a wicketkeeper and at one point held the world record for the highest score by a nightwatchman in a Test – 125 against Zimbabwe in 1999–2000. Boucher is an attacking right-hand batsman who, in the 2007 World Cup, briefly held another record by hitting 50 off 21 deliveries against The Netherlands. As a wicketkeeper he is safe and efficient rather than showy. He has been a regular vice-captain of the Test team and has captained the side in four matches, including a win over Australia.

Test batting and fielding

T	I	NO	R	HS	Av.	100	50	Ct	St
124	175	21	4659	125	30.25	5	29	449	22

First-class batting and fielding

M	I	NO	R	HS	Av.	100	50	Ct	St
186	271	38	7715	134	33.11	9	46	627	36

ODI batting and fielding

M	I	NO	R	HS	Av.	100	50	Ct	St
275	203	52	4397	147*	29.11	1	26	381	19

JACQUES HENRY KALLIS
(b.1975) *Western Province and Middlesex*

Bowlers have to battle for Jacques Kallis's wicket every inch of the way. Fast scoring doesn't interest him, runs do – often selfishly, some say. So what? As a right-hand batsman he is one of the modern greats. Add to that effective fast-medium bowling that is quicker than it looks and excellent slip-fielding and he is, by a considerable distance, South Africa's finest ever all-rounder. Oddly enough, he doesn't much like bowling so it's probably with reluctance and despite himself that he has become the only man to score 9000 runs and take 200 wickets in both Tests and ODIs. His batting is not exciting to watch, just ruthlessly effective, beauty sacrificed to accumulation – five centuries in five Tests in 2003–4, five in four Tests in 2007. But he can attack when the mood is on him – in 2005 he scored 50 off 24 balls against Zimbabwe – it's just that the mood isn't on him very often.

Test batting and fielding

T	I	NO	R	HS	Av.	100	50	Ct
129	218	32	10,092	189*	54.25	30	51	141

Test bowling

T	I	B	R	W	BBI	BBM	Av.
129	215	16,860	7951	257	6–54	9–92	30.85

First-class batting and fielding

M	I	NO	R	HS	Av.	100	50	Ct
220	360	50	16,527	200	53.31	47	89	207

First-class bowling

M	B	R	W	BBI	Av.
220	25,655	11,933	393	6–54	30.36

ODI batting and fielding

M	I	NO	R	HS	Av.	100	50	Ct
287	273	51	10,057	139	45.30	16	71	105

ODI bowling

M	B	R	W	BB	Av.
287	9706	7805	246	5–30	31.72

FAR LEFT *Shaun Pollock is chaired off the field in Durban by Andre Nel (left) and captain Graeme Smith after playing his final Test for South Africa, 12 January 2008.*

CHAPTER 7
CRICKET IN THE WEST INDIES

THE DOMESTIC GAME IN THE CARIBBEAN, PLUS TEST AND FIRST-CLASS RECORDS OF THE WINDIES' ALL-TIME GREATS

The West Indies cricket team consists of multi-racial players from a group of English-speaking Caribbean countries, not all of whom always agree about who should be in the side. Inter-island rivalry is fierce, as evidenced in the competition for the first-class domestic trophy, the Carib Beer Cup as it is now called.

Colloquially, the West Indies are known as the Windies, although in the 1970s and 80s, when the team had some of the most ferocious fast bowlers the game has ever seen, the only windy people to be spotted were the opposing batsmen.

The first combined West Indies team came together in the mid-1880s and in 1886 toured Canada and the United States. In the 1890s representative sides were chosen to play against visiting English tourists. But it was not until 1926 that the West Indies Cricket Board joined the ICC and not until 1928 that the Windies played their first Test (against England).

FROM CONSTANTINE TO SOBERS

The first West Indies star was the all-rounder Learie Constantine. He was swiftly joined by another great, George Headley, who was called 'the black Bradman', although West Indians preferred to think of Bradman as 'the white Headley'. But for many years the side was dominated, and always captained, by white men such as John Goddard and Frank Stollmeyer. In 1950, however, non-whites – the spinners Sonny Ramadhin and Alf Valentine, along with the legendary 'three W's', Frank Worrell, Clyde Walcott and Everton Weekes – dominated when the West Indies trounced England. Soon after, as Worrell became the first regular black captain (and led his side in the first tied Test at Brisbane in 1960), Lance Gibbs became the first spinner to take 300 Test wickets and Gary Sobers proved himself the finest all-rounder the game has ever seen, white players failed to get a look in, for no other reason than that they weren't good enough. So when Brendan Nash was picked in 2008 he was the first white man to play for the Windies since Geoffrey Greenidge in 1973.

REIGN OF THE FAST MEN

For many years West Indies were known as 'the calypso cricketers' because they played the game dashingly, excitingly and with a smile. Indeed, a calypso was written in 1950 to celebrate the deeds of Ramadhin and Valentine. But under Worrell and from the 1960s onwards, with the advent of a long line of terrifyingly fast bowlers, their cricket became tougher. As their rivals' wickets and stricken batsmen tumbled, West Indies might still have been smiling and singing but nobody else was. Sheer survival became the most pressing problem against quicks like Wes Hall and Charlie Griffith (who fractured the skull of the Indian batsmen Nari Contractor and was twice no-balled for throwing

FAR LEFT West Indian fast bowler Fidel Edwards (centre) is enveloped by his team-mate Dwayne Bravo after taking the wicket of century-maker Phil Jaques (108) to end a first-wicket stand of 223 between Jacques and Simon Katich, third Test match vs Australia at Bridgetown, Barbados, 14 June 2008. Darren Sammy celebrates in the background.

hell? Andy Roberts, Michael
Holding, Colin Croft and
Joel Garner, the four fast
bowlers who spearheaded the
West Indies' pace attack in the
late 1970s and early 1980s,
photographed during the first
Test match against England
at the Queen's Park Oval,
Port-of-Spain, Trinidad,
18 February 1981. Geoff
Boycott, who batted against
them during the 1980–1 Test
series, commented that the
only way to prepare to face
Roberts, Holding and Co.
was to 'stand in the fast lane
of the M1 motorway and
dodge the traffic'.

during a controversial career), not to mention their successors in the 1970s, 80s and 90s – men like Andy Roberts, Michael Holding, Joel Garner, Malcolm Marshall, Curtly Ambrose and Courtney Walsh, usually hunting in packs.

And to accompany an apparently endless supply of outstanding fast bowlers there came a batch of excellent batsmen – Rohan Kanhai, Clive Lloyd, Alvin Kallicharran, Gordon Greenidge, Viv Richards, Desmond Haynes and Richie Richardson. In those decades of an intimidating four-man fast attack, supported by some of the finest batsmen in the game, the West Indies were the best team in the world. They faltered a little in the late 1960s and again against Australia in 1975–6 when Dennis Lillee and Jeff Thomson were at their best. But apart from that they twice (in 1984 and 1985–6) inflicted a five-nil 'blackwash' on England (see the Windies Wizards, pages 251–258) and so dominated Australia that between 1973 and 1995 the Aussies didn't win a single series in the Caribbean and only the 1975–6 one at home.

HOW ARE THE MIGHTY FALLEN

But in the late 1990s came the hard times. They had Brian Lara, of course, plus Shivnarine Chanderpaul, Courtney Walsh and Curtly Ambrose but precious little back-up. In 1998–9 they lost 5–0 in South Africa, and in 2000 they lost to England in England for the first time since 1969. Less than a year later – when Walsh and Ambrose had retired and the well of great fast bowlers had dried up – they were whitewashed by Steve Waugh's side in Australia.

Of late, the Windies have been a shadow of the team they once were. In part this was because the West Indies Cricket Board (WICB) was either slow to recognize, or because of the islands' declining economy unable to deal with, the fact that the game, internationally, had now become totally professional.

Then, too, thanks to the influence of television, football and basketball grew more popular and interest in cricket declined. In 2006 a Texas tycoon, Sir Allen Stanford (see pages 298–303), whipped up much enthusiasm with a tournament in Antigua offering a prize of $1 million to the winning team. But this was Twenty20 cricket and in some ways Stanford's enterprise was as ominous as it was encouraging. By 2008, Twenty20 was threatening to dominate the game everywhere.

From Shell Cup to Carib Cup

Meanwhile, the domestic competition – the like of which only became feasible with the introduction of cheap air travel – started out as the Shell Cup in 1965–6, since when it has changed its form and its title on several occasions. At different times it has been contested as a round-robin, a round-robin with a final and a round-robin with a semi-final and a final.

The Shell Cup became the Red Stripe Cup, then the President's Cup, the Busta Cup and now the Carib Beer Cup. Whatever it's called it has been won outright by Barbados 18 times, followed by Jamaica (7), Guyana (5), Trinidad & Tobago (4), Leeward Islands (3) and by Combined Islands once. Barbados, Leeward Islands, Guyana and Trinidad have also shared the title at various times.

As with the first-class competition, so with the one-day cup. From its inception in 1972–3, various sponsors have come and gone, so have non first-class teams like Canada, Bermuda and the USA (who beat Barbados in 2000–1). It began as the Banks Cup and is now the KFC Cup. The most successful sides are Guyana with nine wins and Trinidad and Tobago with eight.

In 2008 the West Indies languished in seventh place among the Test-playing nations. That year they had drawn two Tests in New Zealand but had been beaten at home for the first time by Sri Lanka. Their roster of outstanding players had dwindled to barely a handful, chief among them Chanderpaul, named player of the year by the ICC. Meanwhile, the previously munificent Stanford, now hotly pursued by the FBI and the American Securities and Exchange Commission for alleged financial transgressions, had other things on his mind than the well-being of West Indian cricket.

Early in 2009, however, matters improved when West Indies, captained by a newly mature and responsible Chris Gayle, defeated England one-nil in a Test series in the Caribbean to regain the Wisden Trophy for the first time since 2000 and record their first win in any Test series, anywhere, since 2004. It was too early, perhaps, to predict a return to the glory, glory days but the future was certainly looking brighter.

HOWZAT! I once asked David Gower whether he was ever afraid when facing a four-pronged 90 mph West Indian attack. 'Well, not afraid exactly,' he said, with typical Gower understatement, 'but you do become a little anxious.'

Considering the small population, the West Indies have produced a disproportionate number of great cricketers – these, for example, among…

THE BATSMEN

GEORGE ALPHONSO HEADLEY
(1909–83) *Jamaica*

George Headley, 'the Black Bradman', was and remains one of the greatest West Indian batsmen. In his first Test, against England in 1929–30, he scored 21 and 176, in his third 114 and 112 and in his fourth 223. Headley played only against England and Australia, never seemed to offer a hurried shot, never had a bad series and was the first man to score two centuries in a Test at Lord's, in the 1939 series. The Second World War effectively spelt the end for his Test career when he was in his prime, although he did play a few games afterwards and in 1947–8, against England, was the first black man to captain the West Indies. He was a right-hand batsman, light on his feet and particularly strong off the back foot, with reflexes so sharp that, according to Len Hutton, he could play the ball later than any other batsman. If you were listing the top 10 batsmen of all time, Headley would have to make the squad. His son Ron played twice for West Indies and his grandson, Dean, was a fast bowler for England.

Test batting and fielding

T	I	NO	R	HS	Av.	100	50	Ct
22	40	4	2190	270*	60.83	10	5	14

(An occasional leg-spinner, Headley took 0–230 in Tests)

First-class batting and fielding

M	I	NO	R	HS	Av.	100	50	Ct
103	164	22	9921	344*	69.86	33	44	76

First-class bowling

M	B	R	W	BBI	Av.
103	3845	1842	51	5–33	36.11

FRANK MORTIMER MAGLINNE WORRELL
(1924–67) *Barbados and Jamaica*

Frank Worrell began as a left-arm spinner for Barbados before developing into one of the West Indies' finest batsmen. Even more importantly he was his country's first full-time, black captain, who welded the Windies into the most powerful team in the world. He was a great right-hand batsman, lithe and elegant, a more-than-useful fast-medium or slow left-arm bowler and an inspiring skipper. Such was his stature that when he died of leukaemia three years after being knighted for his services to cricket, he was honoured with a memorial service in Westminster Abbey. Perhaps his greatest achievement was to shatter forever the racist myth that a black man could not captain a cricket side.

BELOW *Frank Worrell (left) and Everton Weekes, who steered the West Indies to their first series win in England in 1950. All of the famous 'three W's' (the other being Clyde Walcott) hailed from Bridgetown, Barbados.*

Test batting and fielding

T	I	NO	R	HS	Av.	100	50	Ct
51	87	9	3860	261	49.48	9	22	43

Test bowling

T	I	B	R	W	BBI	BBM	Av.
51	82	7141	2672	69	7–70	7–70	38.72

First-class batting and fielding

M	I	NO	R	HS	Av.	100	50	Ct
208	326	49	15,025	308*	54.24	39	80	139

First-class bowling

M	B	R	W	BBI	Av.
208	26,740	10,115	349	7–70	28.98

EVERTON DE COURCEY WEEKES
(b.1925) *Barbados*

Immortalized as one of 'the three W's' and statistically the best of them, Everton Weekes was a stocky, swift-footed and attacking right-hand batsman. He made his Test debut against England in 1948 and in 1948–9 against England and India scored centuries in five consecutive innings during a run that consisted of seven consecutive scores of 50 or more and brought him 1000 Test runs in only 12 innings, one fewer than Bradman. In 1956 he made three consecutive hundreds against New Zealand. He was the first West Indian to score 3000, then 4000 Test runs. A persistent thigh injury obliged him to retire from Test cricket when he was 33. In 1995 he was the last of the 'three W's' to be awarded a knighthood.

Test batting and fielding

T	I	NO	R	HS	Av.	100	50	Ct
48	81	5	4455	207	58.61	15	19	49

(Weekes, who bowled leg-spin, took 1–77 in Tests)

First-class batting and fielding

M	I	NO	R	HS	Av.	100	50	Ct
152	241	24	12,010	304*	55.34	36	54	124

(In 1951-2 in New Zealand Weekes, as stand-in wicketkeeper, made one stumping against Wellington)

First-class bowling

M	B	R	W	BBI	Av.
152	1125	731	17	4–38	43.00

CLIVE HUBERT LLOYD
(b.1944) *Guyana and Lancashire*

Even more than Worrell, Clive 'The Big Cat' Lloyd was responsible for the dominance of West Indies cricket. Standing 6' 5", shambling, moustachioed and bespectacled, he was a left-hand middle-order batsman of immense power and a panther-like fielder in the covers with arms so long he looked as if he could play marbles standing up. He was also a useful right-arm medium-pace bowler. A great cricketer anyway and the captain who decreed, after leading his team to a 5–1 drubbing by Australia in 1975–6, that henceforth his attack should consist entirely of lethally fast bowlers. As a result his record as captain included a run of 26 games without defeat and 11 successive victories, not to mention the five-nil 'blackwash' of England in 1984. A cousin of Lance Gibbs, he twice led West Indies to victory in the World Cup (see page 297) and was also captain of Lancashire.

Test batting and fielding

T	I	NO	R	HS	Av.	100	50	Ct
110	175	14	7515	242*	46.67	19	39	90

(Lloyd also took 10 Test wickets for 622 runs)

First-class batting and fielding

M	I	NO	R	HS	Av.	100	50	Ct
490	730	96	31,232	242*	49.26	79	172	377

First-class bowling

M	B	R	W	BBI	Av.
490	9551	4104	114	4–48	36.00

ODI batting and fielding

M	I	NO	R	HS	Av.	100	50	Ct
87	69	19	1977	102	39.54	1	11	39

(In ODIs Lloyd took 8 wickets for 210, average 26.25)

CUTHBERT GORDON GREENIDGE
(b.1951) *Barbados and Hampshire*

Wisely favouring his middle name (who wants to be called Cuthbert?) Greenidge became a great, attacking opening batsman, particularly prolific square of the wicket with mighty cuts, pulls and hook shots (see page 253). Along with Desmond Haynes he shared in 16 century stands for the first wicket in Tests and during the 'blackwash' summer of 1984 hit two double-centuries against England, his brutally destructive match-winning 214 not out at Lord's being considered one of the great innings. Nor was he any less prolific for Hampshire, where he and Barry Richards made as good an opening pair as there has ever been. From an English point of view the sad fact is that he began his first-class career with Hampshire and could have qualified for England. Damn!

Test batting and fielding

T	I	NO	R	HS	Av.	100	50	Ct
108	185	16	7558	226	44.72	19	34	96

(Greenidge, right-arm medium, returned figures of 0–4 in Tests)

First-class batting and fielding

M	I	NO	R	HS	Av.	100	50	Ct
523	889	75	37,354	273*	45.88	92	183	516

First-class bowling

M	B	R	W	BBI	Av.
523	955	479	18	5–49	26.61

ODI batting and fielding

M	I	NO	R	HS	Av.	100	50	Ct
128	127	13	5134	133*	45.03	11	31	45

(In ODIs he took 1–45 in 10 overs)

ISAAC VIVIAN ALEXANDER RICHARDS
(b.1952) *Leeward Islands and Somerset*

Viv Richards was the finest batsman of his day and one of the greatest ever. Massively confident, to the point of arrogance, he never deigned to wear a helmet, reckoning such things were for lesser players. And who could say he was wrong, for rarely can there have been a more devastating batsman. He would saunter to the wicket, unnerve the bowler with a glare of cold contempt and then send his best deliveries to all parts of the ground. Sometimes one wonders how he might have fared against his fast-bowling West Indian team-mates who terrified everyone else, but against that Imran Khan thought Richards the best-ever player of genuine pace. He helped West Indies win the first World Cup in 1975 and in 1976 scored 1710 Test runs at an average of 90. From 1980 to 1991 he captained his country 50 times and never lost a series. He batted right-handed, fielded very well, bowled off-

ABOVE *Viv Richards hooks a ball from his friend and Somerset team-mate Ian Botham during the fifth Test against England at the Oval, August 1984.*

spin, is one of only four non-English cricketers to score 100 first-class centuries and was named by the 2000 edition of *Wisden* as one of the Five Cricketers of the Century. Hard to argue with that. In 1999 he was knighted in his native Antigua.

Test batting and fielding

T	I	NO	R	HS	Av.	100	50	Ct
121	182	12	8540	291	50.23	24	45	122

Test bowling

T	I	B	R	W	BBI	BBM	Av.
121	103	5170	1964	32	2–17	3–51	61.37

First-class batting and fielding

M	I	NO	R	HS	Av.	100	50	Ct
507	796	63	36,212	322	49.40	114	162	464

First-class bowling

M	B	R	W	BBI	Av.
507	23,220	10,070	223	5–88	45.15

ODI batting and fielding

M	I	NO	R	HS	Av.	100	50	Ct
187	167	24	6721	189*	47.00	11	45	100

ODI bowling

M	B	R	W	BB	Av.
187	5644	4228	118	6–41	35.83

BRIAN CHARLES LARA
(b.1969) *Trinidad and Tobago and Warwickshire*

Prominent among the batting records Lara holds (and there are many) are these: the highest individual score in Tests and the highest innings in first-class cricket. A left-hander, he's unquestionably one of the greatest batsmen of all time, known to his West Indian fans as 'the Prince of Port-of-Spain.' In Tests he made seven double-centuries, one triple and one quadruple. His 375 against England in 1994 was a world record (until Matthew Hayden eclipsed it with 380 against Zimbabwe) and his 400 not out, also against England, in 2004 made him the only player ever to regain the record. In 1994 he made 501 not out for Warwickshire against Durham, 308 of them in boundaries. Not since Bradman has there been a batsman quite so greedy for runs. During his Test career he scored 20 per cent of all the West Indies' runs and in Sri Lanka in 2001–2 he made an astonishing 42 per cent of

BELOW *Brian Lara shows his delight at regaining his Test batting record, reaching 400 not out against England at the Recreation Ground, St John's, Antigua, 12 April 2004. In the three Tests he played against England at St John's, he averaged an astounding 432.*

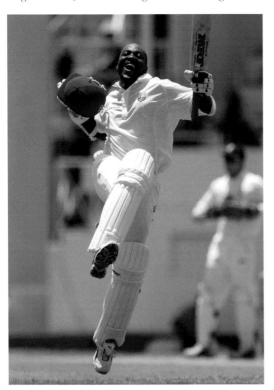

them. Lara was not, though, by any means a dour accumulator; with his high backlift and eagerness to attack he was always thrilling to watch. It was his misfortune to play in and frequently to captain, with only moderate success, a declining West Indian side, whose fate often depended hugely on his personal contributions with the bat. Brian Lara retired from international cricket in 2007, though he continued to play for Trinidad and Tobago and in the Indian Cricket League.

Test batting and fielding

T	I	NO	R	HS	Av.	100	50	Ct
130	230	6	11,912	400*	53.17	34	48	164

(As a leg-spinner he bowled 10 overs in Tests, taking 0–28)

First-class batting and fielding

M	I	NO	R	HS	Av.	100	50	Ct
261	440	13	22,156	501*	51.88	65	88	320

(He took 4 first-class wickets for 416, average 104.00)

ODI batting and fielding

M	I	NO	R	HS	Av.	100	50	Ct
299	289	32	10,405	169	40.48	19	63	120

(His bowling figures were 4–61, average 15.25)

SHIVNARINE CHANDERPAUL
(b.1974) *Guyana, Durham*

Shiv Chanderpaul has little or none of the elegance normally associated with left-handers, favouring a crabby, front-on style that means he scores many of his runs behind the wicket. But he's a bloody hard man to get out – ask any bowler. Four times in Test series he has batted for more than 1000 minutes (around 17 hours) without being dismissed. He scored 62 in his first Test against England in 1994 but it wasn't until his 19th (against India, 1996–7) that he made his first hundred. Since then he has rattled up some remarkable statistics, including averages of 148.66 against England in 2007 and 147.33 against Australia in 2008. Once he gets to the wicket he clings there like a limpet, witness his 104 in West Indies' world-record fourth-innings score of 418 to beat Australia in 2002–3. Yet when the fancy takes him he can score at breathtaking speed – his 100 off 69 balls (also against Australia in 2002–3) is the fourth fastest in Test history. His record as one of the Windies' rotating captains in recent years is not good (one win, three draws in 14 games) but at least he emulated Graham Dowling of New Zealand in hitting a double-century on his debut as skipper. His stance is not perhaps to be recommended to aspiring young batsmen but his bloody-minded determination and concentration certainly are.

Test batting and fielding

T	I	NO	R	HS	Av.	100	50	Ct
119	202	32	8502	203*	50.01	21	52	50

(He has taken 8 wickets for 845 runs with leg spin: best 1-2)

First-class batting and fielding

M	I	NO	R	HS	Av.	100	50	Ct
236	382	66	16,886	303*	53.43	46	86	137

First-class bowling

M	B	R	W	BBI	Av.
236	4634	2453	56	4-48	43.80

ODI batting and fielding

M	I	NO	R	HS	Av.	100	50	Ct
241	226	35	7858	150	41.14	9	53	68

(He has taken 14 wickets for 636: best 3-18)

THE BOWLERS

Against England in 1950 Sonny Ramadhin and Alf Valentine were West Indies' first two bowling heroes but, good as they were, I don't think they were in quite the same league as the following.

LANCELOT RICHARD GIBBS
(b.1934) *Guyana, South Australia and Warwickshire*

Lance Gibbs was the first spinner to take 300 Test wickets – at a remarkable economy rate of 1.98 an over. Certainly he is the West Indies' most successful spin bowler, a tall, slim, long-fingered purveyor of sharp, bouncy off-breaks and later a very good arm

ball. He was a lousy batsman but a fine gully fielder. His finest hours came in 1960–1 against Australia, when he took three wickets in four balls at Sydney and a hat-trick at Adelaide, and in 1961–2 when, at Bridgetown, he reduced India from 149 for 2 to 187 all out, taking the last eight wickets and returning an analysis of 53.3-37-38-8. Between 1967 and 1973 he played for Warwickshire and in 1971 took 131 wickets at 18.89. He was nearly 39 and a couple of years off retirement when he played the first of his few ODIs.

Test bowling

T	I	B	R	W	BBI	BBM	Av.
79	148	27,115	8989	309	8-38	11-157	29.09

Test batting and fielding

T	I	NO	R	HS	Av.	100	50	Ct
79	109	39	488	25	6.97	0	0	52

First-class bowling

M	B	R	W	BBI	Av.
330	78,430	27,878	1024	8-37	27.22

(Gibbs played 3 ODIs, scoring 0* in one innings and taking 2-59, average 29.50)

First-class batting and fielding

M	I	NO	R	HS	Av.	100	50	Ct
330	352	150	1729	43	8.55	0	0	203

WESLEY WINFIELD HALL
(b.1937) *Barbados, Trinidad and Queensland*

Wes Hall was a terrifying right-arm fast bowler (especially in partnership with Charlie Griffith), the forerunner of a long – and at times seemingly endless – line of venomous West Indian quicks from the 1960s onwards. He bowled in excess of 90 mph and at Lord's in 1963 broke Colin Cowdrey's arm. He began as a wicketkeeper-batsman but, after deciding that scaring the life out of other batsmen was more fun, swiftly established himself as the mainstay of the West Indies attack from 1958 to 1969. He remained a useful lower-order batsman and played a significant part in the first tied Test at Brisbane in 1960, hitting a 50 and

HOWZAT! In retirement Wes Hall became an ordained clergymen, advocating that 'every man should help his fellow man'. Battered batsmen might feel that he could have thought of that a bit earlier.

LEFT *The shape of things to come: Wes Hall, the first in a long line of devastating West Indian fast bowlers, in action in 1963.*

Buster Keaton and with a smooth run-up, culminating in an athletic leap, he could, thanks to an enormous pair of shoulders, deliver one of the most vicious bouncers in the game. From the mid-1970s to the early 80s, when the Windies carried all before them, he, Michael Holding, Joel Garner and Colin Croft went about the world happily shattering wickets, batsmen's morale and occasionally their bones. In 1975 and 1979 he was part of the West Indies teams that won the World Cup. He was a thoughtful bowler, often preceding that really nasty bouncer with a slower one to lull the batsman into a fatally false sense of security. No mug with the bat either.

Test bowling

T	I	B	R	W	BBI	BBM	Av.
47	90	11,135	5174	202	7–54	12–121	25.61

Test batting and fielding

T	I	NO	R	HS	Av.	100	50	Ct
47	62	11	762	68	14.94	0	3	9

First-class bowling

M	B	R	W	BBI	Av.
228	42,760	18,679	889	8–47	21.01

First-class batting and fielding

M	I	NO	R	HS	Av.	100	50	Ct
228	291	67	3516	89	15.69	0	10	52

ODI bowling

M	B	R	W	BB	Av.
56	3123	1771	87	5–22	20.35

ODI batting and fielding

M	I	NO	R	HS	Av.	100	50	Ct
56	32	9	231	37*	10.04	0	0	6

bowling the last over with only six runs needed for an Australian victory (see The Great Tied Test, pages 217–219). After retirement he became Minister of Tourism and Sport in the Barbados government.

Test bowling

T	I	B	R	W	BBI	BBM	Av.
48	92	10,421	5066	192	7–69	11–126	26.38

Test batting and fielding

T	I	NO	R	HS	Av.	100	50	Ct
48	66	14	818	50*	15.73	0	2	11

First-class bowling

M	B	R	W	BBI	Av.
170	28,095	14,273	546	7–51	26.14

First-class batting and fielding

M	I	NO	R	HS	Av.	100	50	Ct
170	215	38	2673	102*	15.10	1	6	58

ANDERSON MONTGOMERY EVERTON ROBERTS

(b.1951) *Leeward Islands, Hampshire, New South Wales and Leicestershire*

It took Andy Roberts – the first Antiguan to play for West Indies – only 19 Tests to reach 100 wickets. As deadpan as

JOEL GARNER

(b.1952) *Barbados, Somerset and South Australia*

At 6' 8", 'Big Bird' could generate natural bounce at an alarming speed, the ball – delivered from a great height – seeming to come at the batsman like a thunderbolt from heaven. He also had a very nasty, toe-crushing yorker. His bowling average in Tests is remarkable, in ODIs even better – the best, in fact, of anybody with more than 100 wickets. Against England in the 1979 World Cup final he took 5 wickets for 39. For Somerset he played alongside Viv Richards and Ian Botham: how they failed to win the County Championship with those three is hard to fathom.

Test bowling

T	I	B	R	W	BBI	BBM	Av.
58	111	13,169	5433	259	6–56	9–108	20.97

Test batting and fielding

T	I	NO	R	HS	Av.	100	50	Ct
58	68	14	672	60	12.44	0	1	42

First-class bowling

M	B	R	W	BBI	Av.
214	39,829	16,333	881	8–31	18.53

First-class batting and fielding

M	I	NO	R	HS	Av.	100	50	Ct
214	231	54	2964	104	16.74	1	8	129

ODI bowling

M	B	R	W	BB	Av.
98	5330	2752	146	5–31	18.84

ODI batting and fielding

M	I	NO	R	HS	Av.	100	50	Ct
98	41	15	239	37	9.19	0	0	30

MICHAEL ANTHONY HOLDING

(b.1954) *Jamaica, Lancashire, Derbyshire and Tasmania*

Tall and deceptively slim for a fast bowler, Mikey Holding, aka 'Whispering Death', was even quicker than Roberts. He may well have been the quickest ever. The England bowler Mike Selvey once likened him in his silent, rhythmical, head-swaying run-up to a cobra hypnotizing its prey. In the 1970s and 80s he was an integral part of the most awe-inspiring pace-battery in cricket history, the others including Roberts, Garner, Malcolm Marshall, Sylvester Clark and Colin Croft. On a dead pitch at the Oval in 1976, when no other bowler on either side could make much happen, he took 14 English wickets for 149, the best figures for a West Indian bowler. At Bridgetown in 1981 he bowled what is reckoned to be the greatest over in Test history – five balls, each of increasing pace offering serious threats to Geoff Boycott's health, followed by a sixth, which shattered the wicket. He was a tail-end batsman who made nearly a quarter of his Test runs in sixes and indeed hit more sixes (36) than any other player with fewer than 1000 runs.

BELOW *Always fiercely competitive, Michael Holding kicks over the stumps after his appeal for caught behind is turned down in a 1980 Test against New Zealand.*

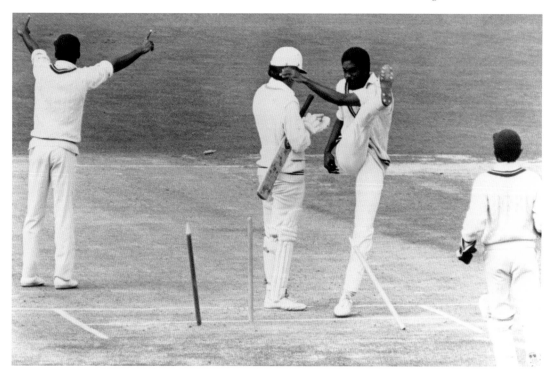

HOWZAT! It's widely believed that during an England–West Indies Test match, with Peter Willey batting and Michael Holding running in to bowl, Brian Johnston announced on BBC Radio's *Test Match Special*: 'The bowler's Holding, the batsman's Willey.' Johnners did say that but, as he told me himself, not actually when he was on air, so the phrase, though it's gone down in folklore, was not heard by *TMS* listeners.

Test bowling

T	I	B	R	W	BBI	BBM	Av.
60	113	12,680	5898	249	8–92	14–149	23.68

Test batting and fielding

T	I	NO	R	HS	Av.	100	50	Ct
60	76	10	916	73	13.78	0	6	22

First-class bowling

M	B	R	W	BBI	Av.
222	38,877	18,233	778	8–92	23.43

First-class batting and fielding

M	I	NO	R	HS	Av.	100	50	Ct
222	283	43	3600	80	15.00	0	14	125

ODI bowling

M	B	R	W	BB	Av.
102	5473	3034	142	5–26	21.36

ODI batting and fielding

M	I	NO	R	HS	Av.	100	50	Ct
102	42	11	282	64	9.09	0	2	30

MALCOLM MARSHALL
(1958–99) *Barbados and Hampshire*

Superlatives are thrown around haphazardly in cricket but those who say Marshall was the finest fast bowler of them all may have a point. He had (just) the best Test average of anyone who has taken 200 wickets or more. He was quite short for a fast bowler but remarkably quick, with a whippy action and a delivery that either skidded or threatened to decapitate the batsman. At Headingley in 1984 he broke his thumb while fielding, batted one-handed and then took 7 wickets for 53 in England's second innings (see page 254); in seven consecutive series from 1982 to 1986 he took at least 21 wickets and in 1988 in England he grabbed 35, including a career-best 7–22 at Old Trafford. After his untimely death from colon cancer the Malcolm Marshall Trophy was introduced as a prize for the leading wicket-taker in every England–West Indies series.

Test bowling

T	I	B	R	W	BBI	BBM	Av.
81	151	17,584	7876	376	7–22	11–89	20.94

Test batting and fielding

T	I	NO	R	HS	Av.	100	50	Ct
81	107	11	1810	92	18.85	0	10	25

First-class bowling

M	B	R	W	BBI	Av.
408	74,645	31,548	1651	8–71	19.10

First-class batting and fielding

M	I	NO	R	HS	Av.	100	50	Ct
408	516	73	11,004	120*	24.83	7	54	145

ODI bowling

M	B	R	W	BB	Av.
136	7175	4233	157	4–18	26.96

ODI batting and fielding

M	I	NO	R	HS	Av.	100	50	Ct
136	83	19	955	66	14.92	0	2	15

COURTNEY ANDREW WALSH
(b.1962) *Jamaica and Gloucestershire*

For some time Walsh played second fiddle to Malcolm Marshall or Curtly Ambrose, though later he and Ambrose formed one of the great opening partnerships, taking 421 wickets between them in 49 Tests. Eventually Walsh ended up with more Test wickets than either of the others and, for a while, more than anyone else in the world. He was not one of the quickest of the Windies' bowlers but he was still impressively fast, had great stamina and guile and, standing 6' 6", could extract considerable bounce. He bowled more overs in Tests (5003.1) than any other

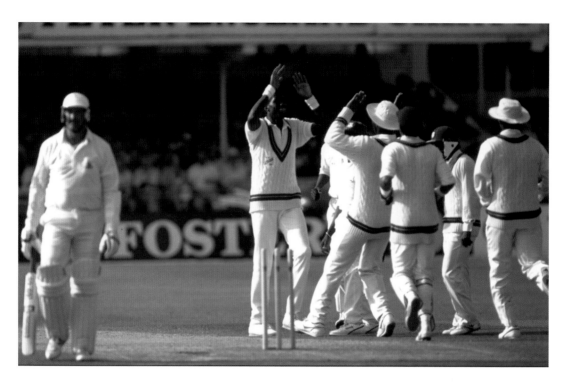

fast bowler and, in first-class matches – many of them for Gloucestershire – had five wickets in an innings more than 100 times and 10 in a match 20 times. In ODIs his best performance was 5 for 1 against Sri Lanka in 1986. A pretty hopeless batsman, he holds the records for most Test ducks (43) and most not outs.

Test bowling

T	I	B	R	W	BBI	BBM	Av.
132	242	30,019	12,688	519	7–37	13–55	24.44

Test batting and fielding

T	I	NO	R	HS	Av.	100	50	Ct
132	185	61	936	30*	7.54	0	0	29

First-class bowling

M	B	R	W	BBI	Av.
429	85,443	39,233	1807	9–72	21.71

First-class batting and fielding

M	I	NO	R	HS	Av.	100	50	Ct
429	558	158	4530	66	11.32	0	8	117

ODI bowling

M	B	R	W	BB	Av.
205	10,822	6918	227	5–1	30.47

ODI batting and fielding

M	I	NO	R	HS	Av.	100	50	Ct
205	79	33	321	30	6.97	0	0	27

CURTLY ELCONN LYNWALL AMBROSE
(b.1963) *Leeward Islands and Northamptonshire*

Another elongated (6' 7") fast merchant, the notoriously taciturn Ambrose had the best economy rate (2.31 runs per over) of any bowler who has taken 400 Test wickets. Along with his longtime opening partner Walsh, he was the last – so far, anyway – of the truly great West Indian quick bowlers. Being bounced at both ends by those two can't have been much fun for any batsman. Among his many remarkable achievements Ambrose took 8 for 45 against England in 1990, had a spell of 7 for 1 against Australia in 1992–3 and in 1993–4 took 6 for 24 in Trinidad when England were blasted away for 46. Like McGrath he seized upon Mike Atherton as his particular bunny, dismissing him 17 times in Tests. His control of line and length was immaculate and when the extreme pace of his youth began to fade he bowled subtle swing and seam.

HOWZAT! An English journalist was once asking Viv Richards about Curtly Ambrose's fitness. Curtly, who happened to be passing by, said: 'You want to know about Curtly, ask Curtly.' 'Okay, Curtly,' said the journalist, 'how are you?' 'Curtly talk to no man,' said Curtly and moved on.

Test bowling							
T	I	B	R	W	BBI	BBM	Av.
98	179	22,103	8501	405	8–45	11–84	20.99

Test batting and fielding								
T	I	NO	R	HS	Av.	100	50	Ct
98	145	29	1439	53	12.40	0	1	18

First-class bowling					
M	B	R	W	BBI	Av.
239	48,798	19,048	941	8–45	20.24

First-class batting and fielding								
M	I	NO	R	HS	Av.	100	50	Ct
239	317	70	3448	78	13.95	0	4	88

ODI bowling					
M	B	R	W	BB	Av.
176	9353	5429	225	5–17	24.12

ODI batting and fielding								
M	I	NO	R	HS	Av.	100	50	Ct
176	96	36	639	31*	10.65	0	0	45

THE ALL-ROUNDERS

LEARIE NICHOLAS CONSTANTINE
(1901–71) *Trinidad and Barbados*

His Test record was inconsistent and not all that impressive but, by the general consent of his contemporaries, Learie Constantine was a great all-rounder, a lightning-fast bowler, a dashing, attacking batsman and a superlative fielder. In 1928 he destroyed Middlesex, who seemed to be sauntering to a win, by taking 7 for 57 in their second innings, then scoring 103 out of 133 in an hour. More importantly, in 1930 he took 4 for 35 and 5 for 87 to help West Indies beat England at Georgetown, and at Port-of-Spain in 1934–5 he levelled the series against England virtually by himself, scoring 90 and 31 and taking

ABOVE *Learie Constantine (left) and his team-mate Wilton St Hill, pictured on tour in England in 1928.*

2 for 41 and 3 for 11 to finish the match with one ball remaining. Between them he and George Headley did more than anyone else to put West Indies cricket on the map. Connie, as he was known, played little first-class cricket but a great deal in the Lancashire leagues, especially for Nelson. After retirement in 1945 he became Trinidad and Tobago's High Commissioner in London, a governor of the BBC and a member of the Race Relations Board and the Sports Council. He was first knighted, then ennobled, ending his days as Baron Constantine of Maraval and Nelson.

Test batting and fielding								
T	I	NO	R	HS	Av.	100	50	Ct
18	33	0	635	90	19.24	0	4	28

Test bowling							
T	I	B	R	W	BBI	BBM	Av.
18	29	3583	1746	58	5–75	9–122	30.10

First-class batting and fielding								
M	I	NO	R	HS	Av.	100	50	Ct
119	197	11	4475	133	24.05	5	28	133

First-class bowling					
M	B	R	W	BBI	Av.
119	17,393	8991	439	8–38	20.48

CLYDE LEOPOLD WALCOTT
(1926–2006) *Barbados and British Guiana*

One of the immortal 'three W's', Walcott was an outstanding right-hand batsman and, despite being unusually tall for the job (6' 2"), a very good wicket-keeper until back problems forced him to give it up. He played for West Indies from 1948 to 1960 and in 1955, against Australia, twice scored two hundreds in a Test and became the first player to make five centuries in a series, while notching up a total of 837 runs at 83.70. Against England in 1953–4 he scored 698 at 87.25. His highest first-class score of 314 not out was made when he was 20 and sharing an unbroken and (then) world-record partnership of 574 with Frank Worrell in an inter-islands match in the West Indies. He hit the ball with thunderous power and when he had to stop wicketkeeping turned, quite effectively, to fast-medium bowling. After he retired he became chairman of the West Indies Cricket Board and in 1997 chairman of the ICC. Like the two other W's he was knighted – Sir Clyde Walcott, Knight of St Andrew in the Order of Barbados.

Test batting and fielding

T	I	NO	R	HS	Av.	100	50	Ct	St
44	74	7	3798	220	56.68	15	14	53	11

Test bowling

T	I	B	R	W	BBI	BBM	Av.
44	22	1194	408	11	3–50	3–50	37.09

First-class batting and fielding

M	I	NO	R	HS	Av.	100	50	Ct	St
146	238	29	11,820	314*	56.55	40	54	174	33

First-class bowling

M	B	R	W	BBI	Av.
146	3449	1269	35	5–41	36.25

FAR RIGHT *Determination is etched on the faces of the swashbuckling West Indian duo of Gary Sobers (right) and Rohan Kanhai (79 Tests and 6227 runs at 47.53) as they come out to bat in 1965. Both men enjoyed illustrious careers in English county cricket as well as at Test level, Kanhai playing for Warwickshire and Sobers for Nottinghamshire.*

GARFIELD ST AUBRUN SOBERS
(b.1936) *Barbados, South Australia and Nottinghamshire*

Right then, what do you say about Gary Sobers? First, he was a genius and a prodigy (he made his Test debut at 17); he was one of *Wisden*'s Five Cricketers of the Century and without any doubt at all he was the greatest all-rounder ever. List the finest left-handed batsmen and Sobers has to be right up near the top. As for bowling, well, there he wasn't quite so great – just bloody damn good, whether opening at a brisk fast-medium, switching to orthodox slow left-arm, or sending down chinamen. And when he wasn't doing any of those things he was one of the best fielders you could hope to see, in particular a superb close-to-the-wicket catcher. On the field there was never a moment when he wasn't involved. If you'd stuck a broom up his backside he would probably have swept the pitch as he went along. Against Pakistan in 1958 he broke Len Hutton's Test record when he scored 365 not out, his maiden Test century. Ten years later, for Notts against Glamorgan and, specifically, Malcolm Nash, he became the first player to hit six sixes in an over. In 1971 his innings of 254 for the Rest of the World against Australia had Don Bradman in raptures. As a captain, however, he was both adventurous and reckless. In Port-of-Spain in 1967–8 his wildly generous declaration enabled England to win the decisive Test. But he was an elegant, powerful batsman, a joy to watch, and a bowler of infinite variety. As with Bradman I doubt if we'll see his like again. In 1975 he was knighted for services to cricket.

Test batting and fielding

T	I	NO	R	HS	Av.	100	50	Ct
93	160	21	8032	365*	57.78	26	30	109

Test bowling

T	I	B	R	W	BBI	BBM	Av.
93	159	21,599	7999	235	6–73	8–80	34.03

First-class batting and fielding

M	I	NO	R	HS	Av.	100	50	Ct
383	609	93	28,314	365*	54.87	86	121	407

First-class bowling

M	B	R	W	BBI	Av.
383	70,789	28,941	1043	9–49	27.74

(He played only one ODI, making a duck and taking 1–31)

When he walked out to bat ... he moved with long strides which, even when he was hurrying, had an air of laziness.
● John Arlott describes Garfield Sobers

WEST INDIES' TEST RECORDS

Tests – played 455; won 152, lost 146, drawn 156, tied 1.
ODIs – played 603; won 326, lost 251, tied 5, no result 21.

The West Indies' highest Test total is 790–3d against Pakistan at Kingston in 1958; their lowest 47 versus England at Kingston in 2004.

Most Test appearances

	T
C.A. Walsh	132
B.C. Lara	130
I.V.A. Richards	121
S. Chanderpaul	119
D.L. Haynes	116

Highest individual Test scores

	R	Opposition	Ground	Match date
B.C. Lara	400*	England	St John's	10 Apr. 2004
B.C. Lara	375	England	St John's	16 Apr. 1994
G.S. Sobers	365*	Pakistan	Kingston	26 Feb. 1958
C.H. Gayle	317	South Africa	St John's	29 Apr. 2005
L.G. Rowe	302	England	Bridgetown	6 Mar. 1974

Highest Test batting averages
(qualification: 15 Tests or more)

	T	Av.
G.A. Headley	22	60.83
E.D. Weekes	48	58.61
G.S. Sobers	93	57.78
C.L. Walcott	44	56.68
C.A. Davis	15	54.20

Most Test centuries

	T	100
B.C. Lara	130	34
G.S. Sobers	93	26
I.V.A. Richards	121	24
S. Chanderpaul	119	21
C.G. Greenidge	108	19

Most Test ducks

	T	I	NO	0s
C.A. Walsh	132	185	61	43
C.E.L. Ambrose	98	145	29	26
M. Dillon	38	68	3	26
F.H. Edwards	41	65	20	18
J. Garner	58	68	14	17
B.C. Lara	130	230	6	17

Brian Lara – holder of the records for the highest individual innings in both Test and first-class cricket – executes a characteristically expansive drive on his way to a century against India in St Lucia, June 2006.

Highest individual run-scorers in Tests

	Span	T	I	NO	R	HS	Av.
B.C. Lara	1990–2006	130	230	6	11912	400*	53.17
I.V.A. Richards	1974–91	121	182	12	8540	291	50.23
S. Chanderpaul	1994–2009	119	202	32	8502	203*	50.01
G.S. Sobers	1954–74	93	160	21	8032	365*	57.78
C.G. Greenidge	1974–91	108	185	16	7558	226	44.72

Note: The most runs in a series (829 at 118.42) were scored by Viv Richards vs England in 1976. Both Clyde Walcott (827 at 82.70 vs Australia, 1954–5) and Gary Sobers (824 at 137.33 vs Pakistan, 1957–8) have also made more than 800 runs in a series.

Highest Test partnerships

	R	W	Opp.	Ground	Match date
C.C. Hunte, G.S. Sobers	446	2	Pakistan	Kingston	26 Feb. 1958
G.S. Sobers, F.M.M. Worrell	399	4	England	Bridgetown	6 Jan. 1960
D.S. Atkinson, C.C. Depeiza	347	7	Australia	Bridgetown	14 May 1955
E.D. Weekes, F.M.M. Worrell	338	3	England	Port-of-Spain	17 Mar. 1954
C.H. Gayle, R.R. Sarwan	331	2	South Africa	St John's	29 Apr. 2005

Highest Test wicket-takers

	Span	T	B	R	W	BBI	Av.
C.A. Walsh	1984–2001	132	30,019	12,688	519	7–37	24.44
C.E.L. Ambrose	1988–2000	98	22,103	8501	405	8–45	20.99
M.D. Marshall	1978–91	81	17,584	7876	376	7–22	20.94
L.R. Gibbs	1958–76	79	27,115	8989	309	8–38	29.09
J. Garner	1977–87	58	13,169	5433	259	6–56	20.97

Note: The best bowling figures in an innings were returned by the off-spinner Jack Noreiga with 9–95 vs India, Port-of-Spain, 1971, and in a match by Michael Holding, who took 14–149 vs England, the Oval, 1976.

Most dismissals by a wicketkeeper in a Test career

	T	W	Ct	St
P.J.L. Dujon	81	270	265	5

Note: R. D. Jacobs took seven catches in an innings vs Australia in 2000. Courtney Browne held nine catches in a match vs England, 1995, and David Murray held nine in a match, against Australia, 1981.

Most catches by a fielder in a Test career

	T	Ct
B.C. Lara	130	164

Note: Brian Lara has twice held 13 catches in a series (vs India 2006 and England 1997–8).

Leading all-rounders (1000 runs [at an average of 20 or more] and 100 wickets)

	T	R	Bat. Av.	W	Bowl. Av.	Tests for 1000/100
C.L. Hooper	102	5762	36.46	114	49.42	90
G.S. Sobers	93	8032	57.78	235	34.03	48

CHAPTER 8
CRICKET IN NEW ZEALAND

THE DOMESTIC GAME IN THE LAND OF THE
LONG WHITE CLOUD, PLUS PROFILES AND
TEST AND FIRST-CLASS RECORDS OF
KIWI ALL-TIME GREATS

New Zealand played their first Test, against England, at home in 1929–30 and – what do you know? – it only took them 25 years to register their first victory, also at home, against West Indies in 1955–6.

Well, New Zealand has a small population (more sheep than people, some say) and, although having a limited number of bodies to choose from doesn't seem to have hindered them much at rugby, it hasn't helped them get a consistently decent Test team together, as their record of having won only about 19 per cent of their matches indicates. The country has around 100,000 cricketers registered by various clubs, only a fifth of the number available to either England or Australia. Even so, it's a hefty enough squad, you might think, from which to find 11 blokes who can play a bit, but general opinion suggests that the standard of club cricket – from which the first-class sides are chosen – is not particularly high.

Nevertheless, New Zealand tend to do rather well in ODIs, having reached the semi-final of the World Cup five times. And despite its shortcomings the domestic first-class competition, originally called the Plunket Shield but now known as the State Championship, has thrown up some excellent players. It was introduced in 1906 but became really serious in 1920–1, since when it has been won 21 times by Auckland, closely pursued by Wellington with 20 victories. Behind them come Canterbury (14), Otago/Southland (13), Central Districts (8) and Northern Districts (6).

In the State Shield, the one-day competition, the positions are somewhat altered. The Canterbury Wizards have won this 13 times and are trailed by Auckland Aces (8), Wellington Firebirds (6), Northern District Knights (5), Central District Stags (3) and Otago Volts (2).

A FAMILY AFFAIR

Perhaps because of the relatively small population, New Zealand cricket has always had strong family connections, the most notable being the Hadlees – father Walter captained the side in the 1930s and 40s, when the star players were the batsmen C.S. Dempster and Martin Donnelly, and was followed by his fast-bowling sons Dayle and Richard (the country's greatest player to date), who performed nobly in the 1970s and 80s. The opening bat Glenn Turner was also one of New Zealand's best assets in the 1970s.

During the 1980s and early 90s the batting brothers Crowe, Jeff and Martin (another outstanding player) also gave considerable service and both captained the Test side. (Their cousin Russell, however, didn't take to cricket and became a Hollywood movie star instead.) Since the 1970s there have also been the Cairnses, Lance and son Chris, the brothers Bracewell, Brendon and John, the Howarths,

Hedley and Geoff, Rodney Redmond and his son Aaron and the identical twins Hamish and James Marshall.

A TEAM IN TRANSITION

In 2007–8 New Zealand Test cricket was much damaged by retirements – those of Chris Cairns, Nathan Astle, Scott Styris and the former captain Stephen Fleming in particular – and the lucrative temptations of India's Twenty20 leagues. The fast bowler Shane Bond, who succumbed to the lure of the rupee in the ICL, was banned from playing for his country again – a carelessly self-inflicted wound, surely, by the Test selectors. His consequent absence from the New Zealand touring team in England in 2008 weakened the side considerably. Daniel Vettori replaced Fleming as captain but while the side continued to thrive in ODIs in 2008 (apart from losing a game to Bangladesh, which is not easy to do) the Test team remained fragile, being beaten home and away by England and also by Australia. Consequently they ended the year only one spot above Bangladesh in the ICC Test rankings.

However, 10 victories in 15 games put them in fifth place, one above England, in the ODI listing and indeed their achievements included a 3–1 series win in England. There was, though, nearly an international incident in the Oval game when the England bowler Ryan Sidebottom barged into Grant Elliott, causing him to be run out. Most people except the England captain Paul Collingwood thought that he (Collingwood) should have called Elliott back to the wicket. He didn't, causing much bitterness between the two teams until Collingwood apologized and resigned the captaincy. Vettori was easily his country's outstanding player, both in Tests and ODIs, and the likes of Jesse Ryder, Tim Southee and the improving Ross Taylor showed promise for the future, but New Zealand remain very much a team in development.

BELOW The University Oval at Dunedin on New Zealand's South Island. In 2007–8 it hosted its first Test match, becoming the country's seventh test venue. But its sylvan setting tells its own story: in December 2008, a washed-out match here against India bought severe criticism of the ground for its siting and lack of facilities. It's worth remembering that it's not just in England that rain stops play…

THE BATSMEN

CHARLES STEWART DEMPSTER
(1903–74) *Wellington and Leicestershire*

'Stewie' Dempster, a short, chunky right-hander, was the first outstanding batsman New Zealand produced. Uncoached, self-taught, he scored New Zealand's first Test century (136) in his country's inaugural series against England in 1929–30. In 1931 he scored another Test hundred at Lord's, then captained the New Zealand team against South Africa in 1931–2 and against England in 1932–3. A neat and tidy player, he was among the half-dozen best batsmen of his time, as his Test record indicates. True, he only played in 10 Tests but no other New Zealander comes close to equalling his average. For business reasons he gave up Test cricket after the 1932–3 season, although he played for Leicestershire from 1935 to 1939 and captained the side for three years. He bowled hardly at all but kept wicket occasionally.

Test batting and fielding

T	I	NO	R	HS	Av.	100	50	Ct
10	15	4	723	136	65.72	2	5	2

First-class batting and fielding

M	I	NO	R	HS	Av.	100	50	Ct	St
184	306	36	12,145	212	44.98	35	55	94	2

(His bowling figures in Tests were 0–10 and in first-class matches 8–300, average 37.50, best 2–4)

MARTIN DONNELLY
(1917–99) *Wellington, Canterbury, Oxford University and Warwickshire*

Largely because of the Second World War, partly for business reasons, Donnelly only played seven Tests and not a whole lot of first-class cricket. Which is a shame, because he was a superb left-hand bat – according to C.B. Fry one of the best he had ever seen – a graceful attacking player with excellent footwork. He was one of the few people to have scored centuries at Lord's for Oxford, the Gentlemen

and his country. After only one first-class match, he toured England with moderate success in three Tests in 1937, aged 19. After the war he was hugely successful for Oxford University and was described as the world's best left-hander, which on New Zealand's 1949 tour of England he may well have been, scoring a magnificent 206 at Lord's. But that was about it. In 1950 he played the last four of his 20 games for Warwickshire and retired.

Test batting and fielding

T	I	NO	R	HS	Av.	100	50	Ct
7	12	1	582	206	52.90	1	4	7

(An occasional left-arm spinner, he took 0–20 in Tests)

First-class batting and fielding

M	I	NO	R	HS	Av.	100	50	Ct
131	221	26	9250	208*	47.43	23	46	76

First-class bowling

M	B	R	W	BBI	Av.
131	3484	1683	43	4–32	39.13

BERT SUTCLIFFE
(1923–2001) *Auckland, Otago and Northern Districts*

Although Sutcliffe was rated alongside Donnelly and Neil Harvey as one of the best left-handers of the post-war era, he never once played on a winning side for New Zealand. That fact alone indicates the burden and responsibility he had to bear as his country's one truly class batsman, once Donnelly had

Test batting and fielding

T	I	NO	R	HS	Av.	100	50	Ct
42	76	8	2727	230*	40.10	5	15	20

(A slow left-armer, he took 4–344 in Tests, at an average of 86.00)

First-class batting and fielding

M	I	NO	R	HS	Av.	100	50	Ct
233	407	39	17,447	385	47.41	44	83	160

(As an occasional wicketkeeper he made one stumping)

First-class bowling

M	B	R	W	BBI	Av.
233	5978	3273	86	5–19	38.05

LEFT *Bert Sutcliffe hits out at the Oval in 1949. Sutcliffe was in his pomp in the four-match Test series, scoring 423 runs at an average of 60.42, including four 50s and a century.*

GLENN MAITLAND TURNER
(b.1947) *Otago and Worcestershire*

A right-hand opening bat, Glenn Turner was a prolific scorer and a hard man to dismiss. He made two hundreds in a match against Australia in 1974, twice carried his bat through a Test innings, scored 1000 runs before the end of May in 1973 and, during a long career at Worcestershire, became the second overseas player (after Bradman) to make 100 centuries. In 1971–2 he hit two double-centuries against the West Indies. His temperament, as a man who played immaculately straight and with an eye to accumulation, was ideally suited to Test cricket, of which he would have played more had he not fallen out for a few years with New Zealand's administrators. Just such a falling-out led to his resignation as captain of the side after 10 matches.

Test batting and fielding

T	I	NO	R	HS	Av.	100	50	Ct
41	73	6	2991	259	44.64	7	14	42

(An off-spinner, he took 0–5 in Tests)

First-class batting and fielding

M	I	NO	R	HS	Av.	100	50	Ct
455	792	101	34,346	311*	49.70	103	148	409

(His bowling record was 5–189, average 37.80)

ODI batting and fielding

M	I	NO	R	HS	Av.	100	50	Ct
41	40	6	1598	171*	47.00	3	9	13

(His ODI bowling figures were 0–0 in one over)

MARTIN DAVID CROWE
(b.1962) *Auckland, Central Districts and Somerset*

Martin Crowe is probably the best right-hand batsman New Zealand has produced. He also captained the side (as his elder brother Jeff had done before him) with some success, especially in ODIs, in the early 1990s. A player of classic technique, he made his Test debut at 19 and was promptly dubbed 'the

departed. He was a player of classic style and great courage. In 1953–4 in South Africa he was hit on the head by a Neil Adcock bouncer, returned heavily bandaged and scored 80 not out in a total of 187. He captained his country four times, retired from Tests when he was 36 but returned in 1965 to make his final Test hundred, 151 not out, against India at Eden Park when he was 41.

HOWZAT! Rodney Redmond made his debut for New Zealand versus Pakistan in 1972–3, scoring 107 and 56. It was his only Test because he could never get used to contact lenses. Why didn't he stick to glasses? His son Aaron made his debut against England in 2008 and scored a duck.

best young batsman in the world', always a hard label to live up to. It was particularly difficult for him on account of a series of injuries, including a broken shin and serious knee problems, but for which his Test record would doubtless have been even better. As it is, his 299 against Sri Lanka in 1991 is the highest score by a New Zealand batsman. The hallmark of his batting, as with all the very best players, was that he seemed to have more time than most people to play his shots – and, at his peak, he could play every shot in the book. He was also a good fielder and a handy right-arm medium bowler, who captained Somerset after the departure of Botham, Richards and Garner in the late 1980s.

Test batting and fielding

T	I	NO	R	HS	Av.	100	50	Ct
77	131	11	5444	299	45.36	17	18	71

Test bowling

T	I	B	R	W	BBI	BBM	Av.
77	35	1377	676	14	2-25	3-107	48.28

First-class batting and fielding

M	I	NO	R	HS	Av.	100	50	Ct
247	412	62	19,608	299	56.02	71	80	226

First-class bowling

M	B	R	W	BBI	Av.
247	79,121	4010	119	5-18	33.69

ODI batting and fielding

M	I	NO	R	HS	Av.	100	50	Ct
143	140	18	4704	107*	38.55	4	34	66

ODI bowling

M	B	R	W	BB	Av.
143	1296	954	29	2-9	32.89

STEPHEN PAUL FLEMING
(b.1973) *Canterbury, Middlesex and Nottinghamshire*

At 23 years and 321 days Fleming was New Zealand's youngest Test captain and went on to become its longest-reigning (80 matches). He was also one of the finest captains in the game as well as a much better batsman than his figures indicate. A graceful left-hander who batted in the upper middle order, he is widely perceived as an under-achiever. For example, although he scored three double-centuries and was the first New Zealander to reach 7000 Test runs, his conversion rate of 50s to 100s was one of the worst among leading batsmen. Nobody, least of all Fleming, could explain that. His stints in English cricket included leading Notts to the County Championship in 2005. He retired from Tests after England's tour of New Zealand in 2007–8 in order to play Twenty20 in the Indian Premier League.

Test batting and fielding

T	I	NO	R	HS	Av.	100	50	Ct
111	189	10	7172	274*	40.06	9	46	171

First-class batting and fielding

M	I	NO	R	HS	Av.	100	50	Ct
247	406	32	16,409	274*	43.87	35	93	340

ODI batting and fielding

M	I	NO	R	HS	Av.	100	50	Ct
280	269	21	8037	134*	32.40	8	49	133

New Zealand's three best and most successful bowlers also happen to be their three most successful…

ALL-ROUNDERS

RICHARD JOHN HADLEE
(b.1951) *Canterbury, Nottinghamshire and Tasmania*

Richard Hadlee was, by a distance, New Zealand's greatest bowler, indeed its greatest cricketer. Actually, he was one of the best right-arm fast bowlers of any time – and not a bad bat either. The son of Walter Hadlee (the former New Zealand captain), brother of Dayle and former husband of Karen (all of them New Zealand Test players), he was extremely quick in his early days, a little slower – but still full of guile – later on, with a wicked outswinger. He modelled his action on that of the great Australian fast bowler Dennis Lillee, bowled very close to the stumps and was the first man to take 400 Test wickets, a target he achieved in only 79 matches (a superb strike rate). He batted left-handed, very aggressively, in the late middle-order and in the 1980s ranked as an outstanding all-rounder alongside Botham, Imran Khan and Kapil Dev. Hadlee also represented Nottinghamshire with distinction between 1978 and 1987. With his smooth run-up, whippy action and side-on delivery, he was the very model of what a fast bowler should be. One of Hadlee's finest Test performances came in the Wellington Test of 1978, when he took 10 wickets to help New Zealand to their first victory over England. His second innings figures were 6 for 46 as the visitors were dismissed for 64. Even more impressive was his 15-wicket haul against Australia at Brisbane in 1985–6. Against England in 1990 he took a wicket with his last ball in Test cricket and that year was knighted for services to the game.

Test batting and fielding

T	I	NO	R	HS	Av.	100	50	Ct
86	134	19	3124	151*	27.16	2	15	39

Test bowling

T	I	B	R	W	BBI	BBM	Av.
86	150	21,918	9611	431	9–52	15–123	22.29

First-class batting and fielding

M	I	NO	R	HS	Av.	100	50	Ct
342	473	93	12,052	210*	31.71	14	59	198

First-class bowling

M	B	R	W	BBI	Av.
342	67,518	26,998	1490	9–52	18.11

ODI batting and fielding

M	I	NO	R	HS	Av.	100	50	Ct
115	98	17	1751	79	21.61	0	4	27

ODI bowling

M	B	R	W	BB	Av.
115	6182	3407	158	5–25	21.56

CHRISTOPHER LANCE CAIRNS
(b.1970) *Canterbury, Northern Districts and Nottinghamshire*

The son of former New Zealand player Lance Cairns, Chris ended with Test averages to rank him up there alongside Ian Botham. He was a right-arm fast-medium bowler and a brutal right-hand batsman, who hit 158 off 172 balls against South Africa in 2004. Until Adam Gilchrist surpassed it he held the record for hitting most sixes (87) in Test matches. At Wellington in 2000 he kept hitting Shane Warne out of the ground and into the street. His overall record – 3000 runs and 200 wickets in Tests – is impressive enough but would have been better still had he not suffered more than his share of injuries, which caused him to miss 55 Tests. Even so, only Hadlee and Daniel Vettori have taken more wickets for New Zealand. As a bowler Cairns's best performance was against the West Indies in 1998 and in ODIs he was only 50 runs short of completing a rare double of 5000 runs and 200 wickets.

Test batting and fielding

T	I	NO	R	HS	Av.	100	50	Ct
62	104	5	3320	158	33.53	5	22	14

Test bowling

T	I	B	R	W	BBI	BBM	Av.
62	104	11,698	6410	218	7–27	10–100	29.40

First-class batting and fielding

M	I	NO	R	HS	Av.	100	50	Ct
21	341	38	10,702	158	35.32	13	71	78

First-class bowling

M	B	R	W	BBI	Av.
217	34,252	18,322	647	8–47	28.31

ODI batting and fielding

M	I	NO	R	HS	Av.	100	50	Ct
215	193	25	4950	115	29.46	4	26	66

ODI bowling

M	B	R	W	BB	Av.
215	8168	6594	201	5–42	32.80

RIGHT *Chris Cairns appeals for the wicket of England's Ashley Giles in the third Test at Trent Bridge, June 2004.*

DANIEL LUCA VETTORI

(b.1979) *Northern Districts, Nottinghamshire and Warwickshire*

Vettori, who ranks high among orthodox left-arm spinners, made himself into an extremely useful all-rounder and succeeded Fleming as New Zealand's captain. As a wicket-taker he relies more on flight, guile and change of pace than sharp spin, which method helped him become only the third New Zealander, after Hadlee and Cairns, to take 200 Test wickets. In 2008 he was number one on the ICC list of ODI bowlers and second among Test all-rounders. At 18 he was the youngest player to represent New Zealand (against England) only three weeks after making his first-class debut. After taking 47 Tests to reach his first 1000 runs he has developed into the best number-eight batsman in the business, his second thousand coming in 22 games at an average of 42.52. His highest score was against Pakistan and his best bowling against Australia in 2000.

Test batting and fielding

T	I	NO	R	HS	Av.	100	50	Ct
83	130	21	2992	137*	27.44	2	18	44

Bowling

T	I	B	R	W	BBI	BBM	Av.
88	142	21,416	9354	285	7–87	12–149	32.82

First-class batting and fielding

M	I	NO	R	HS	Av.	100	50	Ct
139	197	29	4719	137*	28.08	4	28	67

First-class bowling

M	B	R	W	BBI	Av.
139	31,922	14,195	453	7–87	31.33

ODI batting and fielding

M	I	NO	R	HS	Av.	100	50	Ct
239	144	46	1487	83	15.27	0	3	65

ODI bowling

M	B	R	W	BB	Av.
239	11,234	7819	241	5–7	32.44

NEW ZEALAND'S TEST RECORDS

Tests – played 348; won 66, lost 139, drawn 143. In ODIs – played 566; won 245, lost 286, tied 5, no result 30.

New Zealand's highest Test total was 671–4 vs Sri Lanka, Wellington, 1991; the lowest 26 vs England, Auckland, 1955.

Most Test appearances

	T
S.P. Fleming	111
D.L. Vettori	88
R.J. Hadlee	86

Highest individual Test scores

	R	Opp.	Ground	Match date
M.D. Crowe	299	Sri Lanka	Wellington	31 Jan. 1991
S.P. Fleming	274*	Sri Lanka	Colombo (PSS)	25 Apr. 2003
B.A. Young	267*	Sri Lanka	Dunedin	7 Mar. 1997

Highest Test batting averages (qualification: 15 Tests or more)

	T	Av.
J.F. Reid	19	46.28
M.D. Crowe	77	45.36
M.H. Richardson	38	44.77

Note: The most runs in a series (672 at 96.00) were made by Glenn Turner vs West Indies, 1971–2.

Most Test centuries

	T	100s
M.D. Crowe	77	17
J.G. Wright	82	12
N.J. Astle	81	11

Highest Test partnerships

	R	W	Opp.	Ground	Match date
A.H. Jones, M.D. Crowe	467	3	Sri Lanka	Wellington	31 Jan. 1991
G.M. Turner, T.W. Jarvis	387	1	West Indies	Georgetown	6 Apr. 1972
C.S. Dempster, J.E. Mills	276	1	England	Wellington	24 Jan. 1930
S.P. Fleming, J.E.C. Franklin	256	8	South Africa	Cape Town	27 Apr. 2006
N.J. Astle, A.C. Parore	253	8	Australia	Perth	30 Nov. 2001

Highest individual run-scorers in Tests

	Span	T	I	NO	R	HS	Av.
S.P. Fleming	1994–2008	111	189	10	7172	274*	40.06
M.D. Crowe	1982–95	77	131	11	5444	299	45.36
J.G. Wright	1978–93	82	148	7	5334	185	37.82

Most Test ducks

	T	I	NO	0s
C.S. Martin	45	63	30	25
D.K. Morrison	48	71	26	24
S.P. Fleming	111	189	10	16
K.R Rutherford	56	99	8	16
D.L. Vettori	88	130	21	16

Highest Test wicket-takers

		T	B	R	W	BBI	Av.
R.J. Hadlee	1973–90	86	21,918	9611	431	9–52	22.29
D.L. Vettori	1997–2009	88	21,416	9354	285	7–87	32.82
C.L. Cairns	1989–2004	62	11,698	6410	218	7–27	29.40

Note: Richard Hadlee had the best bowling figures in an innings (9–52 vs Australia, 1985), the best in a match (15–123 in the same game) and the most wickets in a series, 33 at 12.15 vs Australia, 1985–6. The best career average was returned by Jack Cowie, who took 45 wickets at 21.53. But he only played in nine Tests.

Most dismissals by a wicketkeeper in a Test career

		T	W	Ct	St
A.C. Parore	1990–2002	67	201	194	7

Note: A.E. Dick claimed 23 victims (21 ct, 2 st) vs South Africa, 1961–2.

Most catches by a fielder in a Test career

	T	Ct
S.P. Fleming	111	171

Leading all-rounders (1000 runs [at an average of 20 or more] and 100 wickets)

	T	R	Bat. Av.	W	Bowl. Av.	Tests for 1000/100
J.G. Bracewell	41	1001	20.42	102	35.81	41
C.L. Cairns	62	3320	33.53	218	29.40	33
R.J. Hadlee	86	3124	27.16	431	22.29	28
D.L. Vettori	88	2992	27.44	285	32.82	47

In the course of his 111 Test matches Stephen Fleming became New Zealand's most successful captain and highest-ever run-scorer.

CHAPTER 9
CRICKET IN INDIA

THE DOMESTIC GAME IN THE
WORLD'S MOST POPULOUS COUNTRY,
PLUS PROFILES AND TEST AND
FIRST-CLASS RECORDS OF INDIA'S
ALL-TIME GREATS

The national sport of India is field hockey, which is odd when you consider that India is probably the powerful cricketing nation in the world – not on the field (though by the end of 2008 it was certainly heading that way) but in its influence over the game internationally and in the fact that, because of the sheer size of the population, the BCCI (the Board of Control for Cricket in India) makes more money from the sale of media rights for the country's matches than any similar organization anywhere else.

The game has been played in India (initially by British sailors) since the early 1700s and now attracts enormous crowds (especially for Twenty20 games) and is infinitely more popular than hockey.

India joined the Imperial Cricket Conference in 1926 and played their first Test match, against England, in 1932. In those days and until partition in 1947 India also included what are now Pakistan and Bangladesh. Before 1932 the best Indian players – K.S. Ranjitsinhji (see also page 72), his nephew K.S. Duleepsinhji and the Nawab of Pataudi – could only experience Test cricket by turning out for England.

GETTING BETTER ALL THE TIME

Success came slowly to the national side, the first Test win against England (at Madras) and the first series victory (against Pakistan) not arriving until 1952. But gradually things got better and by the 1970s India could boast an outstanding batsman in Sunil Gavaskar and four of the world's best spinners in Bishan Bedi, Bhagwat Chandrasekhar, E.A.S. Prasanna and Srinivas Venkataraghavan.

Indeed, India has an enviable record for turning out world-class players from the opening batsman Gavaskar to the all-rounder Kapil Dev and the present bunch of batsmen like Sachin Tendulkar, Rahul Dravid, Sourav Ganguly and such youngsters as Mahendra Singh Dhoni, the wicketkeeper and now captain. The fact that, over the years, the team has tended to lose more Tests than it wins could be down to inter-zonal rivalry among the selectors about who should captain the side and who should be in it in the first place, rather than lack of quality.

India's greatest glory was in 2001 when not only did they beat Steve Waugh's Australians but, at Kolkata, became only the third team in Test history to win after following on, thanks to a majestic double-century by V.V.S. Laxman. This success was pretty well matched by their series win over Ponting's Aussies in 2008, while their finest achievement in ODIs came when they won the World Cup in 1983. They were also beaten finalists in 2003. But at the end of 2008, as India gloried in its financial (about 70 per cent of

FAR LEFT *Indian batsmen V.V.S. Laxman (left) and Rahul Dravid acknowledge the cheers of the crowd as they walk back to the pavilion in Kolkata (Calcutta) on the fourth day of the second Test against Australia, 14 March 2001. In a second innings follow-on, the two batsmen snatched victory from the jaws of defeat with scores of 281 and 180 respectively. India went on to win the series, ending Australia's record run of Test wins. Laxman's marathon innings earned him the nickname (from his initials) of 'Very Very Special'.*

RIGHT *A trio of stars in the Indian cricketing firmament: (left to right) Kapil Dev, a very young Sachin Tendulkar and Mohammad Azharuddin pose before the 1989 Test series against Pakistan. At the tender age of 16, this was Tendulkar's Test blooding – quite literally, as he was hit in the mouth by a ball from Waqar Younis but kept playing. Azharuddin, whose wristy skills brought him 6215 runs and 22 centuries in 99 Tests, fell from grace in 2000 when he was accused of involvement in a match-fixing scandal.*

the world's cricketing revenues stemmed, one way or another, from there) and therefore, in cricketing terms, political clout, appalling terrorism in Mumbai shattered this happy picture. The last two games in the ODI series (England already 5–0 down and heading for a 'brownwash') were cancelled and the Twenty20 Champions League postponed. Thus, if perhaps only temporarily, India joined Pakistan and Sri Lanka (where the government was engaged in continuing strife with the Tamil Tigers) as a dangerous country for teams to visit. But England came to the rescue by returning for a two-match Test series, thus earning the gratitude and even (although in this respect again perhaps only temporarily) the affection of the BCCI, which in recent years had been showing lofty disdain and contempt for the former colonial masters.

At year's end, despite the retirement of Sourav Ganguly and Anil Kumble and despite two painful defeats by Sri Lanka, India could claim to be, if only unofficially, the world's number two Test nation. Old stagers like Tendulkar, Dravid and Laxman were still doing their stuff, Sehwag was in his prime,

Dhoni was showing great flair as a captain and they had unearthed two new potential stars in the opening bat Gautam Gambhir and Ishant Sharma, who could swing the ball both ways at speeds up to 90 mph.

INDIA'S DOMESTIC TROPHIES

Domestically, the main competition is the Ranji Trophy, launched in 1934–5 as 'the Cricket Championship of India', and contested by the various Indian states along with individual cities like Mumbai (or Bombay as it then was) and Hyderabad and sides that have no particular geographical affiliation, such as Railways and Services (armed services, that is, rather than teams made up of waiters, plumbers and electricians). Much of the time this turns out to be a non-contest, having been won 38 times out of 75 by Mumbai, who between 1958–9 and 1972–3 were the victors 15 years in a row. Among the outstanding performances in Ranji Trophy matches was the 443 not out scored by B.B. Nimbalkar for Maharashtra against Kathiawar at Pune in 1948–9.

Traditionally the Indian season kicks off with a match between the previous year's Ranji Trophy winners and the Rest of India for the Irani Trophy. In 1961–2, largely because of the predictable nature of the Ranji Trophy, a second competition, for the Duleep Trophy, was introduced. This is contested by five zonal teams – North, South, East, West and Central – and, in recent years, by a foreign guest side (England Lions, for instance, in 2007–8). To date North Zone have won the Duleep Trophy 17 times and West Zone have won it 16 times, shared trophies included. Since 1973–4 the five zonal teams have also competed for the Deodhar Trophy, which North Zone have won 11 times.

THE WISDOM OF CROWDS

Generally speaking, Indians make up the biggest, most enthusiastic Test match crowds in the world. They are ardent lovers of the game whose cricketing heroes, such as Tendulkar and Dhoni, are up there alongside Bollywood movie stars as objects of public adoration.

The downside of all this is that after setbacks – especially after losses to India's nearest and bitterest rivals, Pakistan – the crowds are inclined to show their displeasure by throwing stones and bottles or even by setting fire to the stands and holding demonstrations in the streets, including the burning of players in effigy. In 1996, when India were losing a World Cup semi-final at Eden Gardens in Kolkata (Calcutta), an armed guard had to be placed at the home of the captain, Mohammad Azharuddin, to protect him from the anger of seriously cheesed-off fans. Matters of selection can inflame passions, too. When Sourav Ganguly was dropped for the Kolkata Test against South Africa in 2005, his home crowd reacted by booing the Indian team and chose to support the opposition instead.

THE LURE OF THE INDIAN PREMIER LEAGUE

Since 2006, when India first took to playing international Twenty20 cricket and went on to win the inaugural Twenty20 World Cup in South Africa the following year, domestic support for this type of cricket has threatened to overwhelm the more traditional forms of the game in India.

In 2007 Zee Telefilms, having been thwarted in bids for the rights to cover the 2003 World Cup and the 2006 ICC Champions Trophy, reacted by creating the Indian Cricket League (ICL), a Twenty20 competition that recruited overseas stars such as Brian Lara, Chris Cairns, Chris Read, Mushtaq Ahmed and Shane Bond. The league was unofficial and the players taking part were banned from Tests and, until wisdom prevailed, from English county cricket, too.

Then, in response to the ICL, the BCCI created the Indian Premier League (IPL), its own official Twenty20 competition – sanctioned by the ICC – and sold the television rights for US$918 million. Thereupon the IPL teams started hurling money at international stars as if they were Premier League footballers: $1.5 million for Dhoni, $1.35 million for Australia's Andrew Symonds, $975,000 for Sanath Jayasuriya and so on. (All right, such wages might be regarded as small change by many Premier League footballers, whose sole accomplishment is the ability to stand on one foot while kicking a ball with the other. But to cricketers they meant wealth hitherto undreamt of.)

International commitments and their contracts with the ECB initially precluded leading English players from this bonanza. But not, surely, for long. Everyone, cricketers included, has to put food on the table and even the ECB could not deny its players the prospect of earning half a million quid or more for a few weeks' knockabout fun in a sunny clime. Once accommodation could be made between the IPL season and players' international commitments it could only be a matter of time before the likes of Pietersen and Flintoff succumbed to the offer of what would amount to a sizeable pension pot. And in February 2009, that's precisely what happened. Kevin Pietersen was sold to Bangalore and Andrew Flintoff to Chennai for $1.55 million each. Ravi Bopara went to King's XI Punjab for $450,000, while Owais Shah and Paul Collingwood were snapped up by Delhi Daredevils for a comparatively modest $275,000 apiece.

For purists (like me) who believe that Test cricket is the most sublime form of the game and that Twenty20 – more popular though it might currently be – is merely an entertaining sideshow, the worry is that it could come to dominate the whole structure of the international game.

HOWZAT! In the early to mid-1990s, when both Mohammad Azharuddin and England footballer Paul Gascoigne were at the peak of their fame, a banner appeared at an England–India Test which read: 'Azha – India's Gazza!'

THE BATSMEN

SUNIL GAVASKAR
(b.1949) *Bombay and Somerset*

A little master of a player, Sunny Gavaskar was a superb right-hand opening bat, the first player to score 10,000 Test runs and at one time holder of the records for most runs and most centuries. (His record of 34 Test centuries stood for almost 20 years until broken by Tendulkar in December 2005.) Compact, elegant and watchful, Gavaskar was almost impossible to get out. Though less than 5' 5" tall he was a great player of fast bowling, even, or especially, that of the fearsome West Indies attack of the 1970s. Against Australia in 1977–8 he scored three consecutive centuries, including two in a match. Later he repeated the two-in-a-match against Pakistan and West Indies to become the first player ever to score two hundreds in a Test three times. Perhaps his greatest innings was against England at the Oval in 1979 when, with India needing 438 to win, he scored 221 to bring his country to within nine runs of victory. (The match was drawn.) Equally adept off both the front and back foot, Gavaskar had all the shots but mostly chose not to play them because, at a time when the Indian team was weak, what it needed from him was resolute defence, and by God, he provided it.

SACHIN RAMESH TENDULKAR
(b.1973) *Mumbai and Yorkshire*

Another titch (about the same height as Gavaskar) and another absolute master of batting, one of the greatest players of all time, up there with Bradman, Richards and Lara. He made his first-class debut at 15 (and scored 100 not out), his Test debut at 16, hit his first Test hundred (against England) at 17 and since then has scored more Test centuries than anyone else, three of them in a row against Australia in 1998, as well as more runs than anyone else – not only in Tests but also in ODIs. His record would be even more remarkable but for elbow and shoulder injuries, and had he not been dismissed 23 times in his nineties in Tests and ODIs. He can play any shot you care to name, although

Sunil Gavaskar batting during his last Test series, against Pakistan, in 1987. One of the greatest opening batsmen in Test history, Gavaskar's game was based on a near-flawless technique and immense powers of concentration.

Test batting and fielding

T	I	NO	R	HS	Av.	100	50	Ct
125	214	16	10,122	236*	51.12	34	45	108

(He bowled right-arm medium or off-spin and took 1-206 in Tests)

First-class batting and fielding

M	I	NO	R	HS	Av.	100	50	Ct
348	563	61	25,834	340	51.46	81	105	293

First-class bowling

M	B	R	W	BBI	Av.
348	1987	1240	22	3-43	56.36

ODI batting and fielding

M	I	NO	R	HS	Av.	100	50	Ct
108	102	14	3092	103*	35.13	1	27	22

(In ODIs he took 1-25)

with advancing years he has become more circumspect. He bats and bowls right-handed and sends down medium-pace, off- or leg-spin, rather expensively and according to need. He was Yorkshire's first overseas signing (not very successfully, though), is the most adored, most sponsored, player in India and very possibly the richest cricketer in the world. Whether he, or Brian Lara, is the greatest batsman of the modern era is open to endless argument. Tendulkar perhaps is the finer technician but less of a match-winner (or match-saver) than Lara – and not so pretty to watch.

Test batting and fielding

T	I	NO	R	HS	Av.	100	50	Ct
156	256	27	12,479	248*	54.27	41	51	100

Test bowling

T	I	B	R	W	BBI	BBM	Av.
156	126	3880	2227	42	3–10	3–14	53.02

First-class batting and fielding

M	I	NO	R	HS	Av.	100	50	Ct
258	407	43	21,318	248*	58.56	68	97	168

First-class bowling

M	B	R	W	BBI	Av.
258	7254	4119	67	3–10	61.47

ODI batting and fielding

M	I	NO	R	HS	Av.	100	50	Ct
425	415	39	16,684	186*	44.37	43	91	129

ODI bowling

M	B	R	W	BB	Av.
425	8015	6806	154	5–32	44.19

RAHUL SHARAD DRAVID
(b.1973) *Bangalore and Kent*

They call him 'The Wall' because he's nearly as difficult to get out as Gavaskar was. A right-hander of classic style, when he sets his mind to it he can bat forever. Like everyone else he has been overshadowed by Tendulkar but in 2001 Dravid (180) and V.V.S. Laxman (281) scored 376 together against Australia to help India, who had followed on, to win the match. In 2002 he hit four consecutive hundreds against England and West Indies and in 2003–4 made double-centuries against New Zealand, Australia and Pakistan. What's more, he's been involved in more century partnerships (72) than anyone else and is a handy wicketkeeper, mostly in one-day matches.

Test batting and fielding

T	I	NO	R	HS	Av.	100	50	Ct
130	225	26	10,486	270	52.69	26	53	179

(An off-spinner, he has taken 1–39 in Tests, best 1–18)

First-class batting and fielding

M	I	NO	R	HS	Av.	100	50	Ct	St
258	427	58	20,405	270	55.29	56	104	313	1

(His bowling figures are 5–273, average 54.60, best 2–16)

ODI batting and fielding

M	I	NO	R	HS	Av.	100	50	Ct	St
333	308	40	10,585	153	39.49	12	81	193	14

(Bowling: 4–170, average 42.50, best 2–43)

VIRENDER SEHWAG
(b.1978) *Delhi and Leicestershire*

Is it a bit premature to ascribe greatness to Sehwag? Maybe, but an average of over 50, with the promise of more to come, puts him among the game's highest

Test batting and fielding

T	I	NO	R	HS	Av.	100	50	Ct
65	112	4	5534	319	51.24	15	17	49

Test bowling

T	I	B	R	W	BBI	BBM	Av.
65	62	2323	1149	29	5–104	5–118	39.62

First-class batting and fielding

M	I	NO	R	HS	Av.	100	50	Ct
128	213	8	10,094	319	49.23	29	36	109

First-class bowling

M	B	R	W	BBI	Av.
128	6954	3582	93	5–104	38.51

ODI batting and fielding

M	I	NO	R	HS	Av.	100	50	Ct
205	200	8	6592	130	34.33	11	35	79

ODI bowling

M	B	R	W	BB	Av.
205	4015	3531	87	3–25	40.58

I don't believe in technique, I believe in performance. ● Virender Sehwag

Virender Sehwag salutes spectators at Chennai (Madras) after making the fastest triple-century in Test history, off just 278 balls, in the first Test against South Africa, March 2008.

achievers. Like his idol Tendulkar he is short and muscular and a pugnacious right-hand bat, particularly effective as an opener. His off-spin bowling's not bad either. His form can be inconsistent – he was dropped from the Test squad in 2007 but came back strongly against Australia that year and, later, against South Africa, made his highest score, thus joining Bradman and Lara as the only batsmen to make two triple-centuries in Tests. In 2008 he thrived more than most against Sri Lanka's new mystery bowler, Ajantha Mendis, his double-century at Galle helping India to win the match. What with all that, plus another match-winning innings against England at Chennai in December 2008 (see pages 226–231), and 11 Test scores of 150 or more, I would say that no, it's not too early to call him great.

THE BOWLERS

BHAGWAT SUBRAMANYA CHANDRASEKHAR
(b.1945) *Karnataka and Mysore*

Despite a withered right arm – the aftermath of childhood polio – Chandra was in the top rank of leg-spinners. An unorthodox one, to be sure. He had an unusually long run-up, bowled at medium pace, didn't turn the leg-break that much and, anyway, was more likely to bowl a sharp googly or flipper than a leggie.

Test bowling

T	I	B	R	W	BBI	BBM	Av.
58	97	15,963	7199	242	8–79	12–104	29.74

(He played one ODI, taking 3–36 and scoring 11*)

Test batting and fielding

T	I	NO	R	HS	Av.	100	50	Ct
58	80	39	167	22	4.07	0	0	25

First-class bowling

M	B	R	W	BBI	Av.
246	53,817	25,547	1063	9–72	24.03

First-class batting and fielding

M	I	NO	R	HS	Av.	100	50	Ct
246	244	114	600	25	4.61	0	0	107

On his day he was a match-winner, as he proved at the Oval in 1971 when his 6 for 38 helped India to a first series win over England. He was an integral part of the great quartet – Bedi, Prasanna and Venkataraghavan being the others – who made Indian spin supreme in the 1960s and '70s. He was a virtually useless batsman and, because of his withered arm, threw left-handed.

BISHAN SINGH BEDI
(b.1946) *Northern Punjab, Delhi and Northamptonshire*

As a left-arm spinner Bishan Bedi had it all – gliding run-up, classically high delivery, flight, loop, bounce, spin, change of pace. His action was about as perfect as it was possible to be. Slim to start with, plump later on but still graceful in movement, he took more first-class wickets than any other Indian bowler, thanks in large part to a successful stint with Northants. His finest series was in Australia in 1977–8 when he took 31 wickets, including his best match figures. An amiable but contentious character, never reluctant to join in – or start – a verbal punch-up, he has been one of the most vociferous critics of Muttiah Muralitharan's bowling action.

Test bowling

T	I	B	R	W	BBI	BBM	Av.
67	118	21,364	7637	266	7–98	10–194	28.71

Test batting and fielding

T	I	NO	R	HS	Av.	100	50	Ct
67	101	28	656	50*	8.98	0	1	26

First-class bowling

M	B	R	W	BBI	Av.
370	90,354	33,843	1560	7–5	21.69

First-class batting and fielding

M	I	NO	R	HS	Av.	100	50	Ct
370	426	111	3584	61	11.37	0	7	172

ODI bowling

M	B	R	W	BB	Av.
10	590	340	7	2–44	48.57

ODI batting and fielding

M	I	NO	R	HS	Av.	100	50	Ct
10	7	2	31	13	6.20	0	0	4

JAVAGAL SRINATH

(b.1969) *Karnataka, Gloucestershire and Leicestershire*

Srinath is arguably the fastest bowler his country has produced and only the second Indian paceman, after Kapil Dev, to take 200 Test wickets. He bowled right arm, mostly at fast-medium, although he was occasionally timed at over 95 mph. His stock deliveries, brisk off the pitch, were in-swingers and off-cutters but he could also reverse-swing the old ball and later developed a good leg-cutter. He made his first-class debut in 1989–90 and did the hat-trick. In 1995 he took 9 for 76 for Gloucestershire against Glamorgan. The effort of trying to extract pace from Indian wickets probably accounted for the injuries which led to the end of his 11-year Test career in 2002.

Test bowling

T	I	B	R	W	BBI	BBM	Av.
67	121	15,104	7196	236	8–86	13–132	30.49

Test batting and fielding

T	I	NO	R	HS	Av.	100	50	Ct
67	92	21	1009	76	14.21	0	4	22

First-class bowling

M	B	R	W	BBI	Av.
147	28,618	14,027	533	9–76	26.31

First-class batting and fielding

M	I	NO	R	HS	Av.	100	50	Ct
147	191	34	2276	76	14.49	0	7	62

ODI bowling

M	B	R	W	BB	Av.
229	11,935	8847	315	5–23	28.08

ODI batting and fielding

M	I	NO	R	HS	Av.	100	50	Ct
229	121	38	883	53	10.63	0	1	32

ANIL KUMBLE
(b.1970) *Bangalore, Karnataka, Leicestershire, Northamptonshire and Surrey*

Though not in Shane Warne's league as a spinner of the ball, Kumble is the second most successful leg-break bowler in Test history and, after Jim Laker, only the second man to take 10 wickets in an innings (versus Pakistan in 1999). He was quickish through the air and tended to spear the ball in rather than flight it, relying more on accuracy, bounce, varied pace and length than sharp turn. If he had a stock ball it was the flipper, although the leggie's customary range of weapons – top-spinners, wrong 'uns and the like – were in his armoury. It's just that he didn't spin them a lot. He was by a long way India's biggest wicket-taker – only Muralitharan and Warne have claimed more victims – and he alone among cricketers has taken all ten in an innings and scored a Test century (versus England, 2007). Mind you, the latter didn't happen until his 118th game. He also holds the record for most caught-and-bowleds (28) in Tests and was the first Indian spinner to take 300 wickets in ODIs.

Test bowling

T	I	B	R	W	BBI	BBM	Av.
132	236	40,850	18,355	619	10–74	14–149	29.65

Test batting and fielding

T	I	NO	R	HS	Av.	100	50	Ct
132	173	32	2506	110*	17.77	1	5	60

First-class bowling

M	B	R	W	BBI	Av.
244	66,931	29,347	1136	10–74	25.83

First-class batting and fielding

M	I	NO	R	HS	Av.	100	50	Ct
244	318	61	5572	154*	21.68	7	17	120

ODI bowling

M	B	R	W	BB	Av.
271	14,496	10,412	337	6–12	30.89

ODI batting and fielding

M	I	NO	R	HS	Av.	100	50	Ct
271	136	47	938	26	10.53	0	0	85

FAR RIGHT *Anil Kumble (seen here in 2008) is Test cricket's third-highest wicket-taker, behind Muttiah Muralitharan and Shane Warne, with 619 victims.*

THE ALL-ROUNDERS

India has produced quite a few, including such accomplished players as Vinoo Mankad and Ravi Shastri. But the best of them all was…

KAPIL DEV
(b.1959) *Haryana, Northamptonshire and Worcestershire*

Kapil was both India's finest pace bowler and a superb all-rounder. He came along at the same time as Botham, Imran Khan and Richard Hadlee and bore comparison with all of them – a right-arm fast-medium bowler, with a fine, in-swinging yorker, and an aggressive, hard-hitting right-hand bat. In 1983 he led India to their only World Cup win, his contribution being 303 runs (average 60.60) and 12 wickets at 20.41 in eight matches. In Tests he was at one time the world's leading wicket-taker. At Lord's in 1990, when Gooch scored 333 and 123, Kapil blasted 77 not out, including four consecutive sixes off Eddie Hemmings, to save the follow-on. In 2002 he beat Gavaskar and Tendulkar to be voted India's Cricketer of the Century.

Test batting and fielding

T	I	NO	R	HS	Av.	100	50	Ct
131	184	15	5248	163	31.05	8	27	64

Test bowling

T	I	B	R	W	BBI	BBM	Av.
131	227	27,740	12,867	434	9–83	11–146	29.64

First-class batting and fielding

M	I	NO	R	HS	Av.	100	50	Ct
275	384	39	11,356	193	32.91	18	56	192

First-class bowling

M	B	R	W	BB	Av.
275	48,853	22,626	835	9–83	27.09

ODI batting and fielding

M	I	NO	R	HS	Av.	100	50	Ct
225	198	39	3783	175*	23.79	1	14	71

ODI bowling

M	B	R	W	BB	Av.
225	11,202	6945	253	5–43	27.45

INDIA'S TEST RECORDS

Tests – played 427; won 98, lost 136, tied 1, drawn 192.   ODIs – played 711; won 344, lost 333, tied 3, no result 31.

India's biggest total in a Test is 705–7d vs Australia, Sydney, 2004; their lowest 42 vs England, Lord's, 1974.

Most Test appearances

	T
S.R. Tendulkar	156
A. Kumble	132
Kapil Dev	131
R. Dravid	130
S.M. Gavaskar	125

Highest individual run-scorers in Tests

	Span	T	I	NO	R	HS	Av.
S.R. Tendulkar	1989–2008	156	256	27	12,429	248*	54.27
R. Dravid	1996–2008	130	225	26	10,486	270	52.69
S.M. Gavaskar	1971–87	125	214	16	10,122	236*	51.12
S.C. Ganguly	1996–2008	109	179	15	6870	239	41.89
D.B. Vengsarkar	1976–92	116	185	22	6868	166	42.13

Highest Test individual scores

	R	Opp.	Ground	Match date
V. Sehwag	319	South Africa	Chennai	26 Mar. 2008
V. Sehwag	309	Pakistan	Multan	28 Mar. 2004
V.V.S. Laxman	281	Australia	Kolkata	11 Mar. 2001
R. Dravid	270	Pakistan	Rawalpindi	13 Apr. 2004
V. Sehwag	254	Pakistan	Lahore	13 Jan. 2006

Highest Test partnerships

	R	W	Opp.	Ground	Match date
M.H. Mankad, P. Roy	413	1	New Zealand	Madras	6 Jan. 1956
V. Sehwag, R. Dravid	410	1	Pakistan	Lahore	13 Jan. 200
R. Dravid, V.V.S. Laxman	376	5	Australia	Kolkata	11 Mar. 200
S.R. Tendulkar, V.V.S. Laxman	353	4	Australia	Sydney	2 Jan. 2004
S.M. Gavaskar, D.B. Vengsarkar	344*	2	West Indies	Kolkata	29 Dec. 197

Highest Test batting averages
(qualification: 15 Tests or more)

	T	Av.
S.R. Tendulkar	156	54.27
V.G. Kambli	17	54.20
R. Dravid	130	52.69
V. Sehwag	65	51.24
S.M. Gavaskar	125	51.12

Most Test centuries

	T	100s
S.R. Tendulkar	156	41
S.M. Gavaskar	125	34
R. Dravid	130	26
M. Azharuddin	99	22
D.B. Vengsarkar	116	17

Note: Tendulkar, with 51 fifties, has made the most scores between 50 and 99.
Gavaskar's 774 at 154.80 vs West Indies, 1970–1, is the record for most runs in a series.

Most Test ducks

	T	I	NO	0s
B.S. Chandrasekhar	58	80	39	23
B.S. Bedi	67	101	28	20
Z. Khan	62	82	20	18
A. Kumble	132	173	32	17
Kapil Dev	131	184	15	16

Highest Test wicket-takers

		T	B	R	W	BBI	Av.
A. Kumble	1990–2008	132	40,850	18,355	619	10–74	29.65
Kapil Dev	1978–94	131	27,740	12,867	434	9–83	29.64
Harbhajan Singh	1998–2008	74	20,585	9698	314	8–84	30.88
B.S. Bedi	1966–79	67	21,364	7637	266	7–98	28.71
B.S. Chandrasekhar	1964–79	58	15,963	7199	242	8–79	29.74

Note: The best match analysis was N.D. Hirwani's 16–136 vs West Indies, Chennai, 1988. Chandrasekhar's haul of 35 wickets at 18.91 vs England, 1972–3, is the best return for a series.

Most dismissals by a wicketkeeper in a Test career

		T	W	Ct	St
S.M.H. Kirmani	1976–86	88	198	160	38

Most catches by a fielder in a Test career

	T	Ct
R. Dravid	130	179

Leading all-rounders (1000 runs [at an average of 20 or more] and 100 wickets)

	T	R	Bat. Av.	W	Bowl. Av.	Tests for 1000/100
Kapil Dev	131	5248	31.05	434	29.64	25
M.H. Mankad	44	2109	31.47	162	32.32	23
I.K. Pathan	29	1105	31.57	100	32.26	28
R.J. Shastri	80	3830	35.79	151	40.96	44

BELOW *Rahul Dravid plays a vintage stroke during the first Test against the West Indies at St John's, Antigua, June 2006. Nicknamed 'The Wall' early in his Test career for his obdurate defence against high-class bowling attacks, Dravid has now entered the pantheon of great Indian batsmen, alongside Sachin Tendulkar and Sunil Gavaskar.*

CHAPTER 10
Cricket in Pakistan

THE DOMESTIC GAME IN PAKISTAN, PLUS
PROFILES AND TEST AND FIRST-CLASS RECORDS
OF PAKISTAN'S ALL-TIME GREATS

Cricket was played in Pakistan long before partition in 1947 while it was still part of British India, but it was not until 1952 that the comparatively new republic was given Test match status, partly thanks to India's recommendation, something India may have regretted ever since, given the nations' prickly relationship. Their first series was against India that year (they lost two-one) and their first tour was to England in 1954 (they drew one apiece). That was a great, albeit unexpected, result, which owed much to the fast bowler Fazal Mahmood taking 12 wickets in the Oval Test.

Their first home game (against India) was at Dacca (Dhaka), which is now in Bangladesh, in 1955, launching a series in which all five matches were drawn, something that had never happened before. But it just goes to show the attritional quality of encounters between Pakistan and India. Since then they have become one of the most gifted, formidable but frequently unpredictable teams in the world. For example, they won the World Cup in 1992 and were runners-up in 1999, but in 2007 they were knocked out after losing to Ireland. The same year they were beaten in the final of the inaugural Twenty20 World Cup by India, which must have been a particularly bitter pill to swallow.

Domestically, the first-class competition is for the Quaid-i-Azam Trophy, introduced in 1953 and, since 1956–7 contested by 12 teams, including three each from Karachi and Punjab. Between them the various Karachi sides have won it 17 times, nobody else more than six.

A CONTROVERSIAL HISTORY

Pakistan's first Test captain was Abdul Kardar, aka Abdul Hafeez when, in his earlier years, he played for India. Since then, either as player or captain or both, he has been succeeded by some pretty remarkable cricketers – Majid and Imran Khan, the leg-spinner Abdul Qadir, Javed Miandad (said by some to be three separate players, Javed, me and dad), Wasim Akram, Waqar Younis, Inzamam-ul-Haq, Mohammad Yousuf and Shoaib Akhtar, who once bowled a ball at 100 mph and may well be the fastest bowler ever. Such claims, however, should be tempered by the fact that there has been much headshaking and sucking of teeth about the legitimacy of his action.

Pakistan and controversy of some kind have always been close neighbours. In 1987 there was the Shakoor Rana affair at Faisalabad, when England's captain Mike Gatting argued with the umpire of that name, who promptly took umbrage and refused to let play continue until an apology had been delivered, thus depriving England of a likely victory.

During the Oval Test in 2006, the umpires Darrell Hair and Billy Doctrove accused Pakistan of tampering with the ball and penalized them

FAR LEFT *Team spirit: Inzamam-ul-Haq of Pakistan gives a pep talk to a huddle of players during the third Test against England at Headingley, 4 August 2006. England ran out 3–0 winners in an ill-tempered series.*

five runs. Skipper Inzamam-ul-Haq and the rest of the team decided this was unjust and over the top and refused to come out after tea, thereby forfeiting the match – the only time this has happened in Test cricket.

Then, during the 2007 World Cup in Jamaica, Pakistan's coach Bob Woolmer died in mysterious circumstances. For some time it was thought he had been murdered and the Pakistan team were among those questioned, though none of them was a suspect. Finally it was decided that his death was accidental. In 2008, with Pakistan beset by economic turmoil and political violence, no Tests were played there. Could things get worse? Yes, sadly, for in March 2009 a coach carrying the visiting Sri Lankan team (who had gallantly, though perhaps foolhardily, replaced India as tourists) was attacked by terrorists during a Test in Lahore. Eight people were killed and seven Sri Lankan players injured. The rest of the tour was immediately cancelled.

Pakistan had been due to co-host the 2011 World Cup but now, as the country looked increasingly like a no-go area, there seemed small chance of that happening. So what the immediate future held for this benighted nation and its cricketers only God knew. But it certainly didn't look good.

RIGHT *England skipper Mike Gatting and Pakistani umpire Shakoor Rana go head-to-head in a notorious incident during the second Test at Faisalabad, 8 December 1987. Simmering bad blood boiled over when Rana (who had already shown himself highly partisan) accused Gatting of cheating for exercising his captain's prerogative of adjusting his field. Australian captain Allan Border later remarked that Pakistan 'seem to have a chip on their shoulder about their cricket'.*

Pakistan has produced a number of great players. Let's take a look at some of…

they called him 'the Little Master' and as Pakistan's first star cricketer he did a very great deal to popularize the game in that country.

THE BATSMEN

HANIF MOHAMMAD
(b.1934) *Bahawalpur and Pakistan International Airlines*

In his time Hanif was as big a legend in Pakistan as Tendulkar was to become in India. He was the country's first great player and the leader of a cricketing dynasty. Three of his brothers (Mushtaq, Sadiq and Wazir) and his son, Shoaib, all played Test cricket. Hanif was an obdurate right-hand opening batsman whose hatred of getting out was equalled only by that of Geoff Boycott. He is most famous (a) for a monumental, 16-hour 337 (during which, incidentally, he was credited with inventing the reverse sweep) to save a match against West Indies in 1957–8 and (b) for being run out for 499 in 1958–9 – a first-class score bettered only by Brian Lara. He was a good fielder, an occasional wicketkeeper and, in Tests, bowled both right-arm off-breaks and left-arm spin, neither with any great success. As a batsman, though,

Test batting and fielding

T	I	NO	R	HS	Av.	100	50	Ct
55	97	8	3915	337	43.98	12	15	40

(His Test bowling record was 1–95, best 1–1)

First-class batting and fielding

M	I	NO	R	HS	Av.	100	50	Ct	St
38	370	44	17,059	499	52.32	55	66	178	12

First-class bowling

M	B	R	W	BB	Av.
238	2766	1510	53	3–4	28.49

JAVED MIANDAD
(b.1957) *Karachi, Sind, Habib Bank, Sussex and Glamorgan*

At 19 Javed became the youngest player to score a century on debut (versus New Zealand, 1976) and, in the same series, the youngest to make a double-century. In all he hit six double-centuries (a Pakistan

BELOW *All hell breaks loose between Javed Miandad and fast bowler Dennis Lillee at Perth, November 1983.*

record), made his highest score against the old enemy, India, and his 50 in the 1992 final helped Pakistan win the World Cup. A gifted right-hander with the attitude of a street-fighter, he was, in short, Pakistan's greatest batsman, a belligerent scrapper who, during a Test in 1983–4, appeared to be trying to hit Dennis Lillee with his bat even while Lillee was apparently trying to kick him. Both as captain and later as Pakistan's coach he often fell out with his own team. He played in all the first six World Cups, starting at 18 as a leg-spinning all-rounder before it became obvious that his greatness lay in batting. He kept wicket occasionally. When he turned out for Glamorgan the locals called him 'the Prince of Wales'.

Test batting and fielding

T	I	NO	R	HS	Av.	100	50	Ct	St
124	189	21	8832	280*	52.57	23	43	93	1

Test bowling

T	I	B	R	W	BBI	BBM	Av.
124	36	1470	682	17	3–74	5–94	40.11

First-class batting and fielding

M	I	NO	R	HS	Av.	100	50	Ct	St
402	632	95	28,663	311	53.37	80	139	341	3

First-class bowling

M	B	R	W	BBI	Av.
402	12,690	6507	191	7–39	34.06

ODI batting and fielding

M	I	NO	R	HS	Av.	100	50	Ct	St
233	218	41	7381	119*	41.70	8	50	71	2

(He took 7 ODI wickets for 297, average 42.42: best 2-22)

INZAMAM-UL-HAQ
(b.1970) *Faisalabad, Lahore, Multan*

Only Javed has scored more Test runs for Pakistan than Inzy, one of the finest right-hand bats of his time. He made important contributions to Pakistan's 1992 World Cup win before establishing himself in the Test side. Ten years later he made his highest score against New Zealand. A portly figure, sensitive about his build, he took unkindly to hecklers likening him to a potato during a match in Canada. He also took unkindly to umpire Darrell Hair's allegations of ball-tampering at the Oval in 2006 and became the first

ABOVE *Inzamam (the 'Sultan of Multan') cuts a ball to the boundary against the West Indies in his home city in 2006. He retired from Test cricket in 2007, having only just failed to beat Javed Miandad's all-time run record.*

captain to forfeit a Test match. But, stroppy or not, he was a powerful and – for his bulk – graceful player, especially against pace. In his 100th Test he scored 184 against India. A lousy runner between the wickets, though, as many of his partners can testify. Still, not even Javed has scored more hundreds for Pakistan.

Test batting and fielding

T	I	NO	R	HS	Av.	100	50	Ct
119	198	22	8829	329	50.16	25	46	81

(A slow left-armer, he bowled nine balls and took 0-8 in Tests)

First-class batting and fielding

M	I	NO	R	HS	Av.	100	50	Ct
245	393	58	16,785	329	50.10	45	87	172

First-class bowling

M	B	R	W	BBI	Av.
245	2704	1295	38	5–80	34.07

ODI batting and fielding

M	I	NO	R	HS	Av.	100	50	Ct
378	350	53	11,739	137*	39.52	10	83	113

(Bowling: 3-64, average 21.33, best 1-0)

MOHAMMAD YOUSUF

(b.1974) *Bahawalpur, Lahore, Lancashire, Pakistan International Airlines*

At the time of writing (spring 2009) Mohammad Yousuf (Yousuf Youhana before he converted from Christianity to Islam in 2005) has the highest Test batting average of any Pakistani. He also holds the world record for most Test runs and centuries in a calendar year (1788 runs, average 99.33, nine hundreds, 2006). A punishing right-hand bat with a splendid technique, he has scored a Test 50 off 27 balls, hit a century in each innings against West Indies (2006) and broke Bradman's record of six hundreds in consecutive Tests by doing it in five matches instead of six. He made two double-centuries (including his highest score at Lahore, 2005) against England, one against Bangladesh and has been dismissed three times in the 190s.

BELOW Mohammad Yousuf kneels in celebration of his second hundred of the match, Pakistan vs the West Indies, third Test, Karachi, 30 November 2006. During this match Yousuf not only broke Viv Richards's long-standing record for the most Test runs in a calendar year, but also established a new record for the most Test hundreds in a year (nine).

Test batting and fielding

T	I	NO	R	HS	Av.	100	50	Ct
79	134	12	6770	223	55.49	23	28	59

First-class batting and fielding

M	I	NO	R	HS	Av.	100	50	Ct
122	202	20	9354	223	51.39	28	44	77

ODI batting and fielding

M	I	NO	R	HS	Av.	100	50	Ct
269	254	40	9242	141*	43.18	15	62	53

(Yousuf's off-breaks are little used. He has bowled one over in Tests (0-3), two balls in ODIs (1-1), and three first-class overs (0-24).)

THE BOWLERS

FAZAL MAHMOOD

(1927–2005) *Lahore, Northern India, Punjab*

Fazal has a secure place in Pakistan cricketing legend as 'the hero of the Oval', because it was there in 1954 that he took 12 for 99 to secure a drawn series and his country's first win over England. The following year he did even better – taking 13 for 114 at Karachi as Pakistan beat Australia for the first time. His first-class career began in Northern India and in fact he was picked to tour Australia with India in 1947–8 but by then Partition had taken place and he opted for Pakistan. He was right-arm fast-medium, similar in style to Alec Bedser, mixing swing and seam with sharp leg-cutters, and his country's first great bowler.

Test bowling

T	I	B	R	W	BBI	BBM	Av.
34	53	9834	3434	139	7-42	13-114	24.70

Test batting and fielding

T	I	NO	R	HS	Av.	100	50	Ct
34	50	6	620	60	14.09	0	1	11

First-class bowling

M	B	R	W	BBI	Av.
112	25,932	8837	466	9-43	18.96

First-class batting and fielding

M	I	NO	R	HS	Av.	100	50	Ct
112	147	33	2662	100*	23.35	1	13	39

PAKISTAN'S TEST RECORDS

Tests – played 337; won 103, lost 89, drawn 145.   ODIs – played 693; won 375, lost 297, tied 6, no result 15.

Pakistan's highest Test total is 708 vs England, the Oval, 1987; the lowest 53 vs Australia, Sharjah, 2002.

Highest individual Test scores

	R	Opp.	Ground	Match date
Hanif Mohammad	337	West Indies	Bridgetown	17 Jan. 1958
Inzamam-ul-Haq	329	New Zealand	Lahore	1 May 2002
Younis Khan	313	Sri Lanka	Karachi	21 Feb. 2009
Javed Miandad	280*	India	Hyderabad (Sind)	14 Jan. 1983
Zaheer Abbas	274	England	Edgbaston	3 June 1971

Most Test appearances

	T
Javed Miandad	124
Inzamam-ul-Haq	119
Wasim Akram	104
Saleem Malik	103
Imran Khan	88

Highest Test batting averages
(qualification: 15 Tests or more)

	T	Av.
Mohammad Yousuf	79	55.49
Javed Miandad	124	52.57
Younis Khan	60	51.80
Inzamam-ul-Haq	119	50.16
Saeed Anwar	55	45.52

Most Test centuries

	T	100s
Inzamam-ul-Haq	119	25
Javed Miandad	124	23
Mohammad Yousuf	79	23
Younis Khan	60	16
Saleem Malik	103	15

Highest individual run-scorers in Tests

	Span	T	I	NO	R	HS	Av.
Javed Miandad	1976–93	124	189	21	8832	280*	52.57
Inzamam-ul-Haq	1992–2007	119	198	22	8829	329	50.16
Mohammad Yousuf	1998–2007	79	134	12	6770	223	55.49
Saleem Malik	1982–99	103	154	22	5768	237	43.69
Younis Khan	2000–9	60	106	7	5129	313	51.80

Highest Test partnerships

	R	W	Opp.	Ground	Match date
Mudassar Nazar, Javed Miandad	451	3	India	Hyderabad (Sind)	14 Jan. 1983
Qasim Umar, Javed Miandad	397	3	Sri Lanka	Faisalabad	16 Oct. 1985
Younis Khan, Mohammad Yousuf	363	3	England	Headingley	4 Aug. 2006
Ijaz Ahmed, Inzamam-ul-Haq	352*	3	Sri Lanka	Dhaka	12 Mar. 1999
Mushtaq Mohammad, Asif Iqbal	350	4	New Zealand	Dunedin	7 Feb. 1973

Highest Test wicket-takers

	T	B	R	W	BBI	Av.
Wasim Akram	1985–2002	104	22,627	9779	414	7–119	23.62
Waqar Younis	1989–2003	87	16,224	8788	373	7–76	23.56
Imran Khan	1971–92	88	19,458	8258	362	8–58	22.81
Abdul Qadir	1977–90	67	17,126	7742	236	9–56	32.80
Danish Kaneria	2000–9	53	15,608	7846	225	7–77	34.87

Note: Abdul Qadir took 9–56 vs England, Lahore, 1987 and Sarfraz Nawaz 9–86 vs Australia, Melbourne, 1979. Imran Khan's 14–116 vs Sri Lanka in 1982 are the best match figures and his 40 at 13.95 vs India in 1982–3 is the largest number of victims in a series.

Most Test ducks

	T	I	NO	0s
Danish Kaneria	53	69	31	23
Waqar Younis	87	120	21	21
Wasim Bari	81	112	26	19
Wasim Akram	104	147	19	17
Inzamam-ul-Haq	119	198	22	14
Mushtaq Ahmed	52	72	16	14

Most dismissals by a wicketkeeper in a Test career

		T	W	Ct	St
Wasim Bari	1967–84	81	228	201	27

Most catches by a fielder in a Test career

	T	Ct
Javed Miandad	124	93

Leading all-rounders (1000 runs [at an average of 20 or more] and 100 wickets)

	T	R	Bat. Av.	W	Bowl. Av.	Tests for 1000/100
Abdul Razzaq	46	1946	28.61	100	36.94	43
Imran Khan	88	3807	37.69	362	22.81	30
Intikhab Alam	47	1493	22.28	125	35.95	41
Wasim Akram	104	2898	22.64	414	23.62	45

BELOW *Pakistan's record Test wicket–taker Wasim Akram and record Test run–scorer Javed Miandad pose in Lahore, November 2000, when former captain Miandad was coaching the national side.*

ABDUL QADIR
(b.1955) *Habib Bank, Lahore and Punjab*

Qadir was the first Pakistani bowler to take 200 Test wickets and in the late 1970s and early 80s, when he was virtually its sole exponent at the top level, he revived the moribund art of leg-spin bowling. He was an attacking bowler – reckoned by Graham Gooch to be quite as good as Shane Warne – who mastered all the leggie's arts, including two different googlies. In 1983–4 his 19 wickets in three matches brought about Pakistan's first series win over England; he took ten in the match at the Oval in 1987, as Pakistan won another series, and surpassed all his previous achievements by returning his best-ever figures, also against England, at Lahore that same year. He was a feisty character with attitude and a fair bat, too.

Test bowling								
T	I	B	R	W	BBI	BBM		Av.
67	111	17,126	7742	236	9-56	13-101		32.80

Test batting and fielding								
T	I	NO	R	HS	Av.	100	50	Ct
67	77	11	1029	61	15.59	0	3	15

First-class bowling					
M	B	R	W	BBI	Av.
209	48,769	22,314	960	9-49	23.24

First-class batting and fielding								
M	I	NO	R	HS	Av.	100	50	Ct
209	247	43	3740	112	18.33	2	8	83

ODI bowling					
M	B	R	W	BB	Av.
104	5100	3454	132	5-44	26.16

ODI batting and fielding								
M	I	NO	R	HS	Av.	100	50	Ct
104	68	26	641	41*	15.26	0	0	21

WASIM AKRAM
(b.1966) *Lahore and Lancashire*

Wasim probably qualifies as an all-rounder but essentially he was a great left-arm fast bowler and, along with Sarfraz Nawaz, a pioneer of reverse swing. He made his Test debut against New Zealand in 1985, having been plucked from obscurity on the insistence of Javed Miandad, and took 10 wickets in his second game. He was a master of line, length and swing, who along with Waqar Younis made up a truly formidable opening attack for his country. In 1992 he was man of the match when Pakistan won the World Cup. He took more wickets in Tests than any other Pakistan bowler and held the world record number in ODIs until Murali pipped him in 2008–9. His highest Test score was against Zimbabwe. For 10 years from 1988 he was the mainstay of Lancashire's bowling but towards the end of his career controversy attended him. In 1992 he and Waqar were suspected of ball-tampering and in 1999 he was accused of match-fixing. In neither case, though, was anything proved.

LEFT *Abdul Qadir on his way to figures of 13 for 101 against England, first Test, Lahore, November 1987.*

[Wasim Akram, career statistics]							
Test bowling							
T	I	B	R	W	BBI	BBM	Av.
104	181	22,627	9779	414	7–119	11–110	23.62
Test batting and fielding							
T	I	NO	R	HS	Av.	100	50	Ct
104	147	19	2898	257*	22.64	3	7	44
First-class bowling							
M	B	R	W	BBI	Av.		
257	50,277	22,549	1042	8–30	21.64		
First-class batting and fielding							
M	I	NO	R	HS	Av.	100	50	Ct
257	355	40	7161	257*	22.73	7	24	97
ODI bowling							
M	B	R	W	BB	Av.		
356	18,186	11,812	502	5–15	23.52		
ODI batting and fielding							
M	I	NO	R	HS	Av.	100	50	Ct
356	280	55	3717	86	16.52	0	6	88

WAQAR YOUNIS
(b.1969) *Karachi, Lahore, Multan and Glamorgan*

Waqar was one of the deadliest of all right-arm fast bowlers. Together, he and Wasim Akram made up just about the most fearsome Test opening attack of the 1990s. Not that he and Wasim always got along well – especially when Wasim was captain and Waqar stayed out of the team for a while. He was extremely quick, maybe one of the quickest ever, had the best strike rate (43.4 balls per wicket) of any bowler who has taken more than 200 Test wickets, was adept at reverse swing and dealt a vicious bouncer and an equally vicious inswinging yorker. Indeed, the yorker – aimed at the batsmen's feet or the base of the stumps, whichever he happened to hit first – was probably his trademark delivery. But for back injuries – the fast bowler's curse – his record, impressive as it is *(see overleaf)*, would have been even better.

BELOW *Waqar Younis hurls himself into a delivery against Australia at Adelaide in 1999.*

HOWZAT! Ian Botham took a highly equivocal view of the Pakistan sides he faced: 'They've always had a lot of talent, a lot of good players, but they're like eleven women. You know, they're all scratching each other's eyes out.'

[Waqar Younis, career statistics]

Test bowling

T	I	B	R	W	BBI	BBM	Av.
87	154	16,224	8788	373	7-76	13-135	23.56

Test batting and fielding

T	I	NO	R	HS	Av.	100	50	Ct
87	120	21	1010	45	10.20	0	0	18

First-class bowling

M	B	R	W	BBI	Av.
228	39,182	21.350	956	8-17	22.33

First-class batting and fielding

M	I	NO	R	HS	Av.	100	50	Ct
228	283	61	2972	64	13.38	0	6	58

ODI bowling

M	B	R	W	BB	Av.
262	12,698	9919	416	7-36	23.84

ODI batting and fielding

M	I	NO	R	HS	Av.	100	50	Ct
262	139	45	969	37	10.30	0	0	35

THE ALL-ROUNDERS

MUSHTAQ MOHAMMAD
(b.1943) *Pakistan International Airlines, Karachi and Northamptonshire*

A younger brother of Hanif, Mushtaq – a leg-spinner and right-hand bat – made his first-class debut at 13 years and 41 days (did his Mummy know what he was up to?), scoring 87 and taking five wickets for 28. He was 15 when he made his Test debut and 17 when he scored his first Test century. Even allowing for the fact that there is some doubt about his actual date of birth, he was still bloody young when he did all those things. He was a prolific and versatile player – the first Pakistani to score 25,000 first-class runs, captain of

Northants when they won the Gillette Cup in 1976, a more attacking batsman than Hanif but just as steadfast in defence and a fine leg-spinner in an age when leg spin was out of fashion. His top score was against New Zealand in 1972–3. Both as batsman and bowler he was worthy of a place in the Test team, which is the hallmark of the best all-rounders.

Test batting and fielding

T	I	NO	R	HS	Av.	100	50	Ct
57	100	7	3643	201	39.17	10	19	42

Test bowling

T	I	B	R	W	BBI	BBM	Av.
57	70	5260	2309	79	5-28	9-119	29.22

First-class batting and fielding

M	I	NO	R	HS	Av.	100	50	Ct
502	843	104	31,091	303*	42.07	72	159	349

First-class bowling

M	B	R	W	BBI	Av.
502	47,226	22,789	936	7-18	24.34

ODI batting and fielding

M	I	NO	R	HS	Av.	100	50	Ct
10	9	3	209	55	34.83	0	1	3

(He bowled 7 overs, taking 0-23)

IMRAN KHAN
(b.1952) *Lahore, Worcestershire, Sussex, New South Wales and Oxford University*

Imran was a right-hand bat and right-arm fast bowler and the finest cricketer Pakistan has yet produced. His bowling average is up there with the best of modern times and his batting was pretty good, too. Indeed, his averages are better than those of Botham, Hadlee and Kapil Dev. He was the pin-up boy of Pakistan cricket, captain of the World Cup-winning team in 1992, a hard-hitting batsman and a very quick bowler. In his final 51 Tests he averaged 50 with the bat and 19 with the ball. He played most of his first-class cricket in England, swanning back home to represent and lead his country. In a 20-year Test career, he was the first Pakistani to take 300 Test wickets and the second fastest player, after Botham (75 Tests compared to 72) to complete the double of 3000 runs and 300 wickets. In 1982 he captained Pakistan to their first series win in England and in 1987 to their first series win in India. In 1995 he married billionaire's daughter Jemima Goldsmith (it didn't last) and on his retirement went into politics, forming his own party and becoming an MP.

BELOW *Pakistan's Imran Khan rounded off an illustrious two decades as an international cricketer by defeating England in the Cricket World Cup in Melbourne in 1992. The team he captained fared well against the all-conquering West Indians in the 1980s, and in 1987 he secured a first series win for Pakistan in England.*

Test batting and fielding

T	I	NO	R	HS	Av.	100	50	Ct
88	126	25	3807	136	37.69	6	18	28

Test bowling

T	I	B	R	W	BBI	BBM	Av.
88	142	19,458	8258	362	8–58	14–116	22.81

First-class batting and fielding

M	I	NO	R	HS	Av.	100	50	Ct
382	582	99	17,771	170	36.79	30	93	117

First-class bowling

M	B	R	W	BBI	Av.
382	65,224	28,726	1287	8–34	22.32

ODI batting and fielding

M	I	NO	R	HS	Av.	100	50	Ct
175	151	40	3709	102*	33.41	1	19	36

ODI bowling

M	B	R	W	BB	Av.
175	7461	4844	182	6–14	26.61

CHAPTER II
CRICKET IN SRI LANKA,
ZIMBABWE AND BANGLADESH

PLUS PROFILES OF SRI LANKA'S
AND ZIMBABWE'S ALL-TIME GREATS

CRICKET IN SRI LANKA

Until 1972 Sri Lanka was called Ceylon and made a nice staging-post for MCC teams on their way by ship to Australia. They'd get off the boat, find their land-legs, casually beat Ceylon in a three-day match at Colombo and go on their way. This was a tradition that had begun with Ceylon's initial first-class match in 1926/7 when the MCC won by an innings.

But in 1981 Sri Lanka was granted Test status and things have been different since then. Not so much at first – they were regarded as something of a pushover in those early days. But they won the World Cup in 1996, much to everyone's surprise, and since then they've been nobody's mugs.

One-day cricket is their forte – World Cup runners-up in 2007, joint winners with India of the 2002 ICC Champions Trophy, 5–0 brownwashers of England in the 2006 NatWest Series and soon afterwards makers of the highest score (443) in ODIs. All right, they were only playing the Netherlands, but nobody else had made that many.

In the early Test days Sri Lanka were particularly noted for elegant, wristy batsmen and lots of people called de Silva, most notable among these being Aravinda de Silva, who scored three Test hundreds before he was 21.

Ranatunga's revolution

The nation's first captain was Bandula Warnapura, who rather screwed up his Test career by joining a rebel tour of South Africa in 1982–3. He was succeeded by Duleep Mendis. But it was under Arjuna Ranatunga that Sri Lanka became a force in international cricket, winning the 1996 World Cup by the expedient of using the heavy-hitting Sanath Jayasuriya to hammer the bowlers in the first 15 overs of fielding restrictions. Nobody else had thought of that. Ranatunga is the man who injected steel into Sri Lanka's backbone. When in 1999 the Aussie umpire Ross Emerson called Muttiah Muralitharan for throwing in an ODI against England, Ranatunga argued vociferously and withdrew his team to the boundary before being persuaded to continue the game. The message was clear: nobody messes with Sri Lanka – not now. Not surprising that when he retired from cricket Ranatunga went into politics.

Sri Lanka's Test record is not unduly impressive, but they have won more than 50 per cent of their ODIs and in either form of the game have become a hard side to beat, especially at home where the pitches seem to turn nicely for Muralitharan and the other spinners. Sri Lanka has had a fine fast-medium left-arm opening bowler in Chaminda Vaas (and gifted batsmen in Mahela

FAR LEFT *The ramparts of the former Portuguese fort at Galle on the southern coast of Sri Lanka make an excellent vantage point for watching cricket at the nearby Galle International Stadium. Here, silhouetted against the setting sun, spectators line the walls during the third and final Test of England's 2007 tour of Sri Lanka. This was the first Test match played at the ground after it was devastated by the Indian Ocean tsunami of 2004.*

Jayawardene and Kumar Sangakkara), but Muralitharan was their match-winner and bowler of most of their overs – until 2008 when the 23-year-old Ajantha Mendis, slow-medium purveyor of a bewildering variety of spin, came along to take 26 Indian wickets in three Tests at 18.38. Towards the end of 2008, despite the protests of Arjuna Ranatunga, then chairman of the cricket board, Sri Lanka, who had only played six Tests that year, cancelled a tour of England the following spring because so many of their players were contracted to the IPL, thus underlining the rapid rise to power of big-money Twenty20 cricket, especially in Asia. On the other hand they did agree to tour Pakistan in spring 2009, only to fall foul of a terrorist attack in Lahore (see page 186).

The domestic first-class competition in Sri Lanka is the Premier Trophy. Inaugurated in 1938, it has gone under various names since. The Sinhalese Sports Club has won it 29 times (one title shared) and the Nondescript Sports Club 13 times (one shared). The 2008–9 winners were were the Colts, their fifth such success.

BELOW *Aravinda de Silva and skipper Arjuna Ranatunga (both in helmets) are mobbed by their team-mates after guiding Sri Lanka to a seven-wicket victory over Australia in the World Cup final in Lahore, 17 March 1996.*

In a comparatively short time as a test-playing nation Sri Lanka have produced a number of extremely fine players. Let's look at…

THE BATSMEN

ARJUNA RANATUNGA
(b.1963) *Sinhalese Sports Club*

Arjuna Ranatunga's claim to prominence lies less in his batting (which fell short) than in his all-round influence on the development of Sri Lankan cricket. At 18 he played in his country's first Test in 1982 and made its first half-century. More significantly, with his innovative and confrontational style of leadership it was he who turned the national team from underdogs to winners and he was always a formidable opponent, especially – as we have seen – when captain, a position he held for 11 years. He was a masterly, if portly, tactician, a left-hand batsman, with a good off-drive and a knack for finding gaps in the field on either side of the wicket. Not a bad right-arm medium bowler either. Razor-sharp fitness was not exactly high on

his agenda and he was much inclined to call for a runner when he'd been batting for a little while and got a bit tired (see also page 280).

ARAVINDA DE SILVA
(b.1965) *Nondescripts, Auckland and Kent*

A very small man (5' 3"), Aravinda de Silva was Sri Lanka's first truly outstanding player, an immortal hero to his fellow-countrymen for scoring a century and taking three wickets in the triumphant 1996 World Cup final. In Tests he made his debut against England in 1984, hit his highest score against New Zealand in 1991 and, in his final game, made another double-century, against Bangladesh, and took a wicket with his last delivery. Twice he scored a hundred in each innings of a Test, on one occasion, versus Pakistan, making 138 and 105, both not out, to become the only player to score two not-out hundreds in the same match. De Silva was a dashing, stylish right-hand bat, a redoubtable hooker and cutter, and a tidy off-spinner. In 1995 he had a terrific season with Kent, hitting 1661 runs at an average of 59.32.

Test batting and fielding

T	I	NO	R	HS	Av.	100	50	Ct
93	155	12	5105	135*	35.69	4	38	47

Test bowling

T	I	B	R	W	BBI	BBM	Av.
93	56	2373	1040	16	2-17	2-20	65.00

First-class batting and fielding

M	I	NO	R	HS	Av.	100	50	Ct
205	295	32	11,641	238*	44.26	25	63	111

First-class bowling

M	B	R	W	BBI	Av.
205	7096	3085	94	5-45	32.81

ODI batting and fielding

M	I	NO	R	HS	Av.	100	50	Ct
269	255	47	7456	131*	35.84	4	49	63

ODI bowling

M	B	R	W	BB	Av.
269	4710	3757	79	4-14	47.55

Test batting and fielding

T	I	NO	R	HS	Av.	100	50	Ct
93	159	11	6361	267	42.97	20	22	43

Test bowling

T	I	B	R	W	BBI	BBM	Av.
93	58	2595	1208	29	3-30	3-34	41.65

First-class batting and fielding

M	I	NO	R	HS	Av.	100	50	Ct
220	343	33	15,000	267	48.38	43	71	108

First-class bowling

M	B	R	W	BBI	Av.
220	9005	3763	129	7-24	29.17

ODI batting and fielding

M	I	NO	R	HS	Av.	100	50	Ct
308	296	30	9284	145	34.90	11	64	95

ODI bowling

M	B	R	W	BB	Av.
308	5148	4177	106	4-30	39.40

SRI LANKA'S TEST RECORDS

Tests – played 184; won 56, lost 67, drawn 61.
ODIs – played 577; won 266, lost 286, tied 3, no result 22.

Sri Lanka's highest Test total is 952–6d vs India, Colombo, 1997; the lowest 71 vs Pakistan, Kandy, 1994.
Note: Sri Lanka's Colombo score is the highest innings total in Test match history.

Most Test appearances

	T
M. Muralitharan	126
S.T. Jayasuriya	110
W.P.U.J.C. Vaas	110

Highest Test batting averages
(qualification: 15 Tests or more)

	T	Av.
K.C. Sangakkara	80	54.99
D.P.M.D. Jayawardene	102	53.23
T.T. Samaraweera	59	51.07

Most Test centuries

	T	100s
D.P.M.D. Jayawardene	102	25
P.A. de Silva	93	20
K.C. Sangakkara	80	18

Most Test ducks

	T	I	NO	0s
M. Muralitharan	126	155	53	32
M.S. Atapattu	90	156	15	22
G.P. Wickramasinghe	40	64	5	17

Most dismissals by a wicketkeeper in a Test career

	Span	T	W	Ct	St
K.C. Sangakkara	2000–9	80	149	129	20

Most catches by a fielder in a Test career

	T	Ct
D.P.M.D. Jayawardene	102	142

Highest individual Test scores

	R	Opp.	Ground	Match date
D.P.M.D. Jayawardene	374	South Africa	Colombo (SSC)	27 July 2006
S.T. Jayasuriya	340	India	Colombo (RPS)	2 Aug. 1997
K.C. Sangakkara	287	South Africa	Colombo (SSC)	27 July 2006

Highest individual run-scorers in Tests

		T	I	NO	R	HS	Av.
D.P.M.D. Jayawardene	1997–2009	102	167	12	8251	374	53.23
S.T. Jayasuriya	1991–2007	110	188	14	6973	340	40.07
K.C. Sangakkara	2000–9	80	132	9	6764	287	54.99

Highest Test partnerships

	R	W	Opp.	Ground	Match date
K.C. Sangakkara, D.P.M.D. Jayawardene	624	3	South Africa	Colombo (SSC)	27 July 2006
S.T. Jayasuriya, R.S. Mahanama	576	2	India	Colombo (RPS)	2 Aug. 1997
M.S. Atapattu, K.C. Sangakkara	438	2	Zimbabwe	Bulawayo	14 May 2004
D.P.M.D. Jayawardene, T.T. Samaraweera	437	4	Pakistan	Karachi	21 Feb. 2009
M.S. Atapattu, S.T. Jayasuriya	335	1	Pakistan	Kandy	28 June 2000

Highest Test wicket-takers

		T	B	R	W	BBI	Av.
M. Muralitharan	1992–2009	126	41,696	16,924	765	9–51	22.12
W.P.U.J.C. Vaas	1994–2009	110	23,204	10,411	354	7–71	29.40
S.T. Jayasuriya	1991–2007	110	8188	3366	98	5–34	34.34

Note: Muralitharan is the country's (and the world's) most successful bowler. Against Zimbabwe at Kandy, 2002, he took 9–51 and vs England at the Oval in 1998 he had 9–65. His overall figures in the same match were 16–220, another Sri Lanka record. (In 126 matches he has taken five wickets in an innings 66 times and ten in a match on 22 occasions.)

Leading all-rounders (1000 runs [at an average of 20 or more] and 100 wickets)

	T	R	Bat. Av.	W	Bowl. Av.	Tests for 1000/100
W.P.U.J.C. Vaas	110	3085	24.48	354	29.40	47

Kumar Sangakkara (left) and Mahela Jayawardene steal another run during their record-breaking third-wicket partnership in the first Test against South Africa at Colombo, 29 July 2006. Their stand of 624 – the highest for any wicket in first-class cricket, and the first instance of a stand of 600 or more in a first-class or Test match innings – set up a crushing victory over the visitors by an innings and 153 runs.

MAHELA JAYAWARDENE
(b.1977) *Sinhalese Sports Club*

Among Jayawardene's achievements are Sri Lanka's highest individual score and, in 2006, captaining the side to a five-nil ODI 'brownwash' of England. Also in that year his 119 at Lord's helped Sri Lanka recover from almost certain defeat to draw the Test. He is an excitingly stylish right-hand bat who, again as captain, led his country to the 2007 World Cup final, which they lost to Australia. He made his debut against India in 1997 when he contributed 66 towards Sri Lanka's world-record total of 952 for 6. While making his own highest score, against South Africa in 2006, he and Kumar Sangakkara shared a stand of 624, the highest for any wicket in the first-class game. He bowls right-arm medium, though not often at the top level, and is a fine close fielder.

Test batting and fielding

T	I	NO	R	HS	Av.	100	50	Ct
102	167	12	8251	374	53.23	25	32	142

(He has taken 5 Test wickets for 273, average 54.60; best 2-32)

First-class batting and fielding

M	I	NO	R	HS	Av.	100	50	Ct
183	288	21	13,960	374	52.28	42	60	232

First-class bowling

M	B	R	W	BBI	Av.
183	2911	1576	51	5-72	30.90

ODI batting and fielding

M	I	NO	R	HS	Av.	100	50	Ct
299	280	29	8042	128	32.03	10	49	159

(He has taken 7 wickets for 558, average 79.71; best 2-56)

THE BOWLERS

MUTTIAH MURALITHARAN
(b.1972) *Kandurata, Kent and Lancashire*

It's hard to know what to say about Murali. He is, and probably always will be, the most successful Test bowler ever, but... With the changes in the Laws his action is certainly legal now but doubts will remain about

ABOVE *Flanked by Thilan Samaraweera (left) and Tillakaratne Dilshan, Muttiah Muralitharan awaits the decision of the third umpire during the second Test between India and Sri Lanka at Galle, 1 August 2008.*

whether it was ever thus and indeed about whether the changes were really necessary except for him. To describe him as a right-arm off-spinner is to overlook his doosra and a great variety of other deliveries. He is a remarkable spinner of the ball with an unusually flexible wrist, happy to bowl marathon spells – the first Sri

Test bowling

T	I	B	R	W	BBI	BBM	Av.
126	218	41,696	16,924	765	9-51	16-220	22.12

Test batting and fielding

T	I	NO	R	HS	Av.	100	50	Ct
126	155	53	1176	67	11.52	0	1	67

First-class bowling

M	B	R	W	BBI	Av.
226	64,914	25,898	1344	9-51	19.26

First-class batting and fielding

M	I	NO	R	HS	Av.	100	50	Ct
226	269	80	2109	67	11.15	0	1	120

ODI bowling

M	B	R	W	BB	Av.
329	17,713	11,485	505	7-30	22.74

ODI batting and fielding

M	I	NO	R	HS	Av.	100	50	Ct
329	154	59	610	33*	6.42	0	0	127

Lankan to reach 100 Test wickets and the fastest of any bowler to 400 and then 500. Whatever you might think of his action (see page 274), he is undoubtedly exciting to watch, forever on the attack, cleverly varying flight, spin and pace, eyeballs bulging, froglike, with enthusiasm and determination. God knows how Sri Lanka would have fared without him; he's probably won more matches single-handed than any other bowler in Test history. And if more than 160 of his wickets were taken against Zimbabwe and Bangladesh, he has also reaped 100-plus against both England and South Africa.

CHAMINDA VAAS
(b.1974) *Basnahira North, Colts, Hampshire, Middlesex and Worcestershire*

Vaas, who also qualifies as a very useful all-rounder, has no rival as Sri Lanka's finest opening bowler. Indeed, until the emergence in 2008 of a new spinner in Ajantha Mendis, Vaas and Muralitharan virtually *were* the Sri Lanka attack. Vaas bowls left-arm fast-medium, swings and seams the ball cleverly and has a most unpleasant late in-dipper. He can reverse-swing it, too, and he's also a pretty skilful left-hand batsman.

Test bowling

T	I	B	R	W	BBI	BBM	Av.
110	192	23,204	10,411	354	7-71	14-191	29.40

Test batting and fielding

T	I	NO	R	HS	Av.	100	50	Ct
110	161	35	3085	100*	24.48	1	13	30

First-class bowling

M	B	R	W	BBI	Av.
193	36,185	16,599	666	7-54	24.92

First-class batting and fielding

M	I	NO	R	HS	Av.	100	50	Ct
193	262	56	5368	134	26.05	4	24	53

ODI bowling

M	B	R	W	BB	Av.
322	15,775	11,014	400	8-19	27.53

ODI batting and fielding

M	I	NO	R	HS	Av.	100	50	Ct
322	220	72	2025	50*	13.68	0	1	60

His bowling helped Sri Lanka to their first overseas Test win (against New Zealand, 1994–5) and against West Indies in 2001–2 he took 26 wickets in three Tests. Twice in ODIs he has done the hat-trick and he was the first person to take eight wickets in an ODI. True, this was against Zimbabwe just as his maiden Test century (in his 97th match) was against Bangladesh, but an eight-for and a hundred are still worth cherishing, whatever the opposition.

THE ALL-ROUNDERS

HASHAN TILLAKARATNE
(b.1967) *Nondescripts*

Hashan Tillakaratne was a talented left-hand bat and, in the early part of his career, a good wicketkeeper, too. Later on he took to bowling right-arm off-breaks, though not so you'd notice it in international matches. Neither as batsman nor 'keeper was he in the very highest class but he was an important figure in the development of Sri Lanka as a force in international cricket. His Test debut was against Australia in 1989 and he kept wicket until 1994, after which he emerged more fully as a Test-class middle-order batsman. In 2003 he was appointed captain of the national team but won only one of 10 matches – though that victory did clinch a series win over England.

Test batting and fielding

T	I	NO	R	HS	Av.	100	50	Ct	St
83	131	25	4545	204*	42.87	11	20	122	2

(In Tests he took 0–25 in 12.4 overs)

First-class batting and fielding

M	I	NO	R	HS	Av.	100	50	Ct	St
252	351	82	13,253	204*	49.26	37	60	275	7

First-class bowling

M	B	R	W	BBI	Av.
252	2726	1368	41	4-37	33.36

ODI batting and fielding

M	I	NO	R	HS	Av.	100	50	Ct	St
200	168	40	3789	104	29.60	2	13	89	6

(He took 6 wickets for 141, average 23.50: best 1–3)

SANATH JAYASURIYA

(b.1969) *Bloomfield Cricket Club,*
Colombo Cricket Club and Somerset

Jayasuriya was a terrific, attacking left-hand bat, stylish
but inclined to hit the ball with uncompromising power.
His venomous attack on the bowling as an opener in the
1996 World Cup revolutionized ODI tactics. He was
also a shrewd left-arm spinner, especially in ODIs, in
which he is the only player to have scored 12,000 runs
and taken 300 wickets, as well as having made the
fastest 50 (off 17 balls). What's more, versus India in
1997 he made what was then his country's highest Test
score, 340. When Ranatunga was sacked in 1999
Jayasuriya took over the captaincy and led the team 38
times before resigning in 2003. Early in 2006 he retired
from Test cricket but later on, at the urging it seemed of
his country's prime minister, he was added to the Sri
Lanka team touring England and performed well in the
five-nil ODI 'brownwash'. His final Test was against
England at Kandy in 2007 when he scored 78.

KUMAR SANGAKKARA

(b.1977) *Central Province, Colombo District,*
Kandurata and Warwickshire

Sangakkara is a world-champion sledger and the best
all-rounder Sri Lanka has produced. He's a graceful,
heavy-scoring, left-hand batsman and self-made
wicketkeeper, who developed into one of the best in
the game. In Tests he handed over the gloves to
Prasanna Jayawardene in 2006 but continues to 'keep
in ODIs. He's ambidextrous and can bowl right-arm
off-spin, though not a lot. As a number three batsman
he's a huge asset to his team, his highest score – 287
against South Africa in 2006 – being only one of five
Test double-centuries. (That 287 was made during
a world-record partnership of 624 with Mahela
Jayawardene.) In style he has been likened to David
Gower, but his approach is much more acquisitive.

Test batting and fielding

T	I	NO	R	HS	Av.	100	50	Ct
110	188	14	6973	340	40.07	14	31	78

Test bowling

T	I	B	R	W	BBI	BBM	Av.
110	140	8188	3366	98	5–34	9–74	34.34

First-class batting and fielding

M	I	NO	R	HS	Av.	100	50	Ct
261	415	33	14,742	340	38.59	29	70	162

First-class bowling

M	B	R	W	BBI	Av.
261	15,113	6719	205	5–34	32.77

ODI batting and fielding

M	I	NO	R	HS	Av.	100	50	Ct
432	420	18	13,151	189	32.71	28	67	121

ODI bowling

M	B	R	W	BB	Av.
432	14,484	11,504	313	6–29	36.75

Test batting and fielding

T	I	NO	R	HS	Av.	100	50	Ct	St
80	132	9	6764	287	54.99	18	30	153	20

First-class batting and fielding

M	I	NO	R	HS	Av.	100	50	Ct	St
165	261	19	11,148	287	46.06	26	54	314	33

ODI batting and fielding

M	I	NO	R	HS	Av.	100	50	Ct	St
246	229	25	7408	138*	36.31	10	48	227	64

HOWZAT! The names of many Sri Lankan players have to be abbreviated
on scoreboards, but surely one of the longest must belong to an all-rounder
who played just one Test, against England in December 2007: Uda Walawwe
Mahim Bandaralage Chanaka Asanka Welegedara.

When Zimbabwe was known as Southern Rhodesia, its cricket team was a humble provincial side that took part in South Africa's Currie Cup and occasionally provided members of that country's Test team – Colin Bland, for instance (1960s), whose speed and accurate throwing revolutionized fielding, and the Pithey brothers, Tony and David (1950s and 60s).

But after achieving independence in 1980 Zimbabwe, with ideas above its station, applied for and was granted Test status. The results have hardly been entirely happy, although their first Test – a draw against India at Harare in 1992 – was not a bad start.

From day one the team was weak by international standards. Yes, Zimbabwe has produced some good cricketers, notably the wicketkeeper-batsman Andy Flower, Dave Houghton (easily the country's second-best batsman, after Flower) the fast bowler Heath Streak and Graeme Hick. (Hick, however, opted to qualify for England.) Another famous Zimbabwean was Duncan Fletcher, who went on to become England's coach. But apart from Murray Goodwin, Flower's brother Grant and the chicken-farmer Eddo Brandes, a useful bowler, there was no depth to the Zimbabwe side. The political situation, with President Mugabe busily trashing his own country, didn't help either.

A NATION IN DECLINE, A TEAM IN DECLINE

At the 2003 World Cup, jointly hosted by Zimbabwe and South Africa, England refused to play in Zimbabwe, thereby forfeiting a match. In the same tournament Andy Flower and the fast bowler Henry Olonga wore black armbands to mourn 'the death of democracy' in their country, were sacked from the team and sought asylum in England.

Thereafter, with players like Goodwin and others announcing early retirement from international cricket, the Test side went into such decline that late in 2003 Matthew Hayden made the then-Test record score of 380 against them in Australia. In 2004 Streak was fired as captain by the Zimbabwe Cricket Union (ZCU) and 14 other players walked out in protest against what they saw as political interference in the team's selection and management. In 2005 Streak and some of the other rebels were reinstated, but results on the pitch continued to be bad – New Zealand bowled them out twice in a day – the political conflict between players and management continued and at the end of the year the new young captain, Tatenda Taibu, retired in despair from international cricket. By then the standard was so low that, in January 2006, Zimbabwe withdrew from

Test cricket, probably to the relief of everyone else in the ICC. With so many players retiring or, like the Flowers, Streak, Goodwin and the spinner Ray Price, choosing to sign for English counties, the quality in the country's first-class competition, the Logan Cup, and in the one-day Faithwear Cup is said by observers to have fallen below club standard.

Zimbabwe continued to play international one-day cricket and enjoyed occasional success. They beat Australia by five wickets in the World Twenty20 Championship in 2007 and defeated West Indies in an ODI during the 2007–8 season. But mostly they still lose.

In 2008, after the appalling farce of the Zimbabwean presidential election, both South Africa and England decided to cut all cricketing ties with the country and the proposed 2009 tour of England was cancelled. As for the future, the hope is that, with a team currently consisting mostly of players in their early 20s, Zimbabwe might have a decent side in time for the 2011 World Cup. At the end of 2008, however, that hope was looking pretty forlorn.

Zimbabwe has produced a handful of pretty decent Test players – among them Houghton, who scored 1464 runs at 43.05 – but only two who have any claim to be a great deal better than that.

ANDY FLOWER
(b.1968) *Mashonaland, Essex and South Australia*

Andy Flower (pictured above) was by a long way the finest batsman and all-rounder ever to play for Zimbabwe – a proficient wicketkeeper and a right-hand batsman of the highest quality, particularly adept at playing spin. (His younger brother Grant, a left-arm spinner, was a useful all-rounder for his country, too.) In 1994–5 Andy Flower led Zimbabwe to their first Test victory against Pakistan and in 2001 scored 142 and 199 not out against South Africa. Later that year he made 540 runs in a series against India. No Zimbabwean has scored as many Test and ODI runs or can boast a better batting average. Oddity note: like many wicketkeepers, when not behind the stumps he

liked to bowl off-spin, not that he did it very well. After ending his international career for political reasons in 2003 (along with Henry Olonga), he continued (with Grant) to play for Essex and had a season with South Australia. Injury in 2006 brought his career to an end and in 2007 he was appointed assistant coach to the England team. After Peter Moores was sacked in January 2009, he became stand-in coach.

Test batting and fielding									
T	I	NO	R	HS	Av.	100	50	Ct	St
63	112	19	4794	232*	51.54	12	27	151	9

First-class batting and fielding									
M	I	NO	R	HS	Av.	100	50	Ct	St
223	372	69	16,379	271*	54.05	49	75	361	21

ODI batting and fielding									
M	I	NO	R	HS	Av.	100	50	Ct	St
213	208	16	6786	145	35.34	4	55	141	32

(His bowling in Tests was 0–4, in ODIs 0–23, in first-class 7–270, average 38.57 best 1–1)

● HOWZAT! The off-spinner John Traicos played three Tests for South Africa versus Australia in 1970. A record 22 years and 222 days later he made his next Test appearance – for Zimbabwe against India. This is the longest period between Tests in history.

HEATH STREAK
(b.1974) *Matabeleland, Hampshire and Warwickshire*

The only Zimbabwean to take first 100 and then 200 Test wickets, Streak, whose international career ended in 2005, is a whole-hearted fast-medium right-arm bowler with great reserves of stamina, a very handy lower-order batsman and an excellent outfielder. For several years his country's attack pretty much consisted of Streak and anyone else around who was willing to turn his arm over. That being so, his record is extremely respectable. After a couple of stints as captain he finally gave up playing for Zimbabwe because of the political situation there and disagreements with the board. In 2005 he was made captain of Warwickshire but resigned the job early in 2007 and left the county at the end of that season. He has since played in the Indian Cricket League.

Test batting and fielding

T	I	NO	R	HS	Av.	100	50	Ct
65	107	18	1990	127*	22.35	1	11	17

Test bowling

T	I	B	R	W	BBI	BBM	Av.
65	102	13,559	6079	216	6-73	9-72	28.14

First-class batting and fielding

M	I	NO	R	HS	Av.	100	50	Ct
175	264	48	5684	131	26.31	6	27	58

First-class bowling

M	B	R	W	BBI	Av.
175	31,117	14,352	499	7-55	28.76

ODI batting and fielding

M	I	NO	R	HS	Av.	100	50	Ct
189	159	55	2943	79*	28.29	0	13	46

ODI bowling

M	B	R	W	BB	Av.
189	9466	7129	239	5-32	29.82

ZIMBABWE'S TEST RECORDS

Tests – played 83; won 8, lost 49, drawn 26.   ODIs – played 350; won 88, lost 248, tied 5, no result 9.

Zimbabwe's highest Test total is 563–9d vs West Indies, Harare, 2001; the lowest 54 vs South Africa, Cape Town, 2005.

Most Test appearances

	T
G.W. Flower	67

Highest individual Test score

	R	Opp.	Ground	Match date
D.L. Houghton	266	Sri Lanka	Bulawayo	20 Oct. 1994

Highest Test batting average (qualification: 15 Tests or more)

	T	Av.
A. Flower	63	51.54

Highest individual run-scorer in Tests

	Span	T	I	NO	R	HS	Av.
A. Flower	1992–2002	63	112	19	4794	232*	51.54

Most Test centuries

	T	100s
A. Flower	63	12

Most Test ducks

	T	I	NO	0s
G.W. Flower	67	123	6	16

Leading all-rounder (1000 runs [average of more than 20] and 100 wickets)

	T	R	Bat. Av.	W	Bowl. Av.	Tests for 1000/100
H.H. Streak	65	1990	22.35	216	28.14	40

Highest Test partnerships

	R	W	Opp.	Ground	Match date
M.W. Goodwin, A. Flower	277*	5	Pakistan	Bulawayo	14 Mar. 1998
G.W. Flower, A. Flower	269	4	Pakistan	Harare	31 Jan. 1995
G.W. Flower, G.J. Whittall	233*	5	Pakistan	Harare	31 Jan. 1995
A.D.R. Campbell, A. Flower	209	4	India	Nagpur	25 Nov. 2000
A.D.R. Campbell, D.L. Houghton	194	3	Sri Lanka	Harare	26 Oct. 1994

Highest Test wicket-taker

	T	B	R	W	BBI	Av.
H.H. Streak 1993–2005	65	13,559	6079	216	6-73	28.14

Note: Paul Strang took 8–109 in an innings vs New Zealand, Bulawayo, 2000 and A.G. Huckle had 11–255 in a match vs New Zealand, Bulawayo, 1997.

Most dismissals by a wicketkeeper in a Test career

	T	W	Ct	St
A. Flower 1992–2002	63	151	142	9

Most catches by a fielder in a Test career

	T	Ct
A.D.R. Campbell	60	60

CRICKET IN BANGLADESH

Bangladesh became the tenth – and, so far, final – Test nation in 2000 when they played their first game at home against India. They lost by nine wickets. Since then it's been an uphill struggle with only one win in 59 games – and that against a Zimbabwe side soon to drop out of Test cricket.

Such a record has led to demands, in this impatient modern age, that they should be deprived of their Test status. But both India and New Zealand took time to adjust to the game at the highest level, so perhaps Bangladesh should be given a little slack, especially as cricket has overtaken football as the most popular game there. Besides, it's a developing country with a population of anything up to 159 million among whom, surely, there must be world-class players in the making.

Okay, they haven't produced any yet but these are early days. And though their Test record makes gloomy reading they have had their moments of glory in ODIs, such as beating Pakistan during the 1999 World Cup and India in the 2007 tournament, recording a win against Australia in the 2005 NatWest Series and beating Zimbabwe several times. And, already, in Mohammad Rafique, they have one of only 15 players in the world to have taken 100 wickets and scored 1000 runs in both Test and one-day internationals.

Bangladesh's professed aim was to become serious contenders in every form of the game by 2010, but given that in September 2008 six of their Test squad and eight other players had joined the Indian Cricket League, thus opting out of the international game, that seemed pretty unlikely. True, they might have beaten New Zealand in a Test that year (but didn't) and true, too, they put up a spirited fight against Sri Lanka by scoring 413 in the fourth innings only to lose by 107 runs.

But then they began 2009 by losing the next Sri Lanka Test by 465 runs, the fifth-biggest spanking in history, and the worry was that eight years on they didn't seem to be any better than they were when they started, although they could claim one record: their captain Mohammad Ashraful had the lowest batting average (23.82) of anyone who had scored five Test centuries.

With Zimbabwe kicked out of the reckoning Bangladesh had become the whipping-boys of Test cricket, albeit no doubt regarded fondly by opposing players anxious to improve their batting and bowling average. Bangladesh have yet to produce anybody with even a remote claim to greatness. And the way things appear to be, that's not going to change any time soon. But they have the population and the enthusiasm. All we can do is wait and see.

RIGHT *The Bangladesh team await the umpire's ruling on a run-out during a one-day international against the other international cricketing minnow, Zimbabwe, December 2006. Bangladesh won all three of the matches in this series.*

BANGLADESH'S TEST RECORDS

Tests – played 59; won 1, lost 52, drawn 6.
ODIs – played 198; won 44, lost 152, no result 2.

Bangladesh's highest Test total is 488 vs Zimbabwe, Chittagong (MAA), 2005; the lowest 62 vs Sri Lanka, Colombo (PSS), 2007.

Most Test appearances

	T
Habibul Bashar	50

Highest individual Test score

	R	Opp.	Ground	Match date
Mohammad Ashraful	158*	India	Chittagong (MAA)	17 Dec. 2004

Highest Test batting average
(qualification: 15 Tests or more)

	T	Av.
Habibul Bashar	50	30.87

Highest individual run-scorer in Tests

	Span	T	I	NO	R	HS	Av.
Habibul Bashar	2000–8	50	99	1	3026	113	30.87

Most Test centuries

	T	100s
Mohammad Ashraful	48	5

Most Test ducks

	T	I	NO	0s
Mohammad Ashraful	48	93	4	15

Highest Test partnerships

	R	W	Opp.	Ground	Match date
Mohammad Ashraful, Mushfiqur Rahim	191	6	Sri Lanka	Colombo (PSS)	3 July 2007
Shahriar Nafees, Habibul Bashar	187	2	Australia	Fatullah	9 Apr. 2006
Javed Omar, Habibul Bashar	167	2	Pakistan	Peshawar	27 Aug. 2003
Tamim Iqbal, Junaid Siddique	161	1	New Zealand	Dunedin	4 Jan. 2008
Mehrab Hossein jnr, Mushfiqur Rahim	144	5	New Zealand	Chittagong (CDS)	17 Oct. 2008

Highest Test wicket-taker

	T	B	R	W	BBI	Av.
Mohammad Rafique	2000–8	33	8744	4076	100	6–77	40.76

Most dismissals by a wicketkeeper in a Test career

	T	W	Ct	St
Khaled Mashud	2000–7	44	87	78	9

Most catches by a fielder in a Test career

	T	Ct
Habibul Bashar	50	22

Leading all-rounder

	T	R	Bat. Av.	W	Bowl. Av.	Tests for 1000/100
Mohammad Rafique	33	1059	18.57	100	40.76	33

CHAPTER 12
SIX OF THE BEST

CRICKET'S GREATEST MATCHES:
FROM JESSOP'S MATCH OF 1902 TO
THE MIRACLE AT CHENNAI, 2008

W e could begin, I suppose, with England versus Australia at the Oval in 1882. You know – Spofforth 14 for 90, death of English cricket, body cremated, Ashes taken to Australia, all that stuff. But we won't; instead we'll leap forward 20 years to another England–Australia Test at the Oval – Jessop's Match, which was even more exciting and, from an English point of view, had a much happier conclusion.

1 JESSOP'S MATCH

ENGLAND VS AUSTRALIA, THE OVAL, 11–13 AUGUST 1902

This followed the Old Trafford Test, which could be called 'Tate's Match', after the wretched Fred of that ilk, whose son Maurice was later to take 155 wickets and score nearly 1200 runs for England. That was Fred's first Test, his only Test, and he emerged from it as the villain of the piece.

This, remember was the Golden Age, the age in England of Ranji, C.B. Fry, Johnny Tyldesley, Sydney Barnes, Gilbert 'the Croucher' Jessop, George Hirst and the young Wilfred Rhodes, and for Australia of Monty Noble, Clem Hill, Victor Trumper, Hugh Trumble and the young Warwick Armstrong.

But for reasons best known to himself, Lord Hawke, chairman of the England selectors, had discarded Fry, Barnes, Hirst and Jessop for Old Trafford and replaced at least one of them with the honest Sussex yeoman Tate, a slow medium off-spinner. 'My God, look what they've sent me!' said the England captain, Archie MacLaren.

In fact, looking at the statistics, Tate didn't have too bad a match. Batting at number 11, he scored 5 not out and 4, had bowling figures of 11-1-44-0 and 5-3-7-2 and held a catch. Unfortunately, he also dropped a catch, a vital catch, the match-losing catch: a skyer from Joe Darling, the Aussie skipper, to square leg where Tate stood under it – and a split-second later, as it hit the ground, over it. Darling and Syd Gregory then put on 54 (out of a total of 86). Even so, when Tate came in to bat for the second time England needed only eight to win. He edged the first ball for four, survived the next two and was bowled by the fourth. England had lost by three runs – series over, Australia leading two-nil with one to play – and according to his contemporaries and history, it was all Fred's fault.

So to the Oval, where Hirst and Jessop were recalled – and just as well. In Australia's respectable first innings Hirst was the pick of the England bowlers with

FAR LEFT *Andrew Flintoff consoles Brett Lee after England's heart-stopping victory over Australia in the second Test at Edgbaston, 7 August 2005 (see pages 223–225). England's triumph – by a margin of just two runs – squared the series 1–1, and set the scene for perhaps the most nail-bitingly thrilling of all Ashes summers. Having turned the tide at Birmingham, England went on to win one of the remaining three Tests and draw the other two, thereby retaking the Ashes 2–1.*

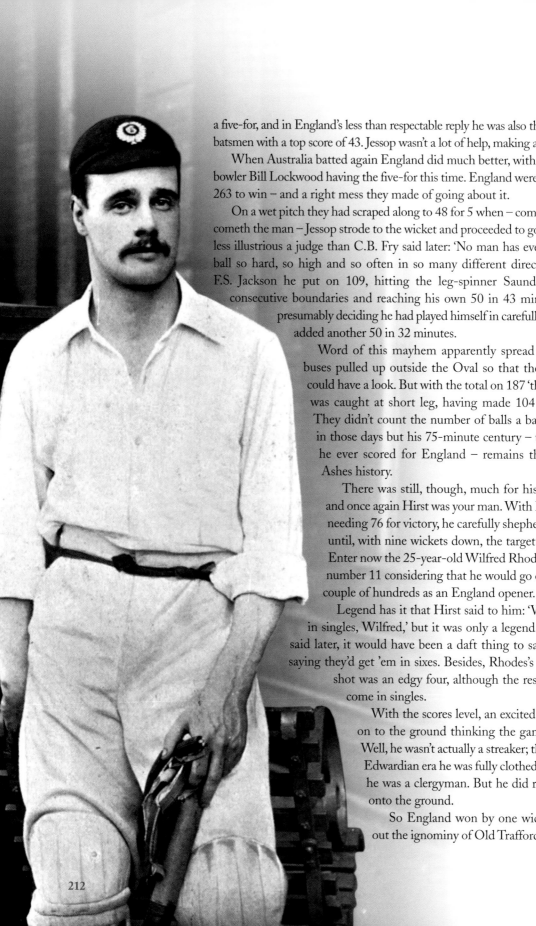

a five-for, and in England's less than respectable reply he was also the pick of the batsmen with a top score of 43. Jessop wasn't a lot of help, making a mere 13.

When Australia batted again England did much better, with the opening bowler Bill Lockwood having the five-for this time. England were left needing 263 to win – and a right mess they made of going about it.

On a wet pitch they had scraped along to 48 for 5 when – cometh the hour, cometh the man – Jessop strode to the wicket and proceeded to go mad. As no less illustrious a judge than C.B. Fry said later: 'No man has ever driven the ball so hard, so high and so often in so many different directions.' With F.S. Jackson he put on 109, hitting the leg-spinner Saunders for four consecutive boundaries and reaching his own 50 in 43 minutes. Then, presumably deciding he had played himself in carefully enough, he added another 50 in 32 minutes.

Word of this mayhem apparently spread so fast that buses pulled up outside the Oval so that the passengers could have a look. But with the total on 187 'the Croucher' was caught at short leg, having made 104 out of 139. They didn't count the number of balls a batsman faced in those days but his 75-minute century – the only one he ever scored for England – remains the fastest in Ashes history.

There was still, though, much for his team to do and once again Hirst was your man. With England still needing 76 for victory, he carefully shepherded the tail until, with nine wickets down, the target stood at 15. Enter now the 25-year-old Wilfred Rhodes, not a bad number 11 considering that he would go on to score a couple of hundreds as an England opener.

Legend has it that Hirst said to him: 'We'll get 'em in singles, Wilfred,' but it was only a legend. As Rhodes said later, it would have been a daft thing to say, as daft as saying they'd get 'em in sixes. Besides, Rhodes's first scoring shot was an edgy four, although the rest did in fact come in singles.

With the scores level, an excited streaker ran on to the ground thinking the game was over. Well, he wasn't actually a streaker; this being the Edwardian era he was fully clothed and anyway he was a clergyman. But he did run excitedly onto the ground.

So England won by one wicket, wiping out the ignominy of Old Trafford. But just as

JESSOP'S MATCH: SCORECARD

Australia: First innings

V.T. Trumper b Hirst	42
R.A. Duff c Lilley b Hirst	23
C. Hill b Hirst	11
J. Darling (capt.) c Lilley b Hirst	3
M.A. Noble c and b Jackson	52
S.E. Gregory b Hirst	23
W.W. Armstrong b Jackson	17
A.J.Y. Hopkins c MacLaren b Lockwood	40
H. Trumble not out	64
J.J. Kelly (wkt) c Rhodes b Braund	39
J.V. Saunders lbw b Braund	0
Extras (b5, lb3, nb2)	10
Total (all out, 123.5 overs)	**324**

Fall of wickets: 1–47, 2–63, 3–69, 4–82, 5–126, 6–174, 7–175, 8–256, 9–324, 10–324
Bowling: Lockwood 24-2-85-1, Rhodes 28-9-46-0, Hirst 29-5-77-5, Braund 16.5-5-29-2, Jackson 20-4-66-2, Jessop 6-2-11-0

Australia: Second innings

Trumper run out	2
Duff b Lockwood	6
Hill c MacLaren b Hirst	34
Darling c MacLaren b Lockwood	15
Noble b Braund	13
Gregory b Braund	9
Armstrong b Lockwood	21
Hopkins c Lilley b Lockwood	3
Saunders c Tyldesley b Rhodes	2
Trumble not out	7
Kelly lbw b Lockwood	0
Extras (b7, lb2)	9
Total (all out, 60 overs)	**121**

Fall of wickets: 1–6, 2–9, 3–31, 4–71, 5–75, 6–91, 7–99, 8–114, 9–115, 10–121
Bowling: Lockwood 20-6-45-5, Rhodes 22-7-38-1, Hirst 5-1-7-1, Braund 9-1-15-2, Jackson 4-3-7-0

England: First innings

A.C. MacLaren (capt.) c Armstrong b Trumble	10
L.C.H. Palairet b Trumble	20
J.T. Tyldesley b Trumble	33
T.W. Hayward b Trumble	0
Hon. F.S. Jackson c Armstrong b Saunders	2
L.C. Braund c Hill b Trumble	22
G.L. Jessop b Trumble	13
G.H. Hirst c and b Trumble	43
W.H. Lockwood c Noble b Saunders	25
A.F.A. Lilley (wkt) c Trumper b Trumble	0
W. Rhodes not out	0
Extras (b13, lb2)	15
Total (all out, 61 overs)	**183**

Fall of wickets: 1–31, 2–36, 3–62, 4–67, 5–67, 6–83, 7–137, 8–179, 9–183, 10–183
Bowling: Trumble 31-13-65-8, Saunders 12-7-79-2, Noble 7-3-24-0

England: Second innings

MacLaren b Saunders	2
Palairet b Saunders	6
Tyldesley b Saunders	0
Hayward c Kelly b Saunders	7
Jackson c and b Trumble	49
Braund c Kelly b Trumble	2
Jessop c Noble b Armstrong	104
Hirst not out	58
Lockwood lbw b Trumble	2
Lilley c Darling b Trumble	16
Rhodes not out	6
Extras (b5, lb6)	11
Total (9 wickets, 66.5 overs)	**263**

Fall of wickets: 1–5, 2–5, 3–10, 4–31, 5–48, 6–157, 7–187, 8–214, 9–248
Bowling: Trumble 33.5-4-108-4, Saunders 24-3-105-4, Noble 5-0-11-0, Armstrong 4-0-28-1

England won by 1 wicket

Tate was unfairly made the scapegoat for the earlier defeat so, it seems to me, Jessop was somewhat overpraised for this victory.

His must have been a thrilling innings, one that any cricket-lover in possession of a time machine would hurry back to watch, and no doubt its value lay not so much in the quantity of runs as in the parlous situation in which he scored them. But, even so, surely Hirst had contributed just as much, if not indeed a lot more. (Come to that, if the result had gone the other way, as it might easily have done, this would undoubtedly have gone down as Trumble's match.)

FAR LEFT *Gilbert Laird Jessop, c.1895. In the words of a contemporary versifier, the fast-scoring Gloucestershire batsman 'wrecked the walls of distant towns when set in an assault'.*

2 LAKER'S MATCH

ENGLAND VS AUSTRALIA, OLD TRAFFORD, 26–31 JULY 1956

Australians can bitch as much as they like, complaining bitterly that the perfidious Poms had done the dirty on them yet again, that the Old Trafford pitch was specially prepared for the greatest of off-spinners, Jim Laker, and therefore they, the opposition, were never in with a fair chance. But the Aussies long ago raised whingeing to an art form and, besides, where's the logic in their argument?

Yes, England had Laker but the Australians were themselves captained by an off-spinner, Ian Johnson, not admittedly in Laker's class but good enough to take 109 wickets in his 45 Tests.

NO TURN FOR THE AUSSIES

The fact is that in this match, played at the end of July 1956, everything depended on the toss and the weather. True, the wicket deteriorated rapidly, even before the end of the first day when little puffs of dust appeared, and very likely the pitch was prepared with spin bowlers in mind. But no groundsman in the world can predict who is going to win the toss, so let us assume that things had gone the other way, that Johnson not May had called correctly and chosen to bat.

If the Aussies had then scored 400-plus, as they might well have done, and their spinners had skittled England would they have whinged? Would they hell.

As it happened England batted first and scored 459, with the Australians muttering darkly about the wicket soon after tea on day one and continuing to do so throughout. But despite the favourable conditions their spinners, Johnson and Benaud, could not make the ball bite and turn either on the first or second day. Laker, however, could.

PERFECT SPIN-BOWLING CONDITIONS

On day two Australia lost 11 wickets in about four hours. They'd followed on 375 runs behind, Laker having taken nine for 37. There was a big storm that night, Friday, and more rain to come over the weekend. With the wickets uncovered in those days very little play was possible.

But, come the Monday, the weather cleared up and on a slow, easy-paced pitch McDonald and Craig took the score to 114 for 2 with only four hours remaining. Then, sadly for them, the sun came out.

That was all Laker needed. From the Stretford End, where he took all his wickets, he was virtually unplayable. The last six batsmen fell for 75 runs and

No bugger ever got all ten when I was at the other end. ● The great Sydney Barnes watches Laker at Old Trafford, 1956

England's champion completed the most amazing feat of bowling in cricket history by finishing the second innings with all 10 for 53 and the match with 19 for 90, setting a record that will surely never be equalled, still less beaten.

Say what you like about the wicket but nobody, except perhaps God, could control the toss or the weather. It just so happened that everything conspired to give Laker the opportunity of a lifetime and he seized it as no bowler had ever done before and no bowler ever will again. Laker's own comment on the match? 'The amazing thing to me,' he said, 'is that Tony Lock only got one wicket.'

LAKER'S MATCH: SCORECARD

England: First innings

P.E. Richardson c Maddocks b Benaud	104
M.C. Cowdrey c Maddocks b Lindwall	80
Rev. D.S. Sheppard b Archer	113
P.B.H. May (capt.) c Archer b Benaud	43
T.E. Bailey b Johnson	20
C. Washbrook lbw b Johnson	6
A.S.M. Oakman c Archer b Johnson	10
T.G. Evans (wkt) st Maddocks b Johnson	47
J.C. Laker run out	3
G.A.R. Lock not out	25
J.B. Statham c Maddocks b Lindwall	0
Extras (b2, lb5, w1)	8
Total (all out, 158.3 overs)	**459**

Fall of wickets: 1–174, 2–195, 3–288, 4–321, 5–327, 6–339, 7–401, 8–417, 9–458, 10–459
Bowling: Lindwall 21.3-6-63-2, Miller 21-6-41-0, Archer 23-6-73-1, Johnson 47-10-151-4, Benaud 47-17-123-2

Australia: First innings

C.C. McDonald c Lock b Laker	32
J.W. Burke c Cowdrey b Lock	22
R.N. Harvey b Laker	0
I.D. Craig lbw b Laker	8
K.R. Miller c Oakman b Laker	6
K. Mackay c Oakman b Laker	0
R.G. Archer st Evans b Laker	6
R. Benaud c Statham b Laker	0
R.R. Lindwall not out	6
L.V. Maddocks b Laker	4
I.W. Johnson (capt) b Laker	0
Extras	0
Total (all out, 40.4 overs)	**84**

Fall of wickets: 1–48, 2–48, 3–62, 4–62, 5–62, 6–73, 7–73, 8–78, 9–84, 10–84
Bowling: Statham 6-3-6-0, Bailey 4-3-4-0, Laker 16.4-4-37-9, Lock 14-3-37-1

Australia: Second innings (following on)

McDonald c Oakman b Laker	89
Burke c Lock b Laker	33
Harvey c Cowdrey b Laker	0
Craig lbw b Laker	38
Mackay c Oakman b Laker	0
Miller b Laker	0
Archer c Oakman b Laker	0
Benaud b Laker	18
Lindwall c Lock b Laker	8
Maddocks lbw b Laker	2
Johnson not out	1
Extras (b12, lb4)	16
Total (all out, 150.2 overs)	**205**

Fall of wickets: 1–28, 2–55, 3–114, 4–124, 5–130, 6–130, 7–181, 8–198, 9–203, 10–205
Bowling: Statham 16-9-15-0, Bailey 20-8-31-0, Laker 51.2-23-53-10, Lock 55-30-69-0, Oakman 8-3-21-0

England won by an innings and 170 runs

3 THE GREAT TIED TEST

AUSTRALIA VS WEST INDIES, BRISBANE, 9–14 DECEMBER 1960

When the West Indies toured Australia in 1960–1 the team was in transition. Weekes and Walcott had gone but they still had Worrell (who was captain), Ramadhin and Valentine, along with the batsmen Conrad Hunte and Rohan Kanhai, a very fast bowler in Wes Hall and a bit of an all-rounder in one Garfield St Aubrun Sobers.

For their part Australia, captained by the wily Richie Benaud, had the batsmen Colin McDonald, Bobby Simpson, Neil Harvey and Norman O'Neill, the all-rounder Alan Davidson and the fast bowler Ian Meckiff, soon to be named-and-shamed as a chucker (see page 272). Two pretty well-balanced sides, then. Everyone agreed that it should be a very entertaining series and so it proved, right from the start.

Brisbane, 9 December 1960, first Test: Worrell won the toss, West Indies batted, made a bit of a mess of it and at one point were 65 for 3. Then Sobers breezed in and soon ensured this would be a memorable Test, whatever the result, with a century in two hours, while Davidson kicked off a remarkable all-round performance with 5 for 135.

Typically undaunted by a pretty formidable total, Australia hit back with an even better one of their own, thanks largely to O'Neill's 181 in 401 minutes. Thereafter things seemed to quieten down a bit. Kanhai and Worrell made fifties, but the star of the Windies second innings was Davidson with 6 for 87. The Aussies were left needing 232 to win on a good wicket. No big deal except that… in no time at all they had collapsed to 92 for 6 with only a couple of all-rounders and the tail to come. At this point, however, those all-rounders – Benaud and the inevitable Davidson – came together to add 134 for the seventh wicket. At 226 Davidson was run out but, hey, seven to win with three wickets in hand – what could possibly go wrong?

Well, what went wrong was this: just before six o'clock on the final day Wes Hall started bowling what, come what may, would be the last over of the match, an eight-ball over in Australia at that time. The Aussies were then 227 for 7. Only six to win now; and with a leg-bye off the first ball that was reduced to five. Benaud faced the second, hooked, and was caught behind by Alexander. Still five to win, but only two wickets left. Meckiff, the incoming batsman, blocked ball three, missed ball four, which went down the leg side, and was called through for a bye by wicketkeeper Wally Grout. Four balls to go, four to win. Grout fended off the fifth ball, a bouncer, towards Rohan Kanhai at square leg. Kanhai tried to catch it, so did Hall in his follow-through; they both missed and the Aussies scampered a run. Three needed off three balls.

Ball six was especially exciting. Meckiff hit it towards the mid-wicket boundary, he and Grout ran two and turned for the third and, if they had made it, winning run. But Conrad Hunte's throw thudded into Alexander's gloves and the bails were off with Grout stranded some distance up the wicket.

So now let's take a deep breath and look at the situation: scores level, Australia needing one to win with one wicket in hand and two balls to go. At the wicket last man Lindsay Kline, scorer of what now seemed a magnificent 3 not out in the first innings. The Brisbane crowd willed him on. 'Never mind three, just one will do, mate,' they murmured, as Kline confidently pushed ball seven towards square leg and set off for the winning single.

But… Joe Solomon, some 15 yards away, scooped up the ball, threw it hard and true at the only stump he could see, and ran out Meckiff by inches.

Thus, for the first time in 84 years, a Test match ended in a tie. Indeed, there has only since been one other – Australia (again) versus India at Madras in 1986.

BELOW Cricketing history is made on 14 December 1960 at Brisbane, as Joe Solomon of the West Indies (out of picture) runs out Australia's Ian Meckiff for 2, resulting in the first-ever tied Test match.

Cricket is first and foremost a dramatic spectacle. It belongs with the theatre, ballet, opera and the dance. ● C.L.R. James

---

—— THE GREAT TIED TEST: SCORECARD ——

West Indies: First innings

C.C. Hunte c Benaud b Davidson	24
C.W. Smith c Grout by Davidson	7
R.B. Kanhai c Grout b Davidson	15
G.S. Sobers c Kline b Meckiff	132
F.M.M. Worrell (capt.) c Grout b Davidson	65
J.S. Solomon hit wkt b Simpson	65
P.D. Lashley c Grout b Kline	19
F.C.M. Alexander (wkt) c Davidson b Kline	60
S. Ramadhin c Harvey b Davidson	12
W.W. Hall st Grout b Kline	50
A.L. Valentine not out	0
Extras (lb3, w1)	4
Total (all out, 100.6 overs)	**453**

Fall of wickets: 1–23, 2–42, 3–65. 4–239, 5–243, 6–283, 7–347, 8–366, 9–452, 10–453
Bowling: Davidson 30-2-135-5, Meckiff 18-0-129-1, Mackay 3-0-15-0, Benaud 24-3-93-0, Simpson 8-0-25-1, Kline 17.6-6-52-3

West Indies: Second innings

Hunte c Simpson b Mackay	39
Smith c O'Neill b Davidson	6
Kanhai c Grout b Davidson	54
Sobers b Davidson	14
Worrell c Grout b Davidson	65
Solomon lbw b Simpson	47
Lashley b Davidson	0
Alexander b Benaud	5
Ramadhin c Harvey b Simpson	6
Hall b Davidson	18
Valentine not out	7
Extras (b14, lb7, w2)	23
Total (all out, 92.6 overs)	**284**

Fall of wickets: 1–13, 2–88, 3–114, 4–127, 5–210, 6–210, 7–241, 8–250, 9–253, 10–284
Bowling: Davidson 24.6-4-87-6, Meckiff 4-1-19-0, Mackay 21-7-52-1, Benaud 31-6-69-1, Simpson 7-2-18-2, Kline 4-0-14-0, O'Neill 1-0-2-0

Australia: First innings

C.C. McDonald c Hunte b Sobers	57
R.B. Simpson b Ramadhin	92
R.N. Harvey b Valentine	15
N.C. O'Neill c Valentine b Hall	181
L.E. Favell run out	45
K.D. Mackay b Sobers	35
A.K. Davidson c Alexander b Hall	44
R. Benaud (capt.) lbw b Hall	10
A.T.W. Grout (wkt) lbw b Hall	4
I. Meckiff run out	4
L.F. Kline not out	3
Extras (b2, lb8, w1, nb4)	15
Total (all out, 130.3 overs)	**505**

Fall of wickets: 1–84, 2–138, 3–194, 4–278, 5–381, 6–469, 7–484, 8–489, 9–496, 10–505
Bowling: Hall 29.3-1-140-4, Worrell 30-0-93-0, Sobers 32-0-115-2, Valentine 24-6-82-1, Ramadhin 15-1-60-1

Australia: Second innings (target: 233)

McDonald b Worrell	16
Simpson c sub (L. R. Gibbs) b Hall	0
Harvey c Sobers b Hall	5
O'Neill c Alexander b Hall	26
Favell c Solomon b Hall	7
Mackay b Ramadhin	28
Davidson run out	80
Benaud c Alexander b Hall	52
Grout run out	2
Meckiff run out	2
Kline not out	0
Extras (b2, lb9, nb3)	14
Total (all out, 68.7 overs)	**232**

Fall of wickets: 1–1, 2–7, 3–49, 4–49, 5–57, 6–92, 7–226, 8–228, 9–232, 10–232
Bowling: Hall 17.7-3-65-5, Worrell 16-3-41-1, Sobers 8-0-30-0, Valentine 10-4-27-0, Ramadhin 17-3-57-1

Match tied

But the first is always the most important and, besides, this was the more dramatic, hinging as it did on a run out rather than the anticlimactic lbw decision that would end the second tie.

They didn't have man of the match awards in 1960 but if they had there could, surely, have been only one possible winner – Alan Davidson, who took 11 wickets in the game, scored 124 runs and took a catch.

4 BOTHAM'S MATCH (OR MAYBE WILLIS'S?)

ENGLAND VS AUSTRALIA, HEADINGLEY, 16–21 JULY 1981

Monday 20 July 1981, mid-afternoon. Game three in the Ashes series. England, already one down, had followed on and were 135 for 7, still 92 runs behind Australia's first-innings total. At the wicket: Ian Botham, now joined by the fast bowler Graham Dilley. As Dilley approached Botham delivered his rallying-cry: 'Let's give it a bit of umpty.' What followed was the stuff of fantasy.

Ah, but first you have to know the background. England had begun the series with Botham as captain but lost the first Test at Trent Bridge and drew the second at Lord's, where Botham bagged a pair and resigned the captaincy moments before the selectors would have stripped him of it anyway.

For Headingley, Mike Brearley – he who, in the words of Rodney Hogg, had 'a degree in people' – was reintroduced as captain and, coincidentally or not, the transformation in Botham was magical.

Australia won the toss, batted first and, thanks to a hundred from the opener Dyson and 89 from the captain Kim Hughes, declared at 401 for 9. The sole encouragement for England was that Botham, who had taken only six wickets in the first two Tests, was the pick of the bowlers with 6 for 95. And in England's miserable reply of 174 he was also the pick of the batsmen with 50. Well, we thought, at least he was showing a bit of form, not that this was much consolation as England followed on 227 runs behind and slumped to 135 for 7. All over bar the shouting, surely.

But now came the umpty, so much belligerent umpty that with Dilley (56) Botham added 117 and with Chris Old (29) a further 67 for the ninth wicket. Fine contributions by both tail-enders but it was Botham's amazing 149 not out, an innings of calculated brutality which included 114 in boundaries, that has gone down in history and even legend. Nobody, not even the great Dennis Lillee, knew where to bowl to him.

Even so Australia were left needing only 130 to win with Ladbroke's offering odds of 500–1 against an England victory. That seemed fair enough unless, of course, Botham could do it again, this time with the ball. As it happened he couldn't but, happily for England, Bob Willis could.

Willis always bowled for England as if for the lives of his loved ones, but this time he was particularly inspired – as inspired indeed as 'Both' had been with the bat – creating havoc among the Aussies and finishing with a magnificent career best of 8 for 43 as Australia were dismissed for 111. Miraculously, England had won by 18 runs.

So, was it Botham's match or Willis's? If, as they say, batsmen save matches but bowlers win them, then you've got to hand it to Willis. On the other hand,

look at Botham's all-round performance – seven wickets for 109, 199 runs for once out and two catches. So, yes, on balance it was Botham's match – or maybe it was Rodney Marsh's. Or Dennis Lillee's.

Odds of 500–1 were too good for red-blooded Aussies to resist, so Marsh and Lillee backed England and, though I have no idea how much they pocketed, financially they must have finished the game miles ahead of everyone else.

BOTHAM'S MATCH: SCORECARD

Australia: First innings

J. Dyson b Dilley	102
G.M. Wood lbw b Botham	34
T.M. Chappell c Taylor b Willey	27
K.J. Hughes (capt.) c and b Botham	89
R.J. Bright b Dilley	7
G.N. Yallop c Taylor b Botham	58
A.R. Border lbw b Botham	8
R.W. Marsh (wkt) b Botham	28
G.F. Lawson c Taylor b Botham	13
D.K. Lillee not out	3
T.M. Alderman not out	0
Extras (b4, lb13, w3, nb12)	32
Total (9 wickets dec, 155.2 overs)	**401**

Fall of wickets: 1–55, 2–149, 3–196, 4–220, 5–332, 6–354, 7–357, 8–396, 9–401.
Bowling: Willis 30-8-72-0, Old 43-14-91-0, Dilley 27-4-78-2, Botham 39.2-11-95-6, Willey 13-2-31-1, Boycott 3-2-2-0

England: First innings

G.A. Gooch lbw b Alderman	2
G. Boycott b Lawson	12
J.M. Brearley (capt.) c Marsh b Alderman	10
D.I. Gower c Marsh b Lawson	24
M.W. Gatting lbw b Lillee	15
P. Willey b Lawson	8
I.T. Botham c Marsh b Lillee	50
R.W. Taylor (wkt) c Marsh b Lillee	5
G.R. Dilley c and b Lillee	13
C.M. Old c Border b Alderman	0
R.G.D. Willis not out	1
Extras (b6, lb11, w6, nb11)	34
Total (all out, 50.5 overs)	**174**

Fall of wickets: 1–12, 2–40, 3–42, 4–84, 5–87, 6–112, 7–148, 8–166, 9–167, 10–174
Bowling: Lillee 18.5-7-49-4, Alderman 19-4-56-3, Lawson 13-3-32-3

England: Second innings (following on)

Gooch c Alderman b Lillee	0
Boycott lbw b Alderman	46
Brearley c Alderman b Lillee	14
Gower c Border b Alderman	9
Gatting lbw b Alderman	1
Willey c Dyson b Lillee	33
Botham not out	149
Taylor c Bright b Alderman	1
Dilley b Alderman	56
Old b Lawson	29
Willis c Border b Alderman	3
Extras (b5, lb3, w3, nb5)	16
Total (all out, 87.3 overs)	**356**

Fall of wickets: 1–0, 2–18, 3–37, 4–41, 5–105, 6–133, 7–135, 8–252, 9–319, 10–356
Bowling: Lillee 25-6-94-3, Alderman 35-3-6-135-6, Lawson 23-4-96-1, Bright 4-0-15-0.

Australia: Second innings (target: 130)

Dyson c Taylor b Willis	34
Wood c Taylor b Botham	10
Chappell c Taylor b Willis	8
Hughes c Botham b Willis	0
Yallop c Gatting b Willis	0
Border b Old	0
Marsh c Dilley b Willis	4
Bright b Willis	19
Lawson c Taylor b Willis	1
Lillee c Gatting b Willis	17
Alderman not out	0
Extras (lb3, w1, nb14)	18
Total (all out, 36.1 overs)	**111**

Fall of wickets: 1–13, 2–56, 3–58, 4–58, 5–65, 6–68, 7–74, 8–75, 9–110, 10–111
Bowling: Botham 7-3-14-1, Dilley 2-0-11-0, Willis 15.1-3-43-8, Old 9-1-21-1, Willey 3-1-4-0

England won by 18 runs

5 Almost the Great Escape

ENGLAND VS AUSTRALIA, EDGBASTON, 4–7 AUGUST 2005

Edgbaston, Sunday 7 August 2005, and one of the most memorable images in cricket: Brett Lee squatting, heartbroken, on the pitch and being consoled by 'Freddie' Flintoff, a rare moment of human warmth and a fitting postscript to a great match (see page 210).

And what a great match it had been, England's all the way – or nearly all the way – until that fourth morning, when Australia were on 175 for 8, needing 282 to win. At the wicket: Shane Warne and Lee, with only Mike Kasprowicz to come. The crowd, a considerable one, had turned up to enjoy maybe 30 minutes' cricket, top whack, before the Aussies' inevitable defeat and then a joyous gloat, leaving plenty of time to hit the pubs before lunch.

It didn't quite work out that way, but… let's go back to the beginning, actually to before the beginning, to the moment when in warm-up practice Glenn McGrath trod on a ball, damaged his ankle and dropped out of the Australian side. What difference did that make? A lot, every Aussie would insist, but who knows?

Besides, despite the loss of his leading fast bowler, Ricky Ponting, the Australian skipper, was confident. His lads were one up after Lord's and 16 years and nine series had gone by since the hapless Poms last held the Ashes. Australia were used to winning, England to losing. No reason to believe that was going to change any time soon. So he won the toss and chose to field.

Big mistake, huge. The England batsmen, shorn of fear and inhibitions, possibly because of McGrath's absence, simply ripped the Australian attack apart and rattled up 407 in 79.2 overs. Marcus Trescothick led the way with 15 fours and two sixes, while Pietersen and Flintoff also dipped greedily into the trough.

On day two, thanks to Langer and Ponting, Australia made a decent reply, but even so England had a handy lead of 99. Now, though, the game began to see-saw quite a bit. Lee, fast and hostile, and Warne, turning the ball hugely from the rough, put the home batsmen in what the Aussies believed to be their proper place – back in the pavilion – only Flintoff scoring more than 20-odd to ease England from 131 for 9 to the modest respectability of 182 all out.

Game on then – 282 to win. A reasonably big ask, as the Aussies would have put it, but by no means impossible. Once again, however, the indomitable Flintoff roared to the rescue, notably claiming Ponting for a duck, as Australia ended day three on 175 for 8. Game on? Nah, game over.

And then came the remarkable morning of day four. Warne, looking to attack and Lee, solidly behind the ball, gradually whittled the deficit down, but

ABOVE *Steve Harmison
(centre) and his England
team-mates express their
delight and relief after the
Durham paceman's last-
gasp dismissal of Michael
Kasprowicz clinched
victory for England in the
second Test at Edgbaston,
7 August 2005.*

even so 62 were still needed when Warne, trying to fend off the ubiquitous
Flintoff, trod on his wicket.

Enter the rabbit Kasprowicz and now, surely, it was only a matter of a ball
or two before England won. But just for once this rabbit had unexpectedly
sharp teeth and slowly, with the help of extras and bowling that, with victory
beckoning, had become too short, too eager, too desperate, the winning total
came ever more clearly into sight.

With 15 needed and the batsmen settled England's last chance seemed to
come and then go. Kasprowicz hit a ball from Flintoff into the air towards third
man where Simon Jones ran for it, dived – and missed. Suddenly, unbelievably,
England seemed to be up to their old trick of snatching defeat from the jaws
of victory.

But then, with Australia needing only three to win, Harmison banged one
in, Kasprowicz flicked at it, the ball hit his glove and looped nicely to Geraint
Jones behind the stumps. But… was the batsman's hand actually holding the
bat at the moment of contact? If it was, he was out; if it wasn't, he was not out.
To a man Australians believe it wasn't, but umpire Billy Bowden thought it
was, and raised the finger of dismissal.

Kasprowicz was distraught, Lee inconsolable, Flintoff hugely sympathetic and England had won by two runs, en route finally to regaining the Ashes.

Was this the greatest Test match, as many – especially those who were there on that last morning – will claim? Quite possibly. Surely it was one of the most exciting and Australia must feel, as did Steve McQueen until he got caught up in all that barbed wire, that they had been on the very brink of what would have been the greatest escape of them all.

—— ALMOST THE GREAT ESCAPE: SCORECARD ——

England: First innings			England: Second innings	
M.E. Trescothick c Gilchrist b Kasprowicz	90		Trescothick c Gilchrist b Lee	21
A.J. Strauss b Warne	48		Strauss b Warne	6
M.P. Vaughan (capt.) c Lee b Gillespie	24		Hoggard c Hayden b Lee	1
I.R. Bell c Gilchrist b Kasprowicz	6		Vaughan b Lee	1
K.P. Pietersen c Katich b Lee	71		Bell c Gilchrist b Warne	21
A. Flintoff c Gilchrist b Gillespie	68		Pietersen c Gilchrist b Warne	20
G.O. Jones (wkt) c Gilchrist b Kasprowicz	1		Flintoff b Warne	73
A.F. Giles lbw b Warne	23		G.O. Jones c Ponting b Lee	9
M.J. Hoggard lbw b Warne	16		Giles c Hayden b Warne	8
S.J. Harmison b Warne	17		Harmison c Ponting b Warne	0
S.P. Jones not out	19		S.P. Jones not out	12
Extras (lb9, w1, nb14)	24		Extras (lb 1, nb9)	10
Total (all out, 79.2 overs)	**407**		**Total (all out, 52.1 overs)**	**182**

Fall of wickets: 1–112, 2–164, 3–170, 4–187, 5–290, 6–293, 7–342, 8–349, 9–375, 10–407
Bowling: Lee 17-1-111-1, Gillespie 22-3-91-2, Kasprowicz 15-3-80-3, Warne 25.2-4-116-4

Fall of wickets: 1–25, 2–27, 3–29, 4–31, 5–72, 6–75, 7–101, 8–131, 9–131, 10–182
Bowling: Lee 18-1-82-4, Gillespie 8-0-24-0, Kasprowicz 3-0-29-0, Warne 23.1-7-46-6

Australia: First innings			Australia: Second innings	
J.L. Langer lbw b S. Jones	82		Langer b Flintoff	28
M.L. Hayden c Strauss b Hoggard	0		Hayden c Trescothick b S. Jones	31
R.T. Ponting (capt.) c Vaughan b Giles	61		Ponting c G. Jones b Flintoff	0
D.R. Martyn run out	20		Martyn c Bell b Hoggard	28
M.J. Clarke c G. Jones b Giles	40		Clarke b Harmison	30
S.M. Katich c G. Jones b Flintoff	4		Katich c Trescothick b Giles	16
A.C. Gilchrist (wkt) not out	49		Gilchrist c Flintoff b Giles	1
S.K. Warne b Giles	8		Gillespie lbw b Flintoff	0
B. Lee c Flintoff b S. Jones	6		Warne hit wkt b Flintoff	42
J.N. Gillespie lbw b Flintoff	7		Lee not out	43
M.S. Kasprowicz lbw b Flintoff	0		Kasprowicz c G. Jones b Harmison	20
Extras (b13, lb7, w1, nb10)	31		Extras (b13, lb8, w1, nb18)	40
Total (all out, 76 overs)	**308**		**Total (all out, 64.3 overs)**	**279**

Fall of wickets: 1–0, 2–88, 3–118, 4–194, 5–202, 6–262, 7–273, 8–287, 9–308, 10–308
Bowling: Harmison 11-1-48-0, Hoggard 8-0-41-1, S.P. Jones 16-2-69-2, Flintoff 15-1-52-3, Giles 26-2-78-3.

Fall of wickets: 1–47, 2–48, 3–82, 4–107, 5–134, 6–136, 7–137, 8–175, 9–220, 10–279
Bowling: Harmison 17.3-3-62-2, Hoggard 5-0-26-1, Giles 15-3-68-2, Flintoff 22-3-79-4, S.P. Jones 5-10-23-1

England won by 2 runs

6 AND THEN CAME SEHWAG

INDIA VS ENGLAND, CHENNAI (MADRAS), 11–15 DECEMBER 2008

This was a Test not quite like any other – not because England lost (everyone expected that), nor even because they nearly won, nor yet because the greatest player in the match won the game while simultaneously bringing up his own hundred, though much of this was remarkable.

More remarkable still, however, was the fact that the Test took place at all, barely a couple of weeks after a terrorist massacre in Mumbai had caused the England squad, five-nil down in the seven-match ODI series, to flee India in a state of some alarm. They regrouped in the safety of Abu Dhabi to consider their options – to return for the two-match Test series, or just say sod it and go home for Christmas shopping? Reports suggested that some, including Flintoff and Harmison, were in favour of the latter, while Pietersen, the England captain, fervently paraphrased US General Douglas MacArthur in crying: 'We shall return!' In the end that was what, unanimously, they decided to do and they reappeared in India, each swathed in bodyguards, to be greeted as heroes.

And indeed their decision was important, not just for the morale of the Indian people at a desperate time, but for the game itself. There was something simply, well, cricket about the fact that these flannelled fools, undaunted by crazed assassins, were prepared to embark on a Test series even while a nation licked the ugly wounds inflicted by those same crazed assassins.

SETTING A DAUNTING TARGET

So then to the Chennai match. India's team, with Amit Mishra and Yuvraj Singh replacing the now-retired Kumble and Ganguly, was as expected. So, too, was England's. Ian Bell, who had done nothing of much note since making 199 against South Africa at Lord's in July, was retained at number three, no doubt leaving Owais Shah – easily England's outstanding batsman in the ODI debacle – to wonder, as he must have done many times before, what on earth he had to do to get into the bloody team, short of putting out a contract on Bell.

The old pals' act dies hard in the England dressing-room, where it was probably argued that Bell, though possibly a touch disappointing of late if what you wanted of a number three was more than the occasional cameo, was, gosh, ever so talented as well as being an awfully good fielder and a frightfully good chap to have around. Shah was not such a good fielder, and also a bit prickly at times, so he was out and Bell stayed in.

Not that it seemed to matter much at first. England batted and Strauss, who had played no serious cricket since September, settled in as though he had never been away, put on 118 with Cook for the first wicket and completed a typically watchful century, punctuated by cuts and sweeps, a stroke at which he had become far more adept in recent years. Naturally, there was a bit of a collapse – Bell failed, so did Pietersen and Collingwood – but ending the day at 229 for 5 England seemed pretty comfortable.

At the end of day two they looked more comfortable still. True, they had lost their last six wickets for only 95 runs – what else is new? – but India were in a precarious position at 155 for 6. Graeme Swann on his Test debut had taken two wickets – Gambhir and Dravid – in his first over and England were on top.

After the third day they must have been cock-a-hoop. India had rallied (from 102 for 5 to 241 all out) but England, after losing three second-innings wickets for 43 – more failures for Bell and Pietersen – had finished on 172 for 3, thanks to Strauss and Collingwood, and were 247 ahead. The next morning Strauss completed his second hundred of the match (the first Englishman to do so in a Test in India), Collingwood notched up one of his own and at 311 for 9 Pietersen declared, leaving India the improbable task of scoring 387 to win, the like of which had only ever been accomplished in Tests three times before.

Mind you, the target could and should have been greater still. After lunch on the fourth day, faced with a slow pitch and a tardy over rate, the England batsmen had opted to defend when they might have been better advised to attack. But even so, no team had ever come close to scoring 387 to win a Test match in India so England were laughing, weren't they? It was, like, up yours to all those critics who had said before the game that the visitors weren't in with a chance.

SEHWAG SHOWS THE WAY

In the context of this or many another Test, 83 might be considered a laudable but not particularly notable score. Sometimes, however, it's not how many you make but how and in what context you make them that counts, and this was one of those occasions.

Formidable though the target was, Sehwag approached the task with the air of one taking part in a friend's benefit match. Inspired perhaps (or maybe not) by Sebastian in *Twelfth Night* – 'There's for you, and there and there!' – he proceeded to smite the England bowling far and wide. With Gambhir chipping in at the other end India had 80 runs on the board by the 12th over, Sehwag's own 50 having taken him all of 32 balls.

His was a glorious exhibition of clean hitting, not slogging but superb batsmanship, and though he slowed up a little – he was finally out to his 68th delivery – this effectively was the innings that won the Test, played with such ease and confidence as to make everyone wonder why 387 should ever have seemed a formidable total to reach. At close of play India were 131 for 1, needing only 256 more to win. Even so, as Mike Atherton suggested in *The Times*, England might not have been too unhappy, hoping perhaps that India's other

Yuvraj Singh embraces Sachin Tendulkar at Chennai, 15 December 2008. Behind them the scoreboard spells out the statistics of India's extraordinary six–wicket victory. Only three teams have made a higher fourth-innings score to win a Test match than India's 387 for 4. England's declaration in Chennai was only the 11th time in Test history that a team has declared in the third innings and lost.

batsmen would try to emulate Sehwag's bombardment and get themselves out. Besides, this was now a fifth-day pitch which, though slow, was taking spin. Surely Panesar and Swann would present some nasty problems.

As it happened all such assumptions were wrong. England got rid of Dravid quite cheaply but, unfortunately for them, that brought Sachin Tendulkar to the crease. With hindsight it now seems inevitable that the hero of all India should choose this highly emotional occasion to play a hero's innings.

Gambhir went and so did Laxman, but by now India needed only 163 more runs to win. This, surely, was the moment for an England breakthrough, for the next man in was the brilliant but flashy Yuvraj Singh, regarded by Pietersen as a 'pie-chucker' when bowling and by the England players generally as a show pony when batting – a man who might well self-destruct, and if he did so quickly who knew what might happen then?

Tendulkar, however, had other ideas. He kept calming his more excitable young partner until Yuvraj had settled down, and showed by example that it wasn't necessary to try to hammer every ball out of sight, for there were plenty of singles and twos to be had by clever placement of the ball.

So the runs came, Yuvraj scoring most of them until wisely easing back to allow Tendulkar to reach the century which the crowd demanded, no doubt fearing that if he himself scored the winning runs, leaving his partner stranded somewhere in the 90s, he might easily find himself relegated from junior hero to the most hated man on the ground.

Sehwag was voted man of the match, one that had been fascinating throughout and could have gone either way before arriving at a thrilling and, in the circumstances, proper conclusion. It might seem heresy to say so but in the overall scheme of things cricket is not that important. It's just a game, after all, albeit the very best of games, but because of its timing this Test had a particular significance, not just for the Indian team but for the nation.

Right then India, bruised and bleeding from the events in Mumbai, needed something as bright, traditional and if you like trivial as a Test match to lift its spirits. And merely by turning up, the England team had shown that the terrorists were not going to frighten people away, that India – like America, Britain, Spain and other countries where terrorism had done its worst – was still open for business.

The fact that the first Test of the series turned out to be a cracker was just a glorious bonus.

--- AND THEN CAME SEHWAG: SCORECARD ---

England: First innings

A.J. Strauss c and b Mishra	123
A.N. Cook c Khan b Harbhajan Singh	52
I.R. Bell lbw b Khan	17
K.P. Pietersen (capt.) c and b Khan	4
P.D. Collingwood c Gambhir b Harbhajan Singh	9
A. Flintoff c Gambhir b Mishra	18
J.M. Anderson c Yuvraj Singh b Mishra	19
M.J. Prior not out	53
G.P. Swann c Dravid b Harbhajan Singh	1
S.J. Harmison c Dhoni b Yuvraj Singh	6
M.S. Panesar lbw b Sharma	6
Extras (lb7, nb1)	8
Total (all out, 128.4 overs)	**316**

Fall of wickets: 1–118, 2–164, 3–180, 4–195, 5–221, 6–229, 7–271, 8–277, 9–304, 10–316
Bowling: Z. Khan 21-9-41-2, I. Sharma 19.4-4-32-1, Harbhajan Singh 38-2-96-3, A. Mishra 34-6-99-3, Yuvraj Singh 15-2-33-1, V. Sehwag 1-0-8-0

England: Second innings

Strauss c Laxman b Harbhajan Singh	108
Cook c Dhoni b Sharma	9
Bell c Gambhir b Mishra	7
Pietersen lbw b Yuvraj Singh	1
Collingwood lbw b Khan	108
Flintoff c Dhoni b Sharma	4
Prior c Sehwag b Sharma	33
Swann b Khan	7
Harmison b Khan	1
Anderson not out	1
Extras (b10, lb13, w2, nb7)	32
Total (9 wickets dec, 105.5 overs)	**311**

Did not bat: Panesar
Fall of wickets: 1–28, 2–42, 3–43, 4–257, 5–262, 6–277, 7–297, 8–301, 9–311
Bowling: Khan 27-7-40-3, Sharma 22.5-1-57-3, Mishra 17-1-66-1, Yuvraj Singh 3-1-12-1, Harbhajan Singh 30-3-91-1, Sehwag 6-0-22-0

India: First innings

G. Gambhir lbw b Swann	19
V. Sehwag b Anderson	9
R. Dravid lbw b Swann	3
S.R. Tendulkar c and b Flintoff	37
V.V.S. Laxman c and b Panesar	24
Yuvraj Singh c Flintoff b Harmison	14
M.S. Dhoni (capt.) c Pietersen b Panesar	53
Harbhajan Singh c Bell b Panesar	40
Z. Khan lbw b Flintoff	1
A. Mishra b Flintoff	12
I. Sharma not out	8
Extras (b4, lb11, nb6)	21
Total (all out, 69.4 overs)	**241**

Fall of wickets: 1–16, 2–34, 3–37, 4–98, 5–102, 6–137, 7–212, 8–217, 9–219, 10–241
Bowling: Harmison 11-1-42-1, Anderson 11-3-28-1, Flintoff 18.4-2-49-3, Swann 10-0-42-2, Panesar 19-4-65-3

India: Second innings

Gambhir c Collingwood b Anderson	66
Sehwag lbw b Swann	83
Dravid c Prior b Flintoff	4
Tendulkar not out	103
Laxman c Bell b Swann	26
Yuvraj Singh not out	85
Extras (b5, lb11, nb4)	20
Total (4 wickets, 98.3 overs)	**387**

Did not bat: Dhoni, Harbhajan Singh, Khan, Mishra, Sharma
Fall of wickets: 1–117, 2–141, 3–183, 4–224
Bowling: Harmison 10-0-48-0, Anderson 11-1-51-1, Panesar 27-4-105-0, Flintoff 22-1-64-1, Swann 28.3-2-103-2

India won by 6 wickets

CHAPTER 13
THE GREAT TEAMS

THE FIVE GREATEST TEAMS IN CRICKET HISTORY: FROM WARWICK'S WONDERS OF 1920-1 TO PONTING'S PARTY-POOPERS OF 2006-7

W hat is a great team? One that includes a generous complement of great players certainly – but more than that it must achieve great things; it must not simply defeat the opposition, it must slaughter them, grind them mercilessly beneath the heel and then spit on the corpse. Simply to win a series is not enough for a great team; it must dominate to such an extent that virtually from day one the other side doesn't have a chance. Some teams – not many – have done that. These five, for instance.

Warwick's Wonders, 1920–1

When England toured Australia in 1920–1 much had changed since the Triangular Tournament of 1912 (see page 18). More than 60 first-class cricketers had died during the Great War, and men like Archie MacLaren, Ranji and C.B. Fry were in their late forties. Even so Fry, who was 48, was invited to captain the touring team but he withdrew because of injury and J.W.H.T. Douglas, 10 years Fry's junior, got the job.

Age didn't seem to matter so much in those days; it was regarded as a sign of maturity rather than decrepitude. Besides, in 1920–1, with so little cricket having been played in recent years and so many players having retired, a sprinkling of veterans was essential to lend experience to both sides. In that respect England might have seemed to have the stronger team, being able to call upon Douglas, Hobbs, the all-rounders Jack Hearne, Frank Woolley and Wilfred Rhodes and the Surrey fast bowler J.W. (Bill) Hitch.

What's more, in the run-up to the series the auspices looked pretty good, England – playing as the MCC, as they did then in non-Tests – had beaten South Australia, Victoria and Queensland and lost only to New South Wales. But, as they were to be reminded, there's an enormous gap between the first-class game and cricket at Test level.

Clash of the debutants

For the opening Test Australia, captained by Warwick Armstrong, who was then 41, had fewer men of experience to call upon – Armstrong himself and the batsmen Charlie Macartney, Warren Bardsley and Charles Kelleway. As the teams took the field at Sydney half the players – four English, seven

LEFT *Baggy green togetherness: Michael Clarke (partly hidden), Andrew Symonds, Justin Langer, Glenn McGrath, Matthew Hayden, Ricky Ponting, Shane Warne and Michael Hussey celebrate as Australia prepare to regain the Ashes in Perth in 2006.*

PRECEDING PAGE
Warwick Armstrong, the
first of only two Australian
captains to subject England
to the humiliation of
an Ashes whitewash,
photographed in 1921.
'Armstrong is portentous,'
wrote an English journalist
that same year. 'He reminds
one … of a character out of
Conrad; there is an air of
suppressed force about him.'

First Test, Sydney,
17–22 December 1920
Australia: 267 (Collins 70; Hearne 3–77)
and 581 (Armstrong 158, Collins 104;
Parkin 3–102).
England: 190 (Woolley 52; Gregory 3–56,
Mailey 3–95) and 281 (Hobbs 59, Hearne 57,
Hendren 56; Kelleway 3–45).
Australia won by 377 runs

Second Test, Melbourne,
31 December 1920–4 January 1921
Australia: 499 (Pellew 116, Gregory 100,
Taylor 68, Collins 64, Bardsley 51).
England: 251 (Hobbs 122, Hendren 67;
Gregory 7–69) and 157 (Woolley 50;
Armstrong 4–26).
Australia won by
an innings and 91 runs

Australian – were making their Test debuts. And pretty quickly it became clear that the home side had the more gifted newcomers. True, England's included 'Patsy' Hendren, who was to become a stalwart of the side, but among the Aussie freshmen were the opener Herbie Collins, who scored 70 and 104 on debut, Arthur Mailey, the leg-spinner, Jack Ryder, who was to average 51.62 in his 20 Tests, Bert Oldfield, the wicketkeeper who was capped 54 times, and most significantly for this and the next series, the new demon fast bowler Jack Gregory.

Australia batted first and England did well in dismissing them for 267. But despite 52 from Woolley and 49 from Hobbs the visitors were all out for 190, Gregory with 3 for 56 and Mailey (of whom it was said that he bowled like a millionaire while his fellow Australian leggie Clarrie Grimmett bowled like a miser) with 3 for 95 immediately making their presence felt. Thereafter Australia took the game – and, as it turned out, the series – by the scruff of the neck.

In the second innings, with Armstrong and Collins scoring centuries and fifties from Kelleway, Macartney, Bardsley and Taylor, the hosts totalled 581. Despite half-centuries from Hobbs, Hearne and Hendren England only managed 281, Kelleway, Gregory and Mailey each taking three wickets, and Australia won by 377 runs.

So to the second Test at Melbourne and more debutants – for England the Warwickshire fast bowler Henry Howell and the Lancashire batsman Harry Makepeace, and for Australia the right-handed batsman Roy Park. Again Australia batted first and this time they notched up 499. The best England bowler was Howell with 3 for 142.

In reply the visitors made 251 (Hobbs top-scored with a century but Gregory took seven wickets) and, following on, managed a total of just 157. Result: a win for Australia by an innings and 91 runs.

GREGORY THE GREAT

Gregory had been spotted as a great prospect – some say by Pelham Warner, in which case Englishmen might feel Warner should have kept his opinions to himself – while playing for the Imperial Forces XI in England at the end of the War. He was 6' 3", 14 stone, immensely strong and reckoned to be the fastest bowler of his day. What's more, as he proved with his century at Melbourne and another scored in 70 minutes in South Africa a year later, he could bat a bit, too.

For the third game at Adelaide he was joined by Australia's latest newcomer, Ted McDonald, thought by some to be even faster than Gregory. McDonald didn't achieve much in this or the last two Tests, taking only six wickets at 65.33; his real impact came in England in the summer of 1921. But his presence alongside Gregory established a principle that all Test nations, circumstances and personnel permitting, have followed ever since – that you open the bowling with fast men. Hitherto it had been not uncommon for the opening attack to consist of a quick at one end and a spinner at the other – a practice that was still seen in English county cricket after the Second World War. But the partnership of Gregory and McDonald emphasized the value of including genuinely fast bowlers and throwing them the ball as soon as possible.

Australia, again batting first, scored 354. And now, for maybe the only time in the series, England, whose latest debutant was the Surrey batsman P.G.H. ('Percy') Fender, batted themselves into a position from which victory might have seemed possible.

Their reply was a sizeable 447 with a century by C.A.G. Russell and good support from Woolley, Makepeace and Douglas. Had these been five-day Tests a draw, at least, would have been guaranteed. But they were not – they were timeless, and the Adelaide match went into a sixth day. So in their second innings, knowing that time didn't matter, Australia hung around for 186 overs, bar one ball. It was too much for England, gallant though their reply of 370 was (Hobbs making another century). By 119 runs, Australia had won again and regained the Ashes.

Back at Melbourne for the fourth Test, England replaced the wicketkeeper Herbie Strudwick with Yorkshire's Arthur Dolphin. It was to be Dolphin's only Test, memorable for him because of that but hardly memorable for England. For once they batted first but failed to make the most of it, their total of 284 being barely adequate.

Australia's reply of 389 put them in the driving seat. England responded with a second-innings 315. Rhodes top-scored with 73 but Mailey, turning, teasing, flighting as expansively as ever, bamboozled all the Englishmen, to take every wicket but Hendren's. The Aussies won by eight wickets.

> **Third Test, Adelaide,**
> **14–20 January 1921**
> **Australia:** 354 (Collins 162, Oldfield 50; Parkin 5–60) and 582 (Kelleway 147, Armstrong 121, Pellew 104, Gregory 78*; Howell 4–115, Rhodes 3–61).
> **England:** 447 (Russell 135*, Woolley 79, Makepeace 60, Douglas 60; Mailey 5–160) and 370 (Hobbs 123, Russell 59, Hendren 51; Mailey 5–142, Gregory 3–50).
> **Australia won by 119 runs**
>
> **Fourth Test, Melbourne,**
> **11–16 February 1921**
> **England:** 284 (Makepeace 117, Douglas 50; Mailey 4–115, Kelleway 3–37) and 315 (Rhodes 73, Douglas 60, Fender 59, Makepeace 54; Mailey 9–121).
> **Australia:** 389 (Armstrong 123*, Gregory 77, Collins 59, Bardsley 56, Fender 5–122; Woolley 3–56) and 211–2 (Gregory 76*, Ryder 52*).
> **Australia won by 8 wickets**

WARWICK'S WHITEWASH

So all that remained to be seen was whether the whitewash – the first ever between these two countries – was on, and of course it was. For the final match E.R. ('Rockley') Wilson of Yorkshire, a slow-medium right-arm bowler, made his first and only Test appearance, bringing the number of Test debutants in the series to 19, 10 of them Australians, and pointing up how many established players had been lost to the game one way or another because of the War.

HOWZAT! Roy Park, of Victoria, who made his debut in the second Test of the 1920–1 series at Melbourne, came in first wicket down and was bowled first ball by Howell. It was the only ball he ever faced in Test cricket. Drop your scorecard and you'd have missed his entire Test career as a batsman.

No matter how much pride was at stake, and there was a lot, England, alas, hardly made a fight of it. They batted first but only managed 204. Australia replied with 392, with Macartney, after a quiet series, finally coming good, aided (inevitably it must have seemed to England) by Gregory. Fender took his second five-for in consecutive Tests. England did better the second time around, but still left Australia needing only 93, which they reached for the loss of one wicket.

Warwick Armstrong, with 464 runs at 77.33 and 9 wickets at 22.66 apiece, had enjoyed a highly successful series, but the true star, the new star of international cricket, was Jack Gregory, who had come from nowhere to make 442 runs at 73.66 and take 23 wickets at 24.17.

So England, tails between their legs, shuffled off home, destroyed and humiliated, but vowing to do better when, next summer, Australia would be the visitors. Unfortunately any such vow failed to take into account the lethal fast-bowling partnership of Gregory and McDonald…

Fifth Test, Sydney,
25 February–1 March 1921
England: 204 (Woolley 53; Kelleway 4–27, Gregory 3–42) and 280 (Douglas 68; Mailey 5–119).
Australia: 392 (Macartney 170, Gregory 93; Fender 5–90) and 93–1 (Bardsley 50*).
Australia won by 9 wickets

FAST MEN ON THE RAMPAGE

The 1921 series in England was the first in which ferociously quick opening bowlers on one side, and the absence of same on the other, made the vital difference. Australia had Gregory (19 wickets at 29.05) and McDonald (27 at 24.74) and England had, well, they had all sorts of people but none as menacing as the Aussie pair.

The influence of these two ensured that Armstrong extended his winning run against England to eight matches in a row. The last two games were drawn because of bad weather and the fact that these were three-day affairs rather than timeless Tests.

For the first game at Trent Bridge England gave first caps to five players – the batsmen Percy Holmes (Yorkshire), Ernest Tyldesley (Lancashire) and Donald Knight (Surrey), the all-rounder Vallance Jupp (Northants) and the Notts leg-spinner Tom Richmond. (In the course of the series England called up 30 different players, not that it made a lot of difference, though it might have done had they been allowed to use all of them in one game.)

In a low-scoring match England, batting first, were skittled for 112 by Gregory and McDonald. Australia replied with 232 but with England

FAR RIGHT Warwick Armstrong (middle row, centre) with his all-conquering Australians, England, May 1921. Jack Gregory and E.A. (Ted) McDonald, Test cricket's first great fast-bowling double-act, stand, respectively, third from left and second from right in the back row. Between them they took 46 English wickets in Australia's 3–0 Ashes-retaining series victory.

managing only 147 at their second attempt the visitors were left needing just 30 to win, which they did without losing a wicket.

During the first Test Tyldesley was hit on the head by a ball from Gregory, which then rebounded onto his wicket, so with one ball he had been pretty well knocked out and also bowled out. Nor was Tyldesley the only casualty of the Aussie fast men. In game after game batsmen were hit in the stomach, on the hands and thumbs, on the head and over the heart. Not until Larwood and Voce knocked the Aussie batsmen around in 1932–3 (see Bodyline, pages 265–269) was so much mayhem inflicted again by two fast bowlers.

The second Test was at Lord's and again the England selectors made wholesale changes, introducing another four new caps – the Gloucestershire batsman Alf Dipper, the all-rounders Alfred Evans (Kent) and Nigel Haigh (Middlesex) and the Middlesex fast bowler Jack Durston. All but Haigh, who played in five Tests, were one-cap wonders. Again the game was completely one-sided – an Aussie win by eight wickets.

> **First Test, Trent Bridge,**
> **28–30 May 1921**
> **England:** 112 (Gregory 6–58, McDonald 3–42) and 147 (McDonald 5–32).
> **Australia:** 232 (Bardsley 66; Woolley 3–46) and 30–0.
> **Australia won by 10 wickets**
>
> **Second Test, Lord's,**
> **11–14 June 1921**
> **England:** 187 (Woolley 95; Mailey 4–55, McDonald 4–58) and 283 (Woolley 93, Tennyson 74*; Gregory 4–76, McDonald 4–89).
> **Australia:** 342 (Bardsley 88, Gregory 52; Durston 4–102) and 131–2 (Bardsley 63*).
> **Australia won by 8 wickets**

TENNYSON TAKES CHARGE

For the Lord's Test England had also brought in the Hon. Lionel Tennyson, Old Etonian, captain of Hampshire and grandson of Lord Alfred of that ilk, the former poet laureate, and after his battling second-innings knock he replaced Douglas, whose losing streak had extended to seven, as captain for the third Test at Leeds. But this was not the only change, for more debutants appeared – the 34-year-old Hampshire wicketkeeper-batsman George Brown, the 35-year-old batsmen Andy Ducat (Surrey) and Harold ('Wally') Hardinge of Kent (another pair of one-cap wonders) and the Somerset left-arm spinner J.C. ('Farmer') White.

Third Test, Headingley,
2–5 July 1921
Australia: 407 (Macartney 115, Armstrong 77, Pellew 52, Taylor 50; Parkin 4-106) and 273 for 7 (Andrews 92; White 3-37).
England: 259 (Douglas 75, Tennyson 63, Brown 57; McDonald 4-105) and 202 (Mailey 3-71).
Australia won by 219 runs

Hobbs, who had missed the first two Tests because of ill health, was also brought back. But by the time Australia had made 407 (with a century by Macartney), Hobbs had succumbed to appendicitis and did not bat in either innings. For a bit it looked as if Tennyson might not either, because while fielding he had split the webbing of his left hand.

But these poets – or anyway their descendants – are made of sterner stuff and Tennyson, damaged hand protected by a wire basket, went in seventh wicket down and added 88 with Douglas. What difference a healthy Hobbs might have made, who knows, but without him England were dismissed for 259.

Test teams didn't hang about in those days. By the close of the second day Australia were already 143 for 2 in their second innings and on day three declared on 273 for 7, leaving England little chance of making 422 to win. They didn't come close – all out (okay, nine out) for 202.

NINTH TIME LUCKY

So within a few months England had been beaten eight times in a row by Armstrong's men, but now came the good news: they didn't lose the ninth game. This was partly because rain washed out the first day's play at Old Trafford, but also because England, batting first this time, scored 362 for 4 on the second day before declaring the next morning.

ABOVE Old Etonian, Great War veteran and grandson of the more famous Alfred. Lionel Tennyson shows bulldog spirit by batting through the pain of an injury to his left hand in the third Test at Leeds, July 1921.

In fact, Tennyson had declared twice – the first time at 341 for 4 just before six o'clock on day two or, and here it becomes complicated, on day one of what had now become a two-day match because a whole day had been lost to rain. Unfortunately, what neither Tennyson nor the umpires knew but Armstrong did – and brought it firmly to everyone else's attention – was that, according to the Laws, you weren't allowed to declare after a certain point on day one of a two-day match. It was therefore decided that the England innings must continue until the next day and, to confuse matters even further, Armstrong, who had bowled the last over before the false declaration, bowled the next one as well – and nobody noticed, although for somebody to bowl two overs in succession is also a contravention of the Laws. But, what the heck, none of it really mattered because there wasn't enough time left for either side to win. If, however, this had been a timeless game England might have been in with a shout. Australia, batting on a rain-affected, uncovered wicket, were dismissed for 175, but soon afterwards everyone agreed it was time to go home.

And so to the Oval, where England introduced their 30th player of the series in the Surrey batsman Andy Sandham. Batting first, they reached 403 for 8 declared, with Mead notching up a hefty 182 not out. Australia's reply was 389 and, rain having caused the odd delay, the game was pretty well over. England went in again to make 244 for 2 but long before the close Armstrong, who believed all Tests should be timeless, had lost interest. At one point he picked up a newspaper that had blown onto the field and read the sports pages while lounging about on the boundary. His cutting explanation for this was 'I wanted to see who we were playing.'

> **Fourth Test, Old Trafford,**
> 23–26 July 1921
> **England:** 362–4 dec. (Russell 101,
> Tyldesley 78*) and 44–1.
> **Australia:** 175 (Parkin 5–38).
> Match drawn
>
> **Fifth Test, the Oval,**
> 13–16 August 1921
> **England:** 403–8 dec. (Mead 182*,
> Tennyson 51; McDonald 5–143) and 244–2
> (Russell 102*, Brown 84, Hitch 51*)
> **Australia:** 389 (Andrews 94, Taylor 75,
> Macartney 61; Parkin 3–82, Douglas 3–117)
> Match drawn

'A TEAM THAT IS PRETTY SURE OF ITSELF'

In these two series Australia undoubtedly had the stronger team but one can't help wondering whether England would have suffered an eight-nil thumping if the selectors had shown a bit more nous. As *Wisden* pointed out, they seemed to be guided in their chopping and changing by current form rather than proven class. They had, for instance, ignored Sydney Barnes for both series. True, he was 47 in 1920 but still a year younger than Fry, who had been offered the captaincy; true, too, that he had returned to Minor Counties cricket but he was apparently bowling as well as ever and, besides, had often been the scourge of Australia in the past. Wilfred Rhodes who, at the Oval in 1926, aged 48, played a large part in regaining the Ashes, was never called upon in 1921.

What's more, though faced with the two fastest bowlers in the world, the selectors ignored George Gunn of Nottinghamshire, who, along with Hobbs and the emerging Herbert Sutcliffe, was probably the best player of quick stuff in the land.

Not that this should detract from the splendour of Australia's performance. Theirs was indeed a great team with strong batting, lavish spin and, of course, Gregory and McDonald. In the first series the all-round brilliance of Gregory made the difference, in the second the combination of him and McDonald. England's batsmen had never encountered their like before. Add to them the enormous weight, both literal and metaphorical, of Warwick Armstrong and you had a side that could confidently have taken on any other from any era.

Armstrong was gifted, arrogant, supremely self-confident and perhaps the first modern cricketer in that he had no truck with the romantic idea that just playing the game was what counted. His attitude was: 'Stuff that – we're here to win,' and he instilled the same belief in his players. As the *Melbourne Herald* said of them: 'Here is a team that is pretty sure of itself.'

In its obituary of Armstrong *Wisden* said that he 'bore himself in a way likely to cause offence, but he invariably carried his desires over all opposition'. Not hard to think of later Australian skippers of whom much the same thing could be said, nor of whom their role model might have been.

Armstrong and his fast bowlers had changed cricket. Gone was the more gentle elegance of the Golden Age and in its place was a harder, tougher mentality for which 'play up, play up and play the game' didn't mean a damn thing if you were on the losing side.

BRADMAN'S INVINCIBLES, 1948

That philosophy was particularly evident in the Australian squad that toured England in 1948. This lot, captained by Don Bradman and forever immortalized in their homeland as 'the Invincibles', had – according to the batsman Bill Brown – only one aim in mind: never to be beaten by anybody. Actually, he said, that was Bradman's aim, but none of the others was likely to gainsay it – except maybe the buccaneering all-rounder Keith Miller, who always seemed to play the game for the sheer love of it and was not overly concerned by who won or lost.

However, the 1948 tour was to be Bradman's swansong, his last hurrah; at 39 he would retire from Test cricket after the final game at the Oval and was determined to go out a winner. And God, who for some reason known only to Himself seemed to have a soft spot for Bradman, made sure this happened.

Australia won the series four-nil and deservedly so, though not without some good fortune. Admittedly Norman Yardley, the England captain, won the toss four times out of five but, against that, the weather had quite obviously put its money on Australia. England had to bat in bad light at Trent Bridge, Lord's and, for a while, the Oval. It never happened to the Aussies. And at Old Trafford, England might even have been in a potentially winning position until the rain came.

HOWZAT! Talking about the so-called pressures of Test cricket, the Australian all-rounder Keith Miller, a wartime fighter pilot, said: 'Pressure? I'll tell you what pressure is – it's being in a Spitfire with a Messerschmitt up your arse. Now that's pressure. Playing cricket is not.'

A TEAM OF ALL THE TALENTS?

Still, no point in brooding over what might have been. The fact is that Bradman's team played 36 matches on tour, won 27 and drew nine. And what a team he had – the classically smooth Ray Lindwall and the more unorthodox but equally quick Miller to open the bowling, backed up by Bill Johnston's left-arm fast-medium and the nagging accuracy of Ernie Toshack's left-arm medium. In the Tests Lindwall and Johnston took 27 wickets each, Miller 13 and Toshack 11. A handful of supporting bowlers were only required to take another 11 between them. Since one of these supports was the off-spinner Ian Johnson, whose seven wickets cost 61.00 apiece, those critics who challenge the Invincibles' claim to be the greatest team ever say that the side lacked an effective spin bowler. As to that, I daresay Bradman would have insisted, as did captains of West Indian teams in years to come, that he didn't *need* a spin bowler. Anyway, had he felt the need he could have called upon two good leg-spinners in Doug Ring, who played in one Test, and Colin McCool, who didn't play in any.

For the batting, there were Arthur Morris and Sid Barnes to open the innings, followed by the Don himself, Lindsay Hassett, Bill Brown (who later

ABOVE The 1948 Australian tourists before the first Test at Trent Bridge, 10 June 1948. Although Bradman's team did not quite manage to equal Armstrong's Ashes whitewash of 1920–1, they achieved something even more extraordinary, remaining undefeated in all 34 first-class matches of their tour of England. 'Invincibles' indeed.

gave way to the 19-year-old prodigy Neil Harvey) and Miller. When required the all-rounder Sam Loxton and the wicketkeeper Don Tallon also contributed valuable runs.

It became ominously apparent on day one of the first Test at Trent Bridge that the series, which followed hard on England's three-nil defeat Down Under in 1946–7, was likely to be one-way traffic. England, batting first, were reduced to 74 for 8. They eventually reached 165, thanks to Laker's 65 in a partnership of 89 with Alec Bedser. Johnston (5 for 36) and Miller (3 for 38) did the damage.

The Aussies eased past this feeble total with only three wickets down, finally reaching 509 – Bradman's top score of 138 almost matched by Hassett's 137. England did much better second time around, scoring 441, based in large part on Compton's 184. But that left Australia needing only 98 to win. With Barnes notching up 64 not out, they achieved it with eight wickets to spare. Bedser dismissed Bradman for a comparatively rare duck in Australia's second innings.

Now for England the chopping and changing began. Australia called up 15 players in the series; England used 21. But Tom Dollery for Joe Hardstaff, Alec Coxon for Charlie Barnett, Doug Wright for Jack Young – none of it made any difference. In the Lord's match England were thrashed again, this time by 409 runs.

First Test, Trent Bridge,
10–15 June 1948
England: 165 (Laker 65; Johnston 5–36, Miller 3–38) and 441 (Compton 184, Hutton 74, Evans 50; Miller 4–125, Johnston 4–147).
Australia: 509 (Bradman 138, Hassett 137, Barnes 63; Laker 4–138) and 98–2 (Barnes 64*).
Australia won by 8 wickets

Second Test, Lord's,
24–29 June 1948
Australia: 350 (Morris 105, Tallon 53; Bedser 4–100) and 460–7 dec. (Barnes 141, Bradman 89, Miller 74, Morris 62).
England: 215 (Compton 53; Lindwall 5–70, Johnson 3–72) and 186 (Toshack 5–40, Lindwall 3–61).
Australia won by 409 runs

COMPTON THE HERO

And so to Manchester, the scene of England's best chance of a win, Compton's heroics and a nasty injury to Barnes. But before anything else happened England's selectors caused a sensation by dropping Hutton and replacing him with George Emmett of Gloucestershire. Hutton's scores in the series to date had been 3, 74, 20 and 13. His opening partner Cyril Washbrook had fared even worse, with 6, 1, 8 and 37, so it must have been a toss-up which of them to discard. England won the toss again and batted first with Emmett contributing 10 and Washbrook 11, a disappointment for him, since he had been averaging 13 until then.

At 28 for 2 Compton joined Bill Edrich and now Lindwall embarked on a series of bouncers, one of them – a no-ball – flying off the edge of Compton's bat as he tried to hook and hitting him on the forehead. This, remember, was in the days before batsmen wore helmets; Compton didn't even wear a cap. He staggered around, bleeding profusely, before being led off to have stitches inserted in the wound.

But when England had fallen to 119 for 5, the hero returned, head swathed in bandages, to score 145 not out before the innings closed on 363. This total included a stand of 15 for the eighth wicket between Compton and the Lancashire fast-medium bowler Dick Pollard. It's only worth mentioning because, in the course of it, Pollard hit the ball an almighty swipe straight into the midriff of Sid Barnes, fielding as usual about five yards from the bat at silly mid-on. The stricken Barnes collapsed and was carried off by four policemen, thus upstaging Compton who had needed no such constabulary assistance, before being taken on a stretcher to hospital.

Like Compo, Barnes pluckily returned to the ground and batted at number six, but collapsed at the wicket when he had scored only one and went back to hospital, there to spend ten days under observation. Not surprisingly, in his absence, Australia's first innings total was modest by their standards, 221.

With a lead of 142 England sniffed victory, but now the weather intervened. No play was possible for a day and a half, and though Yardley declared when the game restarted with England 174 for 3, there was no time left for anything but a draw. Australia batted out the final day to close on 92 for 1.

> **Third Test, Old Trafford,**
> **8–13 July 1948**
> **England:** 363 (Compton 145*; Lindwall 4–99, Johnston 3–67) and 174–3 dec. (Washbrook 85*, Edrich 53).
> **Australia:** 221 (Morris 51; Bedser 4–81, Pollard 3–53) and 92–1 (Morris 54*).
> **Match drawn**

BUSINESS AS USUAL

After these alarums and excursions the series resumed its inevitable course at Headingley. Well, actually, no, for this was a quite remarkable game. For England Hutton was restored in place of Emmett, and Jack Young, the Middlesex left-arm spinner, was dropped. In the event there were many who thought this a mistake, arguing that if Young had been there on a wicket encouraging spin the result might have been different. If nothing else, his presence would have spared Yardley and Compton from having to send down 48 overs between them and Hutton from being required to contribute four overs of so-called leg-spin that cost 30 runs.

The game started well for England, the home side scoring 496, following an opening stand of 168 by Hutton and Washbrook. Bedser's 79, his highest score in Test cricket, was made as nightwatchman. He had come in at 268 for 2 when Washbrook was out and stuck around the next morning to add 161 with Edrich.

At one point England were looking at a potentially enormous score, but 423 for 2 rapidly became 496 all out, good but not that great because in reply Australia made 458, with Neil Harvey making 112 on his Ashes debut. Even so England, who began their second innings with another century opening stand, seemed a good bet if not for a win then at least a draw when they declared at 365 for 8. This left Australia needing 404 to win, a higher score than had ever been made before in a fourth innings to win a Test match.

> **Fourth Test, Headingley,**
> **22–27 July 1948**
> **England:** 496 (Washbrook 143, Edrich 111, Hutton 81, Bedser 79; Loxton 3–55) and 365–8 dec. (Compton 66, Washbrook 65, Hutton 57, Edrich 54; Johnston 4–95).
> **Australia:** 458 (Harvey 112, Loxton 93, Lindwall 77, Miller 58; Bedser 3–92, Laker 3–113) and 404–3 (Morris 182, Bradman 173*).
> **Australia won by 7 wickets**

England captain Norman Yardley (sixth from left) leads the applause for Bradman (far left) as he embarks on his last Test innings in the fifth Test at the Oval, 14 August 1948. The non-striking Australian batsman is Arthur Morris, with the hulking figure of Alec Bedser to his right. Eric Hollies, whose dismissal of Bradman with a second-ball googly ensured that the 'Don' failed to reach the four runs he needed to average 100 in Test cricket, is second from the left.

When Australia were 57 for 1, with the ball lifting and turning sharply, England were looking pretty good. But unfortunately Laker was having a bad day and, without Young to attack from the other end, Compton with his chinamen was the only other spinner of any note available. With Morris and Bradman batting beautifully together and the England fielders having a bad day, that was never going to be enough. Bradman was missed three times and Morris twice as they put on 301 for the second wicket.

By the time Morris was out, the Aussie score was already 358 and the game was virtually over. Although Miller was dismissed cheaply, Bradman and Harvey wrapped things up.

Farewell to the Don

Fifth Test, the Oval,
14–18 August 1948
**England: 53 (Lindwall 6–20) and 188
(Hutton 64; Johnston 4-40, Lindwall 3-50).
Australia: 389 (Morris 196, Barnes 61;
Hollies 5-131).
Australia won by
an innings and 149 runs**

Which brought everyone to the Oval and Bradman's last Test, and what a double anticlimax this turned out to be. Anticlimax number one was England's first innings. On a pitch already saturated by rain with the threat of more to come, Yardley decided to bat first and was rewarded with a derisory total of 53, of which Hutton – last man out – contributed 30. Nobody else got close to double figures, and five players registered ducks. Lindwall took 6 for 20.

Australia's openers more than doubled this pitiful score and when Barnes was out at 117 there came the moment everyone was waiting for – Donald Bradman's final innings in a Test match. His progress to the wicket was accompanied by a standing ovation from the packed crowd and three cheers from the England team.

Then silence as the Warwickshire leg-spinner Eric Hollies bowled the first ball and the great man blocked it. Hollies toddled to the wicket again, tossed the ball up, Bradman played at it and – anticlimax number two – failed to spot the googly and was clean-bowled for nought, thus reducing his overall Test average from 101.39 to a mere 99.94. Not that it really mattered, not in the overall scheme of the match. Even without Bradman's help Australia scored 389 with Morris run out on 196 and Barnes the second-highest scorer with 61, and then the home team, at one time 125 for 2, managed to get themselves all out for 188, proving that middle- and late-order collapses are nothing new for England XIs. Hutton this time made 64, while Johnston claimed four and Lindwall three scalps, Australia winning by an innings and 149.

The crushing 4–0 series win was no more than Australia deserved because they had outplayed England in every aspect of the game. Even without

HOWZAT! Did Bradman get his final duck because, as he claimed, he had a tear in his eye? Not according to the Gloucestershire and England batsman Jack Crapp, who said: 'That bugger Bradman never had a tear in his eye in his whole life.'

Bradman their batting would have been far too strong for England's meagre attack. Seven of their players averaged more than 44 in the Tests.

As for the bowling, England had nobody who came close to the pace of Lindwall and Miller or the accuracy and control of Johnston. (Only Bedser with 18 at 38.22 managed to take 10 wickets or more.) Like Armstrong before him, Bradman had shown that while strong batting can make defeat unlikely it's fast bowling that wins matches – that and a bloody-minded approach that neither seeks nor offers quarter.

THE SUPER SPRINGBOKS, 1970

Australia toured South Africa in 1970 immediately after a somewhat fraught tour of India. The cricket itself wasn't particularly fraught – Australia won the series three-one – but a riot in Bombay, the crowd's invasion of the pitch in Calcutta and stone-throwing in Bangalore had probably been a bit wearing on the nerves. Everyone said it was jolly decent of the Aussies to go through with the South African visit after such a harrowing time.

For their part the South Africans were very grateful. As it turned out this was to be the last series in which they would take part before the anti-apartheid ban later that year. But they were already somewhat starved of international cricket, their most recent series having been in 1966–7 when they had beaten Bobby Simpson's visiting Australians three-one. Now they were hungry for more.

A NASTY SURPRISE FOR AUSTRALIA

The home team then were raring to go and so, said the visiting captain, Bill Lawry, were his men. In the event he was proved right, although not perhaps in the way he had expected, for raring or not, go indeed the Australians went – into total humiliation, which must have come as a nasty surprise.

Australia, with a squad including the fast bowlers Graham McKenzie and Alan Connolly, batters such as Lawry, Doug Walters, Ian Redpath, Keith Stackpole and Ian Chappell, the off-spinner Ashley Mallett and the 'mystery' spinner John Gleeson, who propelled the ball off his middle finger and could turn it equally from leg or off, must have been reasonably confident of victory, since they had enjoyed recent wins against the fading but still quite powerful West Indies as well as India.

But it was their bad luck to come up against the best South African side there has ever been. There were the Pollock brothers, the fast-bowling Peter (father of Shaun) and the majestic left-handed batsman Graeme; then there was Ali Bacher, a fine captain and doughty right-handed bat, along with the all-rounders Eddie Barlow, Trevor Goddard, who scored 2516 runs and took

123 wickets in Tests, and the hugely gifted Mike Procter, who bowled like a 90 mph whirlwind (off the wrong foot, the critics said, though surely that's impossible) and could hit the ball into the next county. And along with all those there was Barry Richards, as yet uncapped but already one of the finest batsmen in the world, potentially perhaps one of the finest of all time. Against this combination, Lawry's lot were never in with a chance.

In the first of the four Tests South Africa, boosted by Barlow's 127 and 57 from their captain, scored 382. In reply Australia were bounced and blasted out by Peter Pollock and Procter for 164, only Walters showing much fight with 73. In the home team's second innings Graeme Pollock kept the fraternal flag flying with 50, but Connolly with five wickets and Gleeson with four restricted South Africa to 232. Not a lot but more than enough. At the second time of asking, Lawry helped Australia to a more respectable 280, but still lost by 170 runs.

> **First Test, Cape Town,**
> **22–27 January 1970**
> **South Africa:** 382 (Barlow 127, Bacher 57; Mallett 5–126) and 232 (G. Pollock 50; Connolly 5–47, Gleeson 4–70).
> **Australia:** 164 (Walters 73; P. Pollock 4–20) and 280 (Lawry 83; Procter 4–47).
> South Africa won by 170 runs

POLE-AXED BY POLLOCK

In the second match Graeme Pollock massacred the Aussie attack with 274 (then the highest Test score by a South African), Richards announced his arrival on the international scene with 140 in his second game, Herbert ('Tiger') Lance chipped in with 61, while Connolly, Gleeson and the fast-medium bowler Eric Freeman all went for more than 100 runs each as South Africa topped the 600 mark. Australia's response was more of a whimper than a retort: a pathetic 157, Paul Sheahan contributing 62 while Barlow took 3 for 24 and Procter, Pollock and Goddard chipped in with a brace of wickets apiece. Australia did better second time around with Redpath and Walters both scoring 74 and Stackpole 71, but South Africa won easily by an innings and 129 runs.

So now Australia, two down with two to play, simply had to win the next two games. Fat chance, although in the third Test at Johannesburg it could be said that they did fractionally better – they only lost by 307 runs.

Following the Durban debacle, Australia did what at the beginning of the tour would have seemed unthinkable – they dropped 'Garth' McKenzie, who had been the mainstay of their attack for several years, and replaced him with Laurie Mayne. Much good it did them. Mayne's match figures at Johannesburg were 3 for 160 from 44.3 overs.

> **Second Test, Durban,**
> **5–9 February 1970**
> **South Africa:** 622–9 dec. (G. Pollock 274, Richards 140, Lance 61).
> **Australia:** 157 (Sheahan 62; Barlow 3–24) and 336 (Redpath 74, Walters 74, Stackpole 71; Procter 3–62, Barlow 3–63).
> South Africa won by an innings and 129 runs

> **Third Test, Johannesburg,**
> **19–24 February 1970**
> **South Africa** 279 (Irvine 79, Richards 65, G. Pollock 52; Gleeson 3–61) and 408 (Barlow 110, G. Pollock 87, Irvine 73; Gleeson 5–125).
> **Australia** 202 (Walters 64; P. Pollock 5–39, Procter 3–48) and 178 (Redpath 66; Procter 3–24, Goddard 3–27).
> South Africa won by 307 runs

RIGHT *Graeme Pollock drives powerfully through extra cover. The left-hander was in imperious form during South Africa's 1970 home series against Australia.*

In cricketing terms Graeme Pollock is a sadist. ● Eddie Barlow on his South African team-mate

WHITEWASHING THE BAGGY GREEN

And so, finally, to Port Elizabeth with South Africa contemplating an unprecedented whitewash of the men in the baggy green caps. This time Australia retained Mayne but also brought back McKenzie. It wasn't a bad Australian side but neither was it particularly strong and maybe they were a little jaded after the tribulations of the India tour. Whatever the excuses, they were simply out of their depth against the gifted Springboks who, right then, were probably the best team in the world.

For the fourth time Bacher won the toss, South Africa batted, Richards and Barlow put on 157 for the first wicket and from then on Australia were always chasing the game. Excellent bowling by Connolly restricted South Africa to 311 in their first innings, but it was still too much for Australia, who could manage only 212. With an encouraging first innings lead of 99, the host country then proceeded to knock up 407 for 8 declared, leaving Australia the

RIGHT *Barry Richards pulls to the boundary while playing for Hampshire, where he formed a longstanding and fruitful opening partnership with the West Indies' Gordon Greenidge in the 1970s. Many commentators consider the sublimely talented Richards to be the greatest loss to Test cricket following South Africa's isolation from international competition.*

The only time an Australian walks is when his car runs out of petrol. ● Barry Richards

impossible task of scoring 507 to win. They never came close, being dismissed for 246 with nobody scoring a fifty and Procter taking six wickets. Another huge win – by 323 runs – for South Africa, despite the golden boy Graeme Pollock contributing only 1 and 4.

This whitewash was and remains South Africa's greatest triumph. The tragedy – no, not the tragedy, nobody died – the pity of it is that, thanks to their government's racist policy none of that splendid Springbok squad ever played Test cricket again, though most of them were in, or approaching, their prime. Indeed, this series represented the entire Test careers of the 24-year-old Richards (508 runs at 72.57) and the 26-year-old Irvine (353 at 50.42).

What might they or the 24-year-old Procter, who ended the series with 209 runs at 34.83 and 26 wickets at 13.57, have achieved had they been born in some less benighted country? As for Graeme Pollock, himself only 26 in 1970, if he had been allowed to continue from where he was obliged to leave off, he could easily have ended up as the most successful batsman, bar Bradman, in the history of the game.

Whatever anyone might say it's impossible to keep politics out of sport (or anything else, come to that) and here their own country's vile politics destroyed the international careers of South Africa's finest team. A bitter thought to dwell upon, although Lawry's Aussies must also have had pretty bitter thoughts as they skulked off home with averted gaze and their baggy green caps pulled low over their eyes.

Fourth Test, Port Elizabeth,
5–10 March 1970
South Africa: 311 (Richards 81, Barlow 73; Connolly 6-47) and 470-8 dec. (Richards 126, Irvine 102, Bacher 73, Lindsay 60; Mayne 3-83).
Australia: 212 (Sheahan 67, Redpath 55; Procter 3-30, P. Pollock 3-46) and 246 (Procter 6-73).
South Africa won by 323 runs

THE WINDIES WIZARDS, 1984–5

From England's point of view the West Indies' dominance of world cricket reached its peak between 1984 and 1986, a period wherein the Windies, mostly under Clive Lloyd, went a record-breaking 27 games without defeat. In 1984 Lloyd brought these all-conquering warriors to England, against whom they had not lost a series for 15 years. Nor was anything about to change.

AN EMBARRASSMENT OF RICHES

The common feature of all the great teams we have looked at so far is that they had two extremely good, extremely quick fast bowlers. Well, Lloyd's squad had not just two but several battalions of them. Somewhere in the West Indies at that time there seemed to be a conveyor-belt that turned out a new quick bowler every hour on the hour. There were so many of them that Lloyd's party left out Wayne Daniel, who would have strolled into any other Test team in the world.

Among those chosen, however, were Malcolm Marshall, Michael Holding (aka 'Whispering Death'), Joel ('Big Bird') Garner, Eldine Baptiste and Winston Davis. And they, along with a batting line-up of Gordon Greenidge, Desmond Haynes, Larry Gomes, Viv Richards and Lloyd himself, were far too good for England. In addition, unlike many West Indian sides of the period, they also had in Roger Harper their best off-spinner since Lance Gibbs. The team was so strong that Davis played in only one Test – called up from Glamorgan to replace the injured Marshall at Old Trafford – while neither Courtney Walsh nor fine batsmen like Richie Richardson and Gus Logie could get into the side at all.

Of the Tests and Texaco Trophy games they lost only one, a one-day match at Trent Bridge. Most significantly, and for England most humiliatingly, they won every Test, so becoming the first tourists to inflict a five-nil whitewash (or, as the West Indians preferred to put it, 'blackwash') on the host nation.

The statistics tell the story. In the Tests the West Indies scored seven hundreds, two by Greenidge (both double-centuries), two by Gomes and one each by Richards, Dujon and Haynes, who otherwise had a poor series (not that anyone really noticed, so well did the rest of his team perform). England managed only four centuries, three by Allan Lamb (who excelled against the Windies despite a patchy Test record overall), the other by Graeme Fowler.

The bowling figures are even more telling. Marshall took 24 wickets at 18.21, Garner 29 at 18.62, Harper 13 at 21.23 and Holding (who, like Marshall, missed one Test) 15 at 22.87. England's best were Paul Allott with 14 at 20.14 and Ian Botham with 19 at 35.10.

BROKEN WICKETS, BROKEN BONES

The downside to the West Indian superiority (ignoring the fact that, from an English point of view, the entire series was a downside) was the excessive use of bouncers by their fast men. Andy Lloyd and Paul Terry both suffered serious injuries as a result and, as *Wisden* put it, batting against the quick bowlers 'became as much an exercise in self-defence as in defence of the wicket'.

In the first Test at Edgbaston the West Indies began as they obviously intended to continue by sweeping away what was, in truth, a fairly average England side. On his debut Warwickshire's Andy Lloyd, opening the innings, lasted for seven overs and 10 runs before being hit on the head by a ball from Marshall. He spent the next five days in hospital and never played Test cricket again. The match result reflected the reality that, following Lloyd's injury, there was only ever one team in it: West Indies won by an innings and 180 runs.

In the series the Windies used only 13 players; Winston Davis and another fast bowler Milton Small coming in for one

First Test, Edgbaston,
14–18 June 1984
England 191 (Botham 64; Garner 4–53)
and 235 (Downton 56; Garner 5–55).
West Indies 606 (Gomes 143, Richards 117,
Baptiste 87*, Lloyd 71, Holding 69;
Pringle 5–108).
West Indies won by
an innings and 180 runs

game each to replace the injured Holding and Marshall. England called up 21, including in the second Test Chris Broad (father of Stuart), who later acquitted himself well in Mike Gatting's Ashes-retaining team of 1986–7. Replacing Lloyd as opening bat alongside Fowler, he made a decent debut, but again England were not good enough, although they did manage a rare first-innings lead and even had the temerity to declare their second innings.

What brought this unusual occurrence about were weather conditions that, until after lunch on the last day, favoured England's swing bowlers rather than the West Indian quicks. At that point it even looked as if England might win but unfortunately, as soon as the skipper David Gower declared, all signs of swing and movement disappeared and the West Indian batsmen – especially Greenidge, with a match-winning double-century – made light work of scoring 344 to win by nine wickets.

> **Second Test, Lord's,**
> **28 June–3 July 1984**
> **England:** 286 (Fowler 106, Broad 55; Marshall 6–85) and 300–9 dec. (Lamb 110, Botham 81; Small 3–40, Garner 3–91).
> **West Indies:** 245 (Marshall 79, Richards 72; Botham 8–103) and 344–1 (Greenidge 214*, Gomes 92*).
> **West Indies won by 9 wickets**

THE MAGIC OF MARSHALL

In the third Test, at Leeds, England were again in contention until about halfway, at which point the superior class of the West Indians and the courage of Marshall overwhelmed them. Marshall was, in every way, the hero of the game. After bowling six overs in England's first innings he suffered a double-fracture of the left thumb when fielding a shot by Broad and was advised not to play again for at least 10 days. He bowled no more in that innings but, with his own side nine wickets down, went in to bat one-handed and help Gomes to his century. That was brave enough; after all England's strike bowlers, Willis and Allott, though not as fast as the West Indian quicks, could certainly discomfort anyone with a broken thumb. But when England batted again Marshall insisted on doing his share of the bowling and returned his best figures in Test cricket. Result: a win for the West Indies by eight wickets. Rubber over.

THE 'BLACKWASH' BECKONS

At Manchester England again flattered only to deceive. At one point on the first day West Indies were 70 for 4 but after that Greenidge, with his second double-century, Dujon and Davis (chosen as a bowler, not a batsman) took control of the game. Then, as if England were not in enough trouble, Davis, the bowler, broke Paul Terry's arm with a short-pitched delivery. Echoing Marshall's courage at Leeds, Terry returned to the wicket at number 11 to try to avoid the follow-on. It didn't work; before being bowled by Garner he saw Lamb to his third consecutive hundred, but that was all. Thereafter it was again one-way traffic resulting in a win for the West Indies by an innings and 64 runs.

For the fifth Test at the Oval, with England facing the second whitewash in their history, Gower called for 'one last effort', a cry that had a ring of desperation about it. It did no good, although when West Indies were 70 for 6 in their first innings the troops seemed to be responding; even after Clive Lloyd had played a captain's innings to rally his men the final score – 190, the Windies' lowest total of the series – was hardly intimidating. But it was still too much for England. Again the fast men took control. Fowler was hit on the arm and retired hurt before returning to make his side's highest score, 31. Second time around the home team again showed a bit of bulldog spirit, reducing the visitors to 132 for 4 before Haynes decided such nonsense had gone far enough and England were left needing 394 to win. Forlorn hope. Against Holding and Garner they caved in, only Botham making more than 50. So the West Indies had won the game by 172 runs and the series by five to zilch.

It's Test cricket, it's tough. If you want an easy game, take up netball. ● Steve Waugh

Malcolm Marshall was pretty much unplayable throughout the 1984 series, but nowhere more so than in the third Test at Headingley, where he ripped through England's batsmen in their second innings, taking 7 wickets for just 53 runs. Here, he unleashes a trademark bouncer that forces Graeme Fowler to take evasive action.

ENGLAND'S CARIBBEAN NIGHTMARE

BELOW *Viv Richards's West Indies squad before the third Test of the 1985–6 series against England, Kensington Oval, Bridgetown, Barbados. In Michael Holding (front row, third from right), Malcolm Marshall (back row, far left), Joel Garner (front row, second from right) and Patrick Patterson (back row, third from right), the West Indies class of '86 possessed what may rank as the most terrifying pace attack of all time. And the young Courtney Walsh (tallest in the back row) could bowl a bit, as well...*

Decidedly chuffed by this triumph, Lloyd led his team to Australia where they took the series three-one. Meanwhile England, faced with touring the West Indies in 1985–6 and still led by Gower, who had averaged only 19.00 in the 1984 matches, set about regrouping. And, next summer as they, too, beat Australia three-one they must have felt confident that they had done so.

Nevertheless, bearing in mind that West Indian groundsmen liked to make fast bowlers very happy, the attack they took to the Caribbean was somewhat bizarre. No Willis (who had retired), no Allott (who hadn't) and in their places the fast-medium Neil Foster of Essex, along with the swing bowling of Botham and Richard Ellison of Kent and only one genuine quick in Glamorgan's Greg Thomas. With hindsight it's easy to see that such a line-up, impressive enough in England, would never present many problems to West Indian batsmen in the Caribbean. And so, as again the statistics indicate, it proved.

The bowling figures first. For West Indies (captained, after Lloyd's retirement, by Viv Richards) Garner took 27 wickets at 16.14, Marshall 27 at 17.85, Patrick Patterson – who had displaced Davis and Small (mere trundlers compared with the speed he generated) – had 19 at 22.42 and Holding, who again missed one Test, 16 at 24.06. What a line-up! With that amount of velocity at their disposal – plus Courtney Walsh to step in when Holding wasn't available – the West Indian selectors could happily dispense with the off-spinner Harper for all but two Tests. Who needed to pick locks when you could just kick the door down?

England, however, lacking anything like such firepower, did need a spinner – desperately. And John Emburey did his best with 14 wickets at 32.00; Botham with 11 at 48.63 was the only other bowler to take 10 wickets or more.

And then the batting… For West Indies Haynes scored 469 at 78.16, Richards 331 at 66.20 and Richie Richardson 387 at 55.28. Between them they managed four centuries, Richardson notching two of them. In reply, England's best batsman was Gower with 370 at 37.00, nobody else averaged 30 and they couldn't manage one century among them. Little wonder that the series resulted in another monumental whitewashing, blackwashing five-nothing triumph for West Indies, who had now beaten England 10 times in a row. For the record the results were as follows:

First Test, Kingston, Jamaica, 21–23 February 1986
England 159 (Gooch 51; Patterson 4–30) and 152 (Willey 71; Garner 3–22, Marshall 3–29, Patterson 3–44).
West Indies 307 (Greenidge 58, Gomes 56, Dujon 54; Ellison 5–78) and 5–0.
West Indies won by 10 wickets

Second Test, Port-of-Spain, Trinidad, 7–12 March, 1986
England 176 (Gower 66, Lamb 62; Marshall 4–38, Garner 3–45) and 315 (Walsh 4–74, Marshall 4–94).
West Indies 399 (Richardson 102, Haynes 67, Marshall 62*; Emburey 5–78) and 95–3.
West Indies won by 7 wickets

Third Test, Bridgetown, Barbados, 21–25 March 1986
West Indies 418 (Richardson 160, Haynes 84, Richards 51; Thomas 4–70, Foster 3–76).
England 189 (Gower 66, Gooch 53; Marshall 4–42, Patterson 3–54) and 199 (Garner 4–69, Patterson 3–28).
West Indies won by an innings and 30 runs

Fourth Test, Port-of-Spain, Trinidad, 3–5 April 1986
England 200 (Garner 4–43, Holding 3–52) and 150 (Garner 3–15, Marshall 3–42).
West Indies 312 (Richards 87; Botham 5–71, Emburey 3–62) and 49–0.
West Indies won by 10 wickets

Fifth Test, St John's, Antigua, 11–16 April 1986
West Indies 474 (Haynes 131, Marshall 76, Holding 73, Harper 60) and 246–2 dec. (Richards 110*, Haynes 70).
England 310 (Gower 90, Slack 52, Gooch 51; Garner 4–67, Marshall 3–64) and 170 (Gooch 51, Harper 3–10).
West Indies won by 240 runs

This was about as overwhelming a victory as anyone could wish for. In seven innings out of ten England were blasted aside for fewer than 200 runs, while in each of only five complete innings West Indies scored more than 300. Well, yes, for England there were excuses. In the games running up to the series they were given lousy pitches to play on, while Gatting had his nose smashed by a ball from Marshall in an ODI prior to the Tests, went home to get the damaged proboscis repaired and pluckily returned only to have his

HOWZAT! As a result of these two series David Gower holds a unique record, which he probably won't thank me for reminding you of: he is the only England captain ever to lead his team to two whitewashes.

thumb broken in a game against Barbados. Not that any of this really mattered – except to Gatting, of course. Even a fully fit, unbattered, rampant Gatting in the form of his life wouldn't have made a ha'porth of difference. For the fact is that between 1984 and 1986 the West Indies teams, including as they did in Richards, Greenidge, Lloyd, Marshall, Garner and Holding some of the finest cricketers of the last 50 years, were far too strong for any other country in the world. And in this series they simply squeezed the spirit out of a despondent England.

PONTING'S PARTY-POOPERS (OR FLINTOFF'S FLOPS), 2006–7

It is a time-honoured tradition among the Australian press to enquire of each visiting England captain, purely, of course, in an earnest quest for knowledge: 'Is this the worst flamin' Pommie team ever to reach these shores?'

If it had been asked (as it probably was) of 'Freddie' Flintoff in late 2006 it would have saved everybody a lot of time and, in the case of England's followers, heartache if he and the rest of the squad had simply chorused 'Yes!' and got back on the plane to fly home and be done with it.

It would be unjust to label them as individually rotten players, but as a team they managed to notch up some staggeringly rotten results. Well, much the same had been true of Douglas's tourists in 1920–1, but the difference between them and Flintoff's raggedy-arsed army was that Flintoff's lot had regained the Ashes – under a different captain, admittedly – only the previous year and might have been expected to put up a decent fight to retain them.

In the event they did nothing of the kind. All right, Michael Vaughan, the Ashes-winning skipper, was injured and unavailable as was Simon Jones, England's best reverse-swinging fast bowler. And there were doubts about the fitness of Flintoff and Ashley Giles. But James Anderson and Sajid Mahmood had replaced Jones, and the young Alastair Cook was reckoned a handy substitute for Vaughan as opening bat. As for the captaincy, well, was Flintoff really a better bet than Andrew Strauss, who had skippered England rather well against Pakistan the previous summer? Hindsight says no, but then hindsight was always a know-all. Still, all this is academic because Australia, under Ricky Ponting, were in the process of equalling the world record of 16 Test wins in a row and weren't about to let a bunch of Poms interrupt them.

The first shock for England came before the series began when Marcus Trescothick flew home suffering from 'a stress-related illness'. The second came with ball one, on day one, of Test one, which ball – delivered by Steve Harmison – flew straight from his hand into the hands of Flintoff at second slip, to the astonishment of all and the huge amusement of the crowd. From then on Harmison was demoralized and so were England.

AUSTRALIA'S GOLDEN GENERATION

But while castigating England for an inept performance, especially in the second Test, let us also give praise to their opponents. Whether this was a better Australian side than Steve Waugh's, which won 16 straight tests between 1999 and 2001, is difficult to say because, apart from Waugh himself, his twin brother Mark, both of whom had retired, and the fast bowler Jason Gillespie (who was already going off the boil in 2005 anyway), the essential personnel were much the same. Players such as Ponting, Shane Warne, Glenn McGrath, Adam Gilchrist, Matthew Hayden and Justin Langer made the team formidable enough to start with. And though the two Waughs were tough to replace, Australia, as is their custom, managed to do so, with the prolific Mike Hussey and Michael Clarke, while Stuart Clark ensured that Gillespie's absence went unnoticed. In addition, what Ponting's team did and what Waugh's could never manage, was to whitewash England.

Yet, at the outset, England had cause to hope. They had won six recent Test series and stood second only to Australia in the world rankings. Besides, the average age of the Aussie team was 33 – 'Dad's Army', according to England supporters before Harmison's initial delivery – and several were thought to be past their best. On the other hand, with Vaughan and Trescothick absent, only Harmison, Giles and Matthew Hoggard of the England party had ever played a Test in Australia. Knocking on the Aussies might have been, but they had experience on their side – and they made it pay.

Starting the first Test at Brisbane with one run on the board before a single legal ball had been bowled (Harmison's wide) and inspired by an imperious innings from their captain, they made a huge total, could easily have enforced the follow-on, chose not to and proceeded to grind England underfoot, winning by 277 runs.

Well, England lost the first Test in 2005 as well and still came back to take the series. What had been done before could surely be done again and, for a while, it looked as though it might be.

> **First Test, Brisbane,**
> **23–27 November 2006**
> **Australia** 602-9 dec. (Ponting 196, Hussey 86, Langer 82, Clarke 56; Flintoff 4-99) and 202-1 dec. (Langer 100*, Ponting 60*).
> **England** 157 (Bell 50; McGrath 6-50, Clark 3-21) and 370 (Collingwood 96, Pietersen 92; Clark 4-42, Warne 4-124).
> **Australia won by 277 runs**

AUSTRALIA'S ASHES

At Adelaide Flintoff won the toss and, glory be, for once it was England piling on the runs. But with 551 on the board, courtesy of Collingwood's double-century and his solid partnership with Pietersen, Flintoff declared. Now was

this boldness or just hubris? Should he not have batted on to put the game beyond Australia's reach? Was he not aware of the precedent set only three years earlier – on this very ground – when Australia lost to India after scoring 556? Whatever his thinking, it was a terrible mistake. Australia and Ponting himself started scratchily in reply but then the hapless Giles, hampered by a hip injury and soon to fly home anyway because of his wife's illness, dropped Ponting off a sitter. Later it was said, perhaps unkindly, that in that moment he had also dropped the Ashes.

Batting again with only a narrow lead, England should still have made the game safe but instead, mesmerized by Warne, whose figures did not reflect the complete hold he had on them, they batted like a prep school XI playing against their fathers. Another humiliating defeat, this time by six wickets, became inevitable.

Who knows? If England had batted halfway decently in their second innings and drawn the game perhaps they would have gone on to make a fight of it. As it was every vestige of morale seemed to have vanished and at Perth they duly handed back the Ashes having held them for only 462 days. Here they started quite well, dismissing Australia for their lowest all-out total of the series. For once Harmison came good and Monty Panesar, replacing Giles, made an impressive start. But after that it was business as usual as they were out-bowled and out-batted to lose by 206 runs. As a measure of Australia's dominance, in their second innings Gilchrist scored a century off only 57 balls, one ball more than Viv Richard's Test record (against England in 1985–6). In terms of balls faced, if not of time at the crease, Gilchrist's was surely the quickest 100 in Ashes history.

Second Test, Adelaide,
1–5 December 2006
England 551–6 dec. (Collingwood 206, Pietersen 158, Bell 60; Clark 3–75) and 129 (Warne 4–49).
Australia 513 (Ponting 142, Clarke 124, Hussey 91, Gilchrist 64; Hoggard 7–109) and 168–4 (Hussey 61*).
Australia won by 6 wickets

Third Test, Perth,
14–18 December 2006
Australia 244 (Hussey 74*; Panesar 5–92, Harmison 4–48) and 527–5 dec. (Clarke 135*, Hussey 103, Gilchrist 102, Hayden 92; Panesar 3–145).
England 215 (Pietersen 70; Clark 3–49) and 350 (Cook 116, Bell 87, Pietersen 60*, Flintoff 51; Warne 4–115).
Australia won by 206 runs

RICKY'S WHITEWASH

Now all that remained was to see if the impending whitewash could be averted. After the second Test Damien Martyn had surprisingly announced his immediate retirement. Now Warne, needing only one more victim to become the first player to take 700 Test wickets, revealed that he, too, would retire at the end of the series. Thus there was much emotion surrounding the Melbourne Test, which started on Boxing Day after an unusually rainy Christmas (89,155 people watched the first day's play). For this game England dropped wicketkeeper Geraint Jones and replaced him with Chris Read, not that it made much difference. But… avoiding the whitewash: a good sign that Flintoff won the toss and chose to bat? Well, not really, because Warne swiftly took his 700th Test wicket (Collingwood caught off a leg-break) and four more besides and, anyway, just look at the scores. So, another win for Australia, this time by an innings and 99 runs.

And so to the final game at Sydney. This was another emotional occasion, for now it was known that McGrath and Langer would also retire when the series was done. Australia needed that whitewash to see their heroes off in style and they duly got it, although England managed to be reasonably competitive until the third day when, as was now almost to be expected, they were contemptuously brushed aside. Because of England's propensity to collapse they had become known as 'six out, all out'. But in this series it was more like 'five out, all out', since on average their last five wickets acquired 44 runs between them. In this final Test, indeed, it was a case of 'four out, all out' because they lost their last six wickets for 46 runs in the first innings and their last six for 49 in the second, hardly a sign of a team prepared to put up a fight. And a fight is what they did *not* put up, losing the game by 10 wickets.

> **Fourth Test, Melbourne,**
> 26–28 December 2006
> **England** 159 (Strauss 50; Warne 5-39)
> and 161 (Brett Lee 4-47, Clark 3-30).
> **Australia** 419 (Symonds 156, Hayden 153;
> Mahmood 4-100, Flintoff 3-77).
> **Australia won by**
> **an innings and 99 runs**
>
> **Fifth Test, Sydney,**
> 2–5 January 2007
> **England** 291 (Flintoff 89, Bell 71;
> Clark 3-62, McGrath 3-67, Lee 3-75)
> and 147 (McGrath 3-38, Lee 3-39).
> **Australia** 393 (Warne 71, Gilchrist 62;
> Anderson 3-98) and 46-0.
> **Australia won by 10 wickets**

THE GREAT BAGGY GREEN REVENGE

After their Ashes success of 2005 England had been accused of being so carried away as to believe that retaining the urn would be a doddle. I can't believe they were that stupid. They – and their coach Duncan Fletcher – must have realized that playing Australia at home was a whole different ball-game. In 2006–7 they were certainly inept and maybe a little unlucky in that two of their most experienced players, Flintoff and Giles, were never fully fit. But most of all they were beaten by a great team, playing at the top of their form.

The figures – lies, damn lies and statistics – don't always tell the whole story, but here they provide a pretty good picture. The Aussies made nine hundreds, England made three. For Australia, Hussey with 458 runs at 91.60, Ponting with 576 at 82.28, Michael Clarke with 389 at 77.80, Andrew

HOWZAT! Or rather 'Howzis!' for understatement? England's coach, Duncan Fletcher, looking back on the disastrous tour: 'There have been some mistakes with selection. We will reflect on things when we get back, and try not to make the same mistakes again.'

BELOW *Just when you thought it couldn't get any worse… With the Ashes already lost, a grim-faced Andrew Flintoff comes out for the coin-toss with Ricky Ponting at Melbourne on Boxing Day, 2006. The game turned out to be England's heaviest defeat of a disastrous tour.*

Symonds with 232 at 58.00 and Hayden with 413 at 51.62 all averaged more than 50. For England only Pietersen, with 490 at 54.44, managed to do so.

The contrast in the bowling figures is just as stark. For Australia Stuart Clark took 26 wickets at 17.03, McGrath 21 at 23.90, Warne 23 at 30.34 and Lee 20 at 33.20. England's best was Hoggard with 13 at 37.38, followed by Panesar with 10 at 37.90, Flintoff 11 at 43.72 and Harmison 10 at 61.40.

The only Englishman who, had he been eligible, might have been remotely considered for a place in the Australian team was Pietersen. And whom might he have replaced? Hard to think of anybody, except possibly Symonds, who was only picked after Martyn's retirement and whose bowling (though better than Pietersen's) was hardly used.

THE BEST OF THE BEST?

Which of these all-conquering teams was the greatest? Pretty well impossible to say; they played in different eras and different conditions. In some eras the wickets were covered, in others they were not. For some teams conditions favoured the bowlers, for others the batsmen.

You could argue that Bradman's team and the West Indian sides lacked a great spinner, or that Ponting had no great truly fast bowler to call upon. But against that each captain could say: 'I didn't need those things – just look at the results.'

You could also ask the question: how would Ponting's team have fared against Armstrong's if transplanted to 1920–1, or Bradman's against the West Indies in the mid-1980s? Again, of course, it's impossible to say, but I have a firm belief that great players in one era would still be great players in any other; they would simply adapt to the circumstances in which they found themselves. It may be, for instance, that Bradman's overall Test average might not have been nudging 100 if he had been obliged to play several series against a four- or five-man West Indian pace attack, but I bet it would still have been a lot higher than anyone else's.

One more thought: if you could pick players in their prime from each of these great sides, what sort of XI would you come up with? Well, here's one that I would back to play and beat a Test team from Mars, no matter how many arms and legs the Martians might have:

1   **Gordon Greenidge (West Indies)**
2   **Barry Richards (South Africa)**
3   **Don Bradman (Australia, capt.)**
4   **Viv Richards (West Indies)**
5   **Graeme Pollock (South Africa)**
6   **Keith Miller (Australia)**
7   **Jack Gregory (Australia)**
8   **Adam Gilchrist (Australia, wkt)**
9   **Shane Warne (Australia)**
10   **Michael Holding (West Indies)**
11   **Malcolm Marshall (West Indies)**

There's a team that contains Test century-makers all the way down to number eight, with a near-century maker in Warne at nine and two useful tail-enders in Holding and Marshall. It also has ferocious pace aplenty and the world's greatest spinner in Warne, plus a bit of off-spin from Viv Richards as back-up. Ideally, perhaps, there should be a second front-line spinner and, for overcast conditions, a swing bowler, but you can't have everything.

CHAPTER 14
CRICKET CRISES
AND CONTROVERSIES

FROM BODYLINE TO PACKER,
FROM MATCH-FIXING TO SLEDGING

C ricket and controversy may not be joined at the hip exactly but they know each other only too well. Sometimes controversy stems from comparatively mild causes like drink ('Freddie' Flintoff and the pedalo, for example) and leads to nothing much more than a lot of indignant tut-tutting. But sometimes, too, it boils up into a crisis, as in the Basil D'Oliveira affair, that threatens to split the game. What follows is a bunch of controversies, or crises, that have led to more than indignation, if not quite to apoplexy, and in one case almost threatened to rip the British Empire apart. And that case, of course, was…

BODYLINE

Bodyline bowling (cue concerted booing from all Australians) had its genesis in something much more innocuous – leg theory, a system devised in the 1920s by Fred Root of Worcestershire. Root was a fast-medium bowler who attacked leg stump and moved the ball in towards the batsman's body. All perfectly legal.

It was the way Douglas Jardine, England's captain on the 1932–3 tour of Australia, adapted this theory specifically to neuter the threat of Don Bradman that made it potentially lethal. Seriously irritated, indeed alarmed, by Bradman's feat of scoring 974 runs at 139.14 in the 1930 Test series in England, Jardine scrutinized the Don's method in search of weaknesses and decided that he was windy against the fast stuff. As Corporal Jones of *Dad's Army* might have put it: 'He doesn't like it up 'im, sir.'

PUTTING THE FRIGHTENERS ON BRADMAN
Thus convinced, Jardine convened a dinner at the Piccadilly Hotel in London, the others present being Arthur Carr, captain of Nottinghamshire, and Carr's two very fast bowlers, Harold Larwood and Bill Voce. And there they came up with a scheme to bowl extremely quick, short deliveries on leg stump that would rear up into the batsman and virtually force him either to take evasive action or to play into a packed legside cordon of close fielders.

It worked. Before the Test series began the MCC (as England touring teams were then called) played matches against an Australian XI and New South Wales, and Bradman was given a thorough going-over. Faced with this new line of attack he either ducked or withdrew to leg and tried to cut the ball off the stumps. Either way, he did not look happy and, coincidentally or not, he dropped out of the first Test at Sydney (which England won) because of illness.

FAR LEFT *Australian captain Bill Woodfull ducks to avoid a sharply rising ball from Harold Larwood during the fourth Test at Brisbane, February 1933, with a posse of short legs in attendance. Such a field would not be permitted today. As a consequence of Bodyline, a law was introduced in 1947 to limit the number of fielders on the leg side: 'The number of on-side fielders behind the popping crease at the instant of the bowler's delivery shall not exceed two. In the event of an infringement of this rule by the fielding side, the square-leg umpire shall call "No Ball".'*

RIGHT *Miracle at Melbourne: Bradman plays his first ball from Bill Bowes onto his stumps, second Test, Melbourne, 30 December 1932, to record the only golden duck of his prodigious career.*

In the first innings of the second Bradman played on, first ball, to an innocent enough delivery from Bill Bowes – the only golden duck of his Test career. In the second innings, however, he made 103 (his only century of the series) and Australia won the match.

Although Bradman had not been physically hurt, some of his team-mates had received painful blows to the body – at a time, remember, when the helmets and body armour that batsmen wear today had not been invented. So by now the whole of Australia was enraged by 'Bodyline' – shorthand for 'on the line of the body', coined by Hugh Buggy of the *Melbourne Herald* when covering the Sydney Test. Three of England's four fast bowlers – Larwood, Voce and Bowes – employed the method; the fourth, 'Gubby' Allen, refused. But then Allen, like Jardine, was an amateur and allowed to have his own opinions. Professionals like Larwood, whistled up from the Nottinghamshire coal-mines, were not. Opinion in the rest of the squad was divided, with amateurs like Bob Wyatt, the vice-captain, and the Nawab of Pataudi and senior pros such as Wally Hammond and Les Ames being against it.

HOWZAT! As Jardine waved flies away from his face in the Sydney Test, a wag on the Hill shouted: 'Leave our flies alone, Jardine – they're the only flamin' friends you've got out here.' Another time, as Jardine was being heavily barracked, 'Patsy' Hendren said to him: 'They don't seem to like you very much over here, Mr. Jardine.' 'It's f***ing mutual,' said Jardine.

But Jardine, resplendent in his multi-coloured Harlequin cap and oblivious to the insults hurled at him by the crowds, was not to be deterred. Australia hated Jardine, a thin-lipped patrician with an aquiline profile, scion of a wealthy Scottish legal family, born in Bombay (Mumbai), educated at Winchester and Oxford and utterly contemptuous of everything Aussie. The Australian batsman Jack Fingleton perhaps summed up his fellow countrymen's feelings most neatly when he described the England captain as 'a dour, remorseless Scot, 130 years after his time. He should have gone to Australia in charge of a convict hulk.' Australians hated the ferociously quick Larwood, too, although when he emigrated to Australia later in life all was forgiven and they welcomed him.

Crisis point was reached in the third Test, at Adelaide, when first Bill Woodfull, Australia's captain, was struck over the heart by a ball from Larwood and then Bert Oldfield, their wicketkeeper, suffered a fractured skull when he top-edged another Larwood delivery onto his head. 'Well bowled, Harold!' said Jardine, loudly, as Woodfull collapsed as if shot. Ironically, Bodyline was not being used on either occasion. It was straightforward fast bowling that undid the batsmen. Didn't matter, though. The crowd was incensed and when Pelham Warner, the England manager, went to the changing-room to commiserate with him, Woodfull said: 'I don't want to see you, Mr. Warner. There are two teams out there. One is trying to play cricket and the other is not.'

UNSPORTSMANLIKE? MOI?

Alarmed by what was going on, during the match the Australian Board of Control (ABOC) cabled the MCC in London to complain bitterly that Bodyline was threatening 'the best interests of the game', and was 'unsportsmanlike'. They added that unless it was stopped it was 'likely to upset the friendly relations existing between Australia and England'. This came as something of a surprise at Lord's. The British press had not even mentioned 'Bodyline'. To them – and therefore their readers, including probably the MCC – this stuff was just 'fast leg theory', something they were all familiar with. So what was the fuss about? What turned mild astonishment into near-apoplexy at the MCC was the 'unsportsmanlike' bit.

Unsportsmanlike? Them? The MCC, guardians of all that was noblest in the noblest of all

BELOW *Bill Woodfull grimaces in pain as a Larwood thunderbolt strikes him in the chest.* Wisden *described the 'Battle of Adelaide' (as the dramatic third Test match of the 1932–3 series became known) as 'probably the most unpleasant Test ever played … the whole atmosphere was a disgrace to cricket'.*

games? Well, naturally, they sent off a snotty reply which deprecated any reference to unsportsmanlike behaviour and ended tartly with: 'If … you consider it desirable to cancel the remainder of the programme we should consent, but with great reluctance.'

That shoved the ABOC in between a rock and a hard place. The hatred of Jardine and company had generated lucrative receipts at the turnstiles. There was no way the ABOC wanted the tour called off. What, and lose all that money? But Jardine and his team had threatened to withdraw from the last two Tests unless the accusation of unsporting behaviour was retracted. What's more, the mounting antagonism between the two countries was seen by the Australian government as a genuine threat to Anglo-Australian relations and, more seriously, to Anglo-Australian trade (England being a major market for Aussie goods).

A THREAT OF SANCTIONS

So, with a bit of nudging from the Australian prime minister Joseph Lyons, who pointed out the economic hardships that could ensue if the British public decided to boycott Australian produce, the ABOC caved in and sent another cable to the MCC withdrawing all allegations of bad sportsmanship but insisting that Bodyline was 'not in the best interest of cricket'.

Thus the tour went on with Bradman, when facing the Bodyline attack, hopping about between off and leg sides of the wicket even before the ball was bowled and causing Warwick Armstrong to declare: 'To put the matter bluntly, he was frightened of fast bowling.'

He might well have been and it would be hard to blame him since he was the main target of Bodyline. Even so he ended the series with 396 runs at 56.57, a poor return for him but one that would have fulfilled a lifetime's ambition for many a batsman in an Ashes contest. Larwood finished with 33 wickets at 19.51 as England won the series four-one.

The bad taste left by Bodyline lingered on and, although there was never a serious danger that Australia might, in protest, leave the Empire, relations between the two countries continued strained pretty well up to the Second World War. J.H. Thomas, Britain's Cabinet Secretary for the Dominions, declared in a speech: 'No politics ever introduced in the British Empire ever caused me as much trouble as this damn Bodyline bowling.'

It was indeed a nasty, ruthless business and the Laws were changed to make sure it never happened again, although much later on there were some – disgruntled batsmen in particular – who said they couldn't see a

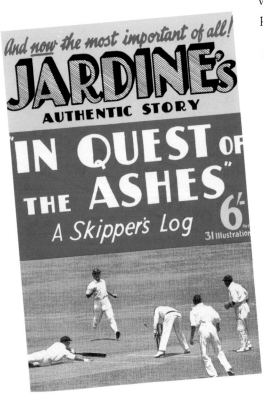

HOWZAT! During the series Jardine complained to Woodfull that one of the Australian players had called him a bastard. Woodfull took this very seriously and, leading Jardine into the Australian changing-room, said to his team: 'All right, listen you lot! Which one of you bastards called this bastard a bastard?'

whole lot of difference between Bodyline and the four-pronged West Indian pace attack of the 1970s and 80s. Actually, there was one significant difference – it was no longer legal to pack the legside field, especially behind the wicket (see caption, page 265).

Who, though, suffered most as a result of Jardine's tactics? Woodfull and Oldfield both recovered from their wounds, while Bradman, who in fact skittered about so nimbly as to avoid being hit by any express delivery, swiftly reclaimed his position as the game's greatest-ever batsman. Jardine went on to captain England against the West Indies in 1934, was himself subjected to Bodyline bowling by Learie Constantine and Manny Martindale and, to his credit, stood up to it unflinchingly to score 127, his only Test century.

The sole victim, indeed the scapegoat for the whole unpleasant affair, was, as it turned out, Harold Larwood, who was asked, unforgivably, by the MCC to sign an apology for his bowling. He refused, saying quite rightly that as a humble pro he was only doing what his amateur captain had ordered. Such insubordination was not acceptable to the MCC and Larwood never played for England again.

THE PACKER REVOLUTION, 1977–9

In the late 1970s Kerry Packer, a pugnacious bruiser of a man with the appearance of a heavyweight boxer who had somewhat gone to seed, was the most hated person in world cricket. Well, no, that really needs a bit of qualification – professional cricketers liked him rather a lot; it was the cricketing establishments who treated him as though he shared a coffin with Count Dracula.

A powerful Australian media mogul, Packer had attempted in 1976 to buy the exclusive television rights to cricket in Australia for his Channel Nine network. He had handsomely outbid the state-owned Australian Broadcasting Corporation (ABC), which had been televising cricket, pretty well un-challenged, for years, but he had been turned down by the Australian Cricket Board (ACB) out of loyalty to its long-term partners.

So Packer said the hell with it and decided to defy both the ACB and the ABC by setting up his own rival and, he hoped, ultra-glamorous cricketing competition, World Series Cricket (WSC).

BELOW *Kerry Packer in 1977, the year he launched World Series Cricket. The flamboyant Australian entrepreneur was reviled by cricket's establishment for causing a damaging schism in international cricket in the late 1970s, but is now revered by cricketers, especially in Australia, for having hugely bettered their financial lot.*

PACKER GETS HIS MEN

To this end he hired the England captain Tony Greig, already a cricketing mercenary in that he had left South Africa to qualify for England, to act as his liaison officer and sign up the best-known cricketers in the world. Greig went about his work during the Centenary Test at Melbourne in March 1977, stealthily recruiting – under an oath of secrecy as strong as the Mafia's *omertà* – most of the best players on either side. When the Australian touring party arrived in England for that summer's Ashes series, 13 of their 17-strong Test squad were already Packer's men.

Indeed, by the time news of the impending WSC was leaked by an Australian journalist in May 1977 – or, anyway, soon after this revelation – Packer had already signed no fewer than 35 of the world's leading players, including England's Greig, Alan Knott, John Snow and Derek Underwood, West Indians Viv Richards, Michael Holding, Clive Lloyd and Andy Roberts, South Africa's Mike Procter, Barry Richards and Graeme Pollock, and Pakistan's Imran Khan and Mushtaq Mohammad, not to mention Greg Chappell, Dennis Lillee and numerous other Aussies.

Naturally the world's cricketing establishments reacted angrily, offering the curled lip of disdain to such defectors. These they regarded as disloyal bounders seduced from what, clearly, they should have regarded as their solemn duty to their boards of control by Packer's trivial promise of a hell of a lot more money than those, by contrast, miserly boards were prepared to offer.

Nevertheless, the ICC attempted to patch matters up by meeting Packer and his advisers at Lord's in June, 1977, but these negotiations came to naught when Packer demanded, and was denied, exclusive Australian TV rights when the ABC contract came to an end after the 1978–9 season.

So now attempts were made to ban said defectors from international and county cricket; but that didn't work either because three of the players, Greig, Procter and Snow, backed by Packer, challenged the decision in the High Court in London. The hearing went on for seven weeks and at the end of it the judge Mr Justice Slade decreed that any such ban would be a contravention of the right to work.

MAKING UP THE RULES

But still the Establishment fought on, saying that (yah, boo!) Packer couldn't call his WSC games Test matches and (sucks to you!) he couldn't use the Laws of Cricket either because they were the copyright of the MCC. Nor was he allowed to hire any of the traditional cricket grounds in Australia.

So he got Richie Benaud to draw up a list of rules for the forthcoming 'Supertests' – they sound much swankier than Test matches, don't they? – leased football stadia, a trotting track and the Sydney Showground to stage the games, and provided them with innovatory 'drop-in' pitches that had been prepared elsewhere and transported to the match grounds.

The initial series of games involving the WSC Australians, the West Indies and a Rest of the World XI began in December 1977. The first season was not very successful, drawing only modest crowds. But Packer now had over 50 cricketers under contract and gradually opposition to him weakened. That opposition was strongest in England but even there the counties were happy to keep WSC players on their books.

In WSC's second season, 1978–9, Packer's strength grew, as did the size of the crowds and the television audiences. Now he was granted permission to stage matches at the Sydney Cricket Ground, where he had floodlights installed for the day–night games, and – had he so wanted – at the Gabba (Brisbane) and the Adelaide Oval. But he preferred to keep the big games to Sydney and Melbourne and ignore the other major stadia, while sending a secondary side, the Cavaliers, to tour up-country regions where cricket of such standard was rarely seen. And at the end of the season he staged a series of Supertests and one-day games between his Australians and the West Indies in the Caribbean, which was a financial boon to the West Indies Cricket Board.

ABOVE *WSC World XI captain Tony Greig before the grand final 'Supertest' against Australia at the floodlit Sydney Cricket Ground, February 1979. The pastel-coloured kit and razzmatazz led cricket's traditionalists to lambast World Series Cricket as a 'circus' and as 'the pyjama game'.*

PEACE BREAKS OUT

As it turned out this was the end of WSC on the field, the last game being a drawn Supertest in Antigua in April 1979. By then the venture had cost Packer a considerable amount of money but the ACB were even worse off. So negotiations were re-opened between the two parties, greatly to Packer's benefit. Under the terms of the 'peace treaty' Packer's Channel Nine acquired exclusive rights to televise Australian cricket and another of his companies was given a 10-year contract to promote and market the game.

On hearing of this the English establishment was seriously cheesed off. As *Wisden* said in its 1980 edition: 'The feeling in many quarters was that when the Australian Board first found Packer at their throats, the rest of the cricket world supported them to the hilt … Now, when it suited Australia, they had brushed their friends aside to meet their own ends.'

Still, the war was over and gradually the WSC rebels were welcomed back into their national folds. Early on, Tony Greig had explained his association with WSC by saying that he thought it could be in the interests of cricket all over the world and, with hindsight, he was right. As a result of the Packer revolution, cricketers became much better paid and many of the WSC innovations were adopted throughout the game – day–night matches, coloured clothing (the birth of the 'pyjama game') and a white ball for ODIs, drop-in pitches and helmets for batsmen.

The latter were introduced after the Australian batsman David Hookes had his jaw shattered by a bouncer from Andy Roberts during a game in December 1977, although the first example – sported by the England batsman Dennis Amiss – was merely a motorcycle helmet and nothing like the designer models batsmen wear today.

So then, Kerry Packer – good thing or bad thing? On the whole, certainly from the players' point of view, a good thing. Cricket traditionally regards change with suspicion, but what the Packer 'revolution' showed was that it's also a resilient game that is able, however reluctantly, to adapt, incorporate new ideas and move on without undue disruption. One can only hope it will cope as well with the latest Twenty20 revolution.

CHUCKING (OR THROWING)

According to Law 24, Clause 3, 'a ball is fairly delivered in respect of the arm if, once the bowler's arm has reached the level of the shoulder in the delivery swing, the elbow joint is not straightened partially or completely from that point until the ball has left the hand. This definition shall not debar a bowler from flexing or rotating the wrist in the delivery swing.'

Right. Lots of players have fallen foul of this one. In Test cricket chuckers go all the way back to Ernie Jones, the successor to Spofforth as Australia's fastest bowler. His first delivery in the Lord's Test of 1892 was described in the newspapers as 'very difficult to distinguish from a throw' and in the Ashes series of 1897–8 he achieved the distinction of becoming the first Test bowler to be no-balled for throwing – both at Sydney and Adelaide. Not that it made much difference; he carried on bowling and, who knows, throwing throughout the series and finished up with 22 wickets as Australia won four-one.

Another Australian, the left-arm fast bowler Ian Meckiff, was less fortunate. Having taken 17 wickets in four Tests against England in 1958–9 despite a suspect action, at the first Test against South Africa in Brisbane in December 1963, he was called by umpire Colin Egar for throwing four times in his only over and was promptly taken off, never to be seen in first-class cricket again. Similarly the South African Geoff Griffin, having done the hat-

trick against England at Lord's in 1960, was then no-balled 11 times in the same innings by umpire Frank Lee and never played in another Test.

Others who have fallen foul of the throwing laws include the England fast bowler Harold Rhodes and the West Indian quick Charlie Griffith; more recently the Sussex and England bowler James Kirtley was briefly suspended in 2005 while he worked to improve his action. Two Pakistani bowlers, Shabbir Ahmed and Shoaib Akhtar, were also suspended for throwing but reinstated when it was decreed that they had satisfactorily sorted themselves out.

MURALI AND THE CASE OF THE
UNUSUAL HYPEREXTENSION

But the mother of all throwing controversies concerns Muttiah Muralitharan, the Sri Lankan off-spinner with the extraordinary action. No fewer than three umpires in Australia – Tony Quillan, Ross Emerson and, in the Melbourne Test in 1995, Darrell Hair – have called him for throwing. And after Murali had taken 16 for 220 against England at the Oval in 1998, the England coach David Lloyd made it abundantly clear that he thought the bowler was a chucker. To be fair, however, Lloyd, like another early critic of Muralitharan's action, West Indian Michael Holding, has since changed his mind.

ABOVE *Freeze-frame images of Ian Meckiff's contentious bowling action, during the one and only over he bowled in what proved to be his final Test match, Brisbane, November 1963. The top strip shows him delivering his third ball, the bottom strip his fourth. Though his action is virtually identical in each, the former was ruled a 'no-ball' while the latter was adjudged legitimate.*

Nevertheless, doubts remained. Once, when Murali came in to bat in a Test, the England captain Nasser Hussein said: 'Here comes the chucker.' Adam Gilchrist, Bishan Bedi, Martin Crowe and Terry Jenner (the former Australian leg-spinner and coach to Shane Warne), have all at least suggested that his bowling action was illegal, while Hair described it as 'diabolical' and Emerson said it would be 'an absolute joke' if Murali became – as he has done – cricket's leading Test wicket-taker. His action has been likened to that of a javelin-thrower or a shot-putter.

Now this raises an interesting thought. If he had played for any other country when he was no-balled, would he have been drummed out of Test cricket like Meckiff and Griffin? And was it because of politics that he was not? Sri Lanka were still comparatively new to Tests and their indignation, led by Ranatunga, at the no-balling of Muralitharan was fierce and genuine. If their star bowler had been banned, might they perhaps have opted out altogether, to the extreme embarrassment of the ICC? And is it not possible that, faced with such an outcome, however remote, the ICC decided that allowances should be made? And, in view of the way the Laws were later changed, were in fact made? Pure speculation of course, backed up by no evidence whatsoever, but maybe worth considering.

However, what apparently had Murali done wrong? Well, it seems he has 'an unusual hyperextension of his arm' (whatever that might mean) during delivery. Because of that and the Australian yells of 'No ball!' he was several times subjected to tests, using all manner of scientific equipment, which subsequently cleared him of throwing.

But how conclusive is that? Anyone who threw the ball during a test on his action would have to be crazy. So the disgruntled murmurs continued, especially in 2004 when, during a Sri Lanka–Australia Test, match referee Chris Broad expressed strong doubts about Murali's doosra.

In 2000 the ICC had set an elbow extension limit – 10 degrees for fast bowlers, 7.5 degrees for medium-pacers and 5 degrees for spinners. But after the Murali doosra business they thought again, studied video footage

HOWZAT! During the mid-1950s Tony Lock, the Surrey and England left-arm spinner, went through a chucking phase. During a game at the Oval in 1955 between Surrey and the Rest, his quicker ball beat the defensive shot offered by Doug Insole, of Essex, and hit the stumps. 'Was I bowled or run out?' asked Insole.

of numerous bowlers during the 2004 Champions Trophy in England and discovered, to their astonishment, that an awful lot of people – even the impeccable Glenn McGrath – were capable on occasion, though not often, of extending their elbows by 12 degrees, while Murali's doosra extension could be as much as 14 degrees.

THE ICC's 'CUNNING PLAN'

So they hit upon what Baldrick, of *Blackadder* fame, would have called a 'cunning plan'. They decided that, as of March 2005, all bowlers, regardless of pace, would be allowed to extend their elbows by 15 degrees, thus making Murali's action perfectly legal, whatever he bowled.

Unconvinced, cynical people – and, yes, even cricket has them – have suggested that what the ICC actually did was say to Murali: 'How far would you like to extend your elbow? Fifteen degrees all right for you?' This, of course, is quite untrue but, as Murali makes his way towards 1000 Test wickets – and if he achieves it, it will be a landmark unlikely ever to be surpassed – using an action which, to the naked eye anyway, doesn't seem to have changed much, if at all, over the years, suspicion lingers on.

He is unquestionably an intelligent, thinking cricketer, a great flighter of the ball and, because of an unusually flexible wrist, a great spinner of it, too, in both directions. But, however many records he may achieve, he seems doomed to be regarded as suspect by many people who believe the laws were changed largely to suit him and that, without special dispensation, he would have been no-balled out of Test cricket a long time ago.

Hang on, though – what difference does it make if you bowl with a perfectly straight arm or one that only straightens at the point of delivery? Well, why not try it yourself? First, bowl an off-break while keeping your arm as straight as you can get it. Then bowl another, this time straightening your arm at the very last moment, and see how much more spin and turn you get. Similarly with fast bowling: the later the arm is straightened, the faster the delivery. Right now the matter rests. Murali and everyone else around the Test arena is officially legal. But what if another exciting bowler turns up whose elbow extension exceeds 15 degrees? Will the figure be raised to 16 or even 20? Let us hope not – because, if so, everyone would be bowling like a javelin-thrower or a shot-putter.

FAR LEFT *Muttiah Muralitharan at net practice. When bio-mechanical tests carried out at the University of Western Australia cleared the Sri Lankan spin wizard of throwing, the former Australian leg-spinner Kerry O'Keeffe commented: 'Boy George would be considered straight at the University of Western Australia.'*

MATCH-FIXING

This has been with us even longer than the throwing controversy. As we have seen, back in 1817 William Lambert was banned for life for match-fixing in England (see page 15) and in the first decade of this century 10 players have been banned for varying lengths of time for similar offences.

Of them the best known are Salim Malik of Pakistan, Hansie Cronje of South Africa, and Mohammad Azharuddin and Ajay Sharma of India; all were ordered to serve life bans, though the ban on Malik was overturned by a Pakistani court in 2008. Most recently the West Indian Test player Marlon Samuels was banned for two years in May 2008, for associating with a bookmaker and 'receiving money or benefit or other reward that could bring him or the game of cricket into disrepute'.

Essentially, match-fixing consists of offering players money, either to provide insider information or to underperform and lose a match. For example, Malik, a former Pakistan captain, allegedly offered Shane Warne, Tim May and Mark Waugh £130,000 each to throw a Test against Pakistan in 1994. They did not accept, but Malik also claimed that he could fix any match during England's then-forthcoming tour of Pakistan for £500,000.

The biggest match-fixing scandals blew up in May 2000. At the hearing which resulted in the banning of Malik, other prominent Pakistan players, among them Wasim Akram, Mushtaq Ahmed and Waqar Younis, were fined for their failure to co-operate with the judicial enquiry into match-fixing.

Later in 2000 Mohammad Azharuddin, the former India captain and one of the country's best batsmen, received his life ban for admittedly fixing three ODIs while the Board of Control for Cricket in India also banned Ajay Sharma for 'consorting with bookmakers'.

THE REACH OF THE BOOKIES

At the root of match-fixing lies gambling, especially in India and Pakistan where betting on cricket runs to millions, possibly billions, of pounds every year. The paymasters are bookmakers. Azharuddin, for instance, was alleged to have received large sums of money from one bookie in return for fixing games.

But perhaps the biggest match-fixing scandal involved the South African captain Hansie Cronje. In April 2000, Delhi police claimed to have a recording of a conversation between Cronje and the representative of an Indian betting syndicate in which match-fixing was discussed. Cronje denied it but later admitted accepting between $10,000 and $15,000 from a London-based bookie for 'forecasting' – though not 'fixing' – results.

Then, at the King Commission hearing in June, it was revealed that Cronje had offered $15,000 each to his team members Herschelle Gibbs and the bowler Henry Williams to underperform in an ODI at Nagpur that year. Neither man did so and neither received any money. A week later Cronje

finally coughed – in 1996, he said, Azharuddin had introduced him to an Indian bookie who gave him $30,000 to persuade his team to lose a Test match on the final day. Since South Africa were already 127 for 5 and chasing a target of 460 he didn't bother talking to anyone (they were all out for 180 anyway), but simply pocketed the money, along with a further $50,000 from the bookie during the tour for providing 'team information'.

Then, during the rain-affected fifth Test against England at Centurion in January 2000, he was offered money by a bookie to declare South Africa's innings and make a game of it. Three days' play had been lost to the weather when South Africa batted and, to everyone's surprise, declared on 248 for eight. Well, not everyone's. In order, as he and the bookie put it, to 'make a game of it' in the limited time left, Cronje had approached the England captain Nasser Hussain suggesting a double forfeiture of innings. Hussein, who was entirely innocent of any skulduggery, agreed and forfeited England's first innings, whereupon Cronje forfeited South Africa's second. England then scored 251 for 8 and won the match.

Everyone said what a jolly good sporting encounter this had been, unaware that, as a reward for his scheming, Cronje had toddled off with R50,000 and, somewhat bizarrely, a new leather jacket.

On 11 October 2000, Cronje was banned from cricket for life, and a year later his appeal against the decision was dismissed. On 1 June 2002 he was killed when the plane in which he was a passenger crashed into the Outeniqua mountains in South Africa.

Faced with all these scandals the ICC had, in 2000, set up the Anti-Corruption and Security Unit (ACSU), headed by Lord Condon, former commissioner of the London Metropolitan Police. It continues to be charged with investigating signs of corruption in cricket, although since the Cronje affair nothing of significance has come to light. So does that mean match-fixing has been stamped out? I wouldn't bet on it. Where large sums of money are on offer there's always a fair chance of somebody being tempted.

SLEDGING

Sledging is the art of verbally distracting, unsettling or abusing a batsman to make him lose first his concentration and then his wicket. Sometimes amusing, often offensive, the practice of sledging has probably been going on since the game began. It's certainly easy to imagine W.G. Grace giving the verbals to an opposing batsman. But the Australians can lay claim to introducing it as a major weapon in modern Test cricket. Ian Chappell has said that the word itself is Australian, first used in South Australia around 1964 and deriving from the description of a bloke who swore in the presence of women as being as 'subtle as a sledge-hammer'. (Australian sheilas, you understand, are sensitive creatures of a delicate nature, unused to rude words.) Well, who knows? Whatever the derivation, the Aussies raised sledging to an art form, particularly under their captain Steve Waugh, who described it as a tactic of 'mental disintegration'.

Sledging is usually done by wicketkeepers, close fielders and bowlers – especially fast bowlers, whose follow-through can bring them virtually into the batsman's face, there to hiss imprecations, four-letter words and insulting comments about the opponent's obvious ineptitude. Occasionally this can misfire. Example: Mervyn Hughes to Robin Smith: 'You can't f***ing bat!' Smith promptly sent the next ball to the boundary. 'We make a good pair, Merv,' he said. 'I can't f***ing bat and you can't f***ing bowl.'

Insults about opponents' physical condition are also popular. Example: As the South African right-hander Daryll Cullinan went in to bat against Australia, Shane Warne, who regarded Cullinan as his personal rabbit, said he'd been waiting two years for the chance to get him out again. Cullinan looked at the portly Warne and offered the neat rejoinder: 'Looks like you spent the whole time eating.'

HOWZAT! During a Test in the West Indies, Aussie quickie Merv Hughes kept glaring at Viv Richards. 'Don't you be glaring at me,' said Richards. 'This is my island, my culture, and in my culture we just bowl.' A little later Hughes dismissed him. 'In my culture,' he said, 'we just say eff off.'

HOWZAT! In another Australia–West Indies Test, Malcolm Marshall was bowling to David Boon who kept playing and missing. Finally Marshall walked up to him. 'Well, David,' he said, 'are you going to get out now or do I have to bowl round the wicket and kill you?'

But jibes of that sort can also misfire. Example: Glenn McGrath, contemptuously, to the plump Zimbabwean Eddo Brandes: 'Why are you so fat?' Brandes: 'Because every time I f*** your wife she gives me a biscuit.'

The wicketkeeper, especially when standing up to the stumps, is usually the sledger-in-chief, encouraging the bowlers with exaggerated shouts of admiration, such as 'Oh, well bowled, Shane!' even if Warne had just delivered a long-hop that somehow escaped punishment, while constantly informing the batsman that he is useless, was almost certainly born out of wedlock and has an unfaithful wife. Example: Rodney Marsh to the incoming Ian Botham: 'G'day, Beefy, how are your wife and my kids?' Quick as a flash and witty with it, 'Both' replied: 'The wife's fine, the kids are retarded.' Not bad.

Close fielders act as a kind of chorus to the 'keeper, frequently chipping in with their own insults and sneers, though they don't always come out on top. Example: James Ormond coming in to bat for England in an Ashes Test in 2001 was greeted by slip-fielder Mark Waugh with: 'Stone me, look who it is! Mate, you're not f***'ing good enough to play for England.' 'Maybe not,' said Ormond, 'but at least I'm the best player in my family.'

The arch-practitioner Steve Waugh himself rather enjoyed being sledged – it fired him up. Knowing this, Mike Atherton, England's captain during the 1997 Ashes series, decided that Waugh was not to be sledged. Arriving at the wicket to total silence Waugh said: 'Okay, you're not talking to me, are you? Well, I'll talk to myself then.' And, as Atherton wrote in his autobiography *Opening Up,* he did – 'for 240 minutes in the first innings and 382 minutes in the second'.

Imran Khan once said: 'You don't get good players out by sledging.' Possibly so, but against a background of continuous derision – particularly in an away Test with the home crowd baying for his dismissal – it's extremely difficult for a batsman to concentrate on the job in hand. And sometimes the insults can become so unpleasant as to be interpreted as racist. Australians don't like this any more than anybody else.

During India's 2007–8 tour of Australia, the home side's black all-rounder Andrew Symonds complained that the Indian off-spinner Harbhajan Singh had called him 'a big monkey'. If true, this was way beyond the limit. Harbhajan denied saying any such thing and his batting partner at the time, Sachin Tendulkar, backed him up. Nevertheless, the match referee Mike Procter upheld the charge and Harbhajan was given a three-match suspension for racial abuse.

FAR LEFT *Merv Hughes (left) subjects the hapless Graeme Hick to a torrent of sledging during the 1993 Ashes series. In a 2006 interview, Hughes was frank and unrepentant about his gamesmanship: 'Yeah, I targeted certain players and Hick was one of them. His performance in '93 suggests that it wasn't a bad plan.'*

HOWZAT! Once, when Australia were playing South Africa, Shaun Pollock was bowling and Ricky Ponting was playing and missing. After a bit… 'Hey, Ricky,' said Pollock, 'this is the ball – it's round, red and weighs about five ounces.' Ponting hit the next one out of the ground. 'Hey, Shaun,' he said, 'you know what it looks like, now go and find it.'

This was greeted with such outrage by the Indian tourists that an international incident almost ensued, with the Indian players threatening to cancel the rest of their Australian visit.

Fortunately, an appeal found in Harbhajan's favour after he explained that he had not called Symonds a monkey at all: he had merely said something in Hindi, which might have sounded like 'monkey' and was admittedly very rude, but was certainly not racial.

Whatever. Also beyond the limit was the verbal confrontation between Essex captain Ronnie Irani and Hampshire's Shane Warne during a county match in 2004, when Irani accused Warne of calling his mother a whore. The umpires had to restore order. And if Irani's accusation was correct then Warne had gone way beyond sledging into the realms of the crass, crude and deeply offensive. So, too, did Ian Healy, the former Australian wicketkeeper who, after Arjuna Ranatunga had called for a runner, said: 'You don't get a runner for being an overweight, fat c**t.'

Sometimes, not too often, it's the batsman who does the sledging, constantly decrying the bowler's efforts. Javed Miandad was said to be a dab hand at this, rabbiting away to put the bowler off his line and length. The danger here, of course, is that it takes only one false shot by the batsman for the laugh to be on him. Example: During the Adelaide Test between Australia and Pakistan in 1991, Javed called Merv Hughes 'a fat bus conductor'. Not long afterwards, Hughes got him out. 'Tickets, please,' he said as Javed walked past him.

For a long time cricketers defended sledging by saying that it was only fun, soon forgotten and 'what's said on the pitch stays on the pitch'. But since the Symonds–Harbhajan incident – following which Matthew Hayden described Harbhajan as 'an obnoxious little weed' during an interview, and the Indian players objected to being called 'bastards' (a term of positive endearment to Aussies) – a feeling has grown in the upper echelons of the game that sledging should be banned. Certainly the Board of Control for Cricket in India has asked the ICC to consider banning it.

Whether that is possible remains to be seen, although the game might be better without it. At best it's puerile, with echoes of the school playground, and at its worst it's unfair, unsporting and often cruel. Either way, it's 'just not cricket' – even if it has been a part of cricket since time immemorial.

LEFT *High noon in Antigua: Australia's Glenn McGrath (right) confronts the West Indian batsman Ramnaresh Sarwan in the fourth Test at St John's, 12 May 2003. Having been hit for 21 runs in just two overs, McGrath tried taunting the batsman by asking: 'What's Lara like in bed, mate?' To which Sarwan replied: 'I don't know – ask your wife.'*

HOWZAT! Finally a good old chestnut involving W.G. Grace, who, having been bowled, merely replaced the bail and stayed where he was, saying to the umpire: 'It was the wind that removed the bail.' The umpire replied: 'Indeed, Doctor, and let us hope the same wind helps your good self on the way back to the pavilion.'

CHAPTER 15
LADIES AND GENTLEMEN

THE RISE OF WOMEN'S CRICKET, AND THE DECLINE OF THE PROFESSIONAL–AMATEUR DIVIDE

S hall we join the ladies? Sorry about that, patronizing I know, but it's what toffs used to say after a swanky dinner. Probably still do. The pudding course disposed of, 'the ladies' were expected to withdraw to the withdrawing-room, leaving their husbands to get pissed on port and tell dirty jokes. After a bit the host would say, 'Shall we join the ladies?' and the blokes would stagger off to find their long-suffering wives.

Well, as they say in revisionist westerns, 'them days is over', and it's a foolhardy man who patronizes women now, especially when it comes to cricket. Women's cricket is a serious business and male chauvinist pigs had better believe it.

For a start, England's women not only regained the Ashes in 2005 but in 2008 actually retained them, which is a heck of a lot more than their humiliated male counterparts can claim.

BLUE AND RED RIBBONS

Goodness knows when women started playing the game but probably the first recorded instance of an all-female match, one that took place in Surrey, occurred in the *Reading Mercury* on 26 July 1745. The report ran as follows:

> *The greatest cricket match that was played in this part of England was on Friday, the 26th of last month, on Gosden Common, near Guildford, between eleven maids of Bramley and eleven maids of Hambledon, all dressed in white. The Bramley maids had blue ribbons and the Hambledon maids red ribbons on their heads. The Bramley girls got 119 notches and the Hambledon girls 127. There was of bothe sexes the greatest number that ever was seen on such an occasion. The girls bowled, batted, ran and catched as well as most men could do in that game.*

And so it has been ever since, though 'the maids' can't be bothered with ribbons in their hair any more. They leave the fancy hairdos to people like Kevin Pietersen (in his earlier, badger-striped days) and Ryan Sidebottom.

The first women's cricket club was formed at Nun Appleton in Yorkshire in 1887 and three years later the first professional women's team, the Original Lady Cricketers, toured the country playing exhibition matches, on which vast sums were wagered by punters in the very considerable crowds. Unfortunately, the team had to disband when the manager (a bloke, naturally) did a runner with all the takings.

But by then cricket for women was not only accepted but approved. As *James Lillywhite's Cricketers' Annual* put it in 1890: 'As an exercise cricket is probably not so severe as lawn tennis, and it is certainly not so dangerous as

FAR LEFT *To the admiring gazes of a clutch of cheerful chaps at a local cricket club, two elegantly turned-out ladies take the field for a village match in August 1954.*

RIGHT *Mary Johnson of Yorkshire and England, who played in 10 Tests for the national women's side between 1948 and 1954, leaps athletically to take a catch, in a staged shot for photographer Bert Hardy of the magazine Picture Post.*

hunting or skating…' In other words, let them get on with it, the little dears won't hurt themselves. Matters became much less patronizing and far more organized with the foundation of the Women's Cricket Association in England in 1926 and of the Australian Women's Cricket Association in 1931, followed in 1934–5 by the first overseas tour – by England to Australia and New Zealand.

TESTING THE WOMEN

The first women's Test match was played between England and Australia in December 1934. The captains were Betty Archdale (England) and Margaret Peden (Australia). England won. Indeed, they won the series three-one and the England all-rounder Myrtle Maclagan scored the first women's Test century in January 1935. Later on that tour Betty Snowball made 189 against New Zealand, still the highest score by an England player. Australia toured England in 1937, the three-match Ashes series being drawn one apiece and then came the War. It wasn't until 1948–9 that England returned to Test cricket and Australia, where they lost the Ashes for the first time.

Tours between England, Australia and New Zealand continued throughout the 1950s. In a remarkable match at St Kilda in 1958, Mary Duggan, the England captain, took 7 for 6 in 14.5 overs as Australia were dismissed for 38. But, as ever, back came the Aussies in the shape of all-rounder Betty Wilson, who took 7 for 7 and skittled England for 35. Then, rubbing salt into the wounds, she made a century in her second innings. The match was drawn and Wilson had become the first person ever to score a hundred and take 10 wickets in a Test. (Incidentally, women's cricket seems to contain more all-rounders than the men's game, doubtless because women are better at multi-tasking.)

South Africa joined the Test-playing nations in 1961 and in 1963 England beat Australia to regain the Ashes. I mention this latter fact because that was the last time they were to beat Australia in a series for 42 years. In 2005, the glory year for English cricket, both sets of Ashes, male and female, were in Australian hands until our lads and lasses came up trumps and shared the famous (notorious?) celebrations in Trafalgar Square. None of the women, however, celebrated with quite the intensity of 'Freddie' Flintoff.

Over the years the number of women's Test nations has grown to 10 – all those countries which have men's Test teams (with the exception of Zimbabwe and Bangladesh) plus the Netherlands and Ireland. In addition, Scotland, Denmark and Japan play ODIs.

Which reminds me...

Women had their own World Cup two years before the men did. Theirs began in England in 1973 and England won, beating Australia in the final at Edgbaston by 92 runs. Since then the tournament has been held, at intervals varying between three and six years, in India, New Zealand, Australia and South Africa. The most frequent winners have been – need you ask? – Australia with five. England have won it twice – the second time at Lord's in 1993 – and New Zealand once.

BELOW *England vs Australia during the three-match series in 1937, which ended one-all. And don't let the skirts fool you – whatever Len Hutton might have said, women take winning the Ashes quite as seriously as men and a lot more seriously than knitting.*

England's captain when they first won the World Cup was Rachael Heyhoe-Flint who, give or take the beard and the belly, might be regarded as the W.G. Grace of women's cricket in England. She was and maybe still is the highest-profile woman in the English game, the first ever to hit a six in a Test match (versus Australia at the Oval, 1963), captain of the England team from 1966 to 1978, one of the first women to be made a life member of the MCC in 1998 and the holder of both the MBE and the OBE for her services to the game.

Most importantly, though, it was her persistent urging (the men at Lord's probably called it 'nagging') that was instrumental in getting the World Cup started in the first place. What's more, she captained England in the first women's Test to be played at Lord's in 1976 and later in that series against Australia rattled up – well, not really, it took her 521 minutes – 179, still the highest score by an Englishwoman in a home Test. Not only was she one of the best players England has had, but for many years she was probably the *only* woman cricketer that most men in this country could name. She is the second highest run-scorer for England, having made 1594 runs at 45.54 in 22 Tests between 1960 and 1979. Oh, and she also played hockey for England.

In 1998 by mutual consent the ECB took over the running of women's cricket in England and in 2005 the International Women's Cricket Council was integrated with the ICC. In 2008 the women's game took a step towards professionalism in England when eight players were contracted under the Cricket Foundation's 'Chance to Shine' scheme to coach girls in schools – a big improvement on the days when members of an England touring party had to contribute towards their own expenses. So what with that and England holding the Ashes, I guess it's now official: women's cricket is a very important part of the game. The maids of Bramley and Hambledon with their hooped skirts and ribbons in their hair wouldn't recognize it.

RIGHT *As captain of the England women's team from 1966 to 1978, Rachael Heyhoe-Flint was unbeaten in six Test series. After retiring from the game (she also played hockey for the national side), she became a sports journalist and broadcaster.*

——— WOMEN'S TEST RECORDS ———

Highest innings total: 596-9d Australia vs England, 1998
Lowest total: 35 England vs Australia, 1958
Most runs in career: 1935 by J.A. Brittin (England), 1979-98
Highest score: 242 by Kiran Baluch (Pakistan) vs West Indies, 2004

Best bowling in an innings: 8-53 by N. David (India) vs England 1995
Best bowling in a match: 13-226 by Shaiza Khan (Pakistan) vs West Indies, 2004
Most wickets in career: 77 by M.B. Duggan (England), 1949-63

England: Played 87; won 19, lost 11, drawn 57.
Australia: Played 67; won 18, lost 9, drawn 40.

But what about the gentlemen?

Until 1962 the Gentlemen (note the all-important capital letter) were superior beings – amateurs who appeared for county or country for the fun of it, without financial remuneration. The professionals, who earned their living from the game, were merely players, except when they turned out against the Gentlemen at which time they, too, were granted a capital letter.

How amateur the amateurs really were is seriously open to doubt. For example, W.G. Grace, who was a Gentleman and therefore an amateur, was known, one way or another, to have made a very handsome living out of playing cricket. And I think we can be confident that his example was not lost on many another Gentleman.

For many years amateurs and professionals did not enter the field of play by the same gate and, just to ensure that Jack knew his place and didn't harbour delusions of being as good as his master, his place in the social order was subtly marked on the scorecards. So Douglas Jardine, an amateur, would appear as D.R. Jardine, but Harold Larwood, a professional, would be Larwood, H. Indeed, there was a famous occasion at Lord's when the announcer informed the crowd that, on the scorecard, 'the name "F.J. Titmus" should, of course,

Dickinsons

have read "Titmus, F.J". Who says the English are class-conscious?

All this differentiation was abandoned in 1962 when the powers-that-be decreed that henceforth there would be no more amateurs or professionals, that all first-class cricketers regardless of where their money came from would be deemed to be pros.

So ended an English tradition that stretched back to the early part of the 19th century – the annual games, sometimes three of them, between the Gentlemen and the Players. Before Test cricket came into being these were the most prestigious matches of the season, in theory pitting the best players in the country against each other. The most frequent venue was Lord's, though games were often played at the Oval and Scarborough.

The first two encounters took place in 1806, but it didn't become an annual fixture until 1819, whereafter – give or take a war or two – the Gentlemen pitted themselves against the Players every year up to and including 1962.

In all, 274 matches were played. Of these the Gentlemen won 68, the Players 125, with 80 games drawn and one (in 1883) tied. That the Gents came out of this lengthy sequence on the sticky end is due, primarily, to the fact that on the whole amateurs, elegant, even languid creatures, preferred batting. So much more aesthetic, you know, so much more, well, gentlemanly.

BELOW *An idealized depiction of cricket's 'Golden Age':* The Players in the Field – Lord's on a Gentlemen v. Players Day, *1895, by a late-Victorian artist named Dickinson. Shown from left to right are: J. Phillips (umpire); Ward, A.; A.E. Stoddart and W.G. Grace (Gentlemen batsmen); Hearne, J.T.; Lohmann, G.A.; Gunn, W.; Shrewsbury, A.; Peel, R.; Briggs, J.; Wheeler (umpire); Sherwin, M. (wicketkeeper); Read, J.M.; Lockwood, W.H. and Attewell, W.*

The sweaty business of bowling, especially fast bowling, was best left, they thought, to horny-handed sons of toil who knew no better. But generally speaking it's bowlers who win matches and so, more often than not, it was the Players who prevailed, even though the Gentlemen would occasionally turn out with 12, 14, 16 or even 18 men. In 1831 the Gents fielded a mere 11, but the Players had only nine and still won by five wickets.

In the 20th century the contests became particularly one-sided, with the Players winning 57 and the Gentlemen only 15 of 130 matches. By then the Players had learned how to bat as well as bowl, and in fact the three highest scores in the whole series were 268 not out by Hobbs, J.B. (1925), 247 by Abel, R. (1901) and 241 by Hutton, L. (1953). For the Gentlemen, W.G. Grace had scored 215 in 1870 and 217 in 1871, but their best effort was C.B. Fry's 232 not out in 1903.

By the time that the Gentlemen versus Players fixture petered out there were so few amateurs around that the games had become predictably one-sided affairs. Of the last 18 matches seven were drawn and the Players won the rest.

As a matter of historical interest, the first match took place at Lord's on 7–9 July 1806. We know that the Players, who batted first, scored 69 and 112 and were beaten by an innings and 14 runs. We know that in the first innings Hampton, J., one of the Players' opening bats, exceeded his own highest first-class score by making 18. We know that W. Lambert made 57 and T.A. Smith 48 for the Gents. We know who took all the catches and made the three stumpings and that Smith and his fellow Gent, A.P. Upton, were run out. We know that in the Players' first innings J. Willes and W. Beldham took at least one wicket each and in their second innings that Lord Freddie Beauclerk also took at least one, while Hammond, J. clean-bowled J. Pontifex, one of the Gentlemen's opening batsmen.

Who the hell took the other 24 wickets we have no idea. Perhaps the scorers couldn't be bothered to identify any bowler they did not instantly recognize. But if they recognized the fielders – which they clearly did – why not the bowlers? Why jot them down, time after time, as 'unknown'? Maybe they felt that bowling, being labourers' work, wasn't worthy of detailed record.

The final game, the 274th, was played at Scarborough on 8–11 September 1962. And here (opposite), as a matter of historical interest, is the scorecard.

ABOVE *Some illustrious names grace the ranks of the Gentlemen's team, Lord's, 1901. Back row (from left to right): W.M. Bradley, A.O. Jones, R.E. Foster, J.R. Mason; middle row (l to r): D.L.A. Jephson, K.S. Ranjitsinhji, G. MacGregor (captain), C.M. Wells, C.B. Fry; seated (l to r): G.L. Jessop, P.L. Warner.*

GENTLEMEN VS PLAYERS: THE LAST SCORECARD

Gentlemen: First innings

A.R. Lewis c Knight b Lock	35
R.M. Prideaux b Knight	17
M.J.K. Smith (capt.) c and b Lock	18
R.C. White b Trueman	24
D. Kirby c and b Barrington	39
A.C. Smith (wkt) c Morgan b Lock	34
R.A. Hutton b Trueman	7
C.D. Drybrough c Gale b Lock	12
G.W. Richardson st Millman b Morgan	68
R.I. Jefferson c Edrich b Morgan	68
O.S. Wheatley not out	3
Extras (b1, w2)	3
Total (all out, 85.1 overs)	**328**

Fall of wickets: 1-27, 2-66, 3-72, 4-130, 5-134, 6-148, 7-188, 8-189, 9-319, 10-328

Bowling: Trueman 12-2-29-2, Knight 8-0-16-1, Lightfoot 15-4-53-0, Lock 20-3-87-4, Morgan 13.1-1-53-2, Barrington 17-1-87-1.

Gentlemen: Second innings

Lewis c Millman b Trueman	0
Prideaux c Lock b Close	25
M. Smith c Millman b Close	33
White c Barrington b Trueman	95
Kirby c Millman b Close	1
A. Smith c Close b Lock	13
Hutton c and b Lock	16
Drybrough c Knight b Lock	16
Richardson c Barrington b Trueman	1
Jefferson not out	3
Wheatley b Trueman	0
Extras (b4, lb9, nb1)	14
Total (all out, 67.5 overs)	**217**

Fall of wickets: 1-1, 2-65, 3-80, 4-82, 5-103, 6-139, 7-212, 8-214, 9-215, 10-217

Bowling: Trueman 9.5-3-11-4, Knight 5-1-8-0. Lock 28-3-126-3, Morgan 4-0-14-0, Close 21-8-44-3

Players: First innings

Edrich, J.H. b Richardson	38
Horner, N.F. c and b Jefferson	30
Gale, R.A. c Richardson b Hutton	31
Barrington, K.F. b Drybrough	100
Close, D.B. c Wheatley b Hutton	9
Lightfoot, A. c Wheatley b Jefferson	11
Morgan, D.C. b Richardson	48
Knight, B.R. b Drybrough	14
Millman, G. (wkt) c Kirby b Jefferson	27
Trueman, F.S. (capt.) c White b Jefferson	19
Lock, G.A.R. not out	1
Extras (b1, lb4, w1, nb3)	9
Total (all out, 80.5 overs)	**337**

Fall of wickets: 1-38, 2-89, 3-102, 4-130, 5-163, 6-274, 7-274, 8-296, 9-336, 10-337

Bowling: Wheatley 7-1-19-0, Jefferson 23.5-2-104-4, Hutton 16-5-42-2, Drybrough 23-0-128-2, Richardson 11-3-35-2

Players: Second innings

Edrich b Hutton	43
Horner not out	49
Gale c and b Wheatley	88
Barrington b Drybrough	25
Knight not out	5
Extras (lb2)	2
Total (3 wickets, 38 overs)	**212**

Did not bat: Close, Lightfoot, Morgan, Millman, Trueman, Lock

Fall of wickets: 1-75, 2-147, 3-193

Bowling: Wheatley 7-0-56-1, Jefferson 11-1-53-0, Hutton 10-2-52-1, Drybrough 7-0-38-1, White 1-0-5-0

Players won by 7 wickets

So the Players were triumphant at the death, as they had been so often. But as the final episode of an historic, if archaic, series the game was a bit of an anti-climax. The cream of English cricket? Hardly that – among those missing from this last encounter were the following: E.R. Dexter, M.C. Cowdrey, D.S. Sheppard, Graveney, T.W., Parfitt, P.H., Allen, D.A., Coldwell, L.J., Stewart, M.J. and Larter, J.D.F. – all of whom had helped England beat Pakistan four-nil that summer.

Would it have been too difficult to persuade them to turn out for this last hurrah, so that the best of English Players could, one final time, tug their forelocks respectfully in the presence of the best of English Gentlemen? And then, no doubt, cheerfully raise two fingers at them...

CHAPTER 16
THE ONE-DAY GAME

LIMITED-OVERS CRICKET
FROM GILLETTE TO TWENTY20

I n the words of Tom Stoppard, cricketer and occasional playwright: 'I don't think I can be expected to take seriously a game which takes less than three days to reach its conclusion.' He was actually giving a gentle put-down to baseball, which is rounders for grown-ups but with a harder ball, a thickish, rounded bat instead of a stick with which to hit it and what look like baskets for the fielders to catch it in. But he could just as easily have been talking about limited-overs cricket (including Twenty20), which has never truly won the hearts of the purists.

The original idea was to produce a faster, shorter and, with luck, more entertaining version of the game which, weather permitting, would be over in one day and in which a draw was not possible. This has certainly led to many exciting finishes, including a number of tied games but, especially in One-Day Internationals (ODIs), there has been increasing criticism that the excitement is limited to the earlier and later overs of an innings with a fair bit of stodge in the middle, when batsmen tend to take fewer risks before chancing their arms at the end.

In ODIs each innings is limited to 50 overs; in List A games – those involving first-class domestic sides – the number can vary between 40 and 60. The differences between one-day cricket and the first-class game include an insistence on at least five bowlers sharing the overs and a restriction on the number any individual bowler may send down. For example, in a 50-overs game nobody can bowl more than 10, in a 40-overs match no more than eight. There is also a much stricter interpretation of a wide ball; in one-day games anything going down the leg side or rising above the batsman's shoulders will be deemed a wide.

FAR LEFT Second leg of the hat-trick: the all-conquering Australians ran out winners in the 2003 ICC World Cup in Johannesburg, South Africa. They had taken the trophy in 1999 in England, and were to repeat the feat in the West Indies in 2007.

LIST A AND ODI CRICKET

One-day games between English county sides began in 1962 when Derbyshire, Leicestershire, Northants and Notts contested the Midlands Cup, which Northants won, playing 65 overs a side. This went down well and next season all the first-class counties took part in the Gillette Cup (won by Sussex) with 60 overs a side. Six years later the John Player Sunday League (40 overs) was introduced and, give or take several changes of names, both competitions have continued ever since, along with another knockout competition, the Benson & Hedges Cup, which has also assumed various different aliases.

But ODIs weren't thought of until 5 January 1971, when Australia played England at Melbourne, and even then the game came about by accident. The teams were supposed to be playing a Test match but rain washed out the first

The one-day game has its critics but you won't find any among the 24,079 people who were at Old Trafford to watch the Gillette Cup semi-final between Lancashire and Gloucestershire. This was a match that began at 11 o'clock in the morning and, without benefit of floodlights, finished just before 9 pm in what seemed almost total darkness.

The Gillette Cup was a 60-overs-a-side affair and Lancashire, under Jack Bond, were particularly good at it, being in the middle of what turned out to be a hat-trick of victories. This, though, was surely the most dramatic game in which they, or any other county side, have ever taken part.

It began quietly enough. Gloucestershire won the toss and made a solid start before, significantly as it was to prove, rain delayed play for an hour at lunch-time. Afterwards Procter scored a handy 65, including a six and nine fours, and the innings closed on a respectable 229 for 6. At that time, before batsmen wielded weapons with the power of howitzers, four an over was regarded as a decent rate of progress.

Because of the rain delay it was already late in the afternoon when Lancashire began their response, one that was equally solid but slow – 17 overs gone before the 50 was raised, whereafter their cause was hardly helped by a mid-innings slump. In very little time 136 for 2 became 163 for 6, and the light was decidedly bad. Nevertheless, Bond elected to play on and he and 'Flat' Jack Simmons, the off-spinner, added 40 valuable runs in seven overs in increasing darkness.

But when Simmons was out at 203 it was already 8.45 pm, the lights were on in the pavilion, the crowd were craning forward, squinting into the night to see what was going on and the incoming David Hughes almost needed a torch to guide him to the wicket. The Gloucestershire players must have been licking their lips as John Mortimore ran in to bowl his off-spinners to the new batsman.

Six balls later, however, they were licking their

that he must have existed on a diet of carrots, had hit the unhappy Mortimore for two sixes, two fours and two twos – 24 runs in total and the game was virtually over.

Therein lies the glory of cricket – a fairly ordinary match suddenly transformed into something wondrous and memorable in the space of a few heroic minutes.

Hughes, inevitably, was named Man of the Match and by the time the ceremonies were over it was well past 10 o'clock and completely dark. The Lancashire lads didn't care, though.

Gloucestershire

R.B. Nicholls b Simmons	5:
D.M. Green run out	2
R.D.V. Knight c Simmons b Hughes	3
M.J. Procter c Engineer b Lever	6:
D.R. Shepherd lbw b Simmons	
M. Bissex not out	2:
A.S. Brown (capt.) c Engineer b Sullivan	
H.J. Jarman not out	
Extras (b2, lb14, w1, nb1)	1
Total (6 wickets, 60 overs)	229

Did not bat: J.B. Mortimore, B.J. Meyer (wkt) J. Davey
Fall of wickets: 1–57, 2–87, 3–113, 4–150, 5–201, 6–210
Bowling: Lever 12-3-40-1, Shuttleworth 12-3-33-0, Wood 12-3-39-0, Hughes 11-0-68-1, Simmons 12-3-25-2, Sullivan 1-0-6-1

Lancashire

D. Lloyd lbw b Brown	3
B. Wood run out	5
H. Pilling b Brown	2
C.H. Lloyd b Mortimore	3
J. Sullivan b Davey	1
F.M. Engineer (wkt) hit wkt b Mortimore	
J.D. Bond (capt.) not out	1
J. Simmons b Mortimore	2
D.P. Hughes not out	2
Extras (b1, lb13, nb1)	1
Total (7 wickets, 56.5 overs)	230

Did not bat: P. Lever, K. Shuttleworth
Fall of wickets: 1–61, 2–105, 3–136, 4–156, 5–160, 6–163, 7–203
Bowling: Procter 10.5-3-38-0, Davey 11-1-23-1. Knight 12-2-42-0 Mortimore 11-0-81-3, Brown 12-0-32-2

Late show: an ecstatic crowd invades the pitch at Old Trafford at the end of Lancashire's epic Gillette Cup encounter with Gloucestershire. Legend has it that match-winner David Hughes sat in a darkened room before taking the field to prepare himself for his innings.

Lancashire captain Jack Bond (left) and the hero of the hour, David Hughes (right).

three days and everyone said, oh, to hell with it, let's scrub the Test and have a one-day game instead. So they did and Australia won by five wickets.

Once the world had grasped the potential of the one-day game as an international event and crowd-pleaser, a competition to find the world champions at this form of the game was inevitable, and the first cricket World Cup was held in England in the summer of 1975 (see opposite).

WHITE BALLS AND PINK TROUSERS

In the early days of ODI cricket the teams used a red ball and were dressed in white as in proper cricket, but then along came Kerry Packer with his World Series Cricket to goose the entire cricketing establishment into a state of panic (see The Packer Revolution, pages 269–272). Among the things he did was to revolutionize the one-day game by dressing his players in multi-coloured uniforms.

At Melbourne on 17 January 1979, the WSC Australians, gleaming in gold, played the WSC West Indians, pretty in pink. Since then one-day games have always been played by teams clad in garish colours and using a white ball – because a red ball delivered by a fast bowler dressed in something equally red would be very difficult to pick up. Packer also brought in dark sightscreens and day–night games played under floodlights.

More recent developments have included the introduction of Powerplays in 2005. This decreed that fielding restrictions – only two fielders outside a 30-yard circle around the pitch – which had for many years applied for the first 15 overs of an innings, would now be imposed for the first ten overs and for

—— ONE-DAY INTERNATIONAL RECORDS ——

Team records

Highest team total	443-9 (50 overs) by Sri Lanka vs The Netherlands, Amstelveen, 2006
Lowest team total	35 (18 overs) by Zimbabwe vs Sri Lanka, Harare, 2004
Highest match aggregate	872-13 (99.5 overs): Australia (434-4) vs South Africa (438-9), Johannesburg, 2005-6
Highest winning run chase	438-9 (49.5 overs) South Africa vs Australia, Johannesburg, 2005-6

Batting records

Highest career total	16,684 by S.R. Tendulkar, India, in 425 matches, 1989–2009
Highest individual score	194 by Saeed Anwar, Pakistan vs India, Chennai, 1996-7
Best career average	55.15 by M.E.K. Hussey, Australia, in 81 innings, 2004-9
Most centuries	43 by S.R. Tendulkar, India, in 415 innings

Bowling records

Most wickets	505 by M. Muralitharan, Sri Lanka, in 329 matches, 1993–2009
Best bowling analysis	8-19 by Chaminda Vaas, Sri Lanka vs Zimbabwe, Colombo, 2001-02

Wicketkeeping record

Most dismissals	472 (417 ct, 55 st) by A.C. Gilchrist, Australia, in 287 matches, 1996-2008

The first cricket World Cup, known as the Prudential Cup after its sponsors and consisting of 60 overs a side, was held in England in 1975. Eight teams took part – England, Australia, India, Pakistan, West Indies and New Zealand (the only six Test-playing nations at the time) plus Sri Lanka and a composite side from East Africa. South Africa were not invited. (Well, they weren't invited anywhere at that time on account of apartheid – and serve them right.) West Indies, with Clive Lloyd making the first hundred in a World Cup final, won it by beating Australia by 17 runs. The next two World Cups were also held in England.

For most of its history the competition has been staged at four-year intervals, though five years separated the World Cups of 1987 and 1992, and three years those of 1996 and 1999. In 1987 the number of overs per innings was reduced from 60 to 50. Coloured clothing made its first appearance in the 1992 World Cup, which also saw the introduction of day–night matches and the use of a white ball, plus further changes to fielding restrictions.

The Test-playing nations, plus those countries granted temporary ODI status by the ICC, qualify automatically for the World Cup. Increasing numbers of non-Test-playing nations (more than 80 of them) are now given a shot at qualifying, and the 2007 competition in the West Indies was a cumbersome and protracted affair. One can only hope things will be more streamlined for the 2011 World Cup (to be jointly hosted – security permitting – by India, Pakistan, Sri Lanka and Bangladesh).

For the record, Australia have won the trophy most often (four times) while England have never won. But, hey, plucky British losers that they are, they've been runners-up three times, an achievement nobody else has equalled.

LEFT *Clive Lloyd holds the Prudential World Cup aloft after the West Indies' victory at Lord's, 1975.*

Year	Host	Final venue	Result
1975	England	Lord's	West Indies (291 for 8 in 60 overs) beat Australia (274 all out in 58.4 overs) by 17 runs
1979	England	Lord's	West Indies (286 for 9 in 60 overs) beat England (194 all out in 51 overs) by 92 runs
1983	England	Lord's	India (183 all out in 54.4 overs) beat West Indies (140 all out in 52 overs) by 43 runs
1987	India, Pakistan	Kolkata	Australia (253 for 5 in 50 overs) beat England (246 for 8 in 50 overs) by 7 runs
1992	Australia, New Zealand	Melbourne	Pakistan (249 for 6 in 50 overs) beat England (227 all out in 49.2 overs) by 22 runs
1996	Pakistan, India, Sri Lanka	Lahore	Sri Lanka (245 for 3 in 46.2 overs) beat Australia (241 for 7 in 50 overs) by seven wickets
1999	England, Scotland, Holland	Lord's	Australia (133 for 2 in 20.1 overs) beat Pakistan (132 all out in 39 overs) by eight wickets
2003	South Africa	Johannesburg	Australia (359 for 2 in 50 overs) beat India (234 all out in 39.2 overs) by 125 runs
2007	West Indies	Barbados	Australia (281 for 4 in 38 overs) beat Sri Lanka (215 for 8 in 36 overs) by 53 runs on Duckworth–Lewis method

two blocks of five overs (Powerplays), which the fielding captain could use as he wished. This was amended in October 2007 to allow the fielding captain to have three fielders outside the circle during one of the sets of Powerplays. Oh, and now the batting side can choose when to introduce either the second or the third Powerplay during their innings, while in rain-restricted matches the number of Powerplay overs is reduced. What with all that, and the inscrutable Duckworth–Lewis method of determining the outcome of those weather-affected matches, what was meant to be a simple game is becoming ever more complicated.

RAISING THE RUN RATE

Nevertheless, since its inception the one-day game has provided a great deal of entertainment and has affected the way Test cricket is played. Even in the grittier, more intense atmosphere of a five-day match, slow run-rates (two or so an over used to be almost commonplace) are no longer acceptable. In the shorter version of the game there is every chance that runs will be scored at five, six or even eight or more an over, and with batsmen now working out like weightlifters and armed with ever-heavier bats there is an expectation that Test players, too, will get on with it and smite the ball more lustily. And to a very large extent this expectation has been fulfilled, particularly by the powerful Australian teams of recent years. After all, men like Matthew Hayden, built like a heavyweight boxer, are hardly going to plod around at the crease like Geoffrey Boycott.

ODIs have now become a vitally important part of the international game, not least because spectators, particularly in the Indian subcontinent, prefer them even to Test cricket. Over the years Test and domestic first-class cricket have learnt to co-exist amicably enough with the 40-to-60-over game. But in 2008 the very existence of all of them came under threat with the advent of…

TWENTY20

We've already seen (see Cricket in India, page 174) how this latest form of the game developed internationally. Since then, as the Indian Premier League (IPL) proved a great success, the buccaneering Allen Stanford, glorying in his self-appointed status as the philanthropic saviour of West Indian cricket (this, of course, in the palmy days before Special Agent Plod of the FBI set the bloodhounds on him) predicted that Twenty20 could become the most popular game in the world. Because it's short (matches take only three hours to complete), fast and furious, he thought even America, where the attention-span of the average sports fan is slightly less than that of the average goldfish, could become addicted.

THE HECTIC HISTORY OF TWENTY20

But before we go into the possible long-term effects of Twenty20, let's see how it all began. This form of mini-cricket was introduced in England by the ECB as an inter-county competition, won by Surrey Lions, in 2003. It caught the public imagination at once. A year later the first Twenty20 match at Lord's, Middlesex versus Surrey, was watched by 26,500 people, the largest attendance for any county game, bar one-day finals, since 1953. The following year Australia played New Zealand in Auckland in the first Twenty20 international. The players thought it was a joke – they dressed up in 1980s uniforms, wore wigs and false facial hair and, just to raise a laugh, Glenn McGrath bowled underarm in imitation of the infamous occasion in 1981 when Greg Chappell ordered his brother Trevor to do just that at the end of a tight ODI between the same countries.

ABOVE *Afro-Kiwi: New Zealand's Hamish Marshall in hair-raising form at the first-ever Twenty20 international, against Australia in Auckland, 17 February 2005. Marshall and his team-mates got into the carnival spirit, sporting retro 80s coiffures and wearing a vile beige strip for the occasion.*

Nobody's laughing now. India won the first Twenty20 World Cup in South Africa in 2007, thus engendering the enthusiasm which Indians carried into their support of the IPL. There were already Twenty20 tournaments in most countries anyway, but the blanket television coverage of the IPL with its cast of all-star players aroused enormous international interest.

In June 2008, the pushy Stanford arrived at Lord's by helicopter like some visiting potentate to announce a series of $20 million, winner-take-all matches between his All-Stars XI and England to begin on November 1 that year in Antigua. He was greeted with some reverence by the ECB chief executive, David Collier and, just to add hype to an occasion that hardly needed any, opened a box containing $20 million before the goggling eyes of four cricketing knights – Ian Botham, Garfield Sobers, Viv Richards and Everton Weekes – and a couple of more common people in Curtly Ambrose and Nasser Hussain.

Further developments swiftly followed. A Twenty20 Champions League was announced for December 2008, in India, with Rupert Murdoch's ESPN Star Sports paying £513 million for the television rights over 10 years. This was later called off after the Mumbai terrorist outrage. India, Australia and South Africa, the organizers of the league, would each have submitted two teams and Pakistan one, with Middlesex, the domestic Twenty20 champions, representing England. Joint organizers the three nations may have been, but it was clearly India who were calling the shots. Kent, runners-up to Middlesex, were debarred from taking part because their team included people who had played in the unofficial Indian Cricket League (ICL). This because the ICC had agreed with the Board of Control for Cricket in India (BCCI) that the ICL was unofficial and its players should be shunned by all right-thinking (i.e. BCCI- and IPL-thinking) people.

For this reason New Zealand dropped Shane Bond and Bangladesh banned its own ICL players from all official cricket. Sri Lanka, however, did allow five of their ICL players and an umpire to take part in the domestic game. But even Sri Lanka drew the line at permitting ICL cricketers to play in international matches, while the ECB decreed that in certain circumstances ICL players would not be eligible for country cricket in 2009. So by the autumn of 2008 official Twenty20 seemed to be having things all its own way with a Twenty20 league set to replace the Pro40 in England and the very real possibility that in the near future such matches at international level could replace ODIs.

Twenty20: the downside

Given that, worldwide, the public has shown a keen taste for such cricket, where's the problem? Well, the problem comes with the money. ODIs and other earlier forms of one-day cricket were never a threat to Tests or the domestic first-class game because they didn't pay that well. Twenty20 does. The signing-on fees for players in the initial IPL were astronomical by cricketing standards – in some cases several hundred thousand pounds for a few weeks' work.

BELOW The trappings of American Football come to cricket, as cheerleaders in Australian and England colours strut their stuff before a Twenty20 international between the two sides at Sydney, 9 January 2007. Could that faint hum in the background be the sound of W.G. spinning in his grave?

England's players were unable to take part in the first season of the IPL because of their central contracts with the ECB and a Test series in New Zealand (March 2008). Mind you, with those central contracts and lucrative sponsorship deals, they weren't exactly paupers, but even so several of them rather fancied dipping their own snouts in the IPL trough. And, of course, in 2009 this came to pass when Pietersen and Flintoff both signed up for $1,550,000 apiece.

Two dangers immediately come to mind – first, the imbalance the money could cause among players. For example, a class batsman, proven in Test cricket but not considered for international Twenty20s, could easily find himself sharing the county dressing-room with a lesser but far richer player than himself (because that player had signed up for the IPL). It would be understandable if such a situation led to resentment.

Secondly, as the influence of Twenty20 spreads, unless a way can be found to make the IPL and similar leagues fit in with Test schedules, star players might start retiring early from Test cricket in order to cash in.

To an extent that has already happened. The New Zealand tourists of 2008, for instance, arrived in England without their former captain Stephen Fleming, Nathan Astle, Scott Styris, Shane Bond and Craig McMillan, all of whom might well have been in the party if they hadn't opted instead for league cricket in India. Then Mahendra Singh Dhoni, India's one-day captain at the time and later the Test captain as well, opted out of the Test series against Sri Lanka, citing exhaustion caused in part by playing 16 IPL matches in six weeks; several Bangladeshi players announced their retirement from the international game in order to play in the ICL and Sri Lanka's sports minister instructed the country's cricket board to allow any Sri Lankan players with IPL contracts to skip the tour of England in 2009 so that they could honour their previous commitments.

At that time the Sri Lanka board, seriously cash-strapped, was discussing a $70 million deal with the BCCI that would seem to put it totally in thrall to India and especially India's Twenty20 cricket. With little more than a Sri Lankan second XI likely to be available, Sri Lanka's 2009 tour of England was cancelled and the West Indies agreed to tour instead.

TEST CRICKET UNDER THREAT

So what happened to those earnest pledges by all members of the ICC, including the BCCI, that Test cricket would always be paramount everywhere? On the eve of the first – and the way things are, surely the last – Stanford $20 million match Kevin Pietersen announced stoutly that, 'Twenty20 is here to stay and is the future of coloured clothes cricket, but white clothes separate the men from the boys. Tests are the pinnacle.' But he was beginning to sound like someone shouting in the wilderness.

HOWZAT! Test cricket's ability to baffle the Latin temperament is exemplified by this plaintive question from Rafael Benitez, Liverpool FC's Spanish manager: 'How can you tell your wife you're just popping out to play a match and then not come back for five days?'

Geoffrey Boycott came closer to the truth when he said, in a radio interview in October 2008, that Test cricket was in trouble. Attendances at Test matches, except in England, were dwindling fast; even for the India–Australia series in late 2008, normally an eagerly-awaited event, the crowds were modest compared with the numbers who would turn out for Twenty20.

In one respect, though, Pietersen was right: Test cricket *does* separate the men from the boys. But in the future how many men will be playing the game? Unless all forms of cricket can be fitted into the year without their schedules impinging on each other there's surely a danger that talented young players of the future might not bother with the comparatively underpaid daily grind of domestic first-class cricket and go straight to Twenty20 instead. Loadsamoney, not too much graft and, in India especially, the prospect of stardom, adulation, sponsorship and even more money. All very well, but players reared only on Twenty20, however gifted they might be, are unlikely to acquire the technique, patience and concentration required for Test cricket and so the classical form of the game would suffer.

In a radio interview just before the Stanford match Graham Gooch, admittedly a bit of an Eeyore among cricketers, took this prospect further when he said, gloomily, that he could foresee Twenty20 competitions developing into a year-long, golf-style world tour in which players would opt out of every other form of the game to follow the sun and the money. If, perish the thought, that were to happen, it's not entirely impossible that the first-class game could vanish altogether and we would be left with this hybrid, the cricketing equivalent of constantly stuffing our faces with hamburgers instead of sitting down to a balanced meal. And that's a prospect to dread.

THE $20 MILLION MATCH

But what of Sir Allen Stanford's initial Twenty20-for-$20-million match? Admittedly, enabling each member of the winning team to trouser a tidy $1 million (worth about £619,000 at the time) was upping the ante a bit, but the concept was by no means entirely novel. Back in the late 17th century games were played in Sussex for 50 guineas a head and in 1735 Frederick, Prince of Wales, captained a side that played for – and lost – a pot of £1000.

The preamble to the $20 million game in Antigua took the form of a series of warm-up matches involving the Stanford All-Stars, England, Trinidad and Tobago and Middlesex (England's domestic Twenty20 champions). During this build-up England seemed to moan a lot – about the pitch (too slow), the floodlights (too low), Stanford wandering in and out of their changing-room as if he owned the place (which, in fact, he did) and on one occasion bouncing Emily Prior, the pregnant wife of England's wicketkeeper, on his knee.

No doubt they – to say nothing of their wives and girlfriends – were moaning a hell of a lot more after the total humiliation they suffered in the money game: all out for 99, beaten by 10 wickets by a motley collection of West Indians captained by Chris Gayle.

Altogether Kevin Pietersen and company appeared to have lost the plot. Didn't prepare enough (unlike Stanford's team, who trained for six weeks), didn't know whether they were playing for England or just the money ('just the money,' said Alastair Cooke, one of the younger and wiser members of the squad) and didn't like the carnival atmosphere surrounding the event. Lord Maclaurin, former chairman of the ECB, likened the whole thing to a pantomime.

And so it was, with England standing in for the Ugly Sisters and Stanford, complaining bitterly that nobody seemed to love him any more despite all he had done, seeming about as popular as Baron Hardup (which, I suppose, he could become if the allegations against him in America turn out to be true).

Meanwhile, Gayle and company were no doubt, quite literally, laughing all the way to the bank. And good for them.

BELOW *Big bucks bonanza: Chris Gayle and cricket's then sugar daddy Allen Stanford in jubilant mood after the Stanford Superstars crushed a woeful England side to win the infamous $20 million match at the Stanford Cricket Ground, St John's, Antigua, 1 November 2008.*

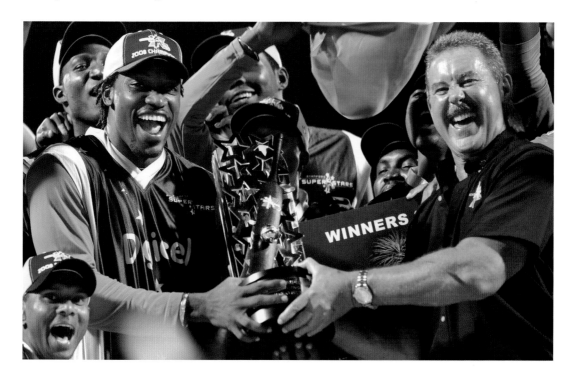

"Caught"

22. If the ball, from a stroke of the bat... be held .. although .. hugged to the body of the catcher :— The STRIKER is out.

Copyright of "Perrier" Water

CHAPTER 17
DOLLIES
AND DOOSRAS

THE LANGUAGE OF CRICKET:
FROM AGRICULTURAL SHOT
TO ZOOTER

What's cricket all about? Dead simple really. Just consider this thumbnail sketch of cricket as explained to a foreigner, probably an American (since they seem to find the game particularly hard to follow). It was first printed on tea towels in England in the 1980s and sums up the game perfectly:

You have two sides, one out in the field and one in. Each man that's in the side that's in goes out and when he's out he comes in and the next man goes in until he's out. When they are all out the side that's out comes in and the side that's been in goes out and tries to get those coming in, out. Sometimes you get men still in and not out. When a man goes out to go in, the men who are out try to get him out, and when he is out he goes in and the next man in goes out and goes in. There are two men called umpires, who stay out all the time and they decide when the men who are in are out. When both sides have been in and all the men have been out, and both sides have been out twice after all the men have been in, including those who are not out, that is the end of the game.

FAR LEFT *'Caught': one of a series of humorous lithographs by Charles Crombie entitled 'The Laws of Cricket', 1905.*

BELOW *Andre Nel appeals for lbw. An English journalist once described the combustible South African as 'the most extravagantly psychotic character ever to grace world cricket'.*

How difficult is that to understand? Still, even when you've grasped those basic principles you also have to comprehend that cricket has a language all of its own, so here – again especially for the benefit of Americans, who may have picked up this book by accident and are completely baffled – are a few useful words and phrases:

Agricultural shot. An ungainly swipe, much favoured by tail-enders, played across the line of the ball, often with eyes tightly shut. If it succeeds the smitten ball might easily end up in the next county. Mostly it doesn't – though it may fetch up in **cow corner** (see below).

Anchor. Usually a top-order batsman who has decided to stay in as long as he can to the benefit of his own batting average, even if it means exposing his partners to nearly all the really hostile bowling.

Appeal. A yell of 'Howzat!' or 'Owzat!' by either bowler or fielder (often all of them) directed at the umpire, usually accompanied by a hostile glare suggesting that even a blind man could see the batsman was out.

Arm ball. A delivery, usually sent down by a spinner, that doesn't deviate one iota and goes straight on. Spinners who claim this as their secret weapon mostly can't turn the ball for toffee.

Backlift. The lifting of the bat before striking, and in some cases before delivery of the ball. Batsmen who do this excessively, especially against very fast bowling, often find their wicket has been shattered while they're still in the process of backlifting. The West Indian batsman Brian Lara had an extravagantly high backlift, but he was a genius. Lesser players emulate him at their peril.

Beamer. An illegal delivery that flies straight towards the batsman's head without bouncing. Usually accompanied by a cry (hardly ever sincere) of 'Sorry!' from the bowler. England's Simon Jones bowled a famous one to Australia's Matthew Hayden in an ODI in 2005…

Block. A cautious defensive shot to stop the ball hitting the wicket, much favoured by Geoffrey Boycott.

Bodyline. See pages 265-269.

Bosie. See **Googly**.

Bouncer. A short-pitched, fast delivery that rears up with the intention of hitting the batsman's head. Not nice to face. It used to be called a 'bumper', in the old days.

Box. Absolutely vital piece of equipment: a sort of triangular object, usually made of strong plastic, to fit into a jockstrap and cover the family jewels. Rachael Heyhoe-Flint, the former England

RIGHT Facing the chin music: Dwayne Bravo leaps extravagantly to avoid a Brett Lee bouncer during a West Indies–Australia encounter in 2008.

women's cricket captain, called the female version 'a manhole cover'.

Buffet bowling. Bowling of such poor quality that the batsmen believe Christmas has come early and help themselves to runs galore.

Bunsen. Short for 'bunsen burner' (rhyming slang for 'turner'), a wicket that takes considerable spin.

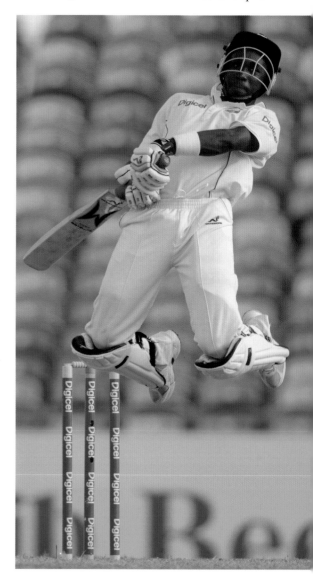

Invariably prepared in Sri Lanka when Muttiah Muralitharan is playing.

Caught. A batsman is out if he hits the ball straight to a fielder, without it bouncing, and said fielder catches it. Unless he's Monty Panesar in which case he might not. Or, indeed, might end up in an entirely different postcode from the ball.

Chinaman. A ball by a left-arm spinner that turns from off to leg, rather than vice-versa. Invented by the West Indian Ellis ('Puss') Achong, who was of Chinese descent (though he may well be the only Chinese person who has ever bowled one).

Chinese cut. No known connection with China at all – merely an ill-timed shot at a ball that takes the inside edge and narrowly shaves the batsman's off or leg stump, often going for four, to the intense fury of the bowler.

Chin music. A series of bouncers designed to rise up just under the batsman's chin. If the ball connects the resulting sound, or music, is appreciated only by the bowler. Well, maybe his fielders, too. West Indian quicks of the 1980s were particularly addicted to it.

Collapse. The loss of several wickets in very quick succession. In the recent past England's batsmen have been particularly adept at it.

Cow Corner. Area between wide long-on and midwicket. So rarely visited by the ball – except from an **agricultural shot** (see above) – that cows could graze there undisturbed.

Death Bowler. Usually brought on in the closing stages of a tight one-day game. Simon Hughes filled this role for Middlesex against Warwickshire in the 1989 NatWest Final. Last over, a few runs

needed and a distraught Hughes is smashed out of the ground by Neil Smith.

Declaration. When a captain decides that his team has scored enough runs either to win or at least draw, and nobody else need go into bat. (Doesn't always work, as Andrew Flintoff discovered in the 2006–7 Ashes series when, in the second Test at Adelaide, he declared England's first innings at 551 for 6, only for Australia to score 513 in reply, then dismiss England the second time around for a pathetic 129 and win by six wickets.)

Dolly. A catch so simple that nobody could possibly drop it. Lots of people do, usually complaining that the sun was in their eyes.

Doosra. The off-spinner's googly, turning from leg to off. Invented by Saqlain Mushtaq of Pakistan and now used most frequently by Muttiah Muralitharan. *Doosra* is a Hindi word meaning 'second' or 'other', in the latter case suggesting something totally unexpected, especially by a batsman who thought an off-break was coming up.

Drinks waiter. Dismissive name for the twelfth man or substitute, who may field but neither bat, nor bowl nor keep wicket. Frequently summoned by imperious batsmen to bring on drinks (or replacement bats or gloves.) Hence his customary disconsolate scowl.

Duck. A score of nought, originally called 'a duck's egg' because that's what nought looks like in the scorebook. Out first ball is a **golden duck**. (See also **king pair** below.)

Duckworth–Lewis. A complicated mathematical method of deciding the result in a rain-affected one-day match. Nobody understands it.

Five-for or **five-fer.** The taking of five wickets in an innings by a single bowler. Also known to admirers of the gorgeous Hollywood actress as a Michelle. (Five-fer, Pfeiffer, see?)

Flipper. An under-spun leg-spinner that doesn't bounce much and doesn't turn much either. The New Zealand-born Australian bowler Clarrie Grimmett invented it. (See also **Zooter.**)

Full toss. A delivery that reaches the batsman without bouncing. Batsmen can't get enough of these (unless of course the full toss is a **beamer**).

BELOW *Clarrie Grimmett: when Bradman told him he was bowling too many flippers, Grimmett promptly dismissed the Don with an orthodox ball and quipped, 'There y'are Don, told you I could bowl a leg break!'*

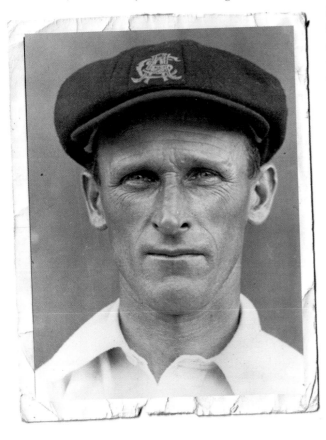

Googly. Deviously cunning: an off-break (to a right-handed batsman) bowled with a leg-break action. Etymology unclear, possible deriving from 'goggle', which is what a batsman does when a ball apparently going harmlessly down the off side removes his leg stump. Invented by B.J.T. Bosanquet, hence known in Australia as a **bosie**, also as a **wrong 'un**.

Half-volley. A delivery that pitches just short of the batsman, who welcomes it with a gleeful cry of 'Come to Daddy!'

Jaffa. A delivery so good as to be unplayable. These are rare, yet somehow almost every batsman you ever meet will insist he was out to a jaffa.

Leg before wicket (LBW). A batsman is out if a ball strikes his body, without first touching either his bat or the hand holding it, and would in the umpire's opinion have hit the wicket. No batsman in the history of the game has ever admitted to being out LBW, always claiming that (a) he hit the ball first or (b) it was quite clearly going miles down the leg side or (c) the umpire should have been issued with a white stick and a guide dog.

List A. The one-day equivalent of first-class cricket. I mention it here only because it crops up elsewhere in this book and you might as well know what it means.

Long hop. A ball that pitches closer to the bowler than the batsman without being fast enough or rising high enough to be a bouncer. Batsmen love these quite as much as **full tosses** (see above).

Military medium. Bowling that is neither fast nor slow nor anything very much, really.

Often hard to score from but likely to induce boredom in spectators and batsmen alike.

Nelson A score, either by a team or an individual, of 111 (or its multiples) is considered unlucky and called a Nelson, after the British admiral. Why? Who knows? The poor devil lost an eye and an arm but apparently had two of all the other vital things that come in pairs. Aussies regard 87 as the unlucky number, presumably because it's 13 short of 100. But in that case why not choose 13 as the unlucky number and be done with it?

Nervous Nineties. A state of anxiety that afflicts batsmen when their score is between 90 and 99 and they long to reach three figures. Saddest victim of the Nervous Nineties was Graeme Hick, who was on 98 not out when Mike Atherton declared England's innings closed against Australia at Sydney in 1994–5.

Nightwatchman. The bloke, usually a tail-ender, sent in near the close of play to save more accomplished batsmen for the next day. The most glorious nightwatchman was Jason Gillespie, who scored 201 not out vs Bangladesh in 2006. His reward? He was never picked for Australia again.

Nurdle. The art of scoring singles by gently nudging the ball into areas where no fielder lurks. England's Graham Thorpe was a dab hand.

Not out. A batsman who has yet to be dismissed. Also the umpire's verbal dismissal of a wrongful **appeal**, the latter frequently leading to foul-mouthed chuntering by the denied bowler.

Out. What a batsman is when, one way or another, he has been dismissed. Most often he will be either bowled, caught, hit wicket, stumped, LBW or run out. He can also be dismissed for handling the ball, hitting it twice, timed out for taking too long to

ABOVE *Graham Gooch uses his right hand to swat away a ball from Australian paceman Merv Hughes that was dropping onto his stumps, Old Trafford, June 1993. Moments later he was given out by umpire Dickie Bird in accordance with cricket's Law 33, which states: 'Either batsman is out Handled the ball if he wilfully touches the ball while in play with a hand or hands not holding the bat unless he does so with the consent of the opposing side.'*

reach the wicket or interfering with the field. Len Hutton was out in the latter way vs South Africa at the Oval in 1951 when, having snicked the ball into the air, he tried to hit it again, thus depriving the South African wicketkeeper Russell Endean of a catch. Hutton said he was trying to stop the ball falling onto his wicket. Oh yeah?

Pair. The scoring of a **duck** in each innings of a match. Very humiliating, especially if it happens on your Test debut as 36 players have discovered so far, including Graham Gooch, who went on to become England's all-time top run-scorer in Tests. The first to 'bag' a pair was Fred Grace (England vs Australia, 1880) and the latest Chris Tremlett (England vs India, 2007). If you get a **king pair** – out first ball in each innings – as Adam Gilchrist did for Australia against India in 2000–1, you should really go and shoot yourself.

Pie-chuckers. A term attributed to former Australian wicketkeeper Rodney Marsh to describe England's bowlers when they were at their worst. Used in 2008 by Kevin Pietersen in reference to the Indian batsman and part-time left-arm spinner Yuvraj Singh. Bit much, really, since Yuvraj's flighted pies had dismissed Pietersen several times. Yuvraj's response: 'Well, a useless bowler getting him out many times would be because of useless batting, I'd say.' Advantage Yuvraj.

Pinch-hitter. A middle- or lower-order batsman sent in to open the innings and promote fast scoring, usually in a one-day match. England try this often, usually with no success at all. Originally a baseball term meaning somebody batting in another's place.

Rabbit. A very poor batsman, usually in the team as a specialist bowler. Phil Tufnell, Monty Panesar, Courtney Walsh, Glenn McGrath and Chris Martin of New Zealand all have to be in the squad. Tufnell, in particular, seemed to prefer playing fast bowling from just behind the square-leg umpire. A rabbit might also be a frontline batsman who keeps getting out to a certain bowler. England's opener Mike Atherton was McGrath's bunny/rabbit, getting out to him a record 19 times.

Reverse-sweep. A shot played by a right-handed batsman (usually down on one knee) as if he were a left-hander. Vice-versa for left-handed batsmen. Mike Gatting once tried this, disastrously, in a World Cup final against Australia. Gloriously re-invented by Kevin Pietersen, who not only switched hands but switched stance to convert himself into a left-handed batsman and hit Muralitharan (in a Test) and Scott Styris of New Zealand (twice in an ODI in 2008) for six. The second time against Styris he switched stance even before the ball was delivered. The purists chuntered miserably about unfair play but the crowds loved it and the MCC said it was perfectly legal, so that's all right then.

Run out. What happens to a batsman when, normally while attempting a run, he fails to reach the crease before the fielding side breaks the wicket. The great Denis Compton was the finest exponent of the run-out, usually of his own batting partners. Any call from him, whether 'Yes!' 'No!' or 'Wait!' was best regarded by his partners as merely a tentative opening to negotiations.

Sticky dog. A drying wicket, almost impossible to bat on and virtually unheard of in this modern age of covered wickets. But in the old days the sight of a sticky dog would convince spinners that there really was a God and turn them all into born-again Christians.

Umpires. Two of them, one at each end, on the field, plus a third somewhere in the pavilion peering at a TV screen, ready to adjudicate when the on-field umpires are baffled. Cheerfully maligned, vilified and abused for their mistakes by onlookers who, unlike the on-field umpires, have the benefit of 20/20 hindsight thanks to slo-mo replays on television. Curiously, though, when the mistakes are in favour of the home team the umpires suddenly become heroes.

Walk. What a batsman should do, without waiting for the umpire's decision, when he knows he has snicked the ball to the wicketkeeper. Most batsmen are totally unfamiliar with the word. Adam Gilchrist was the last Test player known to walk regularly, often to the serious disgruntlement of his team-mates.

Wide. A ball passing so far from the batsman that he cannot reasonably be expected to hit it. This concedes one run as an extra. Steve Harmison's first delivery in the 2006–7 Ashes series was the most notorious, and possibly the widest, wide in cricket history.

Wrong 'un. See **googly**.

Yorker. Usually a very fast delivery aimed to pitch in the batsman's block hole (where he rests his bat while waiting for the ball). Difficult to score from and much used in the closing overs of one-day games. Bloody painful when it lands on your foot.

Zooter. Believed to be a variation on the flipper – a ball that 'zoots' along, barely leaving the ground. Shane Warne claimed to have invented it but it probably doesn't even exist, except in his fertile imagination and, he hoped, in the minds of confused batsmen who might be expecting it, with much trepidation, any time now.

ABOVE AND RIGHT *New Zealand umpire Brent ('Billy') Bowden's antics (above) led his compatriot Martin Crowe to call him 'Bozo the Clown'. Yorkshireman Harold ('Dickie') Bird (right), who umpired 66 Tests from 1973 to 1996, cut an eccentric but less histrionic figure, and was widely respected for the excellence of his judgement.*

CHAPTER 18

So You Want To Be
a Cricketer?

ROUTES INTO THE FIRST-CLASS GAME

O kay, let's assume you're a talented young player besotted by the game, as all right-thinking people are. You've read this far, seen what some of the great names of the past and present have achieved and now you fancy a bit of that. You want to be a professional cricketer – but how do you go about it?

In the old days, starting way back in the 19th century and going on well into the later 20th, a favoured route into the first-class game for promising working-class lads was to get a job on the groundstaff at Lord's. That's how Denis Compton started; so did Ian Botham.

FAR LEFT *Boys playing an impromptu game of cricket in a London street, 1926.*

Join the groundstaff

Botham went for a trial at Lord's, aged 16, in 1971, having already played representative cricket for the English Under-15's schools XI and attracted the attention of Tom Cartwright, the former England bowler who was playing for Botham's home county, Somerset. It was Cartwright who suggested he should be sent to Lord's, where he was duly accepted and spent the next two years as a groundstaff boy.

There he received coaching from Len Muncer and Harry Sharp, both former Middlesex players, and did menial jobs around the ground, such as selling scorecards and working in the Tavern Bar, as well as earning tips by bowling to MCC members in the nets.

Today things have changed, in detail if not in essence. Groundstaff boys are now called MCC Young Cricketers and don't do the menial stuff any more. In a programme led by the MCC's head coach Clive Radley, formerly of Middlesex and England, they are not only coached in all aspects of the game but also attend courses in groundsmanship, scoring, umpiring and IT and take coaching badges themselves. They still act as net bowlers to MCC members but they don't sell scorecards, largely because, in Radley's elegant phrase, 'they made such a piss-hole job of it. They did it deliberately because they didn't want to do it.'

HOWZAT! Beefy's advice to youngsters on the groundstaff: 'Bowl at the batsman's pockets – if they jingle when you hit you know you're only going to get coins for a tip. If they don't you're probably in for a note.'

GET A TRIAL

Every year trials are held at Lord's for promising young cricketers in their middle to late teens, most of whom come with recommendations from schools or clubs. In fact you don't need to be recommended; Radley says: 'We don't reject anyone who writes in.' But the chances of making the grade for those who turn up out of the blue are pretty remote. Indeed, they're not so great even for those who, having arrived recommended, pass the trial and are accepted for the two-year course. Radley reckons that only three, maybe four, of each year's graduates will go on to become professionals. And even then they may not last long.

What makes things even harder is that applicants for the course come not only from all over Britain, but from every other cricket-playing nation as well and competition is fierce. Hamish Marshall (New Zealand) and Darren Sammy (West Indies) were both MCC Young Cricketers.

So that's a tough one to crack. Okay then, what other options are there? Well, direct recommendation from school or club to county has also worked. Jack Russell, the former England wicketkeeper, was recommended to

Gloucestershire by his school sportsmaster, was given trials, made his debut at 17 and joined the county full time the following year.

There's also the MCC School of Merit, which is part-funded by the charitable organization the Lord's Taverners. This is a programme run in the indoor cricket school during the winter for players of particular promise aged 9–19, chosen from schools throughout the country. Graduates include Ashley Giles (Warwickshire), Gareth Batty (Worcestershire) and Ian Blackwell (Somerset), all of whom have represented England.

Try the old school tie

For the more privileged, or academically bright, there was and to an extent still is a smoother way in. Many Test players, including Peter May, Colin Cowdrey, Ted Dexter and more recently Mike Atherton and John Crawley, have made their way into the county and international arenas by way of public schools and, in particular, Oxford or Cambridge universities.

The England batsman Ed Smith, once of Kent, and captain of Middlesex in 2007–8, made his mark at Tonbridge School, alma mater of the Cowdrey clan, and at 17, having been asked to play for Kent's Under-19 side, represented them in a tournament at Oxford, which Kent won. Smith, the man of the match, scored 83 in the final and was promptly offered a contract for the following season with a signing-on fee of £1000. He made his first appearance in the Championship in 1996, aged 18, after a successful season with Cambridge University, for whom he had scored 101 on his first-class debut versus Glamorgan. (As if that wasn't enough he also got a double first in history, which hardly seems fair on the rest of us.) Cricket is a hard game, though; Smith got his chance in the Kent XI at the expense of Graham Cowdrey, an old friend of his family. It was typical of the man, and indeed of his own family as a whole, that Cowdrey was the first to congratulate him.

What you really really want

At this point there's an interesting comparison to be made: both Ed Smith and 'Both' (in *Botham: My Autobiography*) have claimed that by the age of six or seven they were sure they were going to play for England. (Botham probably wasn't entirely certain at which sport he would represent his country, because until his late teens professional football was also an option.)

What this points up – apart from Kipling's shrewd observation that 'the Colonel's Lady an' Judy O'Grady are sisters under their skins' – is that perhaps most of all you really have to want it. Natural talent alone is not enough to get you into the MCC Young Cricketers or, perhaps a more direct way into the game nowadays if you're good enough, the individual counties' academies. What the coaches are looking for, too, are determination, concentration, guts and mental strength. But, hey, not to worry – you have all those things, don't you?

Join an academy

So now what? County academies are, for the most part, new to this country since the turn of the century. The Middlesex academy, for instance, opened in 2003 under Toby Radford, formerly of Middlesex and Sussex, who was later promoted to first XI coach. Anyone can apply for a trial but, again, the best chance of acceptance is to be recommended, either by school or club or by one of the network of independent cricket enthusiasts on whom the counties rely to suggest youngsters worth a good, long look.

The dozen or so who are taken on each year and given extensive coaching and fitness work are regarded as the best young prospects in the county. In addition, most of the academies run age-group sides for boys aged 10–17 and for girls aged under 11, 13, 15 and 17. Here, too, the players are usually nominated by their schools and clubs and, for Middlesex, trials are held at the Finchley Indoor School in November. The county youth system then gives the chosen ones a winter training programme designed by the academy director and overseen by qualified ECB coaches with assistance from past and present professionals. In the summer each youth squad plays a series of competitive matches. The under-13, 14, 15 and 17 squads take part in official ECB competitions. Okay, that's what happens at Middlesex, but other county academies have similar schemes.

Yeah, fine, but does the system work? Well, yes. Citing Middlesex again (because that's the team I support), graduates of the academy include Billy Godleman, who made 113 not out versus Somerset on his County Championship debut, aged 18, in 2007 and the fast-medium bowler Steve Finn.

There are other, more famous, examples from elsewhere. Stuart Broad was associated with the Leicestershire academy from the age of eight, played for the Melton Mowbray Club at Egerton Park from nine until he was 19, and at Oakham School was coached by its director of cricket, Frank Hayes, the former Lancashire and England batsman. But the county connection was probably the most vital in ensuring his early introduction to the first-class game.

So, too, with Alastair Cook, another schoolboy prodigy, who set up run-scoring records at Bedford School where the coach was Derek Randall, and also played for the Maldon Cricket Club. More importantly, though, he was a member of the Essex academy, whose coach was Graham Gooch.

Go private

Now this is all very well but what if, like Ed Smith and Ian Botham, you just know that one day you'll be good enough to play for England, yet the MCC and your county academy have foolishly turned you down? Don't give up – all is not entirely lost because there are things you can do yourself.

Leicestershire, for instance, have an indoor cricket school that can be hired on winter evenings and weekends and there, for a fee, you can receive

BELOW *A fresh-faced Alastair Cook, pictured in 2000 at age 16, when he was still in training at the ECB National Academy.*

HOWZAT! England Test all-rounder Ian Botham had some forthright things to say about cricket's theorists. 'Cricket is full of theorists who can ruin your game in no time,' he remarked in 1980.

coaching, either in groups or individually. Boys and girls aged between 6 and 14 can have coaching in batting and bowling during school holidays, too.

In addition there are several private academies offering courses throughout the year under ECB-qualified coaches. Their aim is to find and develop professional cricketers for the future, so along with winter courses they arrange matches during the summer, which, they say, are watched by county coaches.

There you are then. Any other advice is obvious – practise hard, study the game, get into your school team (always assuming your school playing-field, like so many others, hasn't become a housing estate or a giant supermarket) and join a strong local club. With a bit of luck and a following wind, if you're as good as you (and your Dad) think you are, there's at least a chance that somebody from the county will recognize your talent.

Oh, and if that comes to pass and you become a professional cricketer, how much will you earn? For county players the wage scale currently ranges between upwards of £20,000 and £70,000 a year, but you can make an awful lot more if you're a superstar like Kevin Pietersen or Andrew Flintoff.

Good luck – and watch the ball!

AND NOW THE BAD NEWS...

Great! You've graduated, top of the class, from the county academy and Blankshire have given you a contract – 20,000 quid a year just for playing cricket. You dream of opening the batting at Lord's and scoring a century on debut before lunch but… hang on!

There's an awful lot standing between you and making that hundred, or even getting into the team at all. For a start there are those hardened county pros, understandably reluctant to give up their places to a newcomer. Then there's the overseas player, quite possibly a regular in the Australian Test team. Fortunately, since 2008 there's only one of him instead of the two per county allowed before then.

Still, let's see – six batting places, one taken by the Aussie. Okay, that's five places up for grabs and some of the old pros are only just about hanging on. Plenty of opportunity there, right? Well, no – wrong, because here the sneaky rules about Kolpak players come into the picture.

THE CURIOUS CASE OF MAROS KOLPAK

A Kolpak player is one who, since a European Union edict in 2004, has slithered into the county game via the back door. Maros Kolpak is a Slovak handball player – nothing to do with cricket – who claimed that he was

HOWZAT! Americans have a long history of being baffled by cricket. The novelist Ernest Hemingway hinted at a possibly shaky grasp of its laws when, in 1923, he described the month of April as 'the month cricket players contentedly begin sharpening their stumps'.

unjustly denied employment in Germany. The European Court upheld his claim, saying that although Slovakia wasn't actually part of the European Union it did have trading arrangements with the EU and therefore its citizens had a perfect right to employment in any EU country.

This went down big in places like South Africa, Zimbabwe and various Caribbean islands, which also had trading arrangements with the EU. If Maros could now get a job in Germany, they reckoned, then their cricketers could sign on for English counties, no sweat – and not as overseas players either, or as holders of European passports, but just as good old Kolpak players.

And so it came to pass and the Kolpak players flooded in. Defenders of the system maintained that they would raise the standard of the county game and many of them did – Murray Goodwin (Zimbabwe) has been a stalwart for Sussex, Dale Benkenstein (South Africa) has done much both as batsman and captain for Durham, Hylton Ackerman (South Africa) has given solid service to Leicestershire as has Lance Klusener (South Africa) to Northants.

These and others like Jacques Rudolph (Yorks), Martin van Jaarsveld and Justin Kemp (Kent), Andrew Hall (Northants) and Grant Flower (Essex) are big, or anyway biggish, names. But some of the other Kolpak signings are hardly household names in their own households.

THE COUNTIES' DILEMMA:
TO BUY IN TALENT OR NURTURE IT

The counties are, to put it mildly, in an ambivalent position. They form their academies and claim stoutly that their aim is to produce players for England and then they go and sign a bunch of Kolpaks, saying they need to strengthen the team.

Leicestershire are a case in point. Their team certainly needed some strengthening before the 2008 season began. The previous year they'd finished eighth in the County Championship Division Two and sixth in the Pro40 Division Two. But to sign four new Kolpak players in addition to Ackerman and Claude Henderson (another South African) seemed at the time to indicate not so much weakness as surrender. Indeed, in a game between Leicester and Northants in 2008, no fewer than 15 players turned out who were not eligible for England. A lot of hope that must have given to the academy graduates and other youngsters on both counties' books. (To be fair to Leicestershire, though, as the 2008 season went on they did appear to be striking a balance. Alongside the Kolpaks, they also produced young players of their own – among them 18-year-old Josh Cobb who made 148 not out against Middlesex at Lord's – and could claim to have fielded an average of five England-qualified players under 25, certainly more than any other county could boast.)

The trouble is, however, that there's no limit to the number of Kolpaks a county can sign, unless or until a new interpretation of the EU ruling – that it's meant to encourage freedom of trade, not of labour – is generally accepted and a restriction is agreed upon. At present any of them could, theoretically, turn out a side containing not a single English, or England-eligible, player – a bit like Arsenal in football, until Theo Walcott forced his way into the starting line-up – and therefore having no real connection with this country beyond the fact that it happens to play its matches here.

GOING THE SAME WAY AS FOOTBALL?

A lot of people – English cricketers in particular – are unhappy about this. To play alongside genuine stars such as Ricky Ponting, Shane Warne, Mushtaq Ahmed and Muttiah Muralitharan – to name just a few non-Kolpak overseas players who have turned out in county cricket recently – is one thing. Young English cricketers can learn a lot from them. But where's the advantage in, at best, acting as twelfth man while a journeyman on a Kolpak contract takes the place that could have been yours?

Steve Rhodes, Worcestershire's director of cricket, spoke for many when in April 2008 during a radio interview on BBC Hereford and Worcester he said: 'Where's the opportunity for young English guys? They [Kolpak players] are taking jobs away. Clubs are not breaking the rules but they should give English lads a go.'

He's quite right: clubs are not breaking the rules. It's perfectly legal to employ Kolpak players – but it's not compulsory. Cricket is most popular in England when there's a strong England Test team. (Remember 2005?) But there's not much chance of a strong England Test team if English players can't even get into their county sides.

The situation is not quite as bad as football, where to find more than three or four English players in a top Premiership squad is a novelty. But unless counties choose voluntarily to cut down on Kolpaks and devote more time to nurturing local talent, the pool of future Test players could soon become worryingly shallow.

But, don't despair – there's another option…

THE MINOR COUNTIES

All right, they don't play first-class cricket (except sometimes against touring sides) – that's why they're called minor. (For a short history of Minor Counties cricket, see page 46.) But that didn't stop the great Sydney Barnes (see page 88) who, in the early 20th century, fell out with Lancashire (almost

certainly over money) and played most of his cricket for the Minor County Staffordshire while also turning out for England.

Mind you, the fact that many fine cricketing judges reckon Sydney Barnes might well have been the greatest bowler of all time, no matter who he played for, does make him exceptional, but he is not unique. In 1934–5 David Townsend, an Oxford Blue whose only county side was Durham, who were then also among the minors, appeared in three Test matches for England in the West Indies.

No Minor Counties player has managed that since but, even if it's pretty well impossible now, we know it can be done because it has been done. And we also know that people like W.J. (Bill) Edrich could graduate from Norfolk in the Minor Counties to Middlesex and then to England. The Edriches were a remarkable cricketing family: two of Bill's brothers, Eric and Geoff, played for Lancashire and a third, Brian, for Kent, while their cousin, John, was a prolific opening bat for Surrey and England in the 1960s and 70s. All of them learned their cricket in Norfolk.

So there is hope. If first-class counties have turned you down, see if you can get a Minor County to show interest. And from there, as Bill Edrich proved, it's a small step – well, a giant leap actually – to playing for England. But it's not impossible, that's the thing to remember.

Now at this point impatient young wannabe Test players may say: 'Yeah, but so what? Minor Counties? Mostly amateur stuff. Give or take the odd Barnes, the Edriches or David Townsend, who's ever heard of anyone who played Minor Counties cricket?'

Well, listen up. Jack Hobbs played for Cambridgeshire before going on to glory with Surrey and England. Not only Bill Edrich but also those other Middlesex and England players Peter Parfitt and Clive Radley started out with Norfolk. Chris Read (Notts and England) and Roger Tolchard (Leics and England) began with Devon, while a third England wicketkeeper, Geoff Millman (Notts), had his apprenticeship with Bedfordshire. The current TV pundit and former England coach David Lloyd (Lancs and England) started with Cumberland. Bob Barber (Lancs, Warwicks and England) first played for Cheshire. Tom Dollery (also Warwicks and England) began with Berkshire. Jim Smith (Middlesex and England) was discovered playing for Wiltshire. The double international – cricket and football – John Arnold (Hampshire) was first of all an Oxfordshire player. Jack Ikin (Lancashire and England) was recruited from Staffordshire. And Chris Read's current team-mate at Notts, Charlie Shreck, began with Cornwall.

So don't knock the Minor Counties. Since 1964 many of them have taken part alongside first-class teams in such List A competitions as the Gillette Cup and the Cheltenham and Gloucester Trophy. They play pretty good cricket and one of them could turn out to be your passport to international fame.

FAR LEFT *In 1938, the cricketing family Edrich were able to field an entire XI for charity matches in their native county of Norfolk. This line-up, at Ingham Cricket Club, included four top-flight players: Bill (Middlesex and England), Brian (Kent and Glamorgan), and Eric and Geoff (both Lancashire). Another Edrich, John (b. 1937) later played for Surrey and won 77 caps for England as a gritty opening bat. Between 1934 and 1978, these five most famous Edriches played a total of 1691 first-class matches.*

HOWZAT! Aussie cricket writer Gideon Haigh once explained why the Test spinner Dave Sincock retired young: 'What ground him down was the repetition ... But other factors also bore down on Sincock, such as the burden of bearing the nickname "Evildick".'

Postscript

SO WHAT NOW?

Cricket is a mightily resilient game; it needs to be. Through the centuries, often moaning bitterly over preposterous, new-fangled ideas like three stumps instead of two, it has nevertheless adapted and changed. As the first decade of the new millennium drew to a close, it faced fresh problems. Cricket entered 2009 after a year punctuated by political violence – in Sri Lanka, in Pakistan and in India. Terrorism in Mumbai had caused the curtailment of the India–England one-day series in November 2008, the only sliver of a silver lining in that cloud being that England were saved the indignity of a likely 7–0 drubbing. The England Test squad returned to India in December – though not to Mumbai – for a two-Test series, hailed as heroes and with each player surrounded by more bodyguards than Barack Obama.

England's peaceful return helped settle India's nerves but in March 2009, more horror arrived with a murderous attack in Lahore, Pakistan, on the touring Sri Lanka team. With cricket targeted for the first time, the Subcontinent now seemed unsafe for visiting sides. What impact would that have on control of the world game?

MONEY, MONEY, MONEY, HURRY, HURRY, HURRY

For the moment, that control – ostensibly in the ICC's hands – was actually in India's. The ICC's hands were palsied things, incapable of holding on to anything much, while India's had a firm grasp of the purse strings. Of all the cricket-playing nations India had the most money and therefore the most power. In addition, even though

LEFT *Kevin and his minders: personnel from the paramilitary Indian Special Action Group shadow England's (then) cricket captain Kevin Pietersen during a training session at the M.A. Chidambaram stadium in Chennai, 10 December 2008.*

the Indian Premier League (IPL) was affected, like everyone else was, by the global recession, and was finding it increasingly difficult to attract sponsors, India still controlled the highly lucrative Twenty20 game.

Money has always had a strident voice in cricket, from wagers and gambling in the early years and the trousering of large sums by such so-called amateurs as W.G. Grace, to Stanford's $20 million match and the hefty fees star players can attract in the IPL and the rival Indian Cricket League (ICL).

ABOVE *Cricket's new gladiators: Muttiah Muralitharan (far left), Mahendra Singh Dhoni (centre) and Stephen Fleming (far right) adorn a poster for the IPL team Chennai Super Kings, who also number in their ranks such Test stars past and present as Matthew Hayden, Michael Hussey, Makhaya Ntini and Andrew Flintoff.*

But is money alone the reason for the rapid emergence of Twenty20 and its evident threat to the future of Test cricket? It's certainly a factor and will surely cause the early retirement of a number of international players as they look for lighter, better-paid work than the grind of the first-class game. But perhaps an even more ominous prospect for the future well-being of the longer versions of cricket is the sheer pace of modern life. In an age when the world's financial system can collapse faster than England's middle-order, people want their gratification right now.

Attendances at Test matches have dwindled everywhere, except for the moment in England; but that's not the fault of Twenty20 – it was happening anyway. Most people simply don't have the time to devote three, four or five days to a game of cricket, either at the ground or on the box. Probably few of them ever did, but when time and life moved more slowly it was possible to find the odd day here and a few hours there to follow the progress of a match.

Now – hurry, hurry – everything has to happen all at once, from beginning to end, preferably in the early evening and before the pubs close. And the spectators want immediate action – biff, bang, wallop – fours and sixes and wickets clattering in every over. So they lose the glorious subtlety of the game, so what? This is not a subtle age. This is an age of in-your-face immediacy, and Twenty20 satisfies that.

It's the young, always impatient, who have taken to it most avidly and that's a worry. People brought up on the longer game can enjoy Twenty20 for what it is but keep it in context. If, on the other hand, all you know about cricket is this simplistic, text-message version of it, then you don't really know cricket at all and maybe will never bother to learn. So, will future generations,

HOWZAT! England's series defeat in the Caribbean in spring 2009 prompted former skipper Nasser Hussain to observe: 'It's a graveyard for fast bowlers, county cricket. We need some pace from somewhere.'

if they can even be bothered to read about the game, believe that the likes of Bradman, Richards, Lara, Tendulkar and Pietersen must have been boring because they stayed at the crease for hours, not just a few hectic overs? It hardly bears thinking about.

Incidentally, on a related note, it seemed that something would have to be done about the status of the ICL. Unreasonable, surely, that the ICL and its players should be forever pariahs, the latter cast out from Test cricket simply because the IPL didn't fancy the competition. Was it too much to expect that sooner or later the ICL would be granted official recognition? Bangladesh, in particular, would certainly welcome the chance to stiffen a pitifully weak side by bringing back some of their former Test players.

ENGLAND'S LOST OPPORTUNITY

At the start of 2009, England's position regarding Twenty20 seemed ever more precarious. Of course, it could all have been so different. If the ECB, which introduced the bloody game, had only had the nous to develop it as India has done the power could still lie, as it did in the heyday of the MCC, at Lord's. The words crying and spilt milk come to mind, but there you go. England lost control of Twenty20 and even walked out on a projected $970 million series involving Australia, India and South Africa. In a newspaper article in February, 2009, Lord Marland, who had unsuccessfully challenged Giles Clarke for the chairmanship of the ECB, said that meant 'England has become estranged from cricketing countries that were our traditional allies – and still should be.' Just as pertinently it also meant that India, Australian and South Africa would reap the financial benefits of the series, leaving England with… what? Hard to say, really. No good looking to Stanford for salvation. The ECB was now paying the penalty for having dropped its drawers with a girlish giggle and leapt into bed with this apparently affluent suitor, blithely ignoring the fact that the moustachio-twirling Lothario had already been spurned by Australia, India and South Africa.

In effect, the ECB, like Esau, had sold its birthright – our birthright, actually – for a mess of pottage, only to discover when allegations of massive fraud were made against its presumed benefactor that there was a hell of a lot more mess than there was pottage.

What with that and an urgent need for new sponsors in practically every department of the domestic game – including a replacement for Vodafone who had elected to give up sponsoring the national team – English cricket seemed to be in dire straits both on and off the field.

THE KEV AND PETE SHOW

Having begun 2009 on the back of series defeats by South Africa and India the England camp promptly faced another embarrassment – a huge bust-up between the captain Kevin Pietersen and the coach Peter Moores. It seems the two never got along – clash of personalities, Moores too aggressively I'm-in-charge for Pietersen, who took that amiss, not being noted for his diffidence or lack of self-belief. Not for nothing did the Aussies dub him FIGJAM ('F*** I'm Good, Just Ask Me'), though it's probably unfair to say that he takes two cricket coffins to every match – one for his kit, the other for his ego.

Whatever. Moores wanted things done his way, Pietersen wanted something different and this conflict came to a head when Pietersen said his predecessor Michael Vaughan should be in the West Indies touring party and the selectors, Moores among them, quite rightly said he shouldn't. Vaughan's form both in Tests and the county game had been rubbish in 2008 and he'd played no serious cricket since the end of the summer season. Now Pietersen and Moores went *mano a mano*. Each appeared to think he had the backing of the team and each turned out to be wrong. Some liked Pietersen; some liked Moores: nobody seemed to like both.

Sorting through the conflicting versions of this tale it appears that Pietersen had issued the ECB with what amounted to an ultimatum: either Moores goes or I do. Naturally, the ECB couldn't allow the captain – a new one at that and a South African to boot – to tell them who the coach should be. Nor, contemplating the aggro that would certainly arise in the England dressing-room, could they retain Moores and ask Pietersen, stripped of the captaincy, to serve under him as a mere foot soldier. So a traditional English compromise was arrived at – both would have to go, Moores being fired and Pietersen having his resignation from the captaincy accepted, much to his surprise at first because he didn't seem to know he'd proffered it. The ECB, however, firmly believed he had and that was that. Effectively what had happened was that in issuing his ultimatum Pietersen had performed the neat trick of slaying Moores and blowing his own brains out with the same bullet. Andrew Strauss, who – as anyone gifted with half-decent hindsight maintained – should have been made captain when Michael Vaughan resigned, replaced him, and there the matter rested, although how happy everybody would be with this outcome remained to be seen.

BELOW *Renaissance man? Andrew Strauss regained the England captaincy in January 2009 in the aftermath of the Pietersen–Moores rift. Strauss scored 541 Test runs at 67.62, with three centuries, during England's 2009 tour of the Caribbean. On the debit side, however, he led the team to its first series defeat by the West Indies since 1998.*

ON HOME AND FOREIGN FIELDS

Test cricket had also been having a chequered time. It had ended 2008 on a high note after two exciting, against-the-odds victories – by India against England at Chennai and by South Africa against Australia at Perth. But there had been too many mismatches. Sri Lanka filling their boots at Bangladesh's expense was nobody's idea of a good time, except those Sri Lankans who emerged with much improved averages. What to do? Nobody quite seemed to know. Dropping Bangladesh, like Zimbabwe, from the Test rota was one option; establishing something tantamount to a two-division Test championship was another; but neither seemed entirely satisfactory. For one thing England, only the fifth-strongest nation, would be in danger of ending up in division two if the second option were adopted and that would never do. Maybe the best solution would be fewer, more carefully arranged, Test series.

On the home front, too, English cricket had its problems. As gifted players transferred ever more easily from one county to another, the gap in class between the first and second divisions of the County Championship began to increase. Evidence of that was provided by the ease with which Warwickshire and Worcestershire, relegated in 2007, gained promotion in 2008, the implication being that, fielding much the same teams in the latter year as they did in the former, they found the competition in Division Two pretty undemanding.

As for the question of Kolpak players, the Home Office was looking at ways of tightening the criteria for signing them. In theory, fewer Kolpaks would mean more opportunities for England-qualified players and one could only pray that a by-product of this would be the emergence of some decent spinners.

WHERE HAVE ALL THE SPINNERS GONE?

With the retirement of Warne and MacGill even Australia, especially the squad touring India in late 2008, looked desperate for new spinners. (Jason Krejza may have taken 12 wickets in the fourth Test at Nagpur, but he conceded more runs (358) than any other bowler on debut. This is not exactly match-winning stuff.) England, though, were hardly better off. Their leading spinner was Monty Panesar and critical opinion suggested that he hadn't really progressed much. As Shane Warne rather cruelly said of him: 'He hasn't so much played 33 Test matches as the same Test 33 times.' But until Graeme Swann, who made his debut as second spinner alongside Panasar in India, replaced him during the 2009 series in the West Indies he appeared to have no rivals, although the promising young Yorkshire leggie Adil Rashid was clearly one for the future. (Swann proved to be England's best bowler in the Caribbean, taking 19 wickets in three Tests at 24.05 each.)

During a cricket discussion at the Cheltenham Literary Festival I asked Mike Atherton to explain this dearth of spinners. He said it was because Marcus Trescothick (who was also present) kept hitting them out of the park and breaking their hearts. Actually, it's quite a tenable theory, although Trescothick alone is hardly to blame. These days very few wickets in England – or anywhere, except India and Sri Lanka – are prepared with spinners in mind. On tracks that are either batsman- or seamer-friendly, big hitters such as Trescothick, armed with what look like small tree trunks, can take on the spinners with impunity, confident that, unless it's in the hands of a master like Warne, the ball is unlikely to turn much, let alone do anything outrageous.

In the days of uncovered wickets, spinners were often the main line of attack. No first-class side would take the field without at least two of them. In 1947 Middlesex, the county champions that year, invariably included two leg-spinners (Walter Robins, the captain, and Jim Sims), the left-armer Jack Young and Denis Compton bowling chinamen. On at least one occasion they threw in yet another leg-break bowler, Ian Bedford, as well, making five spinners in one team. Young and Sims each took 100 wickets or more while Robins, Bedford and Compton chipped in with another 106 between them.

Fat chance of anything remotely like that happening now. In first-class matches the – usually lone – spinner's role is mainly one of containment, spearing the ball in on a length rather than flighting it. Paradoxically, however, spinners often thrive in Twenty20, as England discovered to their cost against the Stanford Superstars in November 2008, when the West Indian left-armer Sulieman Benn took three of their wickets. Ironic if, while the first-class game is sadly neglecting one of cricket's most beautiful arts, the spread of Twenty20 were to unearth a whole new crop of its exponents.

CONTINUITY, COMPROMISE AND CHANGE

Which brings us to the big question: where does cricket go from here? Well, inevitably, it will change again. But whether that means Twenty20 taking over or even, due to its very ubiquity, vanishing as fast as it arrived because the public tired of it, remains to be seen. A compromise to be desired would be that, as with Packer and his day–night, pyjama-clad revolution, Twenty20 is absorbed into the wider game, co-existing with first-class and Test cricket rather than usurping them.

Of course, with the Subcontinent – the heartland of the modern game – in violent turmoil and nobody able to predict how things will shake down, the future of Twenty20 might seem pretty small beer. It's not though, not in the long term. The matter still remains to be resolved, but somehow cricket *will* survive and adapt as it always has. And with that in mind, I will happily raise a glass, optimistically half-full, to the greatest game ever devised by man.

OVERLEAF *Cricket on a late-summer afternoon, 1991.*

INDEX

A NOTE ON THE STATISTICS

The cut-off point for the Test, first-class and ODI statistics presented in this book was 14 March 2009. Test, first-class and ODI records presented here therefore include the five Tests of England's January–April 2009 tour of the West Indies (but not the ODI series); the ODIs and two Test matches of Sri Lanka's truncated tour of Pakistan, January–March 2009; the first two Tests of Australia's February–April 2009 tour of South Africa; and the five ODIs of India's February–April 2009 tour of New Zealand (but not the following three-Test series).

In 2005 the ICC ruled that the six-day ICC Super Series Test match played at Sydney in October of that year between Australia and a World XI was an official Test match. This book follows *Wisden Cricketers' Almanack* in including runs scored and wickets taken by Australian participants in that match (since these players were representing their country), but of excluding runs scored and wickets taken in the game by members of the World XI (since they were not). This book also follows *Wisden Cricketers' Almanack* in excluding from the relevant players' Test records the five matches played between England and the Rest of the World in 1970.

Where alternative versions of certain pre-war first-class statistics exist (notably in relation to the career totals of W.G. Grace, C. Blythe, G.H. Hirst, J.B. Hobbs, H. Sutcliffe, F.R. Woolley and W. Rhodes), this book uses the versions of these players' career statistics that appear in *Wisden Cricketers' Almanack.*

ABBREVIATIONS

The following abbreviations are used in the tables of records in Chapters 2 to 11 and in the scorecards and scorecard summaries in Chapters 12, 13, 15 and 16.

Av.	batting or bowling average	NO	not out
b	bowled	ODI	One-Day International
B	balls bowled	Opp.	opponents
BBI	best bowling in an innings	R	runs scored/runs conceded
BBM	best bowling in a match	St	stumped/stumpings made
c	caught	T	number of Test matches played
capt.	captain		
Ct	catches taken	W	wickets taken
d/dec.	innings declared	wkt	wicketkeeper
HS	highest score	*	an asterisk after a batsman's score indicates 'not out'
I	number of innings batted/bowled in		
M	number of matches played		

Please note that in the scorecards in Chapters 12, 15 and 16 the following abbreviations are used to denote Extras:

b	byes	nb	no-ball
lb	leg-byes	w	wide

PICTURE CREDITS

Bridgeman Art Library / Marylebone Cricket Club, London 6–7, 12, 16–17, 20, 24–25, 42, 78, 288–289, Private Collection–Stapleton Collection 304.
Getty Images Allsport/Laurence Griffiths 2–3, 77, Allsport/Adrian Murrell 11, 35, 61, 102–103, 148, 221, 253, 256, 271, 309, Allsport/Graham Chadwick 47, Allsport/Craig Prentis 58, Allsport/Shaun Botterill 74, Allsport/Matthew Ashton 87, Allsport/Clive Mason 138, 316, Allsport/Simon Bruty 160, Allsport/Jack Atley 193, Allsport/John Parkin 198; Mike Hewitt 4–5, 184; Topical Press Agency 9, 80, 237, 320; AFP/Adrian Dennis 10–11, AFP/Carl De Souza 41, AFP/Indranil Mukherjee 116, 158, 182–183, 228–229, 322, AFP/Andrew Yates 189, 305, AFP/Alessandro Abbonizio 167, AFP/Dean Treml 169, AFP/Arko Datta 170, AFP/ Dibyangshu Sarkar 177, AFP/Arif Ali 188, 191, AFP/Asif Hassan 189, AFP/Sanka Vidanagama 200–201, AFP/Lakruwan Wanniarachchi 202, 204, AFP/Farjana Godhuly 209, AFP/Jewel Samad 303, AFP/Emmanuel Dunand 306; Bob Thomas/Popperfoto 14, 15, 18, 21, 23, 28, 50, 53, 70, 75, 79, 99, 110, 115, 122, 123, 129, 175, 192, 212, 268, 290, 310; Hamish Blair 19, 40, 126–127, 136–137, 262, 281, 310; Fox Photos 26–27, 109, 307; Central Press 30, 38–39, 63, 65, 91, 93, 94–95, 98, 104, 118, 119, 120, 133, 134, 151, 164, 216, 233, 241, 244–245, 249, 264, 285, 312, 313; Hulton Archive 33, 62, 72, 81, 82, 88, 89, 110, 266; Steve Lindsell 37; Adam Pretty 40; Popperfoto 45, 55, 57, 90, 98, 112; *Evening Standard* 60, 179, 250; Clive Mason 64, 206; Tom Shaw 66–67, 124, 210; Paul Gilham 71; *Express* 92, 130; Clive Rose 101, 149, 162; Keystone 113, 157, 287, 297; Rischgitz 117; Paul Kane 125; Getty 128, 144, 187, 195, 232, 328–329; Tertius Pickard/Gallo Images 135, 140; Chris McGrath 142; IPC Magazines/*Picture Post* 146; Allsport UK 152, 154, 172; Ezra Shaw 168; Global Cricket Ventures/BCCI 181, 230; Stu Forster 196, 325; Thurston Hopkins 282; Bert Hardy 284; Michael Steele 292, 326; Phil Walter 299; Cameron Spencer 300; Ross Kinnaird 314.
Mary Evans Picture Library 32, 267.
Patrick Eagar 34, 85, 96, 105, 114.
Graham Morris 186.
The Age **Ron Lovitt Fairfax Photos** 218.
David Frith 238.
The Wisden Cricketer 273.
SW Pix 278.

Quercus Publishing has made every effort to trace copyright holders of the pictures used in this book. Anyone having claims to ownership not identified above is invited to contact Quercus Publishing.

Pages 2 and 3: Darren Gough awaits his turn to bat, ODI vs Sri Lanka, Headingley, 2 July 2002.
Pages 4 and 5: the England slip cordon, day four of the first Test match vs South Africa, Lord's, 13 July 2008. (left to right) Strauss, Collingwood, Ambrose, Cook, Pietersen and Anderson.
Endpapers: 'Some Representative Cricketers', Supplement to *The Graphic*, 12 July 1890

This book is for my entire family, none of whom (except Charlie)
is, alas, a cricket fan but all of whom nobly put up with my
obsessive chuntering about cricket for months on end.

ACKNOWLEDGMENTS

My particular thanks to Richard Milbank at Quercus for his unstinting, enthusiastic support and shrewd suggestions; to his nephew James Pickering, as big a cricket nut as I am, for his invaluable help in compiling the statistics; to the lovely Caroline Proud, who is entirely to blame for my being asked to write the book in the first place; to Peter Furtado, with whom it was a pleasure to work on the editing; to Kevan Westbury of Two Associates, who designed the book; to Nick Clark and Peter Lewis, who worked wonders on the page layouts; to Elaine Willis for her excellent picture research; and to my old mate Hunter Davis, whose *Bumper Book of Football* led the way to *Barry Norman's Book of Cricket*. Such mistakes as appear in this volume are almost certainly my fault but, if you should point any out, I shall immediately blame somebody else.

The following titles were invaluable reference sources in writing and researching this book:

Wisden Cricketers' Almanack, various eds. (numerous editions)
Wisden Anthology 1864–1900, ed. Benny Green (1988)
Wisden Anthology 1900–1940, ed. Benny Green (1985)
Wisden Anthology 1940–1963, ed. Benny Green (1988)
Wisden Anthology 1963–1982, ed. Benny Green (1985)
Wisden Anthology 1978–2006: Cricket's Age of Revolution,
    Stephen Moss (2006)
The Playfair Cricket Annual, ed. Bill Frindall (numerous editions)
Barclay's World of Cricket: The Game from A to Z,
    ed. E.W. Swanton (1986)
The Complete Who's Who of Test Cricketers, Christopher
    Martin-Jenkins (1999)
England Test Cricketers, Bill Frindall (1989)
England: The Cricket Facts, Dean Hayes (2006)
Great Cricket Quotes, David Hopps (2006)
Cricket Facts, Figures and Fun, Liam McCann (2007)
The Trivia Lovers' Guide to Cricket (2007)

And not forgetting the online source that is Cricinfo.com – the *Wisden* of the internet. Also – with sceptical reservations – Wikipedia.com.

And finally, I'd like to thank the authors of the following:

Opening Up, Mike Atherton (2002)
Botham: My Autobiography, Ian Botham (2000)
Stiff Upper Lips and Baggy Green Caps, Simon Briggs (2006)
The Fast Men, David Frith (1984)
What Sport Tells Us About Life, Ed Smith (2008)
Coming Back to Me, Marcus Trescothick (2008)

First published in Great Britain in 2009 by
Quercus
21 Bloomsbury Square
London
WC1A 2NS

A CIP catalogue record for this book is available from the British Library

ISBN 978 1 84724 844 2

10 9 8 7 6 5 4 3 2 1

Printed and bound in Portugal

MR. W. W. READ
Surrey

MR. A. P. LUCAS
Essex

MR. S. M. J. WOODS
Somersetshire

MR. A. J. WEBBE
Middlesex

HALL
Yorkshire

PEEL
Yorkshire

SHREWSBURY
Nottingham

LORD HARRIS
Kent

MR. K. J. KEY
Surrey

BARNES
Nottingham

SHERWIN
Nottingham

PILLING
Lancashire

SOME REPRESE